WORLD BANK DISCUSSION PAPER NO. 402

Trade, Global Policy, and the Environment

Per G. Fredriksson, editor

The World Bank
Washington, D.C.

Discussion Papers present results of country analysis or research that are circulated to encourage discussion and comment within the development community. The typescript of this paper therefore has not been prepared in accordance with the procedures appropriate to formal printed texts, and the World Bank accepts no responsibility for errors. Some sources cited in this paper may be informal documents that are not readily available.

The findings, interpretations, and conclusions expressed in this paper are entirely those of the author(s) and should not be attributed in any manner to the World Bank, to its affiliated organizations, or to members of its Board of Executive Directors or the countries they represent. The World Bank does not guarantee the accuracy of the data included in this publication and accepts no responsibility for any consequence of their use. The boundaries, colors, denominations, and other information shown on any map in this volume do not imply on the part of the World Bank Group any judgment on the legal status of any territory or the endorsement or acceptance of such boundaries.

ISSN: 0259-210X

Per G. Fredriksson is a consultant at the World Bank

Library of Congress Cataloging-in-Publication Data

Trade, global policy, and the environment / edited by Per G. Fredriksson.
p. cm. — (World Bank discussion paper ; no. 402)
Papers presented at a World Bank conference in April 1998.
Includes bibliographical references (p.).
ISBN 0-8213-4458-7
1. Free trade—Environmental aspects—Congresses.
2. International trade—Environmental aspects–Congresses.
3. Foreign trade regulation—Environmental aspects—Congresses.
4. Environmental policy—Economic aspects—Congresses. 5. Economic development—Environmental aspects—Congresses. 6. Free trade—Environmental aspects—Developing countries—Congresses.
I. Fredriksson, Per. II. World Bank. III. Series: World Bank discussion papers ; 402.
HF1703.T73 1999
333.7—dc21 99-10251
CIP

Contents

Figures

Tables

Tables *(continued)*

Foreword

We live in an increasingly interconnected world. Trade flows worldwide are growing rapidly and global production patterns are shifting as countries follow their comparative advantage in production via trade. At the same time, however, there is growing concern about potential adverse environmental impacts from increasing trade. Questions such as the following are commonly asked:

- How does trade liberalization influence the environment, and how does environmental policy influence trade flows?
- Does increased economic integration induce a "race to the bottom" whereby policymakers seek to improve the ability of domestic firms to compete with their foreign rivals though the lowering of environmental regulations?
- What are possible ways to avoid or reduce any negative environmental effects from freer trade?
- How do trade measures, such as sanctions, influence a country's decision to participate in global environmental policymaking?

To respond to these concerns policymakers are seeking guidance on the links between trade and their national environment, and appropriate policy responses to address any adverse impacts. This is not an easy task, however. The environmental impacts of the various bilateral, regional, or multilateral trade liberalization programs undertaken are sometimes difficult to anticipate, and thorough analysis often requires large amounts of data. This is particularly true because the impact of trade liberalization is very country-specific. No two countries are identical. With freer trade each country will specialize in (at least somewhat) different sectors than before trade was liberalized. Since the impacts are country-specific, effective policymaking requires that particular attention has to be paid to both the existing policies and future economic structure of a country in order to anticipate outcomes and determine appropriate actions. In addition, policy analysis capacity in developing countries is often weak.

This volume attempts to increase the level and scope of our knowledge about the nexus between trade liberalization, and local and global environmental quality. Several chapters in this volume address these linkages, including the environmental and health effects of trade liberalization and consequent economic growth, the possible inverted U-shaped relationship between growth and emissions, and the effects of trade distortions and environmental policies on environmental damage from sectors such as horticulture and forestry. All of these concerns are linked to the question of sustainable development. How can we ensure that countries grow sufficiently fast to offer their populations improved economic conditions, without causing environmental and health effects that are irreversible?

Another concern often raised in the trade and environment debate is the possible existence of "pollution havens" in developing countries. Will countries with relatively lax environmental regulations end up becoming new hosts for polluting firms migrating from richer countries, with supposedly more stringent controls? Most existing studies have not found strong support for this hypothesis. A number of chapters in this volume add to the debate by studying the importance of wages, subsidies, and capital markets in determining industrial location.

Subsidies, such as those commonly found in the agriculture and energy sectors, often have multiple detrimental effects—on the environment, on government finances, on world market prices, and on competition. There is great scope for so-called "win-win" policies in this area, whereby subsidy reduction or removal is good for both the economy and the environment. This is one area where free-trade proponents and nongovernmental organizations appear to have much in common and could potentially form a strong coalition against protectionist forces.

Not all environmental issues are local. The issue of climate change is one challenging example of a global environmental concern. The costs of emission reductions are borne by populations living today, but the benefits will probably not be enjoyed until several decades from now. How can the global community overcome this problem in an efficient and equitable way? What role does trade policy have in this area? The volume addresses the linkages between trade, trade policies, and international agreements, and also discusses available policy tools to address global environmental problems.

Although this volume does not offer the final solution to all of these issues, it does provide new perspectives and thinking on these topics. The results offered here should help policymakers create improved local and global environmental and trade policies. The importance of these issues can only grow in the future, as the world becomes an increasingly integrated place, and trade flows help ensure improved living standards for all parties.

The World Bank has been pleased to be a part of the dialogue and I would like to express my thanks to Per Fredriksson for leading this effort and editing this volume, to all of the authors and reviewers of the material included here, to the two keynote speakers at the Trade, Global Policy, and the Environment Conference, Daniel Esty (Yale University) and David Reed (World Wide Fund for Nature), and to Sida, the Swedish International Development Agency, for supporting this important work.

John A. Dixon
Environmental Economics and Indicators
The Environment Department
The World Bank

Abstract

This Discussion Paper contains 13 chapters that contribute to knowledge in three broad areas: the environmental effects of trade liberalization and growth, the "pollution-haven" hypothesis, and economic instruments for global environmental problems. Earlier versions of these chapters were presented at a conference held at the World Bank in April 1998. An introductory chapter gives a summary of the findings and policy conclusions.

The chapter by Strutt and Anderson is a case study simulating how Indonesia's environment would be affected by two different reforms: the Uruguay Round and Asian-Pacific Economic Cooperation (APEC) most-favored-nation trade liberalization. The results suggest that air and water pollution would decline as a result of trade-policy reforms. However, incorporating an 0.5 increase in the rate of income growth would mean that APEC liberalization would yield up to 15 percent more air pollution and up to 12 more water pollution by 2020. The authors argue that the economic surplus created could be used for environmental protection.

The chapter by Beghin, Bowland, Dessus, Roland-Holst, and van der Mensbrugghe examines links between Chilean trade policy, atmospheric pollution, and public health in the Santiago metropolitan area. The authors examine three trade policy scenarios: (*i*) Chile's accession to the North American Free Trade Association (NAFTA), (*ii*) Chile's accession to MERCOSUR (Southern Cone Market), and (*iii*) complete trade liberalization with the rest of the world. Unilateral trade liberalization would result in significantly higher economic gains than the former two, but would have a negative effect on the environment and on urban morbidity and mortality. MERCOSUR has a similar, but less intense, effect. NAFTA integration would be environmentally benign in terms of several types of pollution emissions relative to the other trade integration scenarios.

Dean's chapter develops a methodology for estimating the effects of openness on income growth, and of income growth on environmental damage. She uses water-pollution data from Chinese provinces and finds that trade liberalization has both a direct and an indirect effect on emissions growth. Increased trade openness in China directly aggravates environmental damage by inducing an expansion of polluting sectors. However, income growth indirectly reduces emissions.

Hettige, Mani, and Wheeler provide further evidence on the relationship between industrial water pollution and income. They find that total industrial water pollution rises rapidly through middle-income status and remains approximately constant thereafter, not following an inverted-U. Simulations show that during the 1980s the Asian developing economies replaced Organisation of Economic Co-Operation and Development (OECD) countries as the world's largest producers of industrial water pollution.

Markandya, Emerton, and Mwale study the environmental effects in Kenya of removing European Union preferential trading arrangements with Kenyan horticultural production, and of other environmental policy measures. Horticultural production turns out to be largely insensitive to such measures. Chomitz, Griffiths, and Puri study the effect of trade and tax policies on deforestation in the Sahel. The authors' model shows that distortions in kerosene and gasoline prices have almost no impact on the rate of woodland degradation. Only substantial kerosene subsidies induce a shift towards this fuel. Efficiency-enhancing policy reforms, while desirable on economic grounds, may sometimes have less environmental impact than hoped.

One issue that has attracted much attention is whether lower trade barriers will result in a specialization by developing countries in pollution-intensive industries. Mani and Wheeler's chapter argues that such "pollution-haven" effects are insignificant because production is primarily for the domestic market, not for export. The increase in the developing countries' share of dirty-sector production is attributed to a highly income-elastic demand for basic industrial products. As income levels have increased, this elasticity has declined, and the stringency of environmental regulations has been raised.

Two chapters argue that there may be other reasons why researchers have not found strong effects of environmental regulations on plant locations and trade patterns. First, Eliste and Fredriksson present empirical evidence suggesting that producers may have been compensated by policymakers for their environmental protection costs. This may explain the minimal effect on trade flows. Second, Dasgupta, Laplante, and Mamingi argue that making sufficient information available to capital markets may provide financial and reputational incentives to invest pollution-reduction efforts in both developed and developing countries. Developing-country capital markets were found to react favorably to announcements of positive environmental performance. Multinational investments in pollution-intensive sectors in developing countries may be affected by concerns over legal liability and reputational damage.

Multilateral environmental agreements are increasingly seen as crucial policy tools with which to address global environmental problems. The chapter by Martin discusses joint implementation, arguing that increases in fuel efficiency resulting from technology transfers may have important second-round effects. Increased efficiency would lower the price of energy relative to other inputs and lower the price of energy-intensive products relative to other products. If the fuel whose efficiency is being improved is initially the most emissions-intensive, the aggregate effect of price changes may result in an increase in emissions, especially if this fuel continues to be the most polluting variety.

The issue of trade sanctions in international environmental agreements is contentious. Barrett argues that sanctions are more likely to be used when nonsignatories could potentially develop a comparative advantage in pollution-intensive industries. In such cases sanctions against nonsignatories increase the supply of emission reductions and are more likely to be credible. The chapter by Fredriksson and Gaston addresses the issue of "political drag," or "regulatory chill;" that is, the hypothesis that because of exposure to international competition countries may delay the enactment of environmental legislation. Overall, this argument is not supported by data from the 1992 Climate Change Convention. Institutional factors and emissions play a more important role in influencing the likelihood of cooperation on global environmental policymaking, however.

Parry provides a survey of the literature on the "double dividend;" the idea that emission taxes yield a double return by both reducing emissions and raising revenues that can be used to reduce distorting taxes elsewhere in the economy. However, pre-existing tax distortions may render environmental policies more costly. Parry concludes that if the policy raises tax revenues that are used to reduce other taxes, such additional cost can be reduced.

List of Contributors

Keynote Speakers
Daniel Esty, Yale University
David Reed, World Wide Fund for Nature

Authors
Kym Anderson, University of Adelaide
Scott Barrett, London Business School
John Beghin, Iowa State University
Brad Bowland, University of Minnesota
Kenneth M. Chomitz, World Bank
Susmita Dasgupta, World Bank
Judith M. Dean, Johns Hopkins University
Sébastian Dessus, OECD Development Centre
Paavo Eliste, West Virginia University
Lucy Emerton, Policy Research Group, Nairobi
Per G. Fredriksson, World Bank
Noel Gaston, Bond University
Charles Griffiths, U.S. Environmental Protection Agency
Hemamala Hettige, Asian Development Bank
Benoit Laplante, World Bank
Nlandu Mamingi, University of the West Indies
Muthukumara Mani, World Bank
Anil Markandya, University of Bath
Will Martin, World Bank
Dominique van der Mensbrugghe, OECD Development Centre
Sam Mwale, Policy Research Group, Nairobi
Ian Parry, Resources for the Future
Jyotsna Puri, World Bank
David Roland-Holst, Mills College
Anna Strutt, University of Waikato
David Wheeler, World Bank

Discussants
Kym Anderson, University of Adelaide
Scott Barrett, London Business School
Shantayanan Devarajan, World Bank
Ishac Diwan, World Bank
William Easterly, World Bank
Bruce Gardner, University of Maryland
Noel Gaston, Bond University
Jenny Ligthart, International Monetary Fund
Anil Markandya, University of Bath
Alex Mourmouras, International Monetary Fund
Mohan Munasinghe, World Bank
Håkan Nordström, World Trade Organization
David Roland-Holst, Mills College
David Tarr, World Bank
Scott Vaughan, World Trade Organization

Session Chairs
Maureen Cropper, World Bank
John A. Dixon, World Bank
Hossein Farzin, University of California, Davis
Ricardo Melendez-Ortiz, International Centre for Trade and Sustainable Development
Mohan Munasinghe, World Bank
Gunnel Nycander, Swedish International Development Cooperation Agency
John D. Shilling, World Bank
Kamoji Wachiira, Canadian International Development Agency

Chapter 1

Trade, Global Policy, and the Environment

New evidence and issues

Per G. Fredriksson

1. Introduction

The trade and environment debate intensified in the 1990s, in part because of the attention drawn to the issues by the North American Free Trade Agreement (NAFTA) and the Uruguay Round free trade negotiations. Interest has increased further because many proposed solutions to the climate change problem have potential implications for the global trading system. Focus is likely to sharpen as the next multilateral trade negotiation round appears on the horizon, but the debate is often built on little or no empirical evidence. To inform the debate, guide policymakers toward solutions, and help set priorities more empirical work is clearly needed.

This volume is an attempt to further our understanding of the empirical links between trade and the environment. The 13 papers included, which were presented at a World Bank conference in April 1998, focus on three main themes:

1. Effects of trade liberalization and growth on the environment
2. The "pollution haven" hypothesis
3. Economic instruments for resolving global environmental problems.

The papers address a number of different issues within each of the themes, offering new data or new questions and approaches. This introductory chapter provides an overview of the issues raised and the main insights and policy conclusions obtained. In the following section some of the main linkages between trade and the environment are discussed to offer the reader a better understanding of the issues.

2. Background—Scale, Composition, and Technique Effects

Although many issues in the trade and environment debate are contentious, a consensus appears to be emerging on a few matters. Many participants in the debate now agree that (a) more open trade improves growth and economic welfare, and (b) increased trade and growth without appropriate environmental policies in place may have unwanted effects on the environment. However, in some situations more open trade may also reduce pressure on the environment. This ambiguity occurs because trade policy and trade flows have several conflicting effects on both the environment and resource use. It has proven useful to view the various effects of trade liberalization in three categories: *scale, composition,* and *technique effects*. This is now a standard way of thinking about the problem and a helpful tool for analyzing the issues involved. Many of the papers in this volume are devoted to deepening our understanding and empirical knowledge of these effects. Only through a firm understanding of the linkages involved can well-founded policy advice be formulated.

Scale effect

The *scale* effect refers to the fact that more open trade creates greater economic activity, thus raising the demand for inputs such as raw materials, transportation services, and energy. If output is produced and delivered using unchanged technologies, an increase in emissions and resource depletion must follow.

Composition effect

The *composition* effect stems from changes in the relative size of the economic sectors following a reduction in trade barriers. Lowering trade barriers changes the relative prices between goods produced in different sectors, so that producers and consumers face new trade-offs. Countries tend to specialize production in sectors in which they have a comparative advantage; this tendency becomes more pronounced with freer trade. If the difference between abatement costs and the price of resource extraction is sufficiently large—making environmental regulations more important in the determination of comparative advantage—countries with lax regulations are likely to shift away from relatively clean sectors and specialize in more polluting or resource-dependent sectors, thus damaging the environment.

If, on the other hand, the base for international comparative advantage is differences in the supply of labor and capital or in the efficiency of technologies, then the impact of changing sector composition (in response to trade liberalization) on environmental quality and resource extraction will be ambiguous. More open trade encourages countries to shift production into sectors that make heavy use of their relatively abundant factors—sectors in which they have a comparative advantage. The final effect depends on whether the new sector composition is more or less polluting than the original one; that is, it depends on the relative pollution-intensity of the expanding sectors compared to the contracting ones. Developing countries tend to have a comparative advantage in labor-intensive sectors, which are generally cleaner than capital-intensive sectors. But developing countries rich in natural resources may experience an expansion of resource extraction following trade reform. Countries just beginning the industrialization process will naturally experience a rapid increase in the size of the manufacturing sector.

Technique effect

The *technique* effect refers to changes in production methods that follow trade liberalization. Pollution emissions per unit of output do not necessarily stay constant; final intensity depends on a number of subcomponents:

- Since trade liberalization generates increased income levels, demand for environmental quality is also likely to increase. Assuming that this leads to political pressure for more stringent environmental policies and enforcement, the per-unit pollution load will be lower.
- If investment liberalization also takes place, foreign investment may bring modern technologies which are likely to be cleaner than older versions.
- As the relative price of intermediate inputs changes when tariffs are lowered, the input mix chosen by firms is adjusted; the new mix may be more or less pollution-intensive.
- Governments may begin competing for investment and jobs by setting lower environmental standards—a "race to the bottom." However, if foreign consumers demand goods produced with cleaner methods, international trade could reduce pollution intensities, instead stimulating a "race to the top."
- Closely related to the previous point, incentives for lobby groups to pressure governments for more favorable environmental legislation may shift as a result of liberalization. If the sectoral composition effect (discussed above) implies a shift into more pollution-intensive sectors, both industry and environmental interests can be expected to intensify their efforts to receive favors from environmental policymakers—at higher output levels more is at stake, both in terms of profits and environmental degradation.

In sum, the technique effect has an ambiguous effect on pollution and resource extraction, but is generally believed to be positive for environmental quality. In addition, seen from a global perspective, free trade results in a more efficient use of resources; thus fewer raw materials and inputs are used to produce a given amount of output. As noted above, however, the amount of output produced is not constant.

The three main effects described above often have both local and global environmental implications, and their relative importance differs among countries. The final impact of trade liberalization on the environment is therefore ambiguous. A quantification of the relative magnitude of these effects, and their final result, is therefore useful to understand the range of the relative significance of the three effects in different countries.

The country-specific effects point to a need to identify and forecast the effects of existing and future trade and environmental policies—which puts great pressure on policymaking institutions. Sufficient institutional capacity is not always in place to permit environmental problems to be prevented or handled as they arise, underscoring the need for a thorough analysis of future environmental effects as foreign trade continues to open up. The collection of papers in this volume should contribute to an improved analysis of the complex issues involved in such situations.

3. Overview of the Volume Papers

The three sections below provide an overview of the papers contained in this volume, according to the three major themes cited above. At the end of each section the main empirical findings are reiterated.

Effects of trade liberalization and growth on the environment

The six papers addressing the first broad theme study the linkages between trade regimes, growth, and environmental degradation from different perspectives. The first two studies simulate the environmental and health effects of trade liberalization and consequent economic growth. The following two contributions study the inverted-U (or environmental Kuznets curve) and the role of trade openness in this relationship. The last two papers in this section discuss the effects of trade distortions and environmental policies on environmental damage from horticultural production and deforestation.

Trade, Growth, and Environmental and Health Effects. The first two papers in this volume use computerized general-equilibrium models to predict the environmental impacts of trade liberalization. In chapter 2 ("Will Trade Liberalization Harm the Environment? The Case of Indonesia to 2020"), Anna Strutt and Kym Anderson present a case study simulating the ways in which Indonesia's environment in the year 2020 will be affected by two different reforms: the Uruguay Round and most-favored-nation liberalization by Asian-Pacific Economic Cooperation (APEC) countries. The authors focus on the additional environmental damage caused by trade liberalization. An important contribution of the paper is its use of estimates of the likely impact of new technology on emissions; thus incorporating one component of the technique effect.

The authors' results suggest that, at least with respect to air and water, trade policy reforms would in many cases improve the environment and reduce the depletion of natural resources. In the worst cases it would add only slightly to environmental degradation. According to the authors these results would occur even without strengthening enforcement of existing environmental regulations or adding new ones, and even if the reforms stimulate a faster rate of economic growth. This would be the case, they argue, because the textile and apparel sectors would expand as a result of liberalization. The damage caused by trade liberalization is estimated to be only a fraction of the damage that normal projected economic growth and structural change would cause by the year 2020 if trade and environmental policies remained unchanged. However, it should be noted that even without trade liberalization environmental degradation is projected to be substantial. Any further damage could therefore potentially have large marginal effects.

The scenario described above is based on a static model that does not include an increase in the economic growth rate as a result of trade reform. The omission of dynamic effects means that the scale effect is likely to be underestimated. For the case of APEC liberalization the authors therefore extend the analysis by performing a simulation in which Indonesia's income growth increases by an extra 0.5 percent per year as a result of liberalization. This implies that by 2020 air pollution would be 12 to 15 percent greater, and water pollution 6 to 12 percent greater, than otherwise would have been the case. The growth rate is clearly important for the resulting increase in emissions; a 0.5 percent higher growth rate may be conservative. The authors argue that the economic gains from trade reforms and the surplus (which would be much greater if GDP growth increased further) available for adopting well-targeted environmental policies to reduce serious damage would be sufficiently large that aggregate social welfare would almost certainly be improved substantially by liberalization.

For the policymaker the challenge is to make sure that the environmental reforms (in particular in pollution-intensive or resource-extracting sectors) required to make trade reform welfare-improving are put in place *before* severe environmental degradation has occurred; it seems particularly important to target the right sectors. As discussed in chapter 3, the need for *information* to ensure that this take places is great. Failure to take preventive measures may result in substantially higher clean-up costs once damage has occurred.

The paper by John Beghin, and others (chapter 3, "Trade, Environment, and Public Health in Chile: Evidence from an Economywide Model") uses an empirical simulation model to examine links between Chilean trade policy, atmospheric pollution, and public health in the Santiago metropolitan area. The paper recommends a coherent policy that links reform programs in the three areas. It makes an important contribution by explicitly incorporating links from trade to the environment to public health indicators, rather than only measuring pollution incidence or other environmental variables. Thus the toxicity of pollutants is factored into the analysis.

Three trade-policy scenarios are examined and compared with a business-as-usual scenario; (1) Chile's accession to NAFTA; (2) Chile's accession to MERCOSUR (the regional trade agreement between Argentina, Brazil, Paraguay, and Uruguay); and (3) unilateral (complete) trade liberalization by Chile with the rest of the world. Moreover, the paper simulates environmental tax policy reforms assumed to be sufficiently large to reduce a particular pollutant by 25 percent. Unilateral trade liberalization results in significantly higher economic gains (GDP would be 5.6 percent higher than under the business-as-usual scenario) than NAFTA or MERCOSUR accession (+1.4 percent and +0.6 percent, respectively). However, completely free trade also produces a substantial worsening of pollution levels and an expansion of resource-based sectors (resource-based exports increase), partly because it facilitates access to cheaper energy.

NAFTA integration, however, would be environmentally benign in terms of several types of pollution emissions, relative to the other trade-integration scenarios. It reduces environmental damage because it diverts trade flows so that Chile reduces its reliance on cheap energy, unlike the other two scenarios. Joining NAFTA, however, would have little impact on Chile's GDP level.

The authors argue that both the MERCOSUR and unilateral liberalization scenarios would have a significant effect on the environment and on urban morbidity and mortality. Damages due to rising morbidity and mortality are substantial. Unilateral trade liberalization results in damages equal to 13 percent of the income gains arising from free trade. Taxes on air pollutants, however, produce net welfare *gains* from reduced health damages. The authors find that emissions of small particulates, SO_2 and NO_2, have the strongest impact on local mortality and morbidity. These three pollutants appear to be highly complementary; if the level of one is reduced, the other ones will also fall. This implies that if only a few types of pollutants are to be targeted (for budget reasons, for example), the complementary pollutants should be targeted first, given their toxicity. Some pollutants can be reduced at a low cost in relation to GDP. For example, reducing SO_2 by 25 percent (and therefore automatically also particulates and NO_2 by 23 and 25 percent, respectively) would cost 0.2 percent of GDP through 2010; CO_2 reduction is even less costly.

The authors' results point to the highly differing trade and growth effects, and therefore environmental and health effects, of different liberalization programs. Just as the economic welfare effects of trade liberalization programs are highly dependent on the type of reform undertaken, their environmental effects depend on what sectors are liberalized and by how much, as well as on which economies integrate their markets. These factors determine the scale-, composition-, and technique effects, and as the Chile case study shows, they differ substantially according to the liberalization scenario. The chapter argues that the resulting input mix (which depends heavily on the environmental policies in place) is an important factor affecting the environmental outcome of liberalization.

The Environmental Kuznets Curve. A county's trade orientation has important implications for its growth rate. This has led to an intense discussion on the environmental impacts of economic growth. At the heart of this debate is the question of whether economic growth is welfare-improving, when all effects are incorporated. The inverted-U hypothesis offers a hopeful answer to this question. It says that at a certain GDP level, pollution levels fall with further income growth, so that there is no contradiction between economic growth and environmental quality beyond this point. However, although this hypothesis has been found to hold true for several types of pollutants, in other cases it does not. The hypothesis also implies that low-income countries seem destined to go through a substantial worsening of the environment (with the consequent health effects) before things get better.

What are the underlying relationships that determine the effects of income growth on the environment? What role does the trade regime play? If we had the answers to these questions, we would be in a better position to prescribe policy recommendations that could help us cut off the top of the inverted-U and also reduce the income level at which the top of the inverted-U is reached. In short the issue is how to facilitate the transition of low-income countries toward improved environmental quality. Other questions include: How can high-income countries reduce the level of pollutants that are now increasing with income? Are international environmental agreements necessary to control these pollutants?

In chapter 4, "Testing the Impact of Trade Liberalization on the Environment: Theory and Evidence," Judith Dean develops a methodology for estimating the relationship between trade liberalization and industrial emissions. She takes into account the effects of openness on income growth and of income growth on environmental damage. The approach consequently allows for the possibility that trade may have several ambiguous effects on the environment. The literature on both trade and growth and income growth and environmental damage (the inverted-U hypothesis) are thus incorporated into the model. She uses water pollution data from Chinese provinces as an example.

The results support the view that trade liberalization has both a *direct* and an *indirect* effect on emissions growth, and that these effects have opposite impacts. Dean finds that China has a comparative advantage in pollution-intensive goods, so that increased trade openness directly aggravates environmental damage by inducing a specialization in these sectors—a composition effect. Increased openness to trade is also shown to strongly increase income growth. However, income growth has an indirect negative effect on emissions growth, improving pollution levels. This is probably because as demand for environmental quality increases, environmental regulations become more stringent—a technique effect. As argued by Strutt and Anderson in chapter 2, greater growth also yields an economic surplus available to be used for environmental protection measures. As income increases a shift may also take place toward cleaner subsectors within the manufacturing sector. Thus trade liberalization also indirectly mitigates environmental damage. Dean's work improves our understanding of the relationship between trade, income growth, and emissions.

The inverted-U relationship differs between various pollutants, and empirical explanations of the underlying workings of economic development on pollution levels have not yet been developed. More work is needed to understand this process, and for which pollutants it does or does not work. For example, the inverted-U relationship should be more likely to hold for local forms of pollution than for global pollutants, because of free-riding problems. Another problem with existing evidence is that no country has yet been shown to have actually followed the stipulated path.

In chapter 5, "Industrial Pollution in Economic Development: Kuznets Revisited," Hemamala Hettige, Muthukumara Mani, and David Wheeler provide further evidence by testing for a Kuznets relationship between industrial water pollution and economic growth. They separate out three components of the effects of income growth on water pollution. First, the authors ask what happens to the share of manufacturing in total output when income increases. This is clearly important for total industrial pollution. Second, they look at the sectoral composition of relatively clean and dirty sectors within the manufacturing sector; and third, they examine the intensity of industrial pollution (per unit of output). The authors find that manufacturing's share of output, when isolated, follows a Kuznets-type trajectory. Next, sectoral composition gets "cleaner" through the middle-income range and then stabilizes. Finally, water pollution intensity declines strongly with income, confirming Dean's finding in the preceding chapter. The authors attribute this phenomenon in part to stricter regulation as incomes increase, and in part to a shift to more modern (and therefore cleaner) production technology. When they combine the three relationships, however, they do not find a Kuznets-type relationship. Instead, total industrial water pollution rises rapidly through middle-income status and remains approximately constant thereafter. One important question is the level at which water pollution stabilizes: Does this happen before or after a serious impact on humans, fish, and aquatic life has occurred?

To illustrate the implications of their findings, the authors simulate the trends in industrial water pollution for four groups of industrial economies between 1977 and 1989. They find approximately stable emissions in the OECD and ex-COMECON countries (note that the ex-COMECON economies experienced constant or declining incomes during the period), moderate increases in the newly industrialized countries, and rapidly growing pollution in the developing countries of Asia. Their estimates suggest that during the 1980s the latter replaced the OECD economies as the world's largest generator of industrial water pollution. Overall, however, the negative feedback from income growth to pollution intensity was sufficient to keep total world pollution growth to around 15 percent during the 12-year sample period.

Horticulture, Forestry, and Environmental Degradation. Agriculture is an important, but often neglected, sector in many countries, and trade liberalization could offer new opportunities to agricultural producers in developing countries. Their exports are often taxed, thus driving down domestic prices. But trade policies favorable to developing-country producers can also be cited. For example, in chapter 6, Anil Markandya, Lucy Emerton, and Sam Mwale study the environmental effects of the European Union (EU) preferential trading arrangements with Kenyan horticultural producers ("Preferential Trading Arrangements between Kenya and the EU: A Case Study of the Environmental Effects of the Kenyan Horticulture Industry"). The study is particularly timely because the EU and 71 developing countries have begun negotiations for an arrangement to follow the end of the fourth Lomé Convention, in which preferential access to the EU markets was granted. A large share of Kenya's horticultural output is produced by small-scale farmers, and thus contributes significantly to the incomes of the poor, according to the authors.

Horticultural activities are environmentally damaging, however, and the paper analyzes the impact on the environment of two policy changes: the removal of preferential tariffs and the introduction of environmental policies. The analysis shows that horticultural production (land use) is largely insensitive to such measures. The environmental impact was also negligible; damage to the environment was reduced only slightly by either action. The authors argue that the main reason for this is the relatively high profitability of most horticultural production (the area devoted to this production represents a small share of poor farmers' total production). In Kenya it appears that policies that internalize the social costs of environmental damage could fairly easily be implemented, and could also generate revenue that could be used by the government for environmental protection.

The authors, however, do not model the impacts on marginal or other vulnerable producers. They argue that if tariff preferences were removed the strongest impact would be on these producers, who are barely surviving. Some form of social protection would be needed if the preferences were to be altered. One question that arises from the analysis is what effect the policy changes would have on production methods in the remaining productive areas. Overall, the paper suggests that EU preferential trade with Kenya has little effect either on land use or on Kenya's rural environment.

Kenneth Chomitz, Charles Griffiths, and Jyotsna Puri study the effect of trade and tax policies on deforestation in the Sahel in chapter 7 ("Fuel Prices, Woodlands and Woodfuel Markets in the Sahel: An Integrated Economic-ecological Model"). There has long been concern that overexploitation of woodlands for fuels leads to a vicious circle of environmental degradation, rising fuel prices, and increasing poverty. Urban demand for charcoal and fuelwood leads to increased areas of deforestation around urban centers, as open-access forests are used as sources of energy. Urban fuel costs increase, since supplies must be brought in from increasingly distant harvest areas. This process is influenced by the prices of kerosene, LPG (both substitutes for woodfuels), and gasoline or diesel fuel (a major component of the cost of woodfuel production). Fuel prices, in turn, are to a large extent determined by policy; for example, trade policy. Whereas some countries subsidize kerosene with the explicit goal of reducing pressures on forests and woodlands, in other countries the price of modern fuels is above world market prices as a result of petroleum product trade, manufacture, procurement, distribution, and tax policies. The question is the extent to which, for example, trade and tax policies can affect woodland degradation, rural income, and urban fuel consumption.

The authors' model shows that distortions in kerosene and gasoline prices have almost no impact on the rate of woodland degradation. According to their model only substantial kerosene subsidies induce a shift over to kerosene (due to the demand functions used), although such a shift may also occur when woodfuels start to be transported from much greater distances to urban centers. The paper suggests that reductions in policy distortions, while desirable on economic-efficiency grounds, may sometimes have less environmental impact than hoped. Other factors, such as road access, appear to be more important than trade policy. Reductions in gasoline taxes will have distributional effects, shifting rents away from wood harvesters to urban consumers. The authors, however, qualify their conclusions by pointing to the sensitivity of the results to the assumptions made. The difference between short- and long-run effects may also be important.

Summary of Empirical Results

- Combined trade and environmental reforms offer the greatest possibility for positive welfare effects. Pollution abatement that results in significant, positive health effects sometimes costs only a fraction of the surplus created by trade liberalization. Environmental policy reforms that target pollutants that are mutually complementary are more effective, because several pollutants are reduced simultaneously.
- The inverted-U relationship between pollution levels and income holds for some pollutants only. Some types of industrial water pollution appear not to fall, even at high income levels.
- In some developing countries trade liberalization directly aggravates environmental damage through its effect on relative prices and sectors of specialization, but also indirectly mitigates such damage because of the effect of liberalized trade on income growth.
- Different trade liberalization programs have highly differing effects on environmental quality, human health, and resource use. Some liberalization programs may have little effect on environmental degradation. The effects are country- and policy-specific.

The pollution haven hypothesis

One issue that has attracted much attention is whether reduced trade barriers will result in a specialization by developing countries in pollution-intensive industries; that is, will this group of countries become "pollution havens?" For decades commentators have predicted that relatively less stringent environmental regulations in developing countries will lead polluting firms to migrate there from the OECD economies. Economic theory also argues that low-income countries may develop a comparative advantage in pollution-intensive goods, even when environmental damage is taxed in an optimal fashion. The task of distinguishing the empirical effects of environmental regulations from other trends is certainly a difficult one. Most existing empirical studies have found either no, or weak, effects of environmental regulations on trade flows. Chapters eight, nine, and ten present new evidence related to this issue (chapters four and five also touched on the subject).

Industrial Delocation. Muthukumara Mani and David Wheeler find a pattern that initially appears consistent with the pollution havens hypothesis (chapter 8, "In Search of Pollution Havens? Dirty Industry in the World Economy, 1960-1995"). However, they argue that their evidence shows that pollution-haven effects have not been of major importance for a number of reasons. First, consumption and production of pollution-intensive sector products in the developing world have remained roughly equal throughout the period of study. This indicates that production has been primarily for the domestic market, and firms are not taking advantage of lax regulations to export elsewhere. The authors argue that trade is not to blame for any increase in the production of pollution-intensive goods. Nonetheless, production aimed primarily at the home market can still have severe environmental effects.

Second, a significant part of the increase in the dirty-sector production share in developing regions seems to be due to a highly income-elastic demand for basic industrial products. As income levels have risen, this elasticity has declined. Thus further increases in income now yield a smaller effect on demand than at lower GDP levels. Finally, the authors find that the stringency of environmental regulations increases along with incomes. They argue that although pollution havens may appear to have emerged, in practice, like "low-wage havens," they are transient.

Alternative Explanations. Two papers in this volume argue that there may be other reasons why plant locations and trade patterns do not appear to be strongly affected by environmental regulations. The explanation by Paavo Eliste and Per Fredriksson (chapter 9, "The Political Economy of Environmental Regulations, Government Assistance, and Foreign Trade") is based on the theory that firms subject to environmental regulations may have been compensated by policymakers for the associated abatement costs through various types of transfers such as tariffs, production subsidies, or pollution-abatement subsidies. They present empirical evidence from the agricultural sector that supports this hypothesis.

The results indicate that farmers have been successful in the political game of extracting income transfers from other groups in society. The compensation provided for costs associated with environmental regulation implies that producers are unlikely to be facing the true social cost of the damage caused; that is, that the Polluter Pays Principle does not hold. It follows that production in many countries is likely to be greater and more intense than optimal, affecting environmental quality negatively. To the extent that these phenomena have taken place in other sectors, the implication is that regulations are less likely to influence trade and investment patterns.[1]

In "Pollution and Capital Markets in Developing Countries" (chapter 10) Susmita Dasgupta, Benoit Laplante, and Nlandu Mamingi offer a new perspective on environmental regulations and firm location in developing countries through their discussion of the relationship between firms' environmental performance and the behavior of capital markets. Some observers argue that firms in developing countries have little incentive to undertake pollution control because of weak monitoring and enforcement of environmental regulations—where regulations exist. However, the authors argue that if sufficient information is available to capital markets, these markets may provide financial and reputational incentives to invest in appropriate efforts to reduce pollution. The chapter shows that capital markets in several developing countries react favorably to new media announcements of superior environmental performance and negatively to citizens' complaints about firm emissions. High pollution intensity of production may spark concern among investors about the inefficiency of a firm's production process and the risk of future liabilities; it may spur regulators, environmental groups, and a plant's neighbors to increase surveillance; and it may result in the loss of reputation and goodwill. The announcement of sound environmental performance or investment in cleaner technologies has the opposite effect.

It appears that certain conditions are required for this process to work, however. The existence of potential fines or other penalties may play a role in firm and market behavior, if it is the net present value of possible future liabilities to which the market reacts. Moreover, not all polluters are listed on the stock market; for example, publicly owned firms and small firms are generally not motivated by this form of incentive.[2]

These results may contribute to our understanding of the pollution-haven hypothesis. The expected profitability and flow of investments in pollution-intensive sectors in developing countries may have been affected by concerns over legal liability and reputational damage that could influence a multinational worldwide. This would reduce the incentive to relocate to countries with less stringent environmental regulations. It becomes more difficult to find support for the pollution haven hypothesis, because firms that consider relocating to pollution havens in order to take advantage of lax regulations are discouraged from moving.

Summary of Empirical Results

- Developing-country production is primarily for the domestic market, and firms appear not to have taken advantage of lax regulations to export elsewhere. The increase in developing-country, dirty-sector production is, to a significant extent, due to increasing demand for basic industrial products at low income levels.
- Farmers subject to environmental regulations appear to have been compensated for their environmental protection costs through various support programs. This should have mitigated the trade effects of environmental regulations.
- Information on the environmental performance of firms listed on developing country stock markets have significant effects on share prices, at least in the short run.

Global environmental policymaking

The last set of papers focuses on global environmental policymaking. The first two discuss linkages between trade, trade policies, and international agreements; the last two explore policy tools to address global environmental problems.

International Environmental Agreements and Trade Policy. One issue that attracts considerable interest is the use of trade sanctions in international environmental agreements (IEAs). Clearly, the search for enforcement mechanisms is important for IEAs since no supranational enforcer exists. The Montreal Protocol, which is widely seen as very successful in reducing production of chlorofluorocarbons (CFCs), contains provisions for the use of such sanctions. In "The Credibility of Trade Sanctions in International Agreements" (chapter 11), Scott Barrett discusses the general applicability of trade sanctions as a means to enforce an international agreement to provide a global public good, such as CO_2 reduction. He identifies two requirements that must be satisfied for sanctions to succeed in deterring free-riding.

First, given that sanctions are imposed against free-riders, every country must be better off as a signatory than as a nonsignatory. If this condition were satisfied, free-riding would be deterred completely. Second, when free-riding occurs, signatories must be better off by imposing sanctions than by continuing to trade with nonsignatories. If this condition were satisfied, the threat to impose sanctions would be credible. However, the second condition is less likely to be met, because sanctions hurt the countries imposing them as well as those being targeted. The issue of "leakage" is important in this context. If signatories of an IEA reduce their emissions, nonsignatories could develop a comparative advantage in pollution-intensive industries, thus reducing the impact of the IEA on emissions.

Barrett argues that sanctions are more likely to be used—that is, that the second condition is more likely to hold—when the problem of leakage is large. In that case sanctions against nonsignatories increase the supply of emission reductions and are credible, provided that benefits exceed costs. If both conditions hold, the threat of trade sanctions would be sufficient to deter free-riding, and the sanctions would never be employed. Barrett concludes that the sanctions in the Montreal Protocol were effective and credible, but that it represents a special case and sanctions are less likely to work for many other type of IEAs. For example, many more producers are involved in the production of CO_2 than of CFCs.

In chapter 12 ("The Importance of Trade for the Ratification of the 1992 Climate Change Convention") Per Fredriksson and Noel Gaston investigate the relationship between trade flows and delays in ratification of the United Nations Framework Convention on Climate Change (UNFCCC). Their work addresses the hypothesis of "political drag," or "regulatory chill" in environmental policymaking due to trade concerns. This hypothesis, closely related to the "race to the bottom" argument, argues that countries may delay enacting environmental legislation and associated abatement efforts for reasons of international competitiveness, particularly if they are more open to international trade. The authors argue that the speed of ratification is important to the success of an IEA and for countries' bargaining positions in the next negotiation round. Slow ratifiers of the 1992 Climate Change Convention may have gained an upper hand in the 1997 Kyoto bargaining round.

The evidence on the importance of the openness to trade, however, is weak. Whereas increased exports have tended to increase ratification speed, imports have had the opposite effect. The results suggest that exporting countries have been concerned with reputation, whereas importers worry about their competitiveness. However, it should be noted that large exporters are likely to be large importers. In sum the "political drag" argument cannot be supported by this data. The authors also discuss the implications of the results for the use of trade sanctions.

However, a country's ratification of the UNFCCC is found to be more likely, the greater its total CO_2 emissions and, in particular, civil liberties. Apparently, countries that were heavy polluters came under great political pressure, either internally or externally, to ratify the UNFCCC. Political and institutional factors may be substantially more important than trade arrangements in determining participation in global environmental policymaking. Democracies seem to view international norms as important, and to be less likely to shirk their global responsibilities.

Policy Instruments for Global Environmental Policymaking. In chapter 13 ("Achieving Carbon Emission Reductions through Joint Implementation") Will

Martin takes a closer look at joint implementation, one of several ways to coordinate reduction of global CO_2 emissions. Martin's study has implications for the future design of joint implementation projects. The large differences between the cost of reducing such emissions in industrialized and developing countries suggest potentially great scope for lowering overall emission reduction costs by focusing primarily on projects in developing countries. Most joint implementation proposals focus on installing new, more efficient equipment to reduce energy use for a given output level.

Martin argues that such increases in production efficiency could have some important second-round impacts that have thus far been ignored. Increased efficiency would lower the price of energy relative to other inputs and lower the price of energy-intensive products relative to other products. The direct impact of a fuel-price reduction is an increase in consumption of that fuel. In addition substitution effects will generally reduce the use of other fuels and associated emissions. If the fuel being made more efficient is already the least emissions-intensive, the combined impact of a price reduction and other price changes is likely to favor the environment, because relatively more of the relatively cleaner fuel would be consumed. However, if the fuel being made more efficient is initially the *most* emission-intensive, the aggregate effect of such price changes may result in an *increase* in emissions, especially if this fuel continues to be heavily polluting. The final impact of demand shifts on fuel consumption and energy emissions will also depend on how the supply side of energy markets react. If energy supply is inelastic, reductions in energy demand resulting from joint implementation (because of increased efficiency) will reduce the price of energy and stimulate energy use, partially offsetting the initial fall in demand.

In the final chapter Ian Parry surveys the literature on the "double dividend" ("Carbon Abatement: Lessons from Second-Best Economics"). The "double dividend" refers to the idea that emission taxes yield a double return by both reducing emissions and raising revenues that can be used to reduce distorting taxes elsewhere in the economy. Environmental policies can be substantially more costly when their effect on preexisting tax distortions is taken into account, because environmental policies tend to reduce somewhat the overall level of employment and investment in the economy. Preexisting taxes mean that the levels of employment and investment are already below levels needed to maximize economic efficiency. Hence further reductions result in additional efficiency losses. However, if the environmental policy raises tax revenues, and the latter are used to reduce other distortionary taxes, then much of the additional economic cost can be offset. To achieve CO_2 reduction a revenue-raising instrument (such as an emissions tax or auctioned emissions quota) is thus preferable to a nonrevenue-raising instrument (a nonauctioned emissions quota). It is also important to include the potential impact of a given policy instrument on private incentives to develop more energy-efficient technologies (see also Martin's chapter 13).

Many developing countries have segmented labor markets. Part of the labor force may be employed in a formal sector in which taxes are levied, while the other part works in the informal sector which is not covered by the tax system. The effect of the traditional tax system is to distort the allocation of production by implicitly subsidizing the informal sector, since the latter is not taxed. If energy inputs are taxed to reduce carbon emissions and the revenues are used to reduce formal-sector taxes, the tax shift can reduce the effective subsidy to the informal sector. That is, segmented labor markets offer the possibility of a double dividend from environmental tax reform.

Summary of Empirical Results

- The hypothesis that increased trade makes legislatures less willing to enact global environmental policies could not be confirmed. Democratic institutions appear to positively affect legislative action on global environmental issues.
- Joint implementation programs that are aimed at the cleanest fuel are most likely to be favorable to the environment, because the combined impact of price reductions and other price changes stimulate use of the relatively cleaner fuel.
- Environmental policies can be substantially more costly when their effect on preexisting tax distortions is taken into account. Such policies reduce somewhat the overall level of employment and investment in the economy. If an environmental policy raises tax revenues, however, much of the additional cost may be offset.

4. Policy Conclusions and Recommendations

The collection of papers presented here form a follow-up volume to the 1992 World Bank Discussion Paper edited by Patrick Low ("International Trade and the Environment"). Since the publication of the Low volume, a substantial amount of research has been carried out in this area. In particular, much effort has been devoted to documenting the existence of an inverted-U relationship between income and pollution and the effects of environmental regulations on trade patterns.

However, our knowledge on most issues in the area of trade and environment is still quite limited. Some of the reasons for this include serious data limitations and the fact that the underlying theories (for example, the inverted-U) are often underdeveloped. A major factor behind the uncertainties is also the inherent ambiguity of the impact of trade liberalization on environmental quality. Forecasting the relative magnitude of the various effects of trade liberalization for a specific country requires a substantial amount of data and becomes especially complex and uncertain because the final outcome depends on a politically determined policy response at both the national and international level. Although the papers included in the present volume improve our understanding of these complex matters, much work remains to be done. For example, as income growth proceeds in the future, will the relationships discussed change over time, particularly if abatement costs and pollution levels increase substantially?

A few issues, however, appear to be approaching settlement. Advances can be cited in understanding of the appropriateness of trade measures for environmental protection. Most observers now agree that environmental policy, in general, is more efficient and appropriate than trade policy for addressing environmental problems. Trade policy measures have uncertain effects and create their own distortions. Only in special cases, such as international environmental agreements on transboundary pollution issues, is trade policy likely to play a role. Moreover, uniform harmonization of environmental policy across countries is inappropriate, since countries have different pollution problems and dissimilar valuations of environmental damages. Thus different countries require different environmental policies; otherwise new distortions are created. One way to undertake international cooperation and avoid some distortions could be multi-tier harmonization agreements. Such agreements may avoid the free-riding problem that occurs with transboundary pollution problems.

A few policy conclusions can be drawn from the papers in this volume. For example, the ambiguity of environmental effects of trade liberalization places heavy demands on existing institutions charged with environmental policy formulation and implementation—to prevent potential problems and respond as negative effects appear. Therefore, local institutional capacity building on environmental policy is an important priority. This must include the capacity to identify economic trends and to forecast the environmental effects of structural changes. Many environmental impacts of trade liberalization could be addressed at the national or local level by appropriate environmental policies. Coordination of trade and environmental policies is thus important. Appropriate environmental policy responses may also reduce resistance to continued trade reforms, which in turn would offer protectionist interests less ammunition.

Actions to improve environmental quality need not be expensive. Increased dissemination of information has been found to induce capital markets to police environmental performance. This leads to an environmental policy argument for privatization, because nonlisted firms—such as public companies—are not subject to such scrutiny. Reduced subsidies to polluters, such as agriculture and energy producers, would have positive impacts on environmental quality, world market prices, and government finances. The promotion of democratic ideas and practices also has a beneficial effect on environmental policymaking.

Policymakers prefer low-cost options, but they cannot rely only on win-win policies. If the Polluter Pays Principle is to be effective, environmental regulations should be allowed to have economic and trade effects. These have been found to be small or negligible, in particular because abatement costs are relatively low.

Notes

I would like to thank the participants and, in particular, the discussants at the *Trade, Global Policy, and the Environment* conference for many useful suggestions on the papers in this volume. This chapter draws on their insightful comments. I am also grateful to John Dixon, Ola Larsson, Michael Linddal and Alison Rafael for suggestions on this introduction, and to Jim Cantrell for great desktop work. I am solely responsible for all remaining errors. In addition to the papers presented, David Reed, World Wide Fund for Nature, and Daniel Esty, Yale University, addressed the conference as keynote speakers, and their participation is gratefully acknowledged. Support for the conference and this volume was provided by the Swedish International Development Cooperation Agency (Sida) through the funding of the "Trade, Macroeconomic Reform, and the Environment" project, which is gratefully acknowledged.

1. Alternative or complementary explanations for the absence of changes in observed trade patterns include the fact that in most sectors pollution abatement costs are low relative to labor and capital costs, and therefore the cost differentials between countries are necessarily low. Moreover, some pollution-intensive sectors are dependent on access to natural resources, which determines their location; other industries, such as petroleum refineries, tend to locate close to markets. The "Porter Hypothesis" argues that environmental regulations stimulate innovations and improvement of technology, increasing overall productivity in the process.

2. There is some recent evidence that publicly held firms have worse environmental performance than privately held firms (see R. Hartman, M. Huq, and D. Wheeler, "Why Paper Mills Clean Up: Determinants of Pollution Abatement in Four Asian Countries," Policy Research Department Working Paper 1710, Washington, D.C.: World Bank, 1977).

Chapter 2

Will Trade Liberalization Harm the Environment?

The case of Indonesia to 2020

Anna Strutt and Kym Anderson

1. Introduction

Most-favoured-nation (MFN) trade liberalizations will always improve global economic welfare even in the presence of environmental externalities, provided optimal environmental policies are in place (Anderson and Blackhurst 1992; Corden 1997). However, in a world in which national environmental standards differ markedly between countries and international environmental spillovers are significant, globally optimal environmental policies will differ from nationally optimal ones. That, plus the fact that in many (especially developing) countries the enforcement of environmental policies is often less than optimal even from a national viewpoint, raises in some people's minds (for instance, Chichilnisky 1994) the question of whether liberalizing trade between rich and poor countries is desirable. To reduce the risk that this concern leads to excessive opposition to trade liberalization initiatives, and to begin to assess whether the standard gains from trade are sufficient to outweigh any loss in welfare due to added environmental damage, empirical studies of the resource depletion and environmental degradation effects of such reforms are needed.

This paper provides a methodology for doing that and illustrates it with a case study of Indonesia, a large newly industrializing country that is rich in natural resources and committed to taking part in major multilateral and regional trade liberalizations over the next two decades. Section 1 describes how a modified version of the global economy-wide model known as GTAP is used to project the world economy to 2010 and 2020 without and with those trade reforms. (This long-run view allows us to abstract from the disruptions of the current financial and political crisis.) As explained in Section 2, an environmental module is attached to the Indonesian part of that global model so as to measure the effects of structural and policy-induced changes in economic activity on air and water pollution in Indonesia. The results, presented in Section 3, identify the proportional contributions of changes in the aggregate level and composition of output, and in production techniques, to changes in environmental indicators. A base case projection without trade reform is compared with alternative scenarios involving (a) full global implementation of Uruguay Round commitments, and (b) the additional move to MFN free trade by APEC countries by 2020. The paper concludes in Section 4 with a brief summary of results and suggestions for further research.

Projecting the level and composition of output to 2020 without and with trade policy reforms

Rapid economic development and on-going policy reforms in Indonesia and other countries of the world will change substantially the level, composition and location of production and consumption during the next two decades. In this section we project global economic growth and structural changes for the periods 1992-2010 and 2010-2020. We also model the Uruguay Round and APEC trade liberalization commitments over those periods. The Uruguay Round agreements should be fully implemented by 2005, before the end of the first period, and 2010 is the date agreed at Bogor in November 1994 for completion of trade liberalization by APEC industrialised countries. The year 2020 was agreed by Indonesia and other APEC developing countries to be the date for completing their move to free trade, and it also happens to be the end of Indonesia's Second Long Term Development Plan.

For the present purpose of projecting the world economy to 2020 we use the GTAP database and model of national and international markets for all products and countries/regions of the world (see Hertel 1997). There are numerous advantages of using such a global, economy-wide CGE model even if, as with the GTAP model used here, it is comparative static in nature. The economy-wide approach makes explicit the assumed sources of economic growth that expand the demand for and supply of various products; it ensures countries can import only what they can pay for through exporting or borrowing; and it includes in the base scenario the inter-sectoral structural changes that normally accompany economic development. The advantage of using a global model rather than a national one, even though the primary focus of this paper is on results for Indonesia, is that the economic growth and structural and policy changes of other countries can be incorporated explicitly. This ensures that those changes abroad in combination with Indonesia's changes are used to generate new terms of trade for Indonesia. But it also allows the resource depleting effects of international events on Indonesia to be compared with those effects on other economies.

World Bank GDP, labor force, investment and population projections together with the Global Trade Analysis Project (GTAP) Version 3 data base and model are used to generate market projections to the year 2020. The full GTAP model divides the world economy up into 37 sectors and 30 countries or country groups (including the 16 major APEC economies). In order to keep the present analysis and presentation of results tractable, however, the data base is aggregated up to 23 product groups and to 5 regions in addition to Indonesia.

The GTAP model is a standard comparative-static multi-region computable general equilibrium model of the Johansen type that began as the SALTER model developed by the Australian Government in the 1980s but has been hugely improved during the 1990s from its current home at Purdue University in the United States. The model, which is implemented and solved using GEMPACK (Harrison and Pearson 1996), is in use by over one hundred researchers in more than 30 countries on five continents. Hence space is not used here to describe its myriad features and data base.[1]

The model utilizes a representation of consumer demands which allows for differences in both the price and income responsiveness of demand in different regions depending upon both the level of development of the region and the particular consumption patterns observed in that region. In the simulations presented below, many of the East Asian economies are projected to continue to experience very rapid economic growth rates (assuming a reasonably rapid recovery from the present financial crisis), so that the income elasticities of demand play an important role in the model. Non-homothetic preferences are captured through use of a constant difference of elasticities (CDE) function (Hertel and Tsigas 1997). This lies between the commonly used constant elasticities of substitution (CES) function and fully flexible functional forms. Such a demand system enables non-homothetic demand to be calibrated to replicate a pre-specified vector of own-price and income elasticities of demand.

On the supply-side, differences in relative rates of factor accumulation interact with different sectoral factor intensities to drive changes in the sectoral composition of output. The GTAP production system used here distinguishes sectors by their intensities in five primary factors of production: land, other natural resources, unskilled labor, skilled labor, and physical capital. Thus in a region where physical capital is accumulating rapidly, relative to other factors, we expect the capital intensive sectors to expand at the expense of unskilled labor intensive sectors such as agriculture in East Asia. Producers are assumed to choose inputs that minimize production costs subject to separable, constant returns to scale technologies. Constant elasticity of substitution (CES) functions describe substitution possibilities between primary factors and market clearing conditions equate supply with demand for each factor of production. For intermediate inputs, the assumption of a Leontief function implies no substitution between different intermediates or between them and a composite primary factor.

Land and other natural resources (minerals and energy raw materials) are assumed to be sector-specific in this study, except that some movement of land within agricultural sectors and between agriculture and forestry is allowed. It is assumed that 60 percent of value added by capital in each of the natural resource sectors is attributable to the specific factor (following Arndt and others 1997). The single factor labour in GTAP is split into skilled and unskilled labour for this study, whereby the global GTAP database is adjusted using recent estimates of labour payments by skill level (Liu and others 1997, p. 17).[2] A composite capital nest is created for human and physical capital, following Arndt and others (1997).

The present paper follows the methodology used in Hertel and others (1996) and Anderson and Pangestu (1998) but projects the world economy from 1992 not just to 2005 but to 2010 before looking at the long-run effects of Uruguay Round trade policy reforms to be implemented between now and 2005. It does the same from 2010 to 2020, to get a more realistic measure of the long-run effects of APEC reforms. We use a carefully constructed set of Uruguay Round shocks, to take into account the reality that actual reforms in Indonesia and elsewhere, particularly for farm products, will be much less than was earlier expected, thanks to 'dirty tariffication' (see Hathaway and Ingco 1996).

Table 2.1 reports the assumed rates of growth in factors and real GDP (from which the implied rates of total factor productivity growth may be derived) in the reference case for the periods from 1992 to 2010 and 2010 to 2020. Exogenous projections of each region's endowments of physical capital, unskilled and skilled labor, and population are utilized. These are based on combinations of historical data and World Bank projections of the growth in population, labor force, real GDP and investment.[3] It is clear from these estimates that the structure of the world economy will change in a number of important ways in this base case, with the developing countries constituting a considerably larger share of the global economy by 2020. Furthermore, given the particularly high rates of savings and investment in East Asia, the capital-labor ratios of these economies are expected to increase, creating supply-side pressures for changes in the composition of output in these economies (Krueger 1977; Leamer 1987). The relatively high rates of accumulation of human capital in developing economies also are likely to contribute to pressures for structural change as developing countries upgrade the skill-intensity of their product mix. Taking all these things into account and starting with the 1992 baseline, the model generates projections of the world economy assuming no changes to existing trade and other policies. That base scenario is then compared with scenarios involving trade policy reforms.

For Indonesia, the assumed rates of factor and GDP growth are close to government expectations and are in line with past trends. Over the 13 years from 1980, for example, the population and labor force growth rates were a little higher than those being projected here for the 18 years to 2010 (1.7 and 2.3 percent historically compared with assumed rates of 1.4 and more than 2.0 in table 2.1), while the rates of growth of physical capital and real GDP were a little lower than those projected here (7.1 and 5.8 percent historically compared with assumed rates of 7.4 and 6.6 in table 2.1).

The model can be closed with either gross domestic product (GDP) or total factor productivity (TFP) as exogenous targets. Since projections for GDP are available, these are imposed on the model, while total factor productivity is endogenized. Empirical evidence suggests that agriculture has a higher total factor productivity growth rate than other sectors (see Martin and Mitra 1996). Therefore, the assumption made here is that agricultural productivity increases at a rate of 0.7 percent per annum higher than other sectors.

With these and myriad other assumptions including those incorporated in the GTAP model (see Hertel 1997), a projection of the world economy to 2010 is generated assuming no trade policy changes. Then the model is re-run several times: with the Uruguay Round being fully implemented with China first excluded but then included in the WTO (the main difference being whether China is excluded or included in getting expanded access to US and EU textile and clothing markets – see Anderson and others 1997); and then with APEC liberalization commitments also being implemented by 2020. The scenario for 2010 with the Uruguay Round fully implemented is the starting

Table 2.1 Assumptions made in the projections: cumulative [and annual] percentage changes in GDP and factor endowments for the period 1992 to 2020

(a) 1992-2010

Region	*Real GDP*	*Physical capital*	*Unskilled labor*	*Skilled labor*	*Population*
Indonesia	215 [6.6]	260 [7.4]	44 [2.0]	449 [9.9]	27 [1.4]
Other APEC developing economies	202 [6.3]	312 [8.2]	26 [1.3]	167 [5.6]	19 [1.0]
Other developing and transition economies	73 [3.1]	61 [2.7]	43 [2.0]	151 [5.3]	40 [1.9]
APEC high-income economies	66 [2.9]	101 [4.0]	16 [0.8]	150 [5.2]	16 [0.8]
Other high-income economies	55 [2.5]	53 [2.4]	1 [0.1]	394 [9.3]	3 [0.2]

(b) **2010-2020**

Region	*Real GDP*	*Physical capital*	*Unskilled labor*	*Skilled labor*	*Population*
Indonesia	95 [6.9]	135 [8.9]	17 [1.6]	77 [5.9]	14 [1.3]
Other APEC developing economies	72 [5.6]	88 [6.5]	9 [0.9]	51 [4.2]	9 [0.8]
Other developing and transition economies	49 [4.1]	46 [3.9]	29 [2.6]	62 [5.0]	18 [1.7]
APEC high-income economies	27 [2.5]	47 [3.9]	3 [0.3]	53 [4.3]	7 [0.7]
Other high-income economies	28 [2.5]	34 [3.0]	-4 [-0.4]	79 [6.0]	0 [0.0]

Source: Strutt (1998, Ch.4) drawing on Anderson and others (1996), Arndt and others (1997) and, for 2010-2020, Bach (1997).

point from which to project the world economy to 2020. This too is done assuming no further trade policy changes as a base case, and that scenario is then compared with one in which the remaining trade barriers of APEC countries are removed. Indonesia's nominal rates of import protection for each sector at the beginning of each of these reform scenarios are shown in Appendix table A2.1.

How do all these changes affect the world economy? Even without the Uruguay Round being implemented, the real value of global output is projected to increase by 65 percent between 1992 and 2010, and then by a further 35 percent by between 2010 and 2020 after the Uruguay Round is implemented but without any APEC regional liberalization. Developing countries are projected to gain enormously in significance, particularly developing APEC economies which are projected to more than double their share of world output, from 6 to 14 percent during the 1992-2020 period, and treble their share of world trade.

Indonesia in particular is projected to almost treble its contribution to world output (from 0.5 to 1.5 percent), to increase its real volume of output and trade more than six-fold over the projection period, and to change the sectoral shares of its GDP substantially. The latter are summarized in table 2.2. It shows Indonesia's agricultural and other natural resource based sectors continuing to decline in relative importance as textiles and other light manufacturing industries grow. The grain sectors' share of GDP is projected to roughly halve by 2010, for example, and to fall by a further one-third or more in the subsequent decade (columns 5 and 6)—even though the absolute level of output keeps rising in these as in all other sectors (columns 3 and 4). Another example is that while the depletion of natural resources continues, forestry, fishing and mining outputs are projected to grow much less rapidly than aggregate national output.

Table 2.2 Percentage changes in sectoral output levels and in sectoral shares of GDP due to economic growth, Indonesia, 1992-2010 and 2010-2020

Sector	*1992 output (US$b)*	*2010 output (US$b)*	*Change in real value of output 1992-2010 (%)*	*Change in real value of output 2010-2020 (%)*	*Change in sectoral share of GDP 1992-2010 (%)*	*Change in sectoral share of GDP 2010-2020 (%)*
Paddy rice	7.5	14.1	87	35	-41	-31
Other grains	0.8	1.0	23	1	-61	-48
Non-grain crops	12.4	19.5	58	15	-50	-41
Livestock	3.2	6.9	113	36	-32	-30
Forestry	2.5	5.1	100	43	-36	-26
Fisheries	3.8	7.0	85	23	-41	-37
Coal	0.8	1.8	124	49	-29	-23
Oil	7.4	15.8	114	64	-32	-16
Gas	6.1	12.4	103	59	-36	-18
Other minerals	3.1	7.1	131	82	-27	-7
Food processing	24.0	44.7	87	34	-41	-31
Textiles, clothing, leather	14.1	77.4	449	177	74	42
Wood products	7.2	12.5	73	32	-45	-32
Paper products	2.7	11.7	331	132	37	19
Petroleum & coal products	5.3	18.8	253	121	12	13
Chemicals, rubber & plastics	9.4	35.8	282	120	21	13
Non-metallic mineral products	1.9	6.8	267	125	17	15
Other manufactured products	20.0	95.0	375	201	51	55
Electricity, water & gas	2.8	10.2	268	118	17	12
Construction	22.1	75.4	241	125	8	16
Trade & transport	25.0	101.0	304	120	28	13
Other private services	36.2	142.5	293	114	25	10
Other public services	8.6	46.9	447	61	74	-18
Total, all sectors	227.0	769.5	215	95		

Note: The projections for the period to 2010 maintain initial protection data, while those for the period 2010 to 2020 in columns 5 and 7 assume that the Uruguay Round, including China, has been fully implemented by 2010.
Source: GTAP V3 database and authors' model results.

Against these massive structural changes that traditionally accompany economic growth, the model's projected changes caused even by very large policy shocks are relatively modest. Table 2.3 shows, for example, how much additional impact by 2010 the Uruguay Round's implementation would have on the output of different sectors in Indonesia, both without and then with China included, and then how much extra impact the APEC reforms to 2020 would add. Since liberalization is expected to raise GDP growth rates as well,[4] we also simulate the APEC reform assuming each APEC economy's annual GDP growth rate over the 20-year implementation period (2000 to 2020) is half a percentage point higher than in the base case, due to faster total factor productivity growth. The impact of these reforms would have to be judged as rather small in most sectors, relative to the large changes that normal economic growth is projected to

Table 2.3 Percentage changes in sectoral output levels in Indonesia following Uruguay Round and APEC trade reform by 2010 and 2020

	Uruguay Round (without China) 2010	Uruguay Round (with China) 2010	APEC Liberalization 2020	APEC Liberalization 2020 (with extra GDP growth of 0.5% pa in APEC economies)
Paddy rice	-0.6	-0.3	-1.6	5.9
Other grains	3.2	4.7	14.9	22.6
Non-grain crops	-5.1	-4.6	-13.4	-4.5
Livestock	-0.2	0.1	3.1	13.2
Forestry	-3.4	-1.1	-0.2	9.4
fisheries	-1.1	-0.7	-4.1	5.8
Coal	-12.1	-7.1	18.4	31.1
Oil	-5.4	-3.3	0.6	11.9
Gas	-5.4	-3.4	0.7	11.1
Other minerals	-8.1	-5.2	-1.6	8.3
Food processing	-0.6	-0.3	-1.7	5.8
Textiles, clothing, leather	61.9	38.5	-2.6	2.9
Wood products	-6.9	-2.4	1.2	11.5
Paper products	-7.8	-3.7	6.7	17.8
Petroleum & coal products	0.9	0.5	-2.1	7.0
Chemicals, rubber & plastics	1.1	2.5	9.2	20.8
Non-metallic mineral products	-7.5	-4.4	23.8	33.6
Other manufactured products	-19.6	-12.3	-1.9	7.4
Electricity, water & gas	2.5	1.5	1.1	10.7
Construction	0.5	-0.1	-1.5	5.9
Trade & transport	-2.4	-1.3	4.9	16.3
Other private services	-2.0	-1.4	1.3	12.1
Other public services	-0.6	-0.5	-1.0	9.3
Real GDP growth	1.9	1.4	1.2	10.8

Source: Authors' model results.

generate (compare Tables 2 and 3). Nonetheless they bring substantial increases in Indonesia's economic welfare as traditionally measured even by comparative static models such as the one used here: the Uruguay Round with China included boosts real GDP for Indonesia by 1.4 percent (or 1.9 percent if China were to be excluded), and the APEC reform (to 2020) adds another 1.2 percent – even ignoring the likelihood that GDP growth would be accelerated by reform.

However, such welfare measures ignore changes in resource depletion and the environment as a consequence of the increased level and changed composition of Indonesia's output. Many environmental groups would claim that adverse resource depletion and environmental degradation effects of trade policy reform will be substantial, but very few empirical studies have sought to test that hypothesis. On environmental degradation, the following section suggests a way to examine how the changes in the aggregate level of output, the composition of that output and in the inputs and technologies used is likely to impact on air and water pollution levels. The paper then provides some empirical results for Indonesia's environment, followed by a discussion of results on resource depletion.

2. Adding an Environmental Module to the Projections Model

Accompanying economic growth and market reform are changes in the scale of output, in tastes, in the relative size of sectors, and in inputs and production technologies. These can all affect the level of pollution. How can we model these interacting forces and decompose the projected changes in environmental degradation to determine how they drive environmental change?

The model providing the projections of structural change and trade liberalization presented above provides a starting point, to which needs to be added environmental side modules to analyse the implications of these economic changes for environmental degradation.[5] In this paper we use side modules to project environmental outcomes in Indonesia for water use, water pollution and air pollution. The data for the side modules are based on a comprehensive environmental input-output data set prepared by Duchin and others (1993) using data collected in Indonesia for 1985 and 2020 by industry for various types of environmental degradation. The authors use a case study approach to project anticipated changes in technology to 2020. Twelve case studies generated data reflecting the views of experts assuming a continuation of current policies. Specialists such as chemical engineers, hydrologists, environmental scientists, energy experts and agricultural scientists were consulted on the technologies likely to be adopted in coming decades.[6] For water use there are data on the volume of water used and discharged by sector. Four measures of the water pollution content of the effluent are provided: biological oxygen demand (BOD), chemical oxygen demand (COD), dissolved solids (DS), and suspended solids (SS). The available air pollutant indicators are carbon dioxide and oxides of sulphur and nitrogen.

Based on the data from Duchin and others (1993), we assemble a matrix of environmental coefficients to estimate the environmental impact per unit of economic activity in each sector for 1992, 2010 and 2020 by assuming trends in environmental parameters per unit of output are linear over the period 1985-2020. The GTAP 1992 benchmark database for Indonesia is calibrated to this 1992 matrix of total emissions to derive environmental damage coefficients per unit of GTAP sectoral output in that base year. The proportional changes in these environmental coefficients over time are then multiplied by the GTAP 1992 environmental coefficients to obtain GTAP environmental coefficients for 2010 and 2020. This approach captures the expected change in environmental coefficients in a consistent way that is used to augment the GTAP analysis.

Three sources of environmental effects of policy changes are able to be identified: the change in the level of aggregate economic activity, the change in the contribution of each sector to output, and the change in production technology. This decomposition is useful for disentangling the causes of changes in environmental damage.[7] Define the total change in pollution (P) as the sum of the changes in pollution in each sector (P_j):

$$P = \sum_{j=1}^{n} P_j$$

The change in pollution in each sector j is the sum of the "aggregate activity" effect (A°_{j}), the "intersectoral composition" effect (C^{o}_{j}), and the "technology" effect (T_j):

$$P_j = A_j^o + C_j^o + T_j$$

In the aggregate activity effect, increased economic activity leads to increased demand for all goods and services and therefore increased emissions. The change in output due to the aggregate activity effect is the proportional change in aggregate real output in the economy (g) multiplied by the initial output in each sector (X_j). This gives the change in the scale of output in each sector with all sectors growing at the aggregate growth rate of the economy. The change in the scale of output in each sector is then multiplied by the initial environmental coefficient for each sector (E_j^o) to give the change in environmental emissions in each sector due to the aggregate activity effect:

$$A_j^o = X_j * g * E_j^o$$

The second effect is the intersectoral composition effect. Because some sectors are more polluting than others, changes in the composition of output will change pollution, even if aggregate output were to remain constant. The intersectoral effect is measured by allowing the composition of output to change while maintaining aggregate output at its initial level. Some sectors contract and others expand. This has some similarities with Dean's (1996) composition effect, where emissions decrease if income growth shifts preferences toward income elastic cleaner goods, but we model the general equilibrium-determined intersectoral effects. Both producers and consumers respond to the changed incentives, given their behavioural functions and the various constraints on the economy. Demand and supply of each commodity in each region of the world respond to changing relative prices, given the elasticities implicit for each sector. The change in sectoral output due to the intersectoral composition effect is found by multiplying the initial output in each sector by the difference between the proportional change in output in that sector (x_j) and the aggregate proportional change in output in the economy (g) to give the change in the relative size of each sector. This change in the contribution of each sector is multiplied by the initial environmental coefficient for each sector to give that sector's change in environmental emissions due to the intersectoral composition effect, (C_j^o), where

$$C_j^o = X_j * (x_j - g) * E_j^o$$

Thirdly, there is the "technology" effect, which is modelled using Duchin and others' (1993) set of environmental parameters reflecting expert opinion on anticipated changes to production methods. Changes in technology will change the amount of degradation caused by each unit of output in each sector. Total emissions with the new coefficients are compared to total emissions with the old environmental coefficients in place. The first square bracketed term of the following equation reflects the new environmental coefficient (E_j^n) applied to both the aggregate activity and the intersectoral composition components of changes in output. The second square bracketed part of the equation reflects the idea that the initial output in each sector will also be produced using the new technology and will therefore contribute to a change in emissions.

$$T_j = \left[\left(A_j^n - A_j^o\right) + \left(C_j^n - C_j^o\right)\right] + \left[X_j * \left(E_j^n - E_j^o\right)\right]$$

where

$$A_j^n = X_j * g * E_j^n$$

and

$$C_j^n = X_j * (x_j - g) * E_j^n$$

However, for policy changes such as trade liberalization where we start from the appropriate updated database, we assume that the new technology is in place and that the trade reform itself does not change the environmental damage coefficients.

3. Empirical Projections of Environmental Impacts in Indonesia of Structural and Policy Changes to 2020

Projected environmental effects due to growth and structural changes

This section uses the detailed environmental side modules to analyse some of the environmental implications of first the growth and structural changes projected for Indonesia and then the trade policy changes by 2010 and 2020.

Table 2.2 shows the 1992 and projected 2010 output levels for each sector, evaluated at 1992 prices, and the proportional changes in output due to structural changes associated with economic growth projected over that period, assuming no trade policy changes. Changes over the subsequent decade also are shown. With the large growth in the economy projected from 1992 to 2010 and 2010 to 2020, all sectors exhibit increased output levels in Indonesia but some expand much more than others. We use environmental side modules to estimate the effects of these changes in output on air and water pollution.

Air Pollution

Atmospheric emission changes are estimated for carbon dioxide and oxides of sulphur and nitrogen. Table 2.4 lists the initial 1992 level and projected new levels of emissions for 2010 without the Uruguay Round or APEC being implemented, and 2020 after the Round's implementation but without APEC trade reform. Large increases are projected for all of these air pollutants. Since the Indonesian economy is projected to grow by 215 percent between 1992 and 2010 and a by further 95 percent by 2020, this finding is not surprising. Carbon emissions increase by 134 percent in the first projected period and by 56 percent for the decade to 2020. Sulphur oxides increase by 132 and 50 percent and nitrogen oxides increase by 162 and 65 percent.

The aggregate output effect increases each sector's output, while the technology and intersectoral composition effects may add to or dampen the impact of increased aggregate output on emissions. Table 2.5 decomposes these air pollution effects to give a more precise indication of the relative magnitudes of the aggregate activity, the intersectoral composition and the technology effects. The table suggests the aggregate activity effects are the main driving force behind the increase in projected emissions, but that the intersectoral composition effects of structural change adds to that effect for all air pollutants. This is because there is a relatively high increase in the contribution to output of high air polluting sectors such as the electricity, water and gas sector and the trade and transport sector. Sectors that are not very high air polluters, such as agricultural sectors, tend to decline in relative importance.

Table 2.4 Recent and projected levels of atmospheric emissions in the base cases, Indonesia, 1992, 2010, and 2020 (kt)

	1992			*2010*			*2020*		
	carbon	*sulphur*	*nitrogen*	*carbon*	*sulphur*	*nitrogen*	*carbon*	*sulphur*	*nitrogen*
Paddy rice	1	0.0	0.1	2	0.0	0.1	3	0.0	0.2
Other grains	16	0.0	0.9	20	0.0	1.1	21	0.0	1.2
Non-grain crops	241	0.3	14.0	378	0.5	22.0	415	0.5	24.2
Livestock	310	0.4	17.9	677	0.8	39.1	931	1.1	53.8
Forestry	246	0.3	14.4	485	0.6	28.3	682	0.8	39.8
Fisheries	531	0.6	31.1	882	1.1	51.6	1,014	1.2	59.3
Coal	853	25.2	5.8	956	28.2	6.5	589	17.4	4.0
Oil	4,463	53.4	31.1	9,187	109.9	64.0	14,244	170.3	99.2
Gas	4,096	0.8	39.2	6,129	1.2	58.7	7,549	1.5	72.3
Other minerals	409	11.1	1.5	650	17.6	2.4	837	22.7	3.1
Food processing	489	13.0	1.8	752	19.9	2.8	890	23.5	3.3
Textiles, clothing, leather	293	7.7	1.1	770	20.1	3.0	1,160	29.9	4.6
Wood products	481	12.9	1.8	880	23.6	3.2	1,167	31.3	4.2
Paper products	217	6.3	1.5	712	20.8	5.0	1,317	38.9	9.7
Petroleum & coal products	1,305	17.4	8.3	4,047	54.4	25.7	8,302	112.4	52.8
Chemicals, rubber & plastics	3,330	35.6	26.6	5,930	65.9	47.3	4,867	60.8	38.6
Non-metallic mineral products	894	25.6	5.4	2,503	73.0	16.8	4,448	131.9	32.5
Other manufactured products	880	23.0	3.4	1,997	52.0	7.8	2,074	53.5	8.2
Electricity, water & gas	7,843	168.2	102.8	18,045	347.1	241.6	26,637	434.2	366.8
Construction	10,547	69.2	37.9	25,007	164.1	89.9	42,587	279.5	153.1
Trade & transport	10,322	129.8	532.5	30,564	384.5	1,578.4	52,865	665.4	2733.0
Other private services	193	1.2	0.8	559	3.4	2.2	943	5.7	3.7
Other public services	709	4.1	2.8	2,882	16.8	11.4	3,724	21.6	14.8
Total, all sectors	48,668	606	882	114,014	1,405	2,309	177,264	2,104	3,782

Note: 2020 levels include Uruguay Round implementation.
Source: Authors' model results.

While the aggregate activity effect, and to a much lesser extent the intersectoral composition effect, increase air pollution during the period to 2020, many sectors' emissions of carbon and oxides of sulphur and nitrogen grow less rapidly than output because of improvements in energy efficiency. This is shown by the technique effect which is negative for all air pollutants in table 2.5, reflecting the improved technologies expected to become available.

WATER USE AND POLLUTION

Table 2.6 presents water use and water pollution results, calculated for the various sectors using GTAP simulation results and a water use and pollution side module.[8] Manufacturing sectors face two offsetting trends in their use of water. Growth occurs in water-intensive sectors like pulp and paper, but new technologies for conserving water are expected to be adopted over time. Overall there is a significant increase in water uptake in the textiles, other manufacturing and pulp and paper sectors. Even by 2010 these more than double their water use, while household water use increases by almost 50 percent. However increases in water use are dwarfed by the savings in water uptake for paddy rice, which is the largest user of water in our model. That comes from the significantly improved efficiencies anticipated in irrigation delivery systems as well as from the changing inter-

Table 2.5 Decomposition of changes in pollution as a consequence of economic growth and structural changes, Indonesia, 1992-2010 and 2010-2020

1992-2010

	Total pollution change[a]		*Aggregate activity effect*	*Intersectoral composition effect*	*Technology effect*
Carbon (kt)	65,346	[134]	104,607	10,149	-49,409
Sulphur (kt)	799	[132]	1,302	214	-716
Nitrogen (kt)	1,427	[162]	1,897	392	-862
Water in (bm^3)[b]	-12	[-4]	685	-388	-309
Water out (bm^3)	0.8	[126]	1.3	0.7	-1
BOD (kt)	81	[52]	337	176	-433
COD (kt)	341	[64]	1,149	726	-1,534
DS (kt)	-17	[-46]	79	-47	-48
SS (kt)	105	[23]	1,002	638	-1,536

2010-2020

	Total pollution change[a]		*Aggregate activity*	*Intersectoral composition*	*Technology effect*
Carbon (kt)	63,982	[56]	107,244	16,904	-60,166
Sulphur (kt)	707	[50]	1,323	276	-893
Nitrogen (kt)	1,495	[65]	2,165	366	-1,035
Water in (bm^3)[b]	-109	[-36]	296	-167	-236
Water out (bm^3)	0.4	[29]	1.3	1.0	-2
BOD (kt)	-13	[-5]	223	146	-382
COD (kt)	-2	[-0]	822	587	-1412
DS (kt)	-13	[-65]	19	-12	-19.5
SS (kt)	-211	[-37]	545	474	-1231

a. Percentages changes from base case are shown in square parentheses.
b. This does not include the change in household water use.
Source: Authors' model results.

Table 2.6 Recent and projected levels of water use and quality in the base cases, Indonesia, 1992, 2010, and 2020

Base level for 1992

	Water in (millions of m³)	*Water out (millions of m³)*	*BOD (kt)*	*COD (kt)*	*Dissolved solids (kt)*	*Suspended solids (kt)*
Paddy rice	313,072	0	0	0	0	0
Livestock	8	0	0	0	0	0
Food processing	124	97	21	30	37	49
Textiles, clothing, leather	102	102	18	72	0	87
Paper products	217	97	64	217	0	70
Chemicals, rubber, plastics	5	4	0	0	0	0
Other manufactures	307	307	54	216	0	261
Households	10,704	0	0	0	0	0
Total, all sectors	324,538	608	157	534	37	466

2010

	Water in (millions of m³)	*Water out (millions of m³)*	*BOD (kt)*	*COD (kt)*	*Dissolved solids (kt)*	*Suspended solids (kt)*
Paddy rice	300,439	0	0	0	0	0
Livestock	16	0	0	0	0	0
Food processing	132	104	12	17	20	24
Textiles, clothing, leather	278	278	32	127	0	129
Paper products	519	262	111	402	0	83
Chemicals, rubber, plastics	9	9	0	0	0	0
Other manufactures	720	720	82	329	0	334
Households	15,712	0	0	0	0	0
Total, all sectors	317,825	1,372	238	875	20	571

2020

	Water in (millions of m³)	*Water out (millions of m³)*	*BOD (kt)*	*COD (kt)*	*Dissolved solids (kt)*	*Suspended solids (kt*
Paddy rice	190,557	0	0	0	0	0
Livestock	21	0	0	0	0	0
Food processing	104	82	5	7	7	7
Textiles, clothing, leather	460	460	37	147	0	115
Paper products	645	390	115	449	0	37
Chemicals, rubber, plastics	11	10	0	0	0	0
Other manufactures	822	822	65	263	0	206
Households	18,494	0	0	0	0	0
Total, all sectors	211,114	1,764	223	866	7	365

Note: 2020 levels include Uruguay Round implementation.
Source: Authors' model results.

sectoral composition of output. As a consequence, total water withdrawals fall over the projection periods, by 4 percent to 2010 and by a further 36 percent by 2020.

Between 1992 and 2010, we project water discharge to increase by 126 percent, with a further 29 percent increase by 2020 (column 2 of table 2.5). The decomposition in table 2.5 shows that the intersectoral composition effect augments the aggregate activity effect a little. The relative increases are in textiles, pulp and paper and other manufactures, which are all large producers of waste water. However, improved technologies dampen the effect of increases in water discharged.

The water pollution changes we model are biological oxygen demand (BOD), chemical oxygen demand (COD), dissolved solids (DS) and suspended solids (SS). These emissions are assumed to be determined by the quantity of waste water produced. Once we have calculated the proportional change in water output for each sector, we can estimate the change in water pollution by sector. Because of the aggregate activity effect, emissions of all water pollutants except for dissolved solids rise between 1992 and 2010 (table 2.5a). However, emissions rise by significantly less than the proportional increase in total output in Indonesia. This is mainly due to the improved technology assumed to be available in 2010. The intersectoral composition effect for all water pollutants, with the exception of dissolved solids, is positive due to the increased relative significance of the polluting industries. The composition effect in both projected periods moves production into the sectors we model as being the most important producers of water pollutants, particularly textiles, pulp, paper, and other manufactures. For dissolved solids, the composition effect is negative with the reduced significance of the food processing sector.

For the period to 2010, the assumed technology effect offsets over 80 percent of the aggregate activity and intersectoral effects for all water pollutants. And for the period to 2020, the technology effect is sufficiently strong to overturn the positive aggregate activity and intersectoral effects to give a net reduction in pollution for all water pollutants.

Projected environmental effects of Uruguay Round and APEC trade reforms

How much difference will it make to those environmental effects of economic growth to impose on Indonesia and others some trade reforms? The first two columns of table 2.3 show the proportional change in output due to Uruguay Round liberalization, first without and then with the inclusion of China as a WTO member. The second pair of columns show the projected sectoral changes in output due to APEC liberalization. Leaving aside the final scenario in which economic growth is assumed to be boosted by APEC liberalization (discussed separately below), some sectors reduce and other sectors increase their output level because of trade reform, in contrast to the middle columns of table 2.2 for structural change projections where all sectors increase their output. We therefore can expect the composition effects to be much stronger relative to the aggregate activity effects in these reform cases, in contrast to the growth and structural change scenarios discussed above.

The results in table 2.3, coming from a global model, include the effects on output levels in Indonesia of changes in protection and relative prices in other regions. The sector that experiences the greatest proportional increase in Indonesia with Uruguay Round implementation is textiles and clothing, with a 60 percent boost to output anticipated if China is kept out of the WTO, or just under 40 percent if China is able to join. With additional APEC liberalization, the effects on the textile sector are much less pronounced because MFA quotas are assumed to have been already phased out as part of the Round's implementation. The sectors that tend to do well with APEC reform are instead the coal and non-metallic minerals — sectors which Indonesia's own policies tend to discriminate against. The corn (coarse grains) sector also is projected to do well.

What do these output changes do to pollution levels? Again, we consider effects on first air and then water, recognising that emissions will increase in some sectors and fall in others in response to Uruguay Round and APEC trade reforms.

Air pollution

Table 2.7 indicates that a *reduction* in air pollution is projected for Indonesia under Uruguay Round liberalization (including China), rather than the increase feared by environmentalists. The reduction from 2010 baseline levels is 0.6 percent for carbon and sulphur oxides and 1.0 percent for nitrogen oxides. The decomposition in table 2.7 shows that the aggregate activity effect adds to air pollution but the change in the intersectoral composition of output reduces air pollution by more.

When the total change in emissions is examined by sector (table 2.8), we find that the most significant reduction is contributed by the trade and transport sector. The output of textiles rises more than that in

Table 2.7 Decomposition of pollution effects from Uruguay Round trade reform (including China), Indonesia, 2010 (*percent change from 2010 baseline level shown in curved parentheses, percent of the 1992-2010 absolute change is in brackets*)

	Total change	*Aggregate Activity*	*Intersectoral composition*
Carbon (kt)	-733 (-0.6) [-1.1]	1,585 (1.4) [2.4]	-2,318 (-2.0) [-3.5]
Sulphur (kt)	-8 (-0.6) [-1.0]	20 (1.4) [2.4]	-27 (-1.9) [-3.4]
Nitrogen (kt)	-22 (-1.0) [-1.5]	32 (1.4) [2.2]	-54 (-2.3) [-3.8]
Water in (billion m^3)	-0.8 (-0.3) [-7]	4 (1.4) [35]	-5 (-1.6) [-42]
Water out (billion m^3)	0.01 (0.6) [1.1]	0.02 (1.4) [2.4]	-0.01 (-0.8) [-1.3]
BOD (kt)	-2.0 (-0.9) [-2.5]	3 (1.4) [4.1]	-5 (-2.3) [-6.6]
COD (kt)	-6.5 (-0.7) [-1.9]	12 (1.4) [3.6]	-19 (-2.1) [-5.5]
DS (kt)	-0.05 (-0.3) [-0.3]	0.3 (1.4) [1.6]	-0.3 (-1.7) [-2.0]
SS (kt)	5.3 (0.9) [5.0]	8 (1.4) [7.6]	-3 (-0.5) [-2.5]

Source: Authors' model results.

any other sector, but since it is starting from a relatively low base of air emissions, the increase in air pollutants from this sector is more than outweighed by reductions occurring in other sectors. If China is not included in the WTO and hence by assumption does not liberalize its trade, the reductions in Indonesia's air pollution almost double relative to the reductions shown in table 2.7 when China is included. This is primarily because the Indonesian textile and clothing sector does not grow as much when China is included and hence that sector does not pull as many resources away from other more-polluting sectors. However, the greater carbon and other emissions in Indonesia are possibly more than offset by a reduction in emissions in China following its accession to WTO and thereby its assumed greater access to textile markets in the United States and the EU.[9]

With additional APEC trade liberalization, air pollution is projected to increase but, as shown in table 2.9, the increases are only between 2 and 4 percent. Moreover, a small number of sectors drive the results. For example, the trade and transport sector contributes over 45 percent of the increase in air pollution (unreported further decomposition of results in table 2.9). This makes it relatively easy to target that pollution with environmental taxes to reduce the

Table 2.8 Sectoral decomposition of the total change in emissions due to Uruguay Round implementation, Indonesia, 2010

	Carbon (kt)	*Sulphur (kt)*	*Nitrogen (kt)*	*Water in (bm^3)*	*Water out (bm^3)*	*BOD (kt)*	*COD (kt)*	*DS (kt)*	*SS (kt)*
Paddy rice	-0.01	0.00	0.00	-0.78	0.00	0.00	0.00	0.00	0.00
Other grains	0.93	0.00	0.05	0.00	0.00	0.00	0.00	0.00	0.00
Non-grain crops	-17.33	-0.02	-1.01	0.00	0.00	0.00	0.00	0.00	0.00
Livestock	0.95	0.00	0.05	0.00	0.00	0.00	0.00	0.00	0.00
Forestry	-5.09	-0.01	-0.30	0.00	0.00	0.00	0.00	0.00	0.00
Fisheries	-6.35	-0.01	-0.37	0.00	0.00	0.00	0.00	0.00	0.00
Coal	-67.89	-2.00	-0.46	0.00	0.00	0.00	0.00	0.00	0.00
Oil	-301.33	-3.60	-2.10	0.00	0.00	0.00	0.00	0.00	0.00
Gas	-207.77	-0.04	-1.99	0.00	0.00	0.00	0.00	0.00	0.00
Other minerals	-33.86	-0.92	-0.13	0.00	0.00	0.00	0.00	0.00	0.00
Food processing	-2.03	-0.05	-0.01	0.00	0.00	-0.03	-0.05	-0.05	-0.07
Textiles, clothing, leather	296.17	7.71	1.15	0.11	0.11	12.20	48.81	0.00	49.57
Wood products	-21.47	-0.58	-0.08	0.00	0.00	0.00	0.00	0.00	0.00
Paper products	-26.13	-0.76	-0.18	-0.02	-0.01	-4.08	-14.74	0.00	-3.05
Petroleum & coal products	21.45	0.29	0.14	0.00	0.00	0.00	0.00	0.00	0.00
Chemicals, rubber & plastics	150.03	1.67	1.20	0.00	0.00	0.00	0.00	0.00	0.00
Non-metallic mineral products	-108.88	-3.17	-0.73	0.00	0.00	0.00	0.00	0.00	0.00
Other manufactured products	-246.05	-6.40	-0.96	-0.09	-0.09	-10.14	-40.55	0.00	-41.18
Electricity, water & gas	276.08	5.31	3.70	0.00	0.00	0.00	0.00	0.00	0.00
Construction	-27.51	-0.18	-0.10	0.00	0.00	0.00	0.00	0.00	0.00
Trade & transport	-385.10	-4.84	-19.89	0.00	0.00	0.00	0.00	0.00	0.00
Other private services	-7.71	-0.05	-0.03	0.00	0.00	0.00	0.00	0.00	0.00
Other public services	-13.83	-0.08	-0.05	0.00	0.00	0.00	0.00	0.00	0.00
Total, all sectors	-732.75	-7.74	-22.09	-0.78	0.01	-2.05	-6.53	-0.05	5.27

Source: Authors' model results.

impact of trade reform on emissions, should that small increase be considered a problem.

The key point to draw from these results, however, is that the air pollutive effects of even these major trade liberalizations is tiny (at less than 4 percent of the base level), and is especially small compared with the increases that will accompany normal economic growth and structural changes, as can be seen by the numbers in square parentheses in tables 2.7 and 2.9.

Water use and pollution

Water withdrawals are reduced by both trade liberalizations. Table 2.7 shows a reduction in withdrawals of 0.3 percent with Uruguay Round implementation, while table 2.9 shows that water withdrawals reduce by a further 1.6 percent with APEC liberalization. These water use reductions are largely due to a reduction in paddy output.

Most water pollutants also decline with Uruguay Round implementation, as shown in table 2.7. The declines are just under 1 percent for BOD, COD and dissolved solids, but there is an increase of just under 1 percent in suspended solids. For APEC liberalization, table 2.9 reports a 2.4 percent increase in BOD and COD but reductions in solids of between 1 and 2 percent. Thus as with air pollution, these results show that trade reform will at most add only a very small

Table 2.9 Decomposition of pollution effects in Indonesia under APEC liberalization, 2020 (*percent change from 2020 baseline level shown in parentheses, percent of the 1992-2020 absolute change in brackets*)

	Total change	*Aggregate activity*	*Intersectoral composition*
Carbon (kt)	3,736	2,124	1,612
	(2.1)	(1.2)	(0.9)
	[2.9]	[1.6]	[1.3]
Sulphur (kt)	72	25	47
	(3.4)	(1.2)	(2.2)
	[4.8]	[1.7]	[3.1]
Nitrogen (kt)	144	45	99
	(3.8)	(1.2)	(2.6)
	[4.9]	[1.6]	[3.4]
Water in (billion m^3)	-3.0	2.3	-5.3
	(-1.6)	(1.2)	(-2.8)
	[-2.5]	[1.9]	[-4.4]
Water out (billion m^3)	-0.002	0.02	-0.02
	(-0.1)	(1.2)	(-1.3)
	[-0.2]	[1.8]	[-1.9]
BOD (kt)	5.4	2.7	2.7
	(2.4)	(1.2)	(1.2)
	[7.9]	[3.9]	[4.0]
COD (kt)	21.1	10.4	10.8
	(2.4)	(1.2)	(1.2)
	[6.2]	[3.0]	[3.2]
DS (kt)	-0.13	0.09	-0.21
	(-1.8)	(1.2)	(-3.1)
	[-0.4]	[0.3]	[-0.7]
SS (kt)	-4.5	4.4	-8.9
	(-1.2)	(1.2)	(-2.4)
	[-4.2]	[4.1]	[-8.4]

Source: Authors' model results.

amount to water use and pollution, an amount that would not be discernible alongside the increased BOD and COD pollution associated with the general expansion of the economy over time.

What if trade reform boosts economic growth?

The above simulations of trade reform are from a comparative static model and so do not include the impact that trade reform would have in boosting economic growth. Hence it understates the extent of pollution that might result. To get a feel of how large that bias might be, we re-ran the APEC liberalization but assumed that APEC economies' GDPs would grow substantially faster (by half a percentage point per year over the 20-year implementation period to 2020) through a boost to their total factor productivity growth. The impact of APEC reform including that faster growth on the pollution results is shown in table 2.10, based on the output effects summarized in the final column of table 2.3. Not surprisingly, that change in assumption raises the effect of liberalization on pollution. Even so, the numbers are relatively small: air pollution is 12-15 percent greater and water pollution 6-12 percent greater, than would have been the case in 2020 (instead of no more than 4 percent as when we assume no growth effect of APEC reform).

Table 2.10 Decomposition of pollution effects in Indonesia under APEC liberalization, with 0.5 percent p.a. extra GDP growth in APEC economies, 2020 (*percent change from 2020 baseline level shown in parentheses, percent of the 1992-2020 absolute change in brackets*)

	Total change	*Aggregate activity*	*Intersectoral composition*
Carbon (kt)	21,142 (12) [16]	19,091 (11) [15]	2,051 (1) [2]
Sulphur (kt)	283 (14) [19]	227 (11) [15]	57 (3) [4]
Nitrogen (kt)	557 (15) [19]	407 (11) [14]	149 (4) [5]
Water in (billion m^3)	11 (6) [9]	21 (11) [17]	-9 (-5) [-8]
Water out (billion m^3)	0.15 (9) [13]	0.19 (11) [16]	-0.04 (-2) [-3]
BOD (kt)	27 (12) [39]	24 (11) [35]	3 (1) [4]
COD (kt)	104 (12) [31]	93 (11) [28]	11 (1) [3]
DS (kt)	0.4 (6) [2]	0.8 (11) [3]	-0.4 (-5) [-1]
SS (kt)	26 (7) [24]	39 (11) [37]	-14 (-4) [-13]

Source: Authors' model results.

This amount is less than one fifth of the air pollution (and a somewhat larger fraction of the water pollution) that would result from the normal output expansions and structural changes that would take place without reform. Moreover, that extra pollution due to accelerated growth is accompanied by a much greater boost to economic welfare as conventionally measured than when we assume there is no growth effect of trade reform: Indonesia's GDP in 2020 is 10.8 percent higher in this growth-enhancing case, compared with only 1.2 percent higher in the earlier APEC reform case that assumed no growth effect. Clearly this compensates generously for the extra pollution and provides great scope for spending some of that extra income on pollution abatement.

Resource depletion

The impact of trade liberalization on natural resource depletion can be crudely inferred from changes in primary production. In the case of the Uruguay Round, the first column of table 2.11 shows that most primary production is reduced by that liberalization. This suggests that less rather than more depletion of Indonesia's natural resources will take place because of the Uruguay Round reforms. Of course there are some offsetting changes in other economies, but the final column of table 2.11 shows that in aggregate the changes to natural resource use from the Round will be tiny.

4. Conclusions

If present environmental policies remain unchanged, projected economic growth and structural changes over the next two decades would, according to the above simulations, add to environmental degradation and resource depletion in Indonesia. This is not an argument against economic growth of course, but rather for the need to introduce or strengthen the enforcement of environmental and resource policies so as to internalize some of the externalities associated with output and consumption expansion. When optimal environmental (and other) policies are in place and are continually adapted to remain optimal over time, it is necessarily the case that economic growth enhances social welfare. That may not preclude a worsening of environmental degradation or further resource depletion, but at least those changes would be optimal from that society's viewpoint, given the actual or opportunity cost of avoidance or abatement. Likewise, trade reform can contribute to environmental damage and resource depletion, but again that will not be nationally welfare-reducing so long as optimal environmental (and other) policies are always in place.

A concern of some people, though, is that developing countries' environmental and resource policies may not be optimal even nationally, let alone from a global perspective, and that trade liberalization with no change in those environmental and resource poli-

Table 2.11 Percentage changes in resource-sector output levels in various regions of the world following Uruguary Round trade reform (including China), 2010

	Indonesia	*Other APEC developing economies*	*Other developing & transition economies*	*APEC high-income economies*	*Other high-income economies*	*Total world*
Paddy rice	-0.3	2.9	-1.3	-1.0	-3.1	0.48
Non-grain crops	-4.6	4.3	-0.4	2.0	-2.9	0.59
Livestock	0.1	-1.4	-1.6	0.9	1.2	-0.06
Forestry	-1.1	-0.7	-0.1	-0.0	1.9	-0.03
Fisheries	-0.7	-7.4	0.1	-0.4	5.1	-0.21
Coal	-7.1	-0.6	0.2	-0.3	1.0	0.03
Oil	-3.3	-2.9	0.2	0.1	0.4	-0.04
Gas	-3.4	-1.4	0.1	0.5	0.1	0.06
Other minerals	-5.2	-5.0	-0.7	-1.4	1.9	-0.39

Source: Authors' model results.

cies therefore could be bad for the environment. Hence the reason in the present empirical study for looking at trade reform without changing environmental and resource policies.[10]

This case study of Indonesia suggests that trade policy reforms slated for the next two decades in most cases would improve the environment (at least with respect to air and water pollution) and reduce the depletion of natural resources in that country and in the worst cases would add only very slightly to environmental degradation and resource depletion even without toughening the enforcement of existing environmental and resource regulations or adding new ones. The economic gains from the trade reforms and the scope for adopting well-targeted environmental and resource policies to reduce any serious damage are such that social welfare almost certainly is going to be improved substantially by these liberalizations.[11]

Furthermore, a related study (Strutt 1998, Ch. 3) which focuses on land degradation through soil erosion and associated off-site damage draws a similar conclusion. That study incorporates feedback effects of that damage on land productivity and thereby is able to value the loss of production associated with that erosion. Again using GTAP to model the effects of implementing the Uruguay Round agreements, the study finds that the aggregate output expansion and shift in its composition does add slightly to soil erosion, but that the cost of the damage caused by that increased erosion is miniscule, amounting to less than 0.2 percent of the national economic welfare gain (as traditionally measured) from the Uruguay Round liberalization.

Moreover, this study has focused only on one country's resources and environment. The natural resource impact of the Uruguay Round can be seen in table 2.11 to be positive rather than negative in most other regions too. It is negative mainly in Western Europe ('Other high-income economies'), where resource policies are well developed and could easily be adapted to cope with any undesired increase in exploitation. And it happens that when environmental damage occurs in Indonesia because of the change in the composition of its output following trade reform, damage to the environment of other countries is often lessened. A case in point is the inclusion of China in the WTO that (hopefully) allows China greater access to US and EU markets under the Uruguay Round Agreement on Textiles and Clothing: the above results show that this would reduce Indonesia's capacity to expand exports of light manufactures and so keep resources in more-polluting activities in Indonesia – but it would mean China moves away from some of its very pollutive coal-intensive heavy manufacturing, thereby potentially reducing not only local air pollution but also global warming. The latter could be quantified by extending the environmental side modules developed here for Indonesia to other countries and regions of the world included in the GTAP model.[12]

We have set up a framework for modelling and decomposing the major environmental impacts of growth and policy reform in as transparent a way as possible. The results presented here indicate sectors of particular concern, given available information and our choice of model.[13] Needless to say, caution should be used in interpreting the above results, particularly given the still poor quality of environmental data. There are sectors and types of environmental damage that are not adequately represented here.[14] Clearly, this kind of research is in its infancy; there are many future directions and areas where improvements can be made. For example as improved environmental data become available for other regions, the environmental effects in other countries could be traced. In particular, improved modelling of air pollution across countries will be possible with the upgraded energy component of future versions of the GTAP data base.[15] More-direct inclusion of emissions and abatement activities in the GTAP model may also be desirable, rather than having just side modules. Among other things, the model could then be modified to enable induced substitution towards less environmentally damaging output and the adoption of less-polluting technologies when environmental taxes are imposed or increased. Endogenizing environmental policies to income growth,[16] trade policy changes and changes in pollution would be another useful extension, providing a rich future research agenda.

Appendix Table A2.1 Import tariff rates in Indonesia without and with Uruguay Round liberalization, by sector, 2010 (percent)

	2010 base	*2010 after UR*
Paddy rice	9.0	9.0
Other grains	0.0	0.0
Non-grain crops	54.7	38.3
Livestock	4.8	4.8
Forestry	14.4	14.4
Fisheries	29.8	29.8
Coal	5.0	5.0
Oil	0.0	0.0
Gas	5.0	5.0
Other minerals	4.9	4.9
Food processing	12.3	11.3
Textiles, clothing, leather	28.7	22.5
Wood products	34.4	31.0
Paper products	8.0	8.0
Petroleum & coal products	4.7	4.7
Chemicals, rubber & plastics	6.6	6.6
Non-metallic mineral products	14.1	12.9
Other manufactured products	15.6	15.4
Electricity, water & gas	0.0	0.0
Construction	0.0	0.0
Trade & transport	0.0	0.0
Other private services	0.0	0.0
Other public services	0.0	0.0

Source: GTAP data base and authors' model results.

Notes

Thanks are due to Christian Bach, Betina Dima-ranan and Faye Duchin for helpful inputs, and to conference participants at the GETS Trade and Environment Workshop, London, June 1998, the World Congress of Environmental and Resource Economists, Venice, June 1998, and the Trade, Global Policy, and the Environment Conference, particularly Shanta Devarajan, David Roland-Holst, Tom Rutherford and David Tarr, for insightful comments. The authors are also grateful to the Australian Centre for International Agricultural Research (under PN9449) and the World Bank for financial assistance.

1. See Hertel (1997, especially chapters 2 and 3) and McDougall (1997) for detailed descriptions of the GTAP model and data base. Updated information is available at the following website: http://www.agecon.purdue.edu/gtap.

2. Version 4 of the GTAP data base will include this split between skilled and unskilled labour. It will also break out a natural resource input calibrated to the target elasticity of supply in resource-constrained sectors (McDougall 1998).

3. Growth rates for 1992-2010 are adapted from Anderson and others 1997; and Arndt and others 1997, while growth rates for 2010–2020 are adapted from Bach 1997.

4. See, for example, the theoretical reasons presented in Grossman and Helpman (1991), and the rapidly growing empirical evidence presented by Baldwin (1992), Dollar (1992), Edwards (1992), Sachs and Warner (1995), Harrison (1996), and USITC (1997), and the references therein.

5. The approach of augmenting CGE models with environmental side models has been taken by a number of researchers. For example, Bandara and Coxhead (1995) look at soil erosion in a single country model. Perroni and Wigle (1997) use an innovative side model to analyse global externalities and abatement costs with GTAP. There have also been attempts to incorporate environmental equations and parameters more directly into a CGE model (for example, Xie 1996).

6. Other scenarios are also presented where the government is assumed to place heavier emphasis on environmental protection and resource conservation. Since we do not explicitly model improved environmental policies here, only the scenario of current trends is used.

7. The decomposition developed here is in some ways similar to the "scale," "composition," and "technique" effects of income growth on the level of environmental emissions discussed by Dean (1996, 1998), Beghin and others (1997, 1998) also discuss such a three-way decomposition.

8. Increases in household water use are taken from estimates in Duchin and others (1993) and entered exogenously, assuming Indonesia's population increases to 263 million by 2020.

9. When China is excluded, the group of "Other APEC developing economies" (which includes China) expand their output of textiles and clothing by only 8 percent following Uruguay Round implementation, whereas with China included, that sector expands 25 percent (Strutt 1998, chapter 5).

10. For more on modelling the responses of environmental policies to trade reforms (something which has not been attempted in the present study), see the recent paper on Mexican agriculture by Beghin and others (1997).

11. This is not inconsistent with the finding by Lindert (1996) that there is virtually no evidence over many decades of net soil degradation in Indonesia.

12. A new paper by Cole, Rayner, and Bates (1998) applies emission coefficients to another set of Uruguay Round output results using GTAP for the world as a whole and places monetary values on the estimated changes in emissions. While the latter values are open to question of course, their global results nonetheless are consistent with the above findings for Indonesia in suggesting that any increases in pollution from the Uruguay Round are likely to reduce developing countries' welfare gains from liberalization by much less than 2 percent while *raising* the welfare gains to some advanced economies. Another new empirical study by Unteroberdoerster (1998), looks at APEC trade liberalization alone and again finds very small effects on the environment.

13. There are of course more sophisticated methods of projecting economic growth, using endogenous growth and incorporating imperfect competition and scale economies.

14. For example, the most excessive pollutant in Indonesian rivers is faecal coliform which exceeds recommended standards by more than a thousand-fold in some places (World Bank 1990, p. xxxi). We have not been able to include this in our present analysis. Nor have we accounted for the human health effects of pollution (as was done for Chile in Beghin and others 1998).

15. The weakness of the energy data in version 3 of GTAP led us to not focus particularly on energy in the current work. Details of the project aiming to collect consistent data on energy quantity flows, prices and taxes to be incorporated into future versions of the GTAP data base are available at http://www.agecon.purdue.edu/gtap/doe/index.htm.

16. The reasons for expecting citizens to seek a tightening of environmental standards and regulations/taxes on pollution and resource depletion as incomes rise, at least after middle-income status is reached, have been canvassed by, among others, Selden and Song (1994), Grossman and Krueger (1995), and Hettige, Mani, and Wheeler (1998).

References

Anderson, K. and R. Blackhurst, eds. 1992. *The Greening of World Trade Issues.* Ann Arbor: University of Michigan Press and London: Harvester Wheatsheaf.

Anderson, K., B. Dimaranan, T. Hertel and W. Martin. 1997. "Economic Growth and Policy Reform in the Asia-Pacific: Trade and Welfare Implications by 2005." *Asia-Pacific Economic Review* 3(1): 1–18.

Anderson, K., and M. Pangestu. 1998. "Structural Changes in a Reforming World Economy: Implications for Indonesia." *Bulletin of Indonesian Economic Studies* 34(3).

Anderson, K., and A. Strutt. 1996. "On Measuring the Environmental Effects of Agricultural Trade Liberalization." In M.E. Bredahl, N. Ballenger, J.C. Dunmore, and T.L. Roe, eds., *Agriculture, Trade and the Environment.* Boulder and London: Westview Press.

Arndt, C., T. Hertel, B. Dimaranan, K. Huff, and R. McDougall. 1997. "China in 2005: Implications for the Rest of the World." *Journal of Economic Integration* 12(4): 505–47.

Bach, C. 1997. Personal communication.

Baldwin, R. 1992. "Measurable Dynamic Gains from Trade." *Journal of Political Economy* 100(1): 162–74.

Bandara, J.S., and I. Coxhead. 1995. "Economic Reforms and the Environment in Sri Lanka." Agricultural Economics Discussion Paper 27/95, La Trobe University, June.

Beghin, J., B. Bowland, S. Dessus, D. Roland-Holst, and D. Van der Mennsbrugghe. 1998. "Trade, Environment and Public Health in Chile: Evidence from an Economywide Model." Chapter 3 in this volume.

Beghin, J., S. Dessus, D. Roland-Holst, and D. Van der Mennsbrugghe. 1997. "The Trade and Environment Nexus in Mexican Agriculture: A General Equilibrium Analysis." *Agricultural Economics* 17(2-3): 115–31.

Chichilnisky, G. 1994. "North-South Trade and the Global Environment." *American Economic Review* 84(4): 851–74.

Cole, M.A., A.J. Rayner, and J.M. Bates. 1998. "Trade Liberalisation and the Environment: The Case of the Uruguay Round." *The World Economy* 21(3): 337–47.

Corden, W.M. 1997. *Trade Policy and Economic Welfare* (second edition). Oxford: Clarendon Press.

Dean, J. 1996. "Testing the Impact of Trade Liberalization on the Environment." CIES Seminar Paper 96-11, University of Adelaide, August.

Dean, J. 1999. "Testing the Impact of Trade Liberalization on the Environment: Theory and Evidence." Chapter 4 in this volume.

Dollar, D. 1992. "Outward-oriented Developing Economies Really Do Grow More Rapidly: Evidence from 95 LDCs, 1976–1985." *Economic Development and Cultural Change* 40(3): 523–44.

Duchin, F., C. Hamilton, and G. Lange. 1993. *Environment and Development in Indonesia: An Input-Output Analysis of Natural Resource Issues.* Jakarta: BAPPENHAS–Ministry of Forestry for USAID.

Edwards, S. 1992. "Trade Orientation, Distortions and Growth in Developing Countries." *Journal of Development Economics* 39(1): 31–57.

Grossman, G.M., and E. Helpman. 1991. *Innovation and Growth in the Global Economy.* Cambridge: MIT Press.

Grossman, G., and A. Krueger. 1995. "Economic Growth and the Environment." *Quarterly Journal of Economics* 110(2): 353–77.

Hathaway, D.E., and M.D. Ingco. 1996. "Agricultural Liberalization and the Uruguay Round." Ch. 2 in W. Martin and L.A. Winters, eds., *The Uruguay Round and the Developing Countries.* Cambridge and New York: Cambridge University Press.

Harrison, A. 1996. "Openness and Growth: A Time-Series, Cross-Country Analysis for Developing Countries." *Journal of Development Economics* 48(2): 419–47.

Harrison, J., and K. Pearson. 1996. "Computing Solutions for Large General Equilibrium Models using GEMPACK." *Computational Economics* 9: 83–127.

Hertel, T.W., ed. 1997. *Global Trade Analysis: Modeling and Applications,* Cambridge and New York: Cambridge University Press.

Hertel, T.W., W. Martin, K. Yanagishima, and B. Dimaranan. 1996. "Liberalizing Manufactures Trade in a Changing World Economy." Ch. 7 in W. Martin and L. A. Winters, eds., *The Uruguay Round and the Developing Countries,* Cambridge and New York: Cambridge University Press.

Hertel, T.W., and M.E. Tsigas. 1997. "Structure of GTAP." Chapter 2 in T.W Hertel, ed., *Global Trade Analysis: Modeling and Applications.* Cambridge University Press.

Hettige, H., M. Mani, and D. Wheeler. 1998. "Industrial Pollution in Economic Development—Kuznets Revisited." Chapter 5 in this volume.

Krueger, A. 1977. "Growth, Distortions and Patterns of Trade Among Many Countries." Princeton Studies in International Finance, Princeton, NJ.

Leamer, E. 1987. "Paths of Development in the Three Factor n-good General Equilibrium Model." *Journal of Political Economy* 95(5): 961–99.

Lindert, P.H. 1996. "Soil Degradation and Agricultural Change in China and Indonesia." CIES Seminar Paper 96-14, University of Adelaide, September.

Liu, J., T.T. Vo, R. Tyers, and T. Hertel. 1997. "Disaggregating Labor Payments by Skill Level in GTAP." Draft Technical Paper, Center for Global Trade Analysis, Purdue University.

Martin, W., and D. Mitra. 1996. "Productivity Growth in Agriculture and Manufacturing." Mimeo, the World Bank, Washington, D.C., September.

McDougall, R.A., ed. 1997. *Global Trade, Assistance, and Protection: The GTAP 3 Data Base.* Purdue University: Center for Global Trade Analysis.

_____, ed. 1998. *Global Trade, Assistance, and Protection: The GTAP 4 Data Base,* Purdue University: Center for Global Trade Analysis.

Perroni, C., and R. Wigle. 1997. "Environmental Policy Modeling." Chapter 12 in T.W Hertel, ed., *Global Trade Analysis: Modeling and Applications.* Cambridge University Press.

Sachs, J.D., and A. Warner. 1995. "Economic Reform and the Process of Global Integration." *Brookings Papers on Economic Activity* 1: 1–118.

Selden, T.M. and D. Song. 1994. "Environmental Quality and Development: Is There a Kuznets Curve for Air Pollution Emissions?" *Journal of Environmental Economics and Management* 27(2): 147-62.

Strutt, A. Forthcoming. *Economic Growth, Trade Policy, and the Environment in Indonesia.* Draft PhD thesis, University of Adelaide.

Unteroberdoerster, O. 1998. "Trade Policy and Environmental Regulation in the Asia Pacific: A Simulation." Mimeo, Brandeis University, Waltham MA, March.

USITC. 1997. *The Dynamic Effects of Trade Liberalization: An Empirical Analysis.* Publication 3069, Washington, D.C.: U.S. International Trade Commission, October.

World Bank. 1990. "Indonesia: Sustainable Development of Forests, Land, and Water," Washington, D.C.: The World Bank.

Xie, J. 1996. *Environmental Policy Analysis: A General Equilibrium Approach.* Aldershot: Ashgate Publishing Limited.

Chapter 3

Trade, Environment, and Public Health in Chile

Evidence from an economy-wide model

John Beghin, Brad Bowland,
Sébastien Dessus, David Roland-Holst,
and Dominique van der Mensbrugghe

1. Introduction

The policy significance of trade and environment linkages has increased sharply in recent years, largely because of a higher profile in trade negotiations such as the Uruguay Round and the NAFTA. Among academic observers, a consensus has emerged that trade policy is not an adequate tool for environmental protection (Beghin and others 1994), but many other aspects of this linkage remain contentious issues. Unfortunately, there is still relatively little empirical evidence to inform this debate, and this is the main objective of the present paper. In particular, we seek to quantify the direct and indirect effects of environmental taxes, including their revenue, cost, and output effects, as well as their interaction with trade policies and their incidence upon the environment, public health, and elsewhere in the economy. For fast growing developing economies, greater outward-orientation holds great promise in terms of growth and efficiency. Pursuing this goal blindly, however, may jeopardize long-term prosperity because of the environmental costs of such a strategy. Hence, it is essential to assess the environmental impact of trade policy generally and trade liberalization in particular, and to examine how these might be better coordinated with environmental policies to mitigate environmental degradation.

Our paper makes two contributions. Firstly, we explicitly incorporate links from trade to environment to public health indicators, rather than simply measuring pollution incidence or other environmental variables. Secondly, this paper is empirical, and intended to strengthen the basis of evidence for the rapidly evolving policy debate on trade-environment linkages (Beghin and Potier 1997). The present paper gives empirical evidence for Chile, but the methodology can be extended to other countries. Using an applied general equilibrium model, we investigate the interactions between trade and environmental policies, focusing particularly on trade liberalization and coordinated policies of effluent taxation. We provide estimates of emissions for detailed pollution types at the national level, identifying patterns of pollution intensity that emerge with greater outward orientation. Although we estimate increased intensities for several pollutants when trade liberalization is undertaken without concurrent environmental taxes, none of these appear alarming.

A second motivation for the present study is to make more tangible the linkages between economic, environmental, and public health indicators, building upon recent and current work on urban pollution and health in Santiago (World Bank 1994; Ostro and others 1995; O'Ryan 1994). This is an essential step in support of policy formulation that takes more explicit account of economy-environment linkages. Past emphasis in this area has been on resource depletion, which is appropriate but seriously limited, since it omits more direct and immediate personal costs of environmental degradation. We quantify the incremental mortality and morbidity associated with combined economic and environmental polices and their monetary damages. Because its topology, local climate, and economic concentration make this urban area comparable to Mexico City and Jakarta, pollution in Santiago poses a major environmental challenge to Chilean policy makers, now and well into the next century.

In this context, we find that abatement of three air pollutants (small particulates, SO_2, and NO_2 (a determinant of ozone)) has the largest impact on mortality and morbidity and far outweighs the health benefits which might arise from abatement of other air pollutants in Santiago. We also find that Chile's accession to the NAFTA, compared to unilateral trade liberalization, would reduce the emissions of many pollutants and have a relatively benign effect on urban public health. Unilateral liberalization, by contrast, would appear to induce a significant transfer of pollution capacity to Chile from the Rest of the World, adversely affecting the environment and public health. Here the case for coordination with environmental policy is compelling indeed.

Until 1975, Chile represented a textbook case of import-substitution, replete with trade distortions, slow growth, foreign exchange restrictions and resulting misallocation of resources. Following a series of policy reforms under the structural adjustment of the 1980s, Chile has become a thriving outward-oriented economy (Papageorgiou and others 1990; World Bank 1999). Growth of output and exports has been spectacular in natural resource-based industries such as agriculture, fisheries, forestry, and mining sectors in which Chile has traditionally been competitive. These expansions have fostered rising living standards and concerns for the environmental consequences of the resource intensity of the growth (World Bank 1994).

In parallel, urbanization is already well advanced in Chile, where about 85 percent of the population live in or within the vicinity of major cities (for example, Santiago Metropolitan Area and Valparaiso). The income growth and rapid urbanization have outpaced the development of infrastructures such as paved roads, public transportation equipment and sewage treatment systems. Several environmental problems in urban areas are linked to the poor road infrastructure and the use of untreated wastewater used in irrigated agriculture (World Bank 1994).

The infrastructure problem exacerbates air pollution in Santiago by contributing to emissions of suspended particulates and other effluents in the air. This problem combined with unique topological and climatic conditions (thermal inversion) put Santiago in the league of the most-polluted cities in the world. Rising income and health concerns are at odds with this situation. With the assistance of international organizations, Chile has started addressing these environmental problems, especially air and water pollution in Santiago, and the depletion of forest resources (see World Bank 1994).

A critical mass of information has recently been accumulated on urban pollution in Santiago (O'Ryan 1994; Sanchez 1992; Turner and others 1993; and World Bank 1994); we make use of this information when we link national pollution estimates to pollution concentrations in Santiago. Our study is a useful contribution to the existing work on Santiago because it provides estimates of pollution emissions at the national level and of their variations induced by policy changes.

2. The TEQUILA Model

The *T*rade and *E*nvironment E*QUIL*ibrium *A*nalysis (TEQUILA) model is a prototype computable general equilibrium model developed at the OECD development Centre for research on sustainable development. The full model is described in details in Beghin and others (1996). The TEQUILA model is recursive dynamic: each period is solved as a static equilibrium problem given an allocation of savings and expenditure on current consumption. It is multi-sectoral (75 sectors for Chile) with careful disaggregation of natural-resource-based sectors and their forward linkages to manufacturing. Natural resource activities include five agricultural sectors, forestry, fisheries, and five mining/extraction sectors. Their linkages to manufacturing are captured by twelve agricultural processing sectors, four wood-based sectors, four oil-based chemical industries, and eight mineral-based ones.

Output is characterized by CRS technology and the structure of production consists of a series of nested CES functions. Final output is determined from the combination of (non-energy) intermediate inputs and a composite bundle of energy and value added (labor, and capital (machinery and land)). Non-energy intermediate inputs are assumed to be utilized in fixed proportions with respect to total non-energy intermediate demand. The energy-value-added bundle is further decomposed into a labor aggregate, and a capital-energy bundle. Labor demand is further decomposed into ten occupations. The capital-energy bundle is further disaggregated into capital demand and demand for an energy aggregate. The energy bundle is itself decomposed into four base fuel components. In this production structure, emissions are linked to intermediate consumption (inputs) rather than final output. Figure A3.1 in the appendix shows the nested structure of production.

Most existing CGE models investigating pollution issues assume fixed proportion between sectoral output and emissions associated with that sector. By contrast, we posit substitution possibilities between value added, energy and non-energy intermediate goods, which allow the decrease of pollution associated with production if pollution taxes are put in place. This is a major improvement in the incorporation of pollution in economywide modeling.

We econometrically estimate the pollution effluents by sector as being function of energy and input use (Dessus and others 1999). Estimates of these input-based effluents intensities are obtained by matching data from a social accounting matrix disaggregated at the 4-digit ISIC level to the corresponding IPPS pollution database of The World Bank (Martin and others 1991). Emissions are generated by both the final consumption and the intermediate use of polluting goods. Excise/effluent taxes are used to achieve pollution abatement. These taxes are measured as unit of currency per unit of emissions and are uniform taxes *per unit of effluent* for all sectors. Since every sector has different effluent intensities, the pollution tax, expressed *per unit of output*, varies across sectors. The latter taxes are tacked on to the producer price of the polluting commodity.

Pollution by sector is characterized by a vector of 13 measures of various water, air and soil effluents. Pollution intensity varies by sector and with relative prices, since the use of "dirty" inputs is influenced by relative price changes induced by policy intervention. The 13 pollution measures include: toxic pollutants in water, air and land (TOXAIR, TOXWAT, TOXSOL); bio-accumulative toxic metals in air, soil, and water (BIOAIR, BIOWAT, BIOSOL); air pollutants such as SO_2, NO_2, CO_2, volatile organic compounds (VOC), and particulate intensity (PART); and finally, water pollution measured by biological oxygen demand (BOD), and total suspended solids (TSS).

We calibrate the TEQUILA model using a detailed social accounting matrix of Chile for 1992. The model is neoclassical with all markets reaching equilibrium. Trade is modeled assuming goods are differentiated with respect to region of origin and destination. On the import side, we account for the heterogeneity of imports and domestic goods with the CES specification attributed to Armington. We assume a CET specification for domestic output, in which producers are assumed to differentiate between the domestic and export markets. We assume that Chile is a small country. Trade distortions are expressed as *ad valorem* tariffs. This assumption is consistent with the recent tariffication of most trade distortions in Chile following its structural reforms.

3. A Brief Description of the Santiago Health Model[1]

This section briefly describes how we map predicted pollution emissions from our simulations into health effects for residents of Santiago, and then ascribe monetary damages to health impacts of pollution. In summary, the model estimates the change in health status associated with a change in major air pollutants by each of 72 industrial activities in Santiago. Changes in industry emissions used are obtained from the economywide model. The health effects model transforms these emissions data into corresponding changes in health status (such as reduction in PM-10 related mortality). In so doing, the health effects component is used to estimate the potential health damage savings (costs) corresponding to alternative trade and environment policy scenarios analyzed by the economywide model.

In characterizing emissions, we use baseline information on major air pollutants and emission sources. This step involves collecting data on pollutants known to cause significant health problems in Santiago, the corresponding emission sources, and baseline average annual emissions and ambient concentration levels. The data are used to estimate the portion of economywide emissions attributable to Santiago, as well as calibrate the health module of the CGE model to initial conditions.

Dispersion modeling maps effluent emissions into ambient concentration levels, and population-weighted concentration levels are used to determine exposure rates for health impacts. The next step involves calculating the health status response to changes in concentrations of air pollutants. Dose response functions express the change in incidence of mortality/morbidity induced by changes in pollution concentrations (Ostro and others 1995). The figures on health end-points presented in the results section should be interpreted as increases or decreases in mortality and morbidity with respect to the mortality and morbidity that would have prevailed at a predetermined safe standard of pollution concentrations. We look at various morbidity and mortality indicators:

1. Premature mortality due to PM-10, SO_2, and ozone
2. Premature mortality in males of age 40-59 due to lead
3. Respiratory hospital admissions (for PM-10, ozone)
4. Emergency room visit (for PM-10)
5. Restricted activity days (for PM-10)
6. Lower respiratory illness for children population of age less than 17 (PM-10)
7. Asthma symptoms for asthmatic population (for PM-10, ozone)
8. Respiratory symptoms (for PM-10, ozone)
9. Chronic bronchitis in population of age 25 or older (for PM-10)
10. Minor restricted activity days (for ozone)
11. Respiratory symptoms in children population (for SO_2)
12. Chest discomfort in adult population (for SO_2)
13. Respiratory symptoms in adult population (for NO_2)
14. Eye irritation in adult population (for ozone)
15. Number of headache in adult population (for CO)
16. IQ decrement in children population (for lead)
17. Cases of hypertension in adult male population (for lead)
18. Non-fatal heart attacks in male population age 40-59 (for lead).

The last step is to attach a monetary value to the health impact figures. We follow a willingness-to-pay approach to valuing morbidity and loss of life due to a change in mortality, relying on the large body of information and data on such measures for industrialized economies to econometrically estimate these damages for Chile. Damages due to mortality are based on the value of a statistical life, which indicates the aggregate valuation by individuals of reducing the risk of dying. For Santiago, our estimate is roughly .55 million dollars per life, in 1992 (purchasing power parity) US dollars. This estimate corresponds to the value of a life reached in 2010 under the reference business-as-usual scenario (Bowland 1997).

Because of the scarcity of corresponding morbidity estimates available for industrialized countries, our morbidity willingness-to-pay measures are less sophisticated. Available estimates from industrialized countries were simply scaled down to reflect the per capita income differences between Chile and these industrialized countries, expressed in (PPP) 1992 US dollars.

4. Policy Reform Scenarios

The time horizon of the simulations is the period 1992-2010. Every year, savings determine the pool of new investment resources for the *next* period and the model solves for an equilibrium. This equilibrium determines savings going to the new investment pool for the subsequent period. Each period, sectoral resource allocation adjusts to new prices. Labor moves freely across sectors; existing capital is reallocated across sectors, but to a lesser extent due to a partial mobility (vintage capital) assumption in the model. The endogenous variables of interest, which adjust at every period, are sectoral inputs, factor use, and output, consumption, trade, pollution emissions associated with production and consumption. Aggregate real income serves as an approximate gauge of welfare or economic efficiency. We do not attempt to measure the cost of pollution and characterize "externalities" only by the level of pollution emissions estimated in each scenario.

We first define a reference trajectory for the economy based on DRI-McGraw-Hill predictions of GDP growth until 2010. Factor and energy productivity changes are endogenously determined such that the GDP forecast and the model are consistent with each other. All policies are held constant in this reference scenario, called the business-as-usual (BAU) scenario. For the years 1992 to 2010, the model gives a reference trajectory base for output, absorption, trade, and pollution emissions, for this BAU scenario. This is the base or reference trajectory of the economy for our analysis. All reported results are expressed in deviations (in percent) from this BAU scenario and for 2010, which is the final year of the simulation exercise.

The first reform scenario imposes taxes on pollutants, one at the time.[2] Each tax is such that the emissions of the targeted pollutant progressively decrease over time and reach a 25 percent decrease relative to its level in the BAU results by 2010. The phasing in of these taxes is set to obtain gradual reductions of 10 percent in 1995, 15 percent in 2000, 20 percent in 2005, and 25 percent in 2010. The tax rates per unit of effluent are the shadow prices of the quantitative constraints on the pollution emissions.

The second scenario considers a gradual trade integration, combining unilateral trade liberalization through tariff reductions, with a concurrent but modest improvement of terms of trade. Terms of trade are parametric for Chile, assumed to be a small country, and the terms of trade improvement is introduced as an exogenous shock. We assume that export prices increase to simulate this improvement that should result from the integration of trading countries. This is equivalent to an improvement of the terms of trade. We decrease the ad-valorem tariffs, progressively to free trade, from their reference levels (1992) as 90 percent of original tariffs in 1995, 60 percent in 2000, 30 percent in 2005, and no tariff in 2010. Terms-of-trade improvements are expressed as an increase in observed world prices for exports by 2 percent in 1995, 4 percent in 2000, 7 percent in 2005, and 10 percent in 2010. The terms-of-trade assumption allows us to see how the environment is affected by an outward-oriented growth strategy.

We consider analogous regional integration and liberalization scenarios with NAFTA and MERCOSUR countries. Disaggregated data on trade flows allow us to consider these alternative trade liberalization scenarios. In these two other trade scenarios, we remove tariffs and increase export prices following a similar progression as in the previous scenario, but only with respect to trading partners which are members of these two regional agreements. Our objective is to impose a sizable trade shock on the Chilean economy to estimate changes in sectoral composition of production and trade. These changes determine the pollution emitted and induced by the outward trade orientation.

The last group of reform scenarios combines the first two types of reforms. For this last scenario, the objective is to investigate the implications of coordinated trade and environment policies. Analytical results (Copeland 1994; and Beghin and others 1997) imply that the coordinated piecemeal approach -gradual changes of two instruments to correct for trade and environmental distortions- leads to welfare improvements. In the context of joint trade and environmental reforms, efficiency gains are obtained because trade distortions are reduced and because environmental degradation can be reduced as well. Recall we want to investigate the effect of such joint reform on sectoral allocation, trade, and pollution abatement. Free trade removes border distortions (domestic border prices are equal to world prices) and the incentives to change input mixes to abate pollution in production have been altered, compared to the case of the single environmental reform. The differences in the incentive structures lead one to expect contrasting results concerning the indirect abatement achieved via complementarity and substitution among emission types, which occurs under the two scenarios.

5. Results from Policy Reform Simulations

Results follow the sequence of the three reform scenarios: environmental tax reform, trade integration (unilateral liberalization, NAFTA, and MERCOSUR), and then combined trade integration and environmental protection. Results are presented for the final year, 2010, in percent deviations from their BAU values. Table 3.1 summarizes the salient results of the simulations in aggregate. Table 3.2 shows the effects of the various scenarios on pollution emissions. A longer report is available upon request. We first note some stylized facts emerging from the Social Accounting Matrix on sectors which appear to be pollution hotspots in Chile. The following sectors exhibit high intensities and levels for several effluent types: agriculture, sugar refining, mining, chemicals, metals, pottery, electricity, gas, and transportation sectors.

Effluent taxes

Effluent taxes have a small negative impact on growth except for the tax on bio-accumulative emissions released in water (BIOWAT), which has a larger impact (an 8.1 percent decrease in GDP over 18 years with respect to what it would have been under BAU). The effects of these taxes on other aggregate measures of

Table 3.1 Impact of policy reform on aggregate variables

Aggregate variables	Environmental reform: Aggregate abatement of 25 percent by type of effluent emission												
	TOXAIR	*TOXWAT*	*TOXSOL*	*BIOAIR*	*BIOWAT*	*BIOSOL*	SO_2	NO_2	CO_2	*VOC*	*PART*	*BOD*	*TSS*
Real GDP	-0.7	-0.8	-0.7	-0.3	-8.1	-0.3	-0.2	-0.2	-0.1	-0.4	-0.3	-0.7	0.0
Production	0.4	0.3	0.3	0.3	-8.1	0.4	-2.4	-2.4	-0.8	-3.0	-2.6	0.3	-0.1
Consumption	-0.4	-0.5	-0.4	0.0	-1.6	0.0	-1.3	-1.3	-0.2	-1.8	-1.3	-0.4	0.0
Investment	-2.1	-2.6	-2.2	-0.8	-23.2	-0.7	-1.3	-1.3	-0.4	-2.0	-1.5	-2.3	-0.1
Exports	-1.6	-1.9	-1.7	-1.0	-10.2	-0.8	-3.1	-3.1	-0.6	-2.1	-3.2	-1.7	0.0
Imports	-1.2	-1.4	-1.3	-0.7	-9.6	-0.5	-3.0	-3.0	-0.5	-1.7	-3.1	-1.3	0.0
Labor supply	-0.2	-0.3	-0.2	-0.1	-3.1	-0.1	0.2	0.2	0.0	-0.1	0.2	-0.2	0.0
Capital supply	-0.9	-1.1	-0.9	-0.4	-10.4	-0.3	-0.6	-0.6	-0.2	-0.7	-0.7	-1.0	0.0
Real income	-0.3	-0.5	-0.4	0.0	-1.3	0.0	-1.2	-1.2	-0.1	-2.5	-1.2	-0.4	0.0
Absorption	-0.8	-1.0	-0.8	-0.2	-7.1	-0.2	-1.2	-1.2	-0.2	-1.7	-1.2	-0.8	0.0

Aggregate variables	Trade policy reform[a]			Combined NAFTA and environmental policy reform[b]					
	UNILATERAL	*NAFTA*	*MERCOSUR*	*BIOAIR*	SO_2	NO_2	CO_2	*VOC*	*PART*
Real GDP	5.6	1.4	0.6	1.2	1.2	1.2	1.4	0.9	1.1
Production	7.3	1.6	0.6	1.8	-1.1	-1.1	0.7	-1.8	-1.4
Consumption	9.2	2.1	0.9	2.1	0.6	0.6	1.8	-0.1	0.6
Investment	17.7	4.3	1.8	3.5	2.7	2.7	3.7	1.9	2.4
Exports	18.0	3.6	2.7	2.7	0.1	0.1	2.9	1.2	-0.1
Imports	29.1	6.0	3.9	5.3	2.4	2.4	5.3	3.9	2.3
Labor supply	2.0	0.8	0.2	0.7	1.0	1.0	0.8	0.6	1.0
Capital supply	7.2	1.7	0.7	1.4	1.1	1.1	1.5	0.9	0.9
Real income	8.6	2.0	0.8	2.1	0.6	0.6	1.9	-0.9	0.6
Absorption	10.5	2.4	1.0	2.3	1.1	1.1	2.2	0.5	1.0

Table 3.1 Impact of policy reform on aggregate variables *(continued)*

	Unilateral trade with aggregate abatement of 25 percent-by type of effluent emission												
Aggregate variables	*TOXAIR*	*TOXWAT*	*TOXSOL*	*BIOAIR*	*BIOWAT*	*BIOSOL*	*SO_2*	*NO_2*	*CO_2*	*VOC*	*PART*	*BOF*	*TSS*
Real gdp	4.7	4.4	4.7	5.3	-7.4	5.4	5.2	5.2	5.5	4.9	5.0	4.7	5.6
Production	7.8	7.5	7.8	7.9	-5.9	7.9	2.9	2.9	5.5	2.4	2.5	7.8	7.1
Consumption	8.7	8.4	8.7	9.1	6.3	9.1	6.7	6.7	8.6	6.0	6.7	8.6	9.2
Investment	14.4	13.3	14.4	16.9	-21.9	17.1	14.9	14.9	16.6	13.9	14.5	14.3	17.6
Exports	16.4	15.9	16.4	17.0	0.2	17.5	11.7	11.8	16.2	13.5	11.6	16.3	17.9
Imports	27.9	27.4	27.9	28.3	10.5	28.9	22.2	22.3	27.3	24.7	22.2	27.9	29.1
Labor supply	1.7	1.7	1.7	1.8	-2.9	1.9	2.4	2.4	2.2	1.9	2.3	1.7	2.0
Capital supply	6.1	5.7	6.0	6.9	-9.6	6.9	6.2	6.2	6.9	6.0	6.0	6.0	7.2
Rural income	8.2	7.9	8.1	8.6	6.1	8.6	6.2	6.3	8.2	4.4	6.3	8.1	8.6
Absorption	9.3	8.8	9.3	10.3	-1.8	10.3	8.2	8.2	9.9	7.5	8.1	9.3	10.5

a. Reflects unilateral trade liberalization, Nafta integration and Mercosur integration by 2010 with no explicit environmental policy reforms.
b. Reflects combined policy reforms of Nafta integration and aggregate abatement of 25 percent by type of effluent emission.

economic activity tend to be small as well, with the same exception of the tax on BIOWAT. Trade decreases by about 10 percent and investment decreases by 23 percent. The moderate aggregate output effect of the environmental taxes is a result from aggregation. It dissimulates substantial variations at the disaggregated sectoral level and reallocation of resources across sectors.

Next we look at noticeable sectoral output effects, for instance, substantial changes in output occurring in some of the 75 disaggregated sectors included in the model. For the first four taxes (all three toxics, BIOAIR), fish and seafood output increase significantly (increases of 60 to 193 percent). For the same effluent taxes, mining activities decrease sharply (-17 to -60 percent). The tax on BIOWAT, which induces the largest decrease in aggregate output, has a negative effect on virtually all sectors, and it especially has a strong effect on iron, coal, and basic metals (-30 to -59 percent).

Trade contracts with the effluent taxes. At the disaggregated sectoral levels, trade effects are mixed (some decreases, some increases) and moderate. Some exceptions arise: imports and exports of fish increase by over 100 percent for the taxes on toxic pollution; imports of wine and liquors increase by 120 percent with the tax on VOC. The same VOC tax has a strong negative impact on many pollution-intensive manufacturing exports (furniture, chemicals, petroleum refining, and rubber).

The simulation results indicate that the impact of the taxes on pollution abatement is diverse. Strong complementarities are observed in several subsets of the 13 effluent types, despite the clear possibility of substitution among pollution emissions implied by our model since we do not impose any fixed proportions between output and emissions. An increase in the tax on one effluent induces a decrease in another effluent level. All toxics are such a group, so are all bio-accumulative emissions, and NO_2, SO_2 and PART (PM-10). The larger subset of toxics and bio-accumulative emissions follows such a pattern. More intriguing is the presence, in the aggregate, of substitution possibilities among effluents. For example, SO_2 and NO_2 are substitutes for TSS and for bio-accumulative emissions in air and soil.

The tax rates implied by the targeted decrease in emissions are realistic: on average the pollution tax per unit of sectoral output is 4 percent or less for all

Table 3.2 Impact of policy reforms on national effluent emissions

Environmental policy reform	*Aggregate abatement of 25 percent by type of effluent emission*												
	TOXAIR	*TOXWAT*	*TOXSOL*	*BIOAIR*	*BIOWAT*	*BIOSOL*	*SO_2*	*NO_2*	*CO_2*	*VOC*	*PART*	*BOD*	*TSS*
Eeffluent emissions													
TOXAIR	-25.0	-27.4	-25.0	-15.7	-11.9	-14.5	0.9	0.7	0.9	-0.1	0.8	-25.2	0.1
TOXWAT	-22.7	-25.0	-22.7	-13.8	-11.5	-12.8	-0.5	-0.6	0.7	-1.2	-0.5	-22.9	0.1
TOXSOIL	-25.0	-27.4	-25.0	-15.4	-12.2	-14.3	1.1	1.0	1.0	0.0	1.1	-25.2	0.1
BIOAIR	-29.5	-31.5	-29.1	-25.0	-18.7	-19.8	4.4	4.1	-4.5	2.0	0.4	-29.1	-3.0
BIOWAT	-2.0	-2.3	-2.0	-1.7	-25.0	-0.7	-0.3	-0.2	-4.1	-1.5	-3.0	-2.1	-2.0
BIOSOL	-37.3	-39.9	-36.8	-27.3	-13.7	-25.0	4.2	3.8	1.6	3.7	4.1	-36.9	0.0
SO_2	-0.6	-1.4	-0.5	0.4	-5.2	0.2	-25.0	-25.0	-4.1	-10.2	-25.2	-0.5	0.5
NO_2	-0.6	-1.4	-0.5	0.4	-5.2	0.2	-25.0	-25.0	-4.1	-10.1	-25.3	-0.6	0.5
CO_2	0.4	0.3	0.6	-5.1	-29.8	0.6	-8.0	-7.9	-25.0	-4.7	-23.6	0.6	-11.9
VOC	-0.9	-1.5	-0.9	0.1	-4.0	0.1	-3.5	-3.4	-0.6	-25.0	-3.4	-0.9	0.0
PART	-0.6	-1.3	-0.5	-0.2	-7.8	0.2	-23.1	-23.1	-6.2	-9.3	-25.0	-0.5	-0.8
BOD	-24.7	-27.2	-24.8	-15.2	-12.2	-14.0	1.1	0.9	1.0	-0.1	1.1	-25.0	0.1
TSS	0.6	1.2	0.9	-11.7	-55.5	0.2	9.9	10.0	-47.0	0.8	-21.9	0.9	-25.0

	Trade policy reform[a]			*Combined NAFTA & environmental policy reform*[b]					
	UNILATERAL	*NAFTA*	*MERCOSUR*	*BIOAIR*	*SO_2*	*NO_2*	*CO_2*	*VOC*	*PART*
Effluent emissions									
TOXAIR	8.6	-1.0	3.5	-13.9	-0.3	-0.4	-0.2	-1.4	-0.3
TOXWAT	9.5	-0.4	3.3	-11.8	-1.2	-1.3	0.1	-2.1	-1.3
TOXSOL	8.6	-0.8	3.5	-13.5	0.2	0.0	0.1	-1.1	0.1
BIOAIR	8.4	-3.6	8.1	-25.0	1.2	0.9	-8.6	-1.5	-3.2
BIOWAT	14.8	3.6	1.4	1.9	3.2	3.2	-0.9	1.7	0.2
BIO SOL	4.0	-4.8	4.8	-27.7	-0.4	-0.7	-3.4	-0.8	-0.5
SO_2	19.9	3.1	1.6	3.4	-25.0	-25.0	-1.8	-8.4	-25.2
NO_2	19.8	3.2	1.6	3.4	-25.0	-25.0	-1.8	-8.3	-25.2
CO_2	11.8	2.2	0.3	-2.8	-6.7	-6.7	-25.0	-3.2	-24.0
VOC	13.2	3.6	1.2	3.7	-0.4	-0.4	2.9	-25.0	-0.4
PART	18.9	3.1	1.5	2.8	-23.0	-23.0	-4.2	-7.5	-25.0
BOD	8.8	-0.8	3.5	-13.3	0.1	0.0	0.1	-1.1	0.1
TSS	2.8	1.4	-1.2	-10.0	12.6	12.6	-49.3	2.2	-22.8

Table 3.2 Impact of policy reforms on national effluent emissions *(continued)*

	Unilateral trade liberalization with aggregate abatement of 25 percent by type of effluent emission												
National effluent emissions	*TOXAIR*	*TOXWAT*	*TOXSOL*	*BIOAIR*	*BIOWAT*	*BIOSOL*	*SO_2*	*NO_2*	*CO_2*	*VOC*	*PART*	*BOD*	*TSS*
TOXAIR	-25.0	-28.6	-24.9	-10.4	-9.4	-7.9	12.0	11.6	12.3	10.2	11.9	-25.2	8.8
TOXWAT	-21.3	-25.0	-21.2	-7.2	-8.4	-5.0	10.1	9.8	12.1	8.9	10.1	-21.6	9.7
TOXISOL	-25.1	-28.9	-25.0	-10.0	-9.9	-7.6	12.4	12.0	12.4	10.3	12.4	-25.4	8.9
BIOAIR	-28.5	-30.2	-27.9	-25.0	-15.8	-13.8	18.9	18.3	6.3	12.0	13.1	-27.9	5.2
BIOWAT	11.7	10.6	11.7	13.2	-25.0	14.3	13.8	13.9	8.9	11.8	9.8	11.6	12.5
BIOSOL	-44.0	-46.3	-43.4	-29.8	-13.5	-25.0	15.4	14.6	11.2	13.7	15.3	-43.5	4.3
SO_2	18.4	16.2	18.7	20.7	8.9	20.3	-25.0	-24.9	7.2	0.9	-24.9	18.7	20.5
NO_2	18.3	16.2	18.6	20.5	9.0	20.2	-25.1	-25.0	7.2	1.1	-25.0	18.6	20.4
CO_2	11.5	10.7	11.9	7.3	-26.3	12.9	-3.3	-3.2	-25.0	2.8	-26.0	11.9	-1.4
VOC	11.4	10.0	11.5	13.3	5.9	13.4	6.4	6.5	11.4	-25.0	6.7	11.4	13.2
PART	17.5	15.5	17.8	19.0	5.1	19.3	-22.7	-22.6	3.8	1.6	-25.0	17.7	18.1
BOD	-24.7	-28.5	-24.6	-9.5	-9.9	-7.2	12.3	12.0	12.5	10.3	12.4	-25.0	9.0
TSS	2.7	3.5	3.2	-8.6	-63.4	3.5	19.2	19.3	-59.2	4.3	-27.4	3.3	-25.0

a. Reflects unilateral trade liberalization, Nafta integration and Mercosur integration by 2010 with no explicit environmental policy reforms.
b. Reflects combined policy reforms of Nafta integration and aggregate abatement of 25 percent by type of effluent emission.

13 scenarios. The individual tax rates (per sector and by effluent) vary from zero to less than 15 percent for all 13 scenarios, except for the scenario targeting reduction in VOC. In the latter scenario the pollution tax rate on wine and liquors jumps to 52 percent, and the corresponding tax rate on furniture products is 37 percent. These high rates are caused by the fact that these two sectors account for most of the VOC pollution in production.

The decomposition of abatement into scale (aggregate output expansion), composition (composition of GDP), and technique (input substitution) effects reveals interesting results.[3] First, the composition effect seems overwhelming both in the abatement in production and consumption. The effect is more substantial in production than in consumption, that is, imports substitute for domestic output in pollution-intensive sectors. The technical effect in production is moderate, and the scale effect is marginal for most pollutants except for the case of the tax on BIOWAT (production scale effect of -8.1 percent). Surprisingly, a few simulations exhibit positive scale effects in production abatement (all toxics, BIOAIR, BIOSOL, and BOD). Since the scale effect is the aggregation of sectoral output effects over all sectors, the latter result may be due to the expansion of activities that are not intensive in the pollutants being taxed. This expansion, weighted by prices, outweighs the decrease in output in polluting sectors. For example, the taxes on all three toxics decrease mining activities as well as metallic industries, but stimulate fisheries and seafood, and forestry and wood products.

This example shows the limitation of tackling environmental degradation by a single pollution effluent at the time. Abatement of one effluent gives rise to an increase in resource-intensive activities such as forestry and may induce additional degradation and welfare losses if externalities are present in these sectors. This insight reinforces the finding that targeting one specific pollutant can have unintended and damaging consequences on emissions of "substitute" pollutants, and calls for an integrated approach to the design of environmental policies.

In addition, the decomposition of abatement sheds light on the substitutability between effluents. A variety of patterns emerges. Substitution between two effluent types occurs when all three effects are positive (for example, TSS response to tax on TOX-

WAT), or when two or less out of the three effects are positive and larger in magnitude than the remaining effect(s) (for example CO_2 response to BOD tax).

The impact of the effluent taxes on the concentration in Santiago is diverse and to some extent, follows the complementarity/substitution patterns observed for emissions. As shown in table 3.2, all three toxic taxes provide significant decreases in lead (about 10 percent), but nothing else, except for a slight increase in CO concentration (1.1 percent). The three bio-accumulative pollution taxes decrease lead concentrations as well (by 10 to 20 percent). The tax on BIOWAT has negative and sometime large effects on other concentrations as well -remember it is the tax which has the largest negative scale effects among the effluent taxes. Air pollution taxes also produce similar concentration patterns. Emission taxes on either NO_2, SO_2, or PM-10 leads to a substantial decrease in the other two (averaging about 19 percent), and some decrease in CO (averaging about 5 percent). Taxes on CO and VOC also achieve substantial decreases in concentration in Santiago. The taxes on water pollution (BOD, TSS) have marginal impact on most of the concentrations.

As shown in table A3.1, the health endpoints changes are striking for the taxes on SO_2, NO_2, and PM-10. Premature mortality due to PM-10, SO_2 and ozone decreases by more than 30 percent. With these three taxes, most endpoints show improvements with decreases of morbidity of about 30 percent for seven of the morbidity measures. There is a marginal deterioration of morbidity incidence linked to lead (about 1 percent). This result is the consequence of the slight increase in BIOAIR emissions induced by the taxes on SO_2 and NO_2 (around 4 percent).

Table A3.2 presents the health damages reduction induced by the environmental taxes. Figures within parentheses indicate a reduction in damages. The tax on PM-10 induces a decrease in monetary damages equivalent to 0.82 percent of the BAU 2010 GDP; taxes on SO_2 and NO_2 reduce damages by an amount equivalent to 0.65 percent of BAU 2010 GDP. The latter taxes induce net gains as approximated by the loss of aggregate income plus the reduction in damages. These results show the importance of accounting for nonmarket benefits when considering the impact of environmental taxes. The estimated welfare gains are lower-bound estimates because the decreases in morbidity and mortality are only applied to Santiago's population. As suggested by the table some taxes such as the tax on VOC induce negligible net gains in welfare.

Trade integration

We look at two types of trade integration leading to three scenarios: with the world (unilateral liberalization), and regional integration (NAFTA, and MERCOSUR). Unilateral liberalization induces the largest increase in GDP (+5.6 percent), followed by NAFTA (1.4 percent) and MERCOSUR (0.6 percent). These gains are small -they represent the relative gains over 18 years. These small changes originate in the outward-orientation Chile has been following; large gains from liberalization have already occurred. Nevertheless these reforms have more significant positive impacts on aggregate trade and aggregate gross investment.

Moving to disaggregated sectoral output effects, the three trade reforms exhibit sharp contrast. The unilateral trade reform stimulates the output of fruit, forestry, iron, other mining, food processing, wood products, paper, and petroleum refining. Conversely, petroleum and gas production, chemicals, glass and other manufacturing contract with free trade. With NAFTA integration, fruit, agricultural services, other mining, food processing, wine and liquor, would expand significantly, whereas copper, iron, and paper would decrease. Hence, NAFTA integration departs significantly from free trade in terms of international specialization. MERCOSUR integration does not induce any strong effect, except for a major increase in transportation material and a decrease in fish and seafood.

The trade effects of these reforms are as follows. The unilateral reform induces major increases in virtually all sectoral imports and exports, except for imports of chemicals, glass, and other manufacturing. NAFTA integration has a smaller effect on trade than unilateral reform, except for noticeable increases in imports of agriculture and sugar, and smaller increases for livestock, forestry, fish, mining sectors, sugar, wood products, furniture, paper, and plastic; exports of fruits, mining (other than copper, coal, and iron), dairy, wine and liquor, furniture, and pottery.

Finally, the MERCOSUR integration induces increases in imports of agricultural products, iron, oils, sugar, tobacco, petroleum refining, and metals; imports of fish would decrease. On the export side, substantial reductions occur in exports of fish, iron, and seafood; but food processing, chemicals, plastics, and printing expand significantly.

The pollution implications of these trade reforms are next. Unilateral liberalization is pollution intensive, for example, NO_2, SO_2, and PM-10 have an elasticity of 3.5 with respect to GDP increases induced by this unilateral reform. By contrast, MERCOSUR and NAFTA have elasticity values around 2.7 and 2.2 respectively, for the same effluents. NAFTA integration induces decreases in several pollutants (the three toxics, BIOAIR, BIOSOL, and BOD). MERCOSUR induces a decrease in TSS only. The trade diversion of NAFTA integration provides a significant environmental benefit in terms of mitigated emissions, relative to other two trade liberalization scenarios. This is an overlooked insight on trade diversion in presence of externalities. The decrease in effluents under the NAFTA scenario is achieved through strong composition effects in production, outweighing the scale expansion induced by NAFTA. By contrast, the unilateral trade liberalization induces higher intensities in SO_2, NO_2, and PART (PM-10) via strong technical effects towards pollution-intensive input combinations.

Still under free trade, we observe marginal increases for all toxics, BIOAIR, CO_2, VOC, and BOD; we have marginal decreases for TSS, and BIOSOL. Finally, we see substantial increases for PM-10, SO_2, and NO_2. These increases are observed after 18 years of expected growth and hence do not represent anything dramatic. By contrast, NAFTA membership induces decreases in pollution intensity of GDP or production. This difference between the two trade reforms is caused by the cheap energy import occurring under free trade but not under NAFTA.

For the health end-points in Santiago, the unilateral trade liberalization scenario has negative consequences for both mortality and almost all measures of morbidity. Premature mortality due to PM-10, ozone, and SO_2 increases by 25 percent and premature death in males of age 40-59 due to lead increases by 9.2 percent, as shown in table A3.1. Morbidity increases range from 9 percent for cases of hypertension and non-fatal heart attacks to about 26 percent for chest discomfort episodes and respiratory symptoms in children. NAFTA and MERCOSUR induce marginal increases in the health end-points. Although NAFTA decreases several types of emissions, these decreases do not translate into major gains for urban health because these improvements are not relevant for air pollution in Santiago, except for a small improvement in lead concentration. The damages associated with the health incidences are substantial for the unilateral trade liberalization. As suggested by table A3.2, the damages represent 13 percent of the aggregate income gains induced by trade liberalization (damages as percent of gains in GDP). By contrast the damages under the NAFTA scenario are moderate due to the small deterioration of the average health status in Santiago.

Trade integration with environmental protection

In this last set of reforms, we first combine NAFTA reforms and effluent taxes on a subset of pollutants (air pollutants). Then, we consider the unilateral trade liberalization coordinated with effluent tax on one pollutant at the time. The effluent taxes are designed as in the first set of scenarios on environmental reforms (incremental and leading to a 25-percent decrease in emissions of the taxed effluent). The tax rates corresponding to these reforms are slightly higher than in the environmental reforms alone. The average tax rates on pollution, expressed in percent of the producer price per unit of output, do not exceed 5.8 percent. A few individual rates increase sharply. For instance, the tax on TOXWAT emitted by nonmetallic minerals increases to 23.6 percent. As expected, the tax rates on VOC for wine and liquor and for furniture products increase further to 73 and 53 percent, respectively. These increases in tax rates originate in the output and pollution expansion induced by trade liberalization. The pollution expansion requires higher tax rates to be abated back to the level corresponding to a 25 percent decrease with respect to the BAU level.

The aggregate effect of the combined reforms (NAFTA *cum* effluent tax) is small in general, but differs according to the pollutant considered. For example, the effluent tax on CO_2 has practically no effect on aggregate measures, whereas, the tax on VOC has a negative impact on production, consumption and real income. The disaggregated sectoral output variation is more insightful. The iron ore, petro-gas and petroleum refining sectors decrease their activity considerably for several of the effluent taxes. The VOC tax drastically reduces the output of wine and liquors, and of chemicals. Finally, the tax on BIOAIR (lead) induces an expansion of fish, seafood and fruit, but a strong contraction of copper.

The net trade effects of the combined NAFTA and environmental policy reform are next. Specifically, imports of fruits, iron ore, coal, other mining, nonmetallic minerals, electricity and transportation increase for most effluent taxes; conversely, imports of petro-gas and petroleum refining decrease. Exports of fish, iron ore, seafood, food processing, feeds, paper, petroleum refining, glass, nonmetallic minerals, and transportation decrease.

The pollution abatement figures, including the multiplier effects of the tax on pollutants that are not directly targeted by the tax, are surprisingly similar to the abatement figures for the reforms limited to environmental reforms alone. The abatement on the targeted emission is of course exactly similar by design, but the indirect abatement of the other pollutants does not have to be because relative prices are different under the two scenarios. The result is surprising because changing border prices affects specialization and hence pollution. This result is due to the fact that NAFTA integration has a mitigated impact on the Chilean environment.

The impact of coordinated reforms -free trade *cum* environmental taxes- appears almost additive on aggregate output, trade and consumption: the aggregate effect of the coordinated approach is the sum of aggregate effect of the two individual reforms. This is a recurrent result in this type of simulation exercise (Lee and Roland-Holst 1994; Beghin, Roland-Holst, and van der Mensbrugghe 1995, 1997b). However, the disaggregated output and trade figures reveal more interesting, if not surprising, and diverse patterns. For example, iron ore output increases by 51 percent with trade liberalization and decreases by 14 percent with the tax on SO_2. Nonetheless, the combined reform (free trade + SO_2 tax) induces a marginal increase in output of 1.4 percent. This diversity of patterns comes from the difference in relative cost of abatement by increasing imports (composition) and by changing the input mix (technical effect) under different policy regimes. Output of fish, seafood, and wood products increases considerably for several of the free trade *cum* effluent tax scenarios.

Aggregate trade expands less under the coordinated reforms than under the simple unilateral trade liberalization, although some sectoral import induced by the latter reform, grow even more under the coordinated scenario. For instance, imports of fish are larger under the combined scenario than under the free trade scenario. These exacerbated surges are explained by the almost additive effects of the two policies: free trade and environmental protection imply the same international specialization. For example, fish imports increases significantly with the environmental reforms and with free trade. However, the effect under coordinated policies is lower than the sum of the individual one.

The inventory of emissions tends to duplicate the patterns reached under the single effluent tax reform since we target the amount of pollution in a similar fashion (-25 percent for each effluent type). Nevertheless, the substitution between bio-accumulative and toxic pollutants as a group and the air pollutants (SO_2, NO_2, VOC, PM-10, and CO_2) as another group is amplified by free trade. This increased substitution is caused by a selective increase in pollution dictated by the change in relative prices of pollutants when only one type of pollutant is taxed. For instance, the copper and other-mining sectors decrease their activity for the combined scenario targeting toxic and bio-accumulative emissions, but increase their activities under the four coordinated scenarios targeting SO_2, NO_2, PM-10 and CO_2. VOC emissions increase under most scenarios except the one which taxes VOC emissions.

Finally, as indicated by Table A3.1, the urban health impact of the coordinated reforms reflects these stronger substitutions between broad groups of pollutants. Mortality due to air pollution increases dramatically under the combined scenarios involving bio-accumulative and toxic pollution, because the emissions of PM-10, SO_2, and NO_2 are stimulated. Similarly, the morbidity induced by SO_2, NO_2, PM-10 and CO increases under the same combined scenarios. The VOCs-ozone increases have a negative effect on many morbidity measures: increase in restricted activity days, in the number of asthma attacks, respiratory symptoms, in minor restricted activity days, and in eye irritation cases. As shown in the last part of Table A.2, damages reductions under coordinated reforms are less substantial than under the environmental tax alone, because of the substitution forces at work among pollutant types. For example, damages caused by lead pollution are substantial in the coordinated scenario involving a tax on PM-10. Nevertheless, the net welfare gains of combined reforms are much higher than for trade liberalization alone. For example, the tax on PM-10 combined to free trade induces net welfare gains which are 14 percent higher than the net gains under free trade alone.

6. Conclusions

This paper seeks to elucidate linkages between trade, environment, and public health status in an outward-oriented economy. From our results, it is apparent that such linkages are quite complex, and policy makers relying on intuition alone are unlikely to achieve anything close to optimality. Policies in all three areas are clearly interdependent, and better coordination could reduce the social and economic costs of economic growth and environmental mitigation. More detailed empirical work is needed, however, to support such policies.

Trade liberalization scenarios offer different outcomes in terms of growth, international division of labor and environmental consequences. Integration into NAFTA is relatively benign to the environment and has the smallest pollution elasticity with respect to the trade-induced growth (the percentage change in pollution with respect to the percentage change in GDP). Unilateral trade liberalization, with no abatement policy, induces higher growth and patterns of specialization more adverse towards the environment, leading to detrimental impacts on public health in Santiago and considerable monetary damages associated with the negative health impact. MERCOSUR simulations do not indicate substantial changes in income, pollution or public health, except for increased emissions of bio-accumulative pollutants, and small increases in mortality and morbidity linked to lead pollution in Santiago.

Considering effluent taxes alone, the abatement of three pollutants, SO_2, NO_2, and PM-10 achieves the largest decrease in both mortality and morbidity in Santiago. The health damage reduction exceeds the foregone aggregate income and corresponds to a net welfare gain to the Chilean economy.

Coordinated scenarios are well-grounded in economic theory and represent the best of both worlds (efficiency gains from trade, and protected environment); they are characterized by economic expansion and decreases in the emissions of the targeted pollutant as well as its polluting "complements". Nevertheless, emissions of untaxed substitute pollutants increase considerably. These strong substitutions have a negative impact on urban health, with notable increases in mortality and morbidity when toxic and bio-accumulative pollutants are the targets. Further, several natural-resource based sectors expand as well, hence increasing the dimensionality of policy coordination (trade policy, effluent taxes, natural resource management). This is a result specific to our investigation of Chile. By contrast, our analysis of trade and environment linkages in Mexico suggests mostly complementarity between effluent types (Beghin and others 1995, 1997b).

The observed substitutability among pollutant types and its implications for urban health raises two additional coordination and targeting issues. The first one is the coordination of environmental programs targeting subgroups of pollutants (for example, toxic, bio-accumulative, air criteria pollutants). Given the substantial substitutability between these groups, an integrated approach to environmental reform encompassing all major groups of pollutants appears appropriate to avoid unintended environmental degradation or negative health consequence.

The other issue is the hopeful observation that strong complementarities exist within some groups of pollutants and that a policy targeting any pollutant within a group would achieve substantial abatement in most emission types included in the group. This finding is common to most of our case studies and emerges as an empirical regularity in these linkages.

Another regularity shared by this study and the other case studies using the same methodology is the relatively low cost of pollution abatement in terms of foregone aggregate income. In this specific case of Chile and Santiago, we establish this result in terms of welfare. The monetary damages equivalent to the health impact of air pollution are greatly reduced by environmental taxes, especially by the tax on PM-10, NO_2, and SO_2, such that the these welfare gains exceed the loss of GDP induced by the taxes. A net welfare gain emerges. This statement should be qualified because the resource reallocation implied by the effluent taxes is substantial on a sectoral basis and we do abstract from explicit adjustment cost.

The observed substitutability among pollutant types raises two additional coordination and targeting issues. The first one is the coordination of environmental programs targeting subgroups of pollutants (for example, toxic, bio-accumulative, air criteria pollutants). Given the substantial substitutability between these groups, an integrated approach to environmental reform encompassing all major groups of pollutants appears appropriate to avoid unintended environmental degradation.

The other interesting point is the hopeful observation that strong complementarities also exist within some groups of pollutants and that a policy targeting any pollutant within a group would achieve substantial abatement in most emission types included in that group.

Figure A3.1 Production nesting

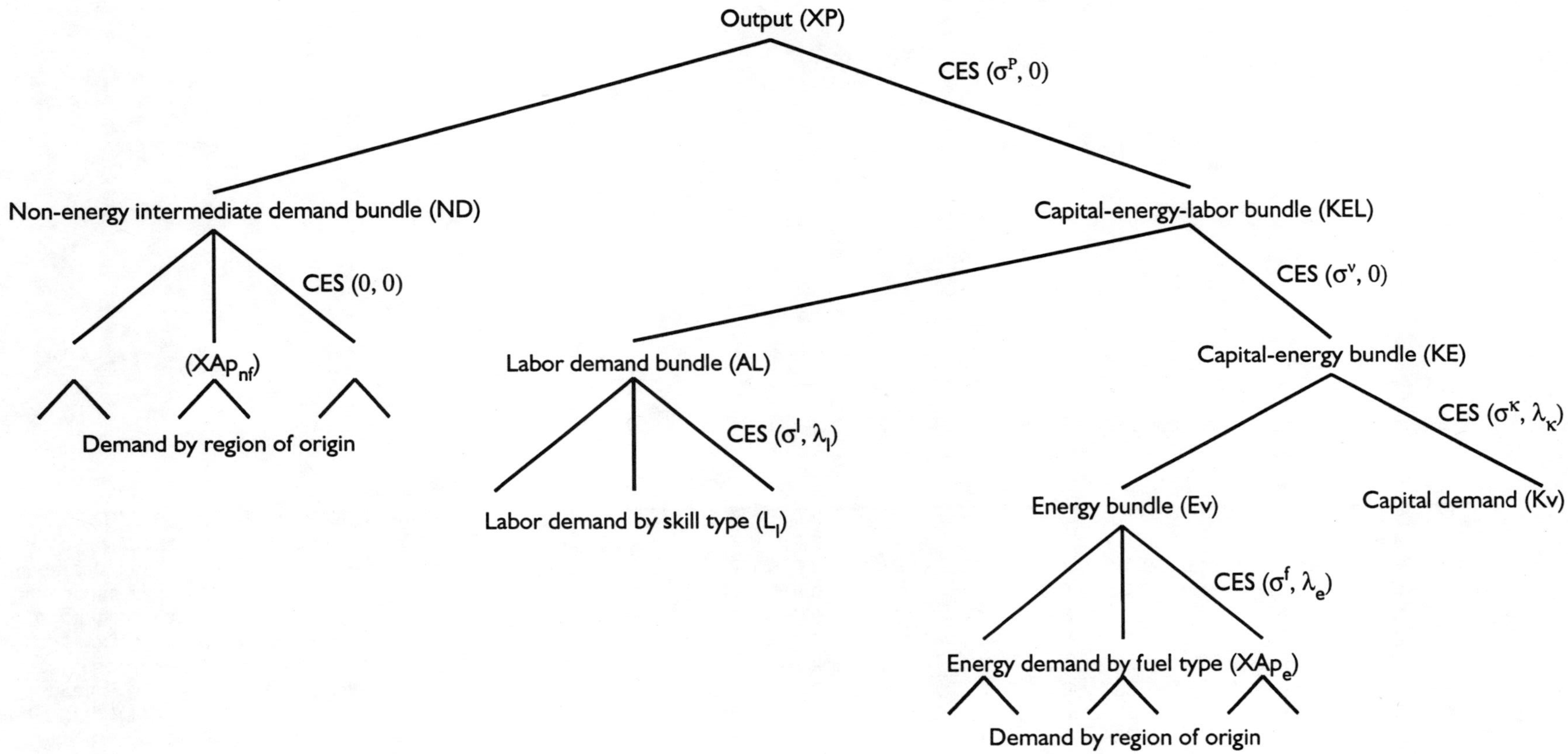

1. Each nest represents a different CES bundle. The first argument in the CES function represents the substitution of elasticity. The elasticity may take the value zero. Because of the putty/semi-putty specification, the nesting is replicated for each type of capital, that is, *old* and *new*. The values of the substitution elasticity will generally differ depending on the capital vintage, with typically lower elasticities for *old* capital. The second argument in the CES function is an efficiency factor. In the case of the *KE* bundle, it is only applied on the demand for capital. In the case of the decomposition of labor and energy, it is applied to all components.
2. Intermediate demand, both energy and non-energy, is further decomposed by region of origin according to the *Armington* specification. However, the *Armington* function is specified at the border and is not industry specific.
3. The decomposition of the intermediate demand bundle, the labor bundle, and the energy bundle will be specific to the level of aggregation of the model. The diagram represents only schematically the decomposition and is not meant to imply that there are three components in the CES aggregation.

Table A3.1 Impact of environmental policy reform on health endpoints for Santiago

	AGGREGATE ABATEMENT OF 25 PERCENT BY TYPE OF EFFLUENT EMISSION											
HEALTH ENDPOINTS	TOXAIR	TOXWAT	TOXSOL	BIOAIR	BIOWAT	BIOSOL	SO_2	NO_2	CO_2	VOC	PART	BOD
Premature Mortality/Year	0.5	-0.4	0.6	0.9	-10.3	1.1	-30.3	-30.3	-7.7	-13.0	-32.4	0.6
Premature Mortality of males age 40-59/Year	-12.6	-13.5	-12.2	-15.8	-24.8	-8.9	1.7	1.6	-10.0	-4.8	-4.8	-12.2
RHA/Year	0.3	-0.4	0.4	0.7	-7.7	0.9	-19.5	-19.4	-5.1	-15.2	-20.9	0.4
ERV/Year	0.5	-0.4	0.7	0.5	-11.6	1.1	-29.3	-29.2	-8.7	-12.6	-32.1	0.6
RAD/Year	0.5	-0.4	0.7	0.5	-11.6	1.1	-29.2	-29.2	-8.7	-12.6	-32.1	0.6
LRI/Year (Children < age 17)	0.5	-0.4	0.7	0.5	-11.6	1.1	-29.2	-29.2	-8.7	-12.6	-32.1	0.6
Asthma Attacks/Year (Asthmatics)	0.3	-0.3	0.3	0.7	-5.7	0.8	-14.4	-14.4	-3.3	-16.5	-15.1	0.3
Respiratory Symptoms/Year	0.4	-0.4	0.5	0.6	-9.1	1.0	-23.0	-22.9	-6.4	-14.3	-24.9	0.5
Chronic Bronchitis/Year	0.5	-0.4	0.7	0.5	-11.6	1.1	-29.2	-29.2	-8.7	-12.6	-32.1	0.6
MRAD/Year	0.2	-0.3	0.2	0.8	-4.0	0.7	-10.0	-9.9	-1.6	-17.7	-10.0	0.2
Respiratory Symptoms/Year (Children)	0.5	-0.6	0.6	1.6	-7.4	1.2	-33.2	-33.1	-5.3	-14.2	-33.4	0.6
Chest Discomfort Episodes/Year	0.5	-0.6	0.6	1.6	-7.3	1.2	-33.1	-33.0	-5.3	-14.2	-33.3	0.6
Respiratory Symptoms/Year (Adults)	0.4	-0.6	0.6	1.5	-7.1	1.1	-32.6	-32.5	-5.2	-13.8	-32.8	0.5
Eye Irritations/Year (Adults)	0.2	-0.3	0.2	0.8	-4.0	0.7	-10.0	-9.9	-1.6	-17.7	-10.0	0.2
Headaches/Year	1.8	1.7	2.0	-8.0	-52.0	1.5	-8.8	-8.7	-42.9	-6.8	-35.4	2.0
IQ decrements	-12.6	-13.5	-12.2	-15.8	-24.8	-8.9	1.7	1.6	-10.0	-4.8	-4.8	-12.2
Cases of Hypertension/1 million males age >20	-12.6	-13.5	-12.2	-15.8	-24.8	-8.9	1.7	1.6	-10.0	-4.8	-4.8	-12.2
Non-fatal Heart Attacks/1 million males age 40-59	-12.6	-13.5	-12.2	-15.8	-24.8	-8.9	1.7	1.6	-10.0	-4.8	-4.8	-12.2

Table A3.1 Impact of trade reform and combined NAFTA and environmental policy reform on health endpoints for Santiago *(continued)*

	TRADE POLICY REFORM*			COMBINED NAFTA AND ENVIRONMENTAL POLICY REFORM**				
HEALTH ENDPOINTS	UNI	NAFTA	MERCOSUR	BIOAIR	SO_2	NO_2	CO_2	VOC
Premature Mortality/Year	24.8	3.2	2.0	3.7	-30.6	-30.6	-5.7	-11.4
Premature Mortality of males age 40-59/Year	9.2	-0.6	8.4	-15.1	1.3	1.2	-11.6	-5.9
RHA/Year	18.7	3.0	1.5	3.4	-18.8	-18.7	-3.0	-14.2
ERV/Year	24.2	3.2	1.9	3.4	-29.5	-29.4	-6.9	-10.9
RAD/Year	24.2	3.2	1.9	3.4	-29.4	-29.4	-6.8	-10.9
LRI/Year (Children < age 17)	24.2	3.2	1.9	3.4	-29.4	-29.4	-6.8	-10.9
Asthma Attacks/Year (Asthmatics)	15.9	2.9	1.3	3.4	-13.3	-13.3	-1.0	-16.0
Respiratory Symptoms/Year	20.7	3.1	1.6	3.4	-22.6	-22.6	-4.4	-13.0
Chronic Bronchitis/Year	24.2	3.2	1.9	3.4	-29.4	-29.4	-6.8	-10.9
MRAD/Year	13.5	2.7	1.1	3.4	-8.4	-8.4	0.8	-17.5
Respiratory Symptoms/Year (Children)	26.4	3.3	2.2	4.5	-33.8	-33.7	-3.1	-12.6
Chest Discomfort Episodes/Year	26.3	3.3	2.2	4.5	-33.6	-33.6	-3.1	-12.6
Respiratory Symptoms/Year (Adults)	25.8	3.3	2.1	4.4	-33.1	-33.1	-3.0	-12.2
Eye Irritations/Year (Adults)	13.4	2.7	1.1	3.4	-8.4	-8.4	0.8	-17.5
Headaches/Year	17.6	3.0	0.2	-5.1	-6.6	-6.5	-43.9	-4.6
IQ decrements	9.2	-0.6	8.4	-15.1	1.3	1.2	-11.6	-5.9
Cases of Hypertension/1 million males age >20	9.2	-0.6	8.4	-15.1	1.3	1.2	-11.6	-5.9
Non-fatal Heart Attacks/1 million males age 40-59	9.2	-0.6	8.4	-15.1	1.3	1.2	-11.6	-5.9

*Reflects unilateral trade liberalization, NAFTA integration and MERCOSUR integration by 2010 with no explicit environmental policy reforms.

**Reflects combined policy reforms of NAFTA integration and aggregate abatement of 25 percent by type of effluent emission.

Note: All figures are percentage changes with respect to base trends in 2010.

KEY: RHA = respiratory hospital admissions; RAD = restricted activity days; MRAD = minor restricted activity days; ERV = emergency room visits; pphm = parts per hundred million; LRI = lower respiratory illness; µg/m3 = micrograms per cubic meter

Table A3.1 Impact of coordinated trade and environmental policy reforms on health endpoints for Santiago. Unilateral trade liberalization with aggregate abatement of 25 percent by type of effluent emission *(continued)*

Premature Mortality/1 million males age 40-59	-5.9	-7.1	-5.2	-14.3	-24.5	0.9	12.4	12.2	-4.7	-1.4	2.5	-5.1	3.5
RHA/Year	18.9	16.8	19.2	20.2	4.9	20.3	-16.5	-16.4	5.8	-7.2	-18.3	19.1	18.2
ERV/Year	24.6	21.9	25.0	25.9	4.0	26.3	-28.5	-28.4	3.4	0.8	-32.3	24.9	22.8
RAD/Year	24.6	21.9	25.0	25.9	4.0	26.2	-28.5	-28.3	3.4	0.8	-32.3	24.9	22.8
LRI/Year (children < age 17)	24.6	21.9	25.0	25.9	4.0	26.2	-28.5	-28.3	3.4	0.8	-32.3	24.9	22.8
Asthma Attacks/Year (Asthmatics)	15.9	14.2	16.2	17.3	5.3	17.2	-10.4	-10.3	7.1	-11.3	-11.1	16.1	15.8
Respiratory Symptoms/Year	20.9	18.6	21.3	22.3	4.6	22.5	-20.8	-20.7	5.0	-4.3	-23.3	21.2	19.9
Chronic Bronchitis/Year	24.6	21.9	25.0	25.9	4.0	26.2	-28.5	-28.3	3.4	0.8	-32.3	24.9	22.8
MRAD/Year	13.3	11.9	13.5	14.7	5.7	14.5	-4.9	-4.8	8.3	-15.0	-4.7	13.4	13.7
Respiratory Symptoms/Year (Children)	26.8	23.7	27.2	29.4	10.8	28.7	-33.3	-33.1	9.3	-0.2	-33.1	27.1	27.4
Chest Discomfort Episodes/Year	26.7	23.6	27.1	29.3	10.8	28.5	-33.2	-33.0	9.3	-0.2	-33.0	27.0	27.3
Respiratory Symptoms/Year (Adults)	26.1	23.1	26.5	28.5	10.7	27.8	-32.8	-32.7	9.0	-0.1	-32.6	26.4	26.7
Eye Irritations/Year (Adults)	13.3	11.9	13.5	14.6	5.7	14.5	-4.9	-4.8	8.2	-15.0	-4.7	13.4	13.7
Headaches/Year	19.0	17.9	19.6	11.0	-49.7	20.4	0.4	0.7	-46.0	4.7	-39.0	19.6	-5.3
IQ decrements	-5.9	-7.1	-5.2	-14.3	-24.5	0.9	12.4	12.2	-4.7	-1.4	2.5	-5.1	3.5
Cases of Hypertension/1 million males age >20		1	2	1	2	0	12	12 2		1	2	1	
Non fatal Heart Attacks/1 million males age 0		1	2	1	2	0	12	12 2		1	2	1	

Table A3.2 Impact of environmental policy reform on mortality and morbidity health damages for Santiago (in millions 1992 PPP$)

	AGGREGATE ABATEMENT OF 25% BY TYPE OF EFFLUENT EMISSION												
HEALTH DAMAGES	TOXAIR	TOXWAT	TOXSOL	BIOAIR	BIOWAT	BIOSOL	SO_2	NO_2	CO_2	VOC	PART	BOD	TSS
Mortality	(16)	(44)	(13)	(13)	(348)	9	(844)	(844)	(240)	(375)	(918)	(13)	(32)
Morbidity	(422)	(467)	(406)	(530)	(1,028)	(286)	(393)	(396)	(474)	(397)	(658)	(407)	(190)
Total	(438)	(511)	(418)	(543)	(1,376)	(276)	(1,237)	(1,240)	(714)	(773)	(1,576)	(419)	(222)
Total (% Chile BAU	(0.23)	(0.27)	(0.22)	(0.28)	(0.72)	(0.14)	(0.65)	(0.65)	(0.37)	(0.40)	(0.82)	(0.22)	(0.12)

Note: All mortality and morbidity figures are valued at a reference level of GDP/capita income in 2010 under BAU in 1992 PPP$.

	TRADE POLICY REFORM*			COMBINED NAFTA AND ENVIRONMENTAL POLICY REFORM**					
HEALTH DAMAGES	UNI	NAFTA	MERCOSUR	BIOAIR	SO_2	NO_2	CO_2	VOC	PART
Mortality	716	88	76	67	(853)	(853)	(187)	(333)	(935)
Morbidity	703	34	317	(457)	(405)	(408)	(494)	(409)	(699)
Total	1,419	122	393	(389)	(1,258)	(1,262)	(682)	(743)	(1,634)
Total (% Chile BAU GDP)	0.74	0.06	0.21	(0.20)	(0.66)	(0.66)	(0.36)	(0.39)	(0.85)

*Reflects unilateral trade liberalization, NAFTA integration and MERCOSUR integration by 2010 with no explicit environmental policy reforms.

**Reflects combined policy reforms of NAFTA integration and aggregate abatement of 25% by type of effluent emission.

	AGGREGATE ABATEMENT OF 25% BY TYPE OF EFFLUENT EMISSION												
HEALTH DAMAGES	TOXAIR	TOXWAT	TOXSOL	BIOAIR	BIOWAT	BIOSOL	SO_2	NO_2	CO_2	VOC	PART	BOD	TSS
Mortality	691	607	704	718	109	755	(804)	(802)	131	11	(901)	701	683
Morbidity	193	109	224	(71)	(764)	452	(3)	(6)	(90)	(79)	(397)	225	488
Total	884	716	927	647	(656)	1,207	(806)	(808)	41	(68)	(1,297)	927	1,171
Total (% Chile BAU	0.46	0.37	0.48	0.34	(0.34)	0.63	(0.42)	(0.42)	0.02	(0.04)	(0.68)	0.48	0.61

Notes: All mortality and mobidity figures are at a reference level of GDP/captia in 12010 under BAU (measured in 1992 PPP$).
Values in parentheses represent welfare gains from policy reform relative to BAU (measured in 1992 PPP$).

Notes

Thanks are due Gunnar Eskeland and Raul O'Ryan for useful discussions. The views expressed in this paper are those of the authors and should not be attributed to their affiliated institutions.

1. The health-module for Santiago is formally presented in Bowland (1997), which describes in full details the different steps and issues involved in the derivation of pollution concentration in Santiago, health impact and monetary damages.
2. Taxing all pollutants simultaneously raises difficulties. First, tracing the effect of any single tax on resource allocation becomes impossible. Second several tax combinations lead to the same decrease in all pollutants, but with different implications on sectoral allocation, consumption and trade.
3. Our decomposition of pollution follows Copeland and Taylor (1994) and Beghin and others (1997), which differs from Grossman and Krueger's (1992). The major difference resides in the technique effect. Grossman and Krueger include technical change in their technique effect; by contrast we consider movements along an iso-production surface away from polluting inputs with given technology.

References

Beghin J., S. Dessus, D. Roland-Holst, and D. van der Mensbrugghe. 1996. "Prototype CGE Model for the Trade and the Environment Program. Technical Specification." *OECD Development Centre Technical Papers* No 116.

_____. 1997. "The Impact of Free Trade and Pollution Taxes on Mexican Agriculture. A General Equilibrium Analysis." *Agricultural Economics* 17: 115–31.

Beghin J., D. Roland-Holst, and D. van der Mensbrugghe. 1994. "The Trade and Environment Nexus: Global Dimensions." *OECD Economic Studies* 23: 167–92.

_____. 1995. "Trade Liberalization and the Environment in the Pacific Basin: Coordinated Approaches to Mexican Trade and Environment Policy." *American Journal of Agricultural Economics* 77: 778–785.

_____. 1997a. "Trade and Pollution Linkages: Piecemeal Reform and Optimal Intervention." *Canadian Journal of Economics* XXX: 442–455.

Beghin J., and M. Potier. 1997. "Effects of Trade Liberalization on the Environment in the Manufacturing Sector." *The World Economy* 20(4): 435–456.

Bowland, B.J. 1997. "Marginal Benefits of Trade and Environmental Policy: Valuing Air Pollution and Health in a Developing Country." Thesis. North Carolina State University, Raleigh.

Copeland, B.R. 1994. "International and the Environment: Policy Reform in a Polluted Small Open economy." *Journal of Environmental Economics and Management* 20: 44–65.

Copeland, B.R., and M.S. Taylor. 1994. "North-South Trade and the Environment." *Quarterly Journal of Economics* 109: 755–87.

Dessus, S., D. Roland-Holst, and D. van der Mensbrugghe. 1994. "Input-based Estimates for Environmental Assessment in Developing Countries." OECD Development Centre Technical Papers, Paris.

Grossman, G.M., and A.B. Krueger. 1992. "Environmental Impact of a North American Free Trade Agreement." CEPR Discussion paper 644, London.

Lee, H., and D. Roland-Holst. 1997. "The Environment and Welfare Implications of Trade and Tax Policy." *Journal of Development Economics* 52(1): 65–82.

Low, P., ed. 1992. *International Trade and the Environment.* World Bank Discussion Paper No 159, Washington D.C.

Martin, P., D. Wheeler, M. Hettige, and R. Stengren. 1991. "The Industrial Pollution Projection System: Concept, Initial Development, and Critical Assessment." Mimeo, The World Bank.

O'Ryan, R.E. 1993. "Cost Effective Policies to Improve Urban Air Quality in Developing Countries: Case Study for Santiago, Chile." Thesis. University of California, Berkeley.

Ostro, B., and others. 1995. "Air Pollution and Mortality: Results from Santiago, Chile." Policy Research Working Paper (No. 1453). The World Bank, Washington D.C.

Papageorgiou, D., A.M. Choksi, and M. Michaely. 1990. *Liberalizing Foreign Trade in Developing Countries. The Lessons of Experience.* World Bank Publications, Washington D.C.

Sanchez, J. M. 1992. "The Costs of Urban Pollution: The Case of Santiago." ILADES/Georgetown University.

Turner, S.H., C.S. Weaver, and M.J. Reale. 1993. "Cost and Emissions Benefits of Selected Air Pollution Control Measures For Santiago, Chile." Final Report Submitted to The World Bank. Engine, Fuel, and Emissions Engineering, Inc: Sacramento, CA.

World Bank. 1994. "Chile: Managing Environmental Problems—Economic Analysis of Selected Issues." Report No. 13061-CH, Washington D.C.

Chapter 4

Testing the Impact of Trade Liberalization on the Environment

Theory and evidence

Judith M. Dean

1. Introduction

Industrial countries have recently raised concerns over whether or not "dirty industries" migrate. The concern has focussed on a perceived loss of comparative advantage in these industries because of more stringent domestic environmental regulations compared to developing countries. Developing countries, in contrast, are concerned that trade liberalization will promote specialization in dirty industries, thus aggravating environmental damage (Dean 1992a, b). In a recent study, Copeland and Taylor (1994) show that, theoretically, lower income in one country can produce a comparative advantage in dirty goods, even if externalities are optimally internalized into production costs.

Very little econometric work has been done on this question (Dean 1992a; Jaffe and others 1995). The work by Tobey (1990) and Grossman and Krueger (1993) suggests that trade flows are unaffected by environmental abundance (environmental control costs). Lucas and others (1992) find that the growth rate of toxic intensity of manufacturing output is lower for rapidly growing open economies compared to those which are closed. Thus openness appears to contribute to cleaner growth.

But the relationship between trade liberalization and environmental damage is more complex than is allowed for in these one-equation models. For a country with a comparative advantage in dirty goods, the static effect of trade liberalization should worsen environmental damage. Yet trade liberalization also raises income. Some would argue that openness actually raises the growth rate of income (Dollar 1992; Harrison 1996; and Edwards 1992). If the inverted-U hypothesis is correct (Grossman and Krueger 1995; Selden and Song 1994), higher incomes eventually result in lower levels of environmental damage. Since the static and dynamic effects of trade liberalization may work in opposite directions, it is possible that increased openness could lower the growth of emissions, and could lower the share of pollution-intensive goods in output, even for a country with a static comparative advantage in those goods.

As a first step in attempting to test the impact of trade liberalization on the environment, this paper develops a simultaneous equations model which incorporates both the static and dynamic interrelationships between trade, environment, and growth. Section 2 outlines the theoretical relationship between trade and the environment, and reviews three econometric studies in light of this relationship. Section 3 sets out a simple multi-equation model which incorporates both the static and dynamic relationships described in section 2. The implications of this for empirical tests are demonstrated in section 4, using the special case of a small country with endogenous factor supply. In this special case, a two-equation simultaneous system is required to capture both the direct and indirect effects of trade liberalization on growth of emissions. This system is then estimated using Chinese provincial data on water pollution for the period 1987–1995. Section 5 discusses the empirical test and presents results.

Preliminary results show strong support for the idea that trade liberalization actually has both a direct and an indirect effect on emissions growth, and that these effects are opposite in sign. It appears that China has a comparative advantage in pollution-intensive goods, and thus increased openness directly aggravates environmental damage. At the same time, increased openness is shown to strongly raise income growth. Income growth itself has a strong negative effect on emissions growth. Thus trade liberalization indirectly mitigates environmental damage.

2. The Links between Trade and the Environment—Econometric Evidence

Theoretically, the impact of trade liberalization on pollution levels is not clear. Consider the use of the environment (reflected by "emissions") as an input into the production process. Using a conventional Heckscher-Ohlin approach, if a country has a relative abundance of "environment," freer trade leads to increased specialization in "environment-intensive" (pollution-intensive) goods. This "composition effect" will tend to increase pollution levels. However, following the Stolper-Samuelson theorem, the price of environment relative to other inputs will be bid up,[1] causing all industries to switch to less pollution-intensive techniques. Thus, the "technique effect" of free trade will lead to a reduction in overall emission levels. The composition effect and the technique effect will have the opposite results on pollution levels, if the country has a relative scarcity of environment.

The critical point to note here is that the stock of environment at any point in time is endogenous, and depends upon the income level of the country. Income growth is thought to have three effects on the existing amount of pollution emissions. Greater economic activity raises demand for all inputs, hence increases emissions (the "scale effect"). However, if people increase their demand for a clean environment as income rises (that is, if clean environment is income elastic), then they will only tolerate higher levels of pollution if the effluent charge is higher. Since higher effluent charges encourage firms to shift toward cleaner production processes, this "technique effect" tends to reduce emissions. Finally, if income growth shifts preferences toward cleaner goods (that is, if clean goods are relatively income elastic), then the share of pollution-intensive goods in output will fall. This "composition effect," therefore, tends to decrease emissions. The inverted-U hypothesis argues that at some income level the scale effect is outweighed by the composition and technique effects, such that an increase in income reduces emissions.

Since freer trade raises income, it directly contributes to increasing pollution levels via the scale effect. However, it thereby induces the composition and technique effects of increased income, both of which tend to reduce pollution levels. If a country is on the right side of the inverted U, then freer trade will tend to reduce the stock of environment, altering that country's comparative advantage. Thus, even for a country with a relative abundance of environment, freer trade may not increase pollution levels. This outcome is even more likely if more open economies actually do grow faster, due to access to better technology or exposure to global competition. They presumably find themselves moving over the inverted-U faster, raising the likelihood that rising incomes will cause pollutant levels to fall.[2]

The few studies which econometrically test the relationship between trade liberalization and the environment focus on the composition effect alone, assuming a fixed stock of the environmental factor. Tobey (1990) and Grossman and Krueger (1993) investigate the impact of environmental regulations on trade flows in the context of a Heckscher-Ohlin-Vanek (HOV) model. The stock of environment is treated as an additional input which, along with labor, capital, and natural resources should affect the pattern of trade. Thus, a relatively large stock of environment (compared to one's trading partners) should give a country a comparative advantage in pollution-intensive goods. For such a country, trade liberalization should lead to increased specialization in these goods, hence aggravating environmental damage.

Tobey sets up a multi-factor, multi-commodity model. Using 1975 data on 23 countries, Tobey predicts net exports of 5 different industry groups which are classified as pollution-intensive.[3] Explanatory variables are the stocks of productive factors, where the stringency of environmental regulations is used as a proxy for the stock of environment. The level of stringency is itself proxied by an index which gives a single ranking to a country. In none of his 5 regressions is the environmental stringency variable significant.[4]

Grossman and Krueger (1993) explain 1987 U.S. imports from Mexico (relative to total U.S. shipments) in 135 industry categories using factor shares as explanatory variables. In this framework, factor shares reflect factor intensity of each industry. Environmental-intensity is proxied by the ratio of pollution abatement costs (operating costs) to total value-added in that U.S. industry.[5] Grossman and Krueger find that U.S. imports from Mexico are indeed lower in industries which are highly capital-intensive (either physical or human). However, pollution abatement costs have no significant impact on U.S. imports from Mexico.

Given the fact that, in all but a handful of U.S. industries, pollution abatement costs as a percent of operating costs are below 1 percent (Low 1992), many authors have argued that these costs are simply too small in importance to influence trade flows. Grossman and Krueger's results suggest that with respect to the United States, Mexico's comparative advantage lies in unskilled-labor-intensive goods. Thus, we would not expect increased openness to cause further specialization in dirty goods unless environment and unskilled labor are complements in production. Based on Tobey's estimates, this seems unlikely. He found that a relative abundance of unskilled labor has a positive significant impact on net exports of only one category of dirty goods—non-ferrous metals.[6]

Lucas, Wheeler and Hettige (1992) (henceforth LWH) focus directly on the toxic intensity of output (rather than on trade flows), where this is measured as aggregate emissions per unit of GDP.[7] The main focus of LWH is to test for an inverted-U relationship between output growth and the pollution-intensity of output. However, for the period 1960-1988, LWH regress the growth of toxic intensity per unit of output on initial per capita income, GDP growth calculated over the same period, and a measure of trade restrictiveness interacted with GDP growth.[8]

LWH find that countries with faster rates of GDP growth had lower rates of increase in toxic intensity over the period. For fast growing low and middle income countries, low levels of trade distortion reduced the growth of toxic intensity further, and during the 1980s actually caused it to fall. On the other hand, a high degree of trade distortion accelerated the growth of toxic intensity of output. Thus, it appears that openness in the trade regime contributes to cleaner growth, by changing the composition of output towards cleaner sectors.[9]

The results from LWH run counter to the popular notion that developing countries have a comparative advantage in pollution-intensive goods (due to lax environmental regulations). There are at least two potential explanations for this result. One is that other primary factors, such as unskilled labor, dictate comparative advantage. If, as the authors suggest, unskilled labor-intensive manufactures are relatively clean, then openness increases specialization in relatively clean goods. The second possibility is that openness increases growth, increasing the likelihood of being on the right side of the inverted U. It is to these two relationships which we now turn.

3. A General Model of Trade and the Environment[10]

A simple simultaneous system is presented in equations (1)–(4) below. This system attempts to capture the multiple ways in which trade can affect the environment (as shown in table 4.1), given that the "stock of environment" is actually endogenous.

$$Y = A(t)h(L, K, E) \quad (1)$$
$$E = f(\tau, Y, \Omega) \quad (2)$$
$$\tau = g(E, Y) \quad (3)$$
$$\Omega = z(t, Y) \quad (4)$$

Equation (1) shows total output (real income, *Y*) as a function of the level of trade restrictions (*t*), the stock of conventional factors of production (*L, K*) and the level of emissions (*E*). Increased openness is assumed to lead to higher total factor productivity (A'<0). Since emissions (or use of the environment) is being treated as an input, the total amount of *Y* is positively related to the equilibrium level of emissions at any point in time. The equilibrium level of emissions is endogenous. From equation (1) one can derive demand for E as a function of the emissions charge (τ), *Y*, and the share of pollution-intensive goods in real output (Ω). This is shown in equation (2). We assume that $f_1<0$, $f_2>0$, and $f_3>0$. Equation (3) is the inverse supply curve for *E* which is derived from individuals' utility function. Utility is assumed to be increasing in goods, but decreasing in emissions. Thus, $g_1>0$ and $g_2>0$.

We expect the composition of output, Ω, to be negatively related to income (z_2<0), as long as clean goods are relatively income elastic. However, the composition of output will also be related to the restrictiveness of the trade regime (t). For a country with a comparative advantage in pollution-intensive goods, z_1<0, since an increase in trade restrictiveness moves resources toward production of relatively cleaner goods.

If we totally differentiate the system in (1)–(4) we can solve for the static effect of trade liberalization on emissions:

$$(dE/dt)\cdot\Delta = -hA'(f_1g_2 + f_2 + f_3z_2) - f_3z_1 \qquad (5)$$

where $\Delta < 0$ is the determinant of the system. The second term on the right side of (5) is the effect of trade liberalization on the demand for environment (as an input) due to a change in the composition of output. If a country's comparative advantage is in pollution-intensive goods, z_1<0, and thus $-f_3z_1$>0. Thus, increased openness would aggravate environmental damage. Counteracting this is the first term which captures the fact that trade raises income. The sum in parentheses shows the technique, scale, and composition effects, respectively, of an increase in income due to trade liberalization. If we are on the "right" side of the inverted U, this sum is negative. With A'<0, the first term is negative. Therefore, even if comparative advantage leads to specialization in pollution-intensive goods, the impact of trade on income could dominate, leading to lower emissions overall.

4. An Alternative Heckscher-Ohlin-Vanek Specification

To illustrate the importance of accounting for the relationships given by (1)–(4) in empirical testing, consider the following special case. Suppose we consider a small country which produces two types of goods, dirty (X_D) and clean (X_C). There is no transborder pollution or consumption pollution. Thus all emissions are generated by production. As in Lopez (1994), production in each sector uses both conventional factors of production (K, L) and E. Rewrite equation (1) as:

$$Y = A(t)h[F(L,K),E] \qquad (1')$$

where $h(\cdot)$ is concave in $F(\cdot)$ and in E, and characterized by constant returns to scale in K, L, and E. The production function in (1′) assumes weak separability between conventional factors of production and emissions. That is, the marginal rate of technical substitution between K and L is assumed to be independent of the level of E. Dirty goods are defined as those which are relatively environment-intensive (pollution-intensive). Thus, production of X_D uses a higher ratio of environment to conventional factors at any given factor price ratio than production of X_C. Let $F(\cdot)$ be an aggregator of the stock of conventional factors.

We assume this country has a relative abundance of environment, and therefore a comparative advantage in dirty goods. The costs of environmental damage are internalized via emissions taxes (τ). Though the country is trading initially, there exists some level of trade restrictions on imports of X_C.

With these simplifying assumptions, we can set out an HOV trade model which captures the relationships in (1)–(4), using the approach developed in Jones (1965). The unit cost functions for X_D and X_C relate goods prices and factor prices:

$$(\hat{\tau} - \hat{w}) = (1/|\theta|)(\hat{p}_D - \hat{p}_C) \qquad (6)$$

where: p_j are domestic prices of good j, j=D,C; w is the wage paid to conventional factors; ^ indicates proportionate change in a variable; θ_{ij} is the share of input i (i=F,E) in unit cost of output j, and $|\theta| = |\theta_{ED} - \theta_{EC}| > 0$. Equation (6) captures changes in the derived demand for inputs as a function of changes in relative goods prices (assuming fixed stocks of factors of production). Since the country is small, changes in the composition of domestic demand do not affect relative outputs nor relative factor demands.

Now from (3) we know that the supply of E is endogenous. Let utility, $U = U(C_D, C_C, E)$ where C_j is consumption of good j. Differentiating U with respect to E one can derive a supply curve for E=$E(\tau, p_D, p_C, Y)$. Let changes in the supply of E be expressed as

$$\hat{E} = \varepsilon_\tau(\hat{\tau} - \hat{w}) - \varepsilon_y\hat{Y} \qquad (7)$$

As in Martin and Neary (1980), ε_τ represents a reduced form supply elasticity with respect to relative factor prices, assuming commodity prices adjust to a change in factor prices. If the supply curve does not bend backward, $\varepsilon_\tau > 0$. The income elasticity of demand for clean environment, $\varepsilon_y > 1$. Thus, a rise in income reduces the amount of emissions individuals are willing to allow.

With constant returns to scale, changes in the composition of output can be expressed as

$$\hat{X}_D - \hat{X}_C = (1/|\lambda|)(\hat{E} - \hat{F}) + \sigma_S|\theta|(\hat{\tau} - \hat{w}) \quad (8)$$

where: σ_S is the elasticity of substitution along the production possibility frontier; λ_{ij} is the share of total i used in producing j, and $|\lambda| = |\lambda_{ED} - \lambda_{LD}| > 0$.

Let income growth be expressed as

$$\hat{Y} = \alpha_E\hat{E} + \alpha_F\hat{F} + \hat{A} \quad (9)$$

where α_i is the share of input i in total output. As in Edwards (1992), suppose at any time T, $A_T = A_o e^{\beta T}$, where β is a linear function of t, and $\beta' < 0$. Then (9) may be written

$$\hat{Y} = \alpha_E\hat{E} + \alpha_F\hat{F} + \beta(t) \quad (10)$$

Substituting (6) into (7) yields the equilibrium rate of change in emissions:

$$\hat{E} = (\varepsilon_\tau/|\theta|)(\hat{p}_D - \hat{p}_C) - \varepsilon_y\hat{Y} \quad (11)$$

Together, equations (10) and (11) form a simple simultaneous system describing the rates of change in equilibrium emissions and equilibrium real income. In this system, trade liberalization affects the growth of emissions in two ways. Recall that changes in changes in the domestic terms of trade $(\hat{p}_D - \hat{p}_C) = (\hat{p}_D^* - \hat{p}_C^* - \hat{t})$ where * represents world prices. Thus, a reduction in trade restrictions will raise the relative price of dirty goods (11), leading to increased specialization in these goods. This should increase the growth of emissions. However, lower levels of trade restrictions will raise factor productivity and thereby income (10). This increase in income will reduce the growth of emissions since it reduces the willingness of individuals to supply the environment as a factor of production at any given t. Estimating a two-equation simultaneous model such as this would allow one to sort out these two effects. Since they work in opposing directions, a one equation model with trade restrictiveness as an explanatory variable may simply yield an insignificant coefficient.

The implications of trade liberalization for the composition of output can be seen by substituting (6), (7), and (10) into (8). With some simplification this yields

$$\hat{X}_D - \hat{X}_C = \tilde{\sigma}_S(\hat{p}_D - \hat{p}_C) - |\lambda|^{-1}Z^{-1}[(1 + \alpha_F\varepsilon_y)\hat{F} + \varepsilon_y\beta(t)] \quad (12)$$

where: $\tilde{\sigma} = \sigma_S + Z^{-1}(\varepsilon_\tau/|\lambda||\theta|)$

$Z = (1 + \varepsilon_y\alpha_E)$

Equation (12) shows that reductions in trade restrictions will again have two opposing effects on the relative growth of the pollution-intensive sector. On the one hand, by increasing the relative price of X_D, trade liberalization induces more than the usual increase in output of X_D, since increased demand for environment raises the equilibrium stock of environment. This is shown by $\tilde{\sigma}_S$, which is the elasticity of substitution along the variable factor production possibility frontier. If backward bending supply curves are ruled out, $\tilde{\sigma}_S > \sigma_S$. Note that this effect is diminished by a feedback effect due to income growth, captured by Z. On the other hand, trade liberalization induces income growth which reduces the equilibrium stock of the environment. This is seen in the third term on the right side of (12). Therefore, increased openness could actually lead to a reduction in the share of pollution-intensive goods in output, if the indirect effect of trade liberalization on income growth, and therefore on the supply of environment, is stronger than the direct effect on the composition of output.

5. An Application to China

Equations (10) and (11) form a system in which income growth and the growth of emissions are determined simultaneously. The hypotheses to be tested are as follows. First, trade liberalization will affect emissions growth "directly," via its effect on the relative price of pollution-intensive goods. If a country has a comparative advantage in those goods, liberalization will raise the growth of emissions. Second, trade liberalization will affect emissions growth "indirectly" via its effect on income growth. If a country's income is high enough such that it is on the "right side" of the inverted *U*, then liberalization will reduce emissions growth. The full impact of trade liberalization on the environment must account for both these effects.

Ideally the system in (10) and (11) should be estimated for a country over time. Because of the lack of any lengthy time series data on emissions, we use pooled Chinese provincial data on industrial water pollution emissions over the period 1987-1995. Data are obtained from a World Bank dataset compiled by David Wheeler and Hua Wang. The focus on water pollution emissions (tons of industrial COD discharge) is in part due to data availability, but also due to the fact that Chinese firms do pay levies on water pollution. Hence, one can argue that to some extent, environmental damage from water pollution is indeed internalized in the costs of the firms. Since emissions data are limited to the industrial sector, income is measured as the value of industrial output in 1990 constant yuan. Data on a broad set of factors of production are not available at the provincial level. Therefore, the traditional factors of production included are simply the labor force and physical capital stock.

No assumption is made as to whether or not China has a static comparative advantage in "pollution-intensive" goods. Changes in relative world prices are simply measured as changes in China's net barter terms of trade. Assessing trade restrictions at an aggregated level is notoriously difficult. For this test, we use the black market premium as a proxy for overall trade restrictiveness. We will attempt some sensitivity tests using alternative measures of overall trade restrictiveness based on actual Chinese tariff and non-tariff barrier data. Although China has some restrictions on trade which differ across provinces, we assume that their effect is mitigated by free inter-provincial trade.

The model in (10) and (11) is estimated using two-stage least squares. Since the average rates of growth of emissions and income across provinces are likely to differ based on variation in the types of industries concentrated in a province, fixed effects were included. Estimation of the model also required correction for both groupwise heteroskedasticity and first order autocorrelation. Table 4.1 reports the results of two specifications of the model.

Specification A uses one variable to capture changes in the domestic terms of trade (as in equation (11)). Thus it restricts the coefficient on changes in the world terms of trade and changes in the black market premium to be the same. Given that the black market premium is an imperfect proxy for changes in overall trade restrictiveness, specification B removes that restriction. Thus, it separates changes in the domestic terms of trade into its two components—changes in the world terms of trade and changes in the black market premium.

These results appear to validate the hypotheses outlined above. In Specification A (the first column) the domestic terms of trade show a strong positive relationship with the growth of emissions. An increase of 1 percent in the relative price of net exports leads to an increase in the growth of emissions of .08 percent. This suggests that China may indeed have a static comparative advantage in pollution-intensive goods. Hence, the direct impact of trade liberalization may indeed be a worsening of the water pollution problem.

At the same time, however, trade liberalization increases the growth of income (second column). The lagged black market premium reflects the overall level of trade restrictiveness at the beginning of period t. A 1 percent reduction in trade restrictiveness produces an increase of .04 percent in the growth rate of income. Turning to column 1 again, we see that a .04 percent increase in the growth rate of income causes a decline in the growth of emissions by $(.22 \times .04) = .0088$ percent. As was argued above, this negative relationship between income growth and emissions growth would reflect the "technique effect." As income rises, people increase their demand for a clean environment, hence imposing higher penalties on water pollution. The indirect role of trade liberalization, via its effect on income growth, is to reduce the water pollution problem.

The results for specification B (third and fourth columns) reinforce those in specification A. It appears that the full effect of changes in the domestic terms of trade on emissions growth can be attributed to changes in openness. This is not surprising, since the world terms of trade for Chinese traded goods changed very little during this period, while the black market premium varied widely over time. The effect of openness on income growth remains the same, while the impact of income growth on emissions growth is slightly more strongly negative.

There are certainly a few anomalies in the results in table 4.1, which suggest that further work needs to be done. First, in both specifications labor force growth has no significant influence on income growth. This

Table 4.1 The impact of openness on growth of emissions

Model:	(A)		(B)	
Dependent variable:	*Emissions growth* [a,b]	*Income growth* [a,b]	*Emissions growth* [a,b]	*Income Growth* [a,b]
Emissions growth	---	-0.02* (-2.08)	---	-0.01 (-1.56)
Income growth	-0.22* (-2.03)	---	-0.29* (-2.21)	---
Domestic Terms of Trade (percent change)	0.08** (4.90)	---	---	---
World terms of trade (percent change)	---	---	0.63 (0.34)	---
Labor force growth	---	0.59 (1.13)	---	0.62 (1.19)
Investment $_{t-1}$	---	0.44** (3.32)	---	0.42** (3.20)
Black market premium $_{t-1}$ (level)	---	-0.04** (-4.69)	---	-0.04** (-4.61)
Black market premium (percent change)	---	---	-0.08** (-3.64)	---
N=168[c]				
Wald test [d]-- chi-square	160.43**	34.41**	179.09**	31.73**

Notes:

t-statistics in parentheses
Black market premia are from World Currency Yearbook. Net barter terms of trade are from World Bank World Development Indicators.
**Significant at the 1 percent level
*Significant at the 5 percent level
[a] All variables are measured in annual percent change except black market premium $_{t-1}$.
[b] Includes fixed effects for provinces. Estimates of the 28 constant terms are not reported. Standard errors corrected for groupwise heteroskedasticity and first order autocorrelation.
[c] Data includes 28 provinces over the period 1987-1995. Due to missing data, 1991 values reflect changes between 1989 and 1991. Hainan and Tibet were excluded due to lack of data.
[d] Tests for the significance of the regression as a whole.

may be due to the use of provincial employment data to measure the labor force as opposed to provincial industrial employment data. It may also reflect the extent to which state owned entreprises dominate industrial production. Second, the growth of emissions itself appears to have either no influence or a negative influence on income growth. This might be due the differing concentrations of pollution-intensive industries across provinces. Future tests will attempt to test for the influence of both state ownership and pollution intensity of industries.

6. Conclusion

Recent events such as NAFTA have brought out concerns on the part of both industrial and developing countries as to the effects of trade liberalization on the environment. For the latter group, concern has focussed on the idea that less stringent environmental standards will imply a comparative advantage in pollution-intensive goods. If so, trade liberalization will harm the environment.

Existing empirical work on this question consists of single equation models which focus on the static relationship between trade and environment. That work found: no relationship between the pattern of trade and relative abundance in environment; a negative relationship between growth of toxic intensity of output and openness. This paper develops an alternative simultaneous equations model which allows for both static effects via comparative advantage, and dynamic effects of trade on income growth and therefore on the growth of emissions. In this way, the literature on trade and growth as well as that on income growth and environmental damage (the inverted-U hypothesis) are incorporated into the model. This highlights the fact that trade liberalization indirectly affects relative factor abundance, since the "stock of environment" is endogenous.

What emerges is a two equation model which simultaneously determines growth of income and growth of emissions. Estimation of this model using Chinese provincial data shows the importance of using a simultaneous model to discern the influence of trade liberalization. Results show that there is indeed both a direct and indirect effect of trade liberalization on emissions growth, and that these effects are of opposite sign. Improvements in the domestic terms of trade lead to increased emissions growth. Hence, the direct impact of trade liberalization would be to aggravate environmental damage. However, results also indicate that increased openness significantly raises the growth of income, and that growth of income has a negative and significant effect on emissions growth. Thus, the indirect effect of trade liberalization is to mitigate environmental damage.

Notes

This paper is a revision and expansion of an earlier study, "Testing the Impact of Trade Liberalization on the Environment," University of Adelaide Centre for International Economic Studies Seminar Paper 96-10. I am most grateful to Bill Lahneman for excellent research assistance, and to Hua Wang, Muthukumara Mani and David Wheeler for their help in obtaining data. Many thanks to Ulrich Kohli and James Riedel, Kym Anderson, Randy Stringer, Rod Ludema, and Mitch Kaneda for helpful suggestions on the earlier study. Thanks are also due to the participants in: The Conference on Trade, Environment, and Growth (August 1996) in Melbourne, Australia; the CIES seminar at the University of Adelaide, Australia; the IEFS session at the ASSA Meetings, January 1997.

1. This is true to the extent that environmental externalities are internalized into production costs.

2. As Birdsall and Wheeler (1992) note, if foreign technology is cleaner, or exports must be cleaner to meet higher foreign standards, then more open economies would see cleaner growth.

3. "Pollution-intensive industries" are those with pollution abatement and control costs per unit of output greater than or equal to 1.85 percent. These 24 SITC industries are then aggregated into 5 industry groups: mining, paper, chemicals, steel, non-ferrous metals.

4. There are a number of shortcomings in this approach. In addition to problems with measuring stringency, using such an index assumes that the regulations in place are actually optimal. If they are not, there is no necessary correlation between environmental endowment and the index. Aggregation may also be a problem. A test run on one country across many industries might allow for environmental stringency to affect the pattern of specialization across industries. Finally, import restrictions on some of these goods might allow domestic industries to absorb the cost of environmental regulations without impacting trade flows.

5. To account for the effects of trade barriers on trade flows the collected tariff rate for each industry is also included. As is well known, however, increases (decreases) in this rate do not necessarily correspond to increased (decreased) restrictiveness in the trade regime.

6. Semi-skilled labor is either unrelated to net exports or significantly negatively related to net exports for the five industry categories he examined.

7. They construct a measure of emissions of 320 types of pollutants from industry *i* per unit of output of *i*. This is then multiplied by the share of industry *i* in GDP (or alternatively manufacturing output), to generate an aggregate measure of emissions per unit of GDP.

8. The trade restrictiveness variable is constructed by grouping countries into seven categories, from least restrictive to most restrictive, based on Dollar's (1992) index of trade distortion.

9. More recently Lucas (1994) finds considerable evidence that increased openness reduces the level of toxic intensity of output, when toxic intensity is measured with respect to individual types of pollutants.

10. The non-technical reader may want to skip sections 3 and 4.

References

Copeland, B.R., and M.S.Taylor. 1994. "North-South Trade and the Environment." *Quarterly Journal of Economics* August: 755–87.

Dean, J. 1992a. "Trade and the Environment: a Survey of the Literature." In P. Low, ed., *International Trade and theEnvironment.* World Bank Discussion Paper No. 159.

Dean, J. 1992b. "Trade Policy and the Environment: Developing Country Concerns." Prepared for the Environment Directorate, OECD.

Dean, J. 1996. "Testing the Impact of Trade Liberalization on the Environment." *Centre for International Economic Studies Seminar Paper 96–10,* University of Adelaide.

Dollar, D. 1992. "Outward-Oriented Developing Economies Really Do Grow More Rapidly: Evidence from 95 LDCs, 1976–1985." *Economic Development and Cultural Change* :523–544.

Edwards, S. 1992. "Trade Orientation, Distortions, and Growth in Developing Countries." *Journal of Development Economics* 39: 31–57.

Grossman, G., and A. Krueger. 1993. "Environmental Impacts of NAFTA." In P. Garber, ed., *The US-Mexico Free Trade Agreement.* Cambridge, MA: MIT Press.

_____. 1995. "Economic Growth and the Environment." *Quarterly Journal of Economics* May: 353–377.

Harrison, A. 1996. "Openness and Growth: a Time-Series, Cross-Country Analysis for Developing Countries." *Journal of Development Economics* 48: 419–447.

Jaffe, A.B., S.R. Peterson, P.R. Portney, and R. Stavins. 1995. "EnvironmentalRegulation and the Competitiveness of U.S. Manufacturing." *Journal of Economic Literature* 33(1): 132–163.

Jones, R. 1965. "The Structure of Simple General Equilibrium Models." *Journal of Political Economy* 73: 557–572.

Lopez, R. 1994. "The Environment as a Factor of Production: the Effects of Economic Growth and Trade Liberalization." *Journal of Environmental Economics and Management* 27: 163–184.

Low, P. 1992. "Trade Measures and Environmental Quality: The Implications for Mexico's Exports." In P. Low, ed., *International Trade and the Environment.* World Bank Discussion Paper No. 159.

Lucas, R.E.B. 1994. "International Environmental Indicators: Trade, Income, and Endowments." Boston University IED Discussion Paper Series No. 46.

Lucas, R.E.B., and others. 1992. "Economic Development, Environmental Regulation and the International Migration of Toxic Industrial Pollution: 1960–88." In P. Low, ed., *International Trade and the Environment.* World Bank Discussion Paper No. 159.

Martin, J., and P. Neary. 1980. "Variable Labour Supply and the Pure Theory of International Trade." *Journal of International Economics* 10: 549–559.

Selden, T.M., and D. Song. 1994. "Environmental Quality and Development: Is There a Kuznets Curve for Air Pollution Emissions?" *Journal of Environmental Economics and Management* 27: 147–162.

Tobey, J. 1990. "The Effects of Domestic Environmental Policies on Patterns of World Trade: An Empirical Test." *Kyklos* 43: 191–209.

Chapter 5

Industrial Pollution in Economic Development

Kuznets revisited

Hemamala Hettige, Muthukumara Mani, and David Wheeler

1. Introduction

A number of recent studies have explored the relationship between economic development and environmental quality. Theoretical papers by Gruver (1976), John and Pecchenino (1992), and Selden and Song (1995) have derived transition paths for pollution, abatement effort and development under alternative assumptions about social welfare functions, pollution damage, the cost of abatement, and the productivity of capital. Empirical studies (Hettige and others 1992; Shafik 1994; Selden and Song 1994; and Grossman and Krueger 1995) have searched for systematic relationships by regressing cross-country measures of ambient air and water quality on various polynomial specifications of income per capita. This extensive body of work has been motivated by several related questions: Does pollution follow a "Kuznets" curve, first rising and then falling as income increases? At what income level does the turnaround occur? Do all pollutants follow the same trajectory? Is pollution reduction in developed economies due primarily to structural change, or to regulation?

The theoretical work has shown that a Kuznets, or inverted-U, relationship can result if a few plausible conditions are satisfied as income increases: Constant or falling marginal utility of consumption; rising marginal disutility of pollution; constant or rising marginal pollution damage; and rising marginal abatement cost. Of course, actual turnaround points depend on the relative magnitudes of the underlying parameters, as well as their signs. Although they are not explicitly captured by the theoretical models, structural change in the economy and more effective regulation are also potentially-important sources of change in pollution.

The empirical results are roughly consistent with a Kuznets curve for conventional air pollutants such as suspended particulates and sulphur dioxide, but the results for water pollution are mixed. In most cases, however, the implied trajectories are sensitive to inclusion of higher-order polynomial terms in income whose significance varies widely. Structural interpretation of the estimates remains ad hoc, since the existing studies have incorporated almost no evidence about actual emissions in developing countries.[1]

This paper attempts to advance the state of the art, using new data on industrial water emissions in developed and developing countries. Our analysis decomposes total industrial pollution into four proximate determinants: National output; the share of industry in national output; the share of polluting sectors in industrial output; and end-of-pipe pollution intensities in the polluting sectors. As most of the previously-cited work has noted (without being able to resolve the issue), declining pollution at higher levels of development must be driven by some combination of income-related changes in the latter three factors.

We investigate these changes in three econometric exercises. Using international panel data, we estimate the effects of economic development on industry's share of total output and the industry share of polluting sectors. To study development-related changes in end-of-pipe pollution intensity, we have collected factory-level data on industrial water pollution from national and regional environmental protection agencies (EPAs) in twelve countries: Brazil, China, Finland, India, Indonesia, Korea, Mexico, Netherlands, Philippines, Sri Lanka, Taiwan (China), Thailand and the United States. Controlling for sectoral differences, we use these data to investigate the effects of income per capita, regulatory strictness and relative input prices on factory-level pollution intensity (pollution/output). In a complementary exercise, we add a measure of regulatory strictness to a cross-country labor intensity equation to test for the impact of regulation on the demand for labor. For our international pollution accounting exercise, these results provide two inputs: A measure of average water pollution intensity for each industry sector (an input to our study of income-related changes in polluting sectors), and an estimate of the change in sectoral pollution intensities as income per capita increases.

We combine our econometric results to simulate the total effect of economic development on industrial water pollution. In this case, we do not find an overall inverse U-shaped relationship. The three factors have very different relationships with income, and their joint product with total output is asymptotic, not parabolic. Industrial water emissions rise until countries attain middle-income status, and then remain approximately constant as they grow richer.

While our results do not support the Kuznets hypothesis for industrial water pollution, they do reveal a striking regularity in cross-country environmental performance. Our plant-level results suggest that pollution and labor intensities with respect to output decline continuously, and at almost exactly the same rate, as income increases. *Thus, sectoral pollution/labor ratios remain approximately constant during the development process.* This finding provides useful leverage for the analysis of pollution trends across countries and over time. As an illustration, we combine our estimated sectoral pollution/labor ratios with panel data on sectoral employment to simulate international trends in industrial water pollution during the past two decades.

The remainder of the paper is organized as follows. Section 2 develops the models which link our three pollution factors to economic development. Section 3 introduces the data used for estimation. Section 4 discusses the results and their implications, while Section 5 provides illustrative estimates of recent water pollution trends in a number of developed and developing countries. Section 6 concludes the paper.

2. Development and Industrial Pollution

The first stages of economic development typically witness the rapid growth of industrial activity and declining environmental quality in densely-populated urban areas. When new industries are pollution-intensive, their emissions can increase local ambient pollutant concentrations to harmful levels. To study this phenomenon, we decompose total industrial emissions in a particular region as follows:

$$P = m(y)Q\rho(y)\eta(y), \qquad (1)$$

where

P = Total industrial pollution
m = Manufacturing share of total output
Q = Total output
ρ = Manufacturing pollution intensity
η = Degree of pollution abatement: $0 < \eta \leq 1$
y = Income per capita

Equation (1) includes three parameters which we hypothesize to be functions of economic development: The manufacturing share of total output (m), the pollution intensity of manufacturing (ρ), and the degree of pollution abatement by industry (η). In this decomposition, the effect of economic development on pollution depends on the signs and the magnitudes of the parameters governing the relations between m, ρ, η and y.

2.1 Manufacturing share of total output

Numerous studies of the relationship between industrialization and economic development have suggested an inverted-U relationship between the manufacturing share of output (m) and income per capita (y).[2] During the first phase of economic growth, m increases as industry expands more rapidly than agriculture. As the economy begins to mature, rapid growth in services becomes the dominant factor and m declines. Over the existing range of national incomes per capita, this relationship can be approximated with a parabolic function:

$$\log m = \alpha_0 + \alpha_1 \log y + \alpha_2 (\log y)^2 \ (a_1 > 0,\ a_2 < 0) \quad (2)$$

Our empirical analysis uses cross-country evidence for the past two decades to estimate this relationship and test its intertemporal stability. We focus particularly on changes in $\delta m / \delta y$ as development proceeds. Controlling for growth in total output, large movements in m will have a significant impact on the trajectory followed by industrial pollution.

2.2 *Sector-weighted pollution intensity*

The sectoral composition of industrial activity has an important effect on its average pollution intensity, or pollution per unit of output. Industrial processes differ greatly in their production of waste residuals which, in turn, have varying potential for creating environmental damage. Abatement costs also differ significantly by industry sector (Dasgupta and others 1996; Hartman and others 1997). Even in well-regulated economies, these factors cause significant intersectoral differences in pollution intensity. For example, metals and cement are generally intensive in harmful air pollutants; food and paper production are disproportionate emitters of organic water pollutants (Hettige and others 1995).

Anecdotal evidence suggests that the sectoral composition of industry follows a 'clean' trend as development proceeds. This could reflect domination of early industrialization by primary industries, which generate heavy pollution loads as they convert bulk raw materials into primary inputs (for example metals, paper, cement, sugar). During the development process, primary indus- tries may lose output share to cleaner industries (for example vehicle and electronics assembly, instruments).[3] In this paper, we test the clean trend hypothesis for industrial water pollution by fitting the following equation to an international panel dataset:

$$\tilde{\rho}_{jt} = \beta_0 + \beta_1 \log y_{jt} + \beta_2 (\log y_{jt})^2,$$
$$\tilde{\rho} = \sum_k s_k \hat{\rho}_k \quad (3)$$

where j, k, t = country, sector and year respectively, and $\hat{\rho}_j$ = average pollution intensity for sector j (see Section 4.3).

2.3 *Pollution abatement*

The marginal cost of abating pollution from industrial sources is a function of the scale of activity, pollutant concentration in process influent,[4] the degree of abatement, and local input prices.[5] In static partial equilibrium, cost-minimizing firms with flexible abatement choices will control pollution to the point where their marginal abatement costs equal the 'price' exacted for pollution by affected parties.[6] Characteristic production scale and process effluent intensity differ significantly by sector, and abatement costs differ by location. Differences in the groups affected by pollution can also lead to significant spatial variation in emissions prices.[7]

Pollution, Employment, Regulation, and Input Prices

Where the environment is 'cheaper' or abatement is more expensive, the pollution intensity of production in a particular sector should be higher, ceteris paribus. However, data scarcity has made it difficult to test the magnitude of these effects, as well as the impact of spatial variation in the prices of capital, labor, energy and materials. At present, we have sufficient data to investigate these relationships in a two-equation demand system:[8]

$$\ln P_j = \alpha_0 + \sum_S \delta_{SP} D_{SP} + \alpha_R \ln R_j + \alpha_K \ln W_{K_j} + \alpha_L \ln W_{L_j} + \alpha_E \ln W_{E_j} + \alpha_M \ln W_{M_j} + \alpha_Q \ln Q_j;$$
$$\ln L_j = \beta_0 + \sum_S \beta_{SL} D_{SL} + \beta_P \ln R_j + \beta_K \ln W_{K_j} + \beta_L \ln W_{L_j} + \beta_E \ln W_{E_j} + \beta_M \ln W_{M_j} + \beta_Q \ln Q_j, \quad (4)$$

where (for country *j*)
P = Plant-level pollution
L = Plant-level employment
D = Vector of dummy variables for S sectors
R = An index of regulatory strictness
$W_{K,L,E,M}$ = Prices of capital, labor, energy and materials
Q = Plant-level output

Our data set, described in the following section, combines information from several sources: plant- and sector-level data on emissions and employment from national and regional EPA's; sector-level information on output and employment from national census bureaus and the World Bank's international database (BESD); and data from BESD on national income, population, and a number of other variables. For cross-country consistency, we use summary data by sector.[9] Plant-level relations between scale (Q) and pollution intensity (P/Q) are not relevant for sectoral aggregates, so we impose the assumption of constant returns ($\alpha_Q = \beta_Q = 1$).[10] This implies estimation of the pollution and labor equations in intensity form, with P/Q and L/Q as the dependent variables.

Using the BESD database, we estimate sectoral average L/Q ratios for each sample country. We construct sectoral average P/L ratios (sectoral pollution intensities w.r.t. labor) from the data provided by national and regional EPA's. We estimate P/Q (pollution intensity w.r.t. output) by multiplying L/Q and P/L for each sector and country. The results permit us to estimate the following equations:

$$\ln\frac{P_j}{Q_j} = \alpha_0 + \sum_S \delta_{SP} D_{SP} + \alpha_R \ln R_j + \alpha_K \ln W_{K_j} + \alpha_L \ln W_{L_j} + \alpha_E \ln W_{E_j} + \varepsilon_j$$
$$\ln\frac{L_j}{Q_j} = \beta_0 + \sum_S \beta_{SL} D_{SL} + \beta_P \ln R_j + \beta_K \ln W_{K_j} + \beta_L \ln W_{L_j} + \beta_E \ln W_{E_j} + \nu_j \qquad (5)$$

In some cases, we have clear prior expectations about parameter signs:

Regulation: Ceteris paribus, we expect stricter regulation to have a negative impact on pollution intensity. We have no clear prior about its impact on labor intensity at the sector level.

Labor Price: We naturally expect increasing wages to reduce the labor intensity of industrial output. The effect of wages on pollution intensity is less transparent. Econometric estimates of KLEM (capital, labor, energy, materials) models has suggested that (K,E) and (L,M) are complements in production, while the pairs KE and LM are gross substitutes.[11] If these relations hold, a wage increase should have the following effects on emissions: (1) Materials use and the volume of polluting residuals should decline; (2) Labor use should decrease in both processing and pollution abatement activities, with some increase in pollution from the latter effect. However, our prior expectation is that the materials-reducing effect should dominate: A wage increase should reduce water pollution intensity.

Energy Price: If labor and energy are gross substitutes in production, then an increase in the price of energy should increase the labor intensity of production. In the case of pollution, an energy price increase will reduce energy use for both processing and pollution abatement. Abatement activity should therefore fall, and water pollution intensity should rise.

Capital Price: A capital price increase should also increase labor intensity. For pollution, an increase in the interest rate or the price of equipment should reduce capital and energy use as well as pollution abatement, while increasing the use of labor and materials in processing. Both reduced abatement and increased materials use should lead to more water pollution.

Pollution Intensity and Economic Development

Regulatory strictness and some input prices (for example, wages) change systematically as per capita income increases. To assess the overall impact of economic development, we also estimate our intensity equations in reduced form:

$$\ln\frac{P_j}{Q_j} = \rho_j = \gamma_0 + \sum_S \delta_{SP} D_{SP} + \rho_y \ln y + \varepsilon_j$$
$$\ln\frac{L_j}{Q_j} = \lambda_j = \gamma_0 + \sum_S \gamma_{SL} D_{SL} + \gamma_y \ln y + \nu_j \qquad (6)$$

These equations have two specific roles to play in our analysis. First, they provide an estimate of ρ_y, the elasticity of end-of-pipe pollution intensity with respect to income per capita. We use this to construct the index η in equation (1). The results also provide estimates of average sectoral pollution intensities (δ_{SP}) across countries. We combine these intensities with our panel data on sector shares by country to construct estimates of $\tilde{\rho}$ for use in equation (3).

3. Data

3.1 Industrial pollution

To our knowledge, this is the first comparative international study of industrial pollution which uses direct observations on emissions. We have obtained the data from environmental protection agencies in Brazil, China, Finland, India, Indonesia, Korea, Mexico, Netherlands, Philippines, Sri Lanka, Taiwan (China), Thailand and the United States. Descriptions of the data sources are provided in the Appendix.

We use the pollution information and complementary employment data to estimate emissions intensities by industry sector in kilograms per day per employee. We focus on organic water pollution because it provides the most plentiful and reliable source of comparable cross-country emissions information. Water pollution data are the most plentiful because developing countries have traditionally begun industrial pollution control programs with regulation of organic water emissions. They are relatively reliable because sampling techniques for measuring water pollution are more widely understood and much less expensive than those for air pollution.

3.2 Environmental regulation

Some comparable measure of regulatory strictness is necessary for estimation of our cross-country equations. However, credible indices of environmental regulation are difficult to find. Even in the United States, comparative analyses of state-level regulatory 'outputs' have generally used input-based measures such as expenditures on monitoring and enforcement, or total employment of inspectors.[12] Such measures may have at least some justification for within-country analyses, since quality- and price-adjustment problems are not too serious. For international comparisons, however, they would be problematic even if comparable data were available. Most developing countries do not have such data, so input-based comparisons are not possible in any case.

A more promising approach has been taken by recent econometric work on the sources of variation in regulatory strictness. This work is helping to identify robust proxies which can be used as instruments in cross-country comparisons. The best instrument is undoubtedly per capita income, which has been shown to affect both formal and informal regulatory pressure on polluters in the United States and Asia (McConnell 1992; Pargal and Wheeler 1996; Hartman and others 1997; Hettige and others 1996; and Wang and Wheeler 1996). Dasgupta and others (1995) have advanced the state of the art by developing quantitative indices of regulatory development from reports filed for the U.N. Conference on Environment and Development (UNCED—Rio de Janeiro, 1992). Their results suggest that international differences in pollution regulation are well-explained by a model which incorporates the effects of per capita income, urbanization, population density, and manufacturing share in national output. We have adopted the Dasgupta model to produce a cross-country pollution regulation index for this paper. Six of our thirteen country cases have actually been scored by the Dasgupta exercise. For the remaining seven cases, we have calculated the pollution regulation index values using the Dasgupta equation.

3.3 Input prices

We have computed wages (in $US 1990 per worker) by ISIC sector from UNIDO's reported sectoral totals for employment and payrolls. Our electricity tariff rates for the OECD and developing countries have been drawn from International Energy Agency data and the World Bank's Power Sheets database, respectively. The World Bank's World Development Indicators database has provided our national real interest rate measures.

3.4 Employment, income, and output

Estimation of equations (2), (3), (5) and (6) requires cross-country data on total output, industrial output, employment, income, population and a number of other variables. We have obtained the relevant panel data from the World Bank's international database (BESD). We have used Summers-Heston estimates as our measure of income per capita.

4. Econometric Results

4.1 Manufacturing share in national output

Table 5.1 reports panel estimates for equation (2). We provide comparable results for OLS, fixed-effects (without time dummies) and random effects models. We prefer the random effects model, but the choice of estimator does not have a major effect on

Table 5.1 Log (manufacturing share of total output) vs. Log (income per capita), 1975–1994

Independent variables	*OLS*	*Fixed effects*	*Random effects*	*OLS*	*Fixed effects*	*Random effects*
Log income	0.9195	0.5147	0.5726	1.3585	0.7719	0.9402
	(2.483)	(1.815)	(2.076)	(7.934)	(6.815)	(8.323)
Log income squared	-0.0442	-0.04268	-0.0364	-0.0704	-0.05988	-0.0622
	-(1.796)	-(2.185)	-(1.923)	-(6.446)	-(8.772)	-(8.988)
Log income time	0.07527	0.0450	0.0511	---	---	---
	(1.993)	(3.126)	(3.456)			
Log income squared time	-0.0045	-0.0028	-0.0032	---	---	---
	-(1.858)	-(3.154)	-(3.538)			
Time	-0.3194	-0.1614	-0.1911	-0.0120	0.0146	0.0062
	-(2.196)	-(2.762)	-(3.205)	-(4.224)	(6.612)	(3.190)
Constant	-6.1460	-3.3256	-4.074	-7.9373	-4.2714	-5.3585
	-(4.480)	-(3.254)	-(4.095)	-(12.013)	-(8.897)	-(11.415)
Number of observations	1136	1136	1136	1136	1136	1136
Number of time periods	16	16	16	16	16	16
Adjusted R-squared	0.299	0.151	0.015	0.297	0.171	0.003

Note: t-statistics in parentheses.

the results. They are consistent with an inverted-U model for manufacturing share in national output. Our results also suggest some structural change in the relationship, since the interactions of time with income and income squared both satisfy classical significance criteria. During the past two decades, the 'inverted-U' appears to have steepened somewhat and shifted downward.

To illustrate the implied relationship, we have calculated median manufacturing shares by income class for all 1,717 observations in our sample. The result (figure 5.1) suggests that manufacturing share rises steeply with income until a country reaches middle-income status;[13] from around 10 percent in countries with less than $1000 per capita (Summers-Heston income, in $US 1990) to around 25 percent in countries with incomes of $5,000–$6,000. Then the manufacturing share slowly declines to around 20 percent in countries with $20,000 or more.

4.2 Changes in sectoral composition

Table 5.4.2 reports results for our analysis of changes in sectoral composition. We have employed panel techniques to estimate equation (3) in log-log form, using the log of share-weighted average BOD intensity as the dependent variable. Again, the fixed-effects and random-effects estimates tell the same story: As income per capita increases, overall pollution intensity declines because relatively 'clean' sectors grow more quickly. However, our results suggest that the *rate* of decline also decreases. We find no evidence of a structural change, except for a very slight (but significant) upshift in compositional pollution intensity.

Figure 5.1 Manufacturing share in GDP vs. per capita income, 1975-1994

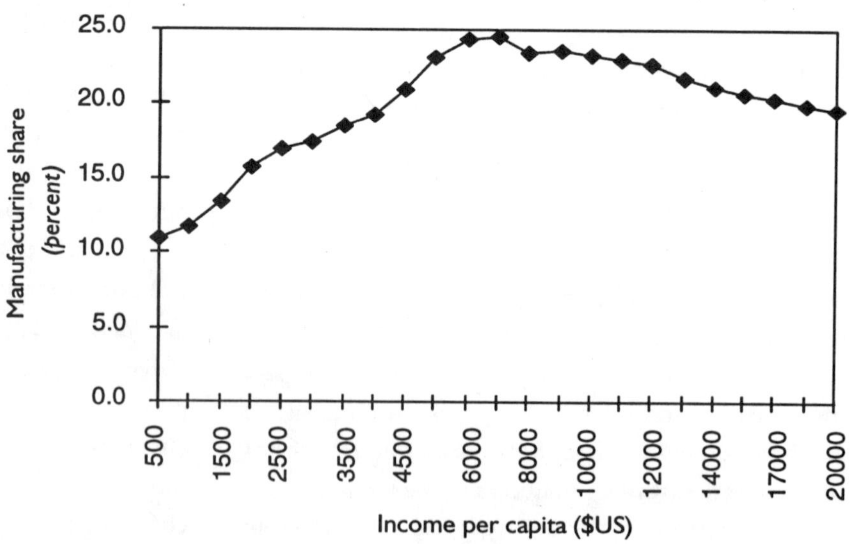

Table 5.2 Log (sector-weighted BOD intensity) vs. Log (income per capita), 1975–94

Independent variables	*OLS*	*Fixed effects*	*Random effects*	*OLS*	*Fixed effects*	*Random effects*
Log income	0.2846	-0.3903	-0.3709	-0.0236	-0.5362	-0.5283
	(1.018)	-(3.566)	-(3.427)	-(0.184)	-(12.719)	-(12.616)
Log income squared	-0.0234	0.01749	0.0164	-0.0019	0.0269	0.0267
	-(1.321)	(2.459)	(2.344)	-(0.249)	(11.050)	(10.974)
Log income time	-0.0117	-0.00736	-0.0071	---	---	---
	-(0.416)	-(1.214)	-(1.171)			
Log income squared time	0.0009	0.0005	0.0004	---	---	---
	(0.578)	(1.398)	(1.374)			
Time	0.03203	0.0319	0.0300	0.0034	0.0055	0.0051
	(0.278)	(1.232)	(1.161)	(2.166)	(6.402)	(6.351)
Constant	0.6935	3.4369	3.3470	1.7679	3.9912	3.9435
	(0.633)	(8.168)	(8.035)	(3.373)	(21.143)	(20.989)
Number of observations	928	928	928	928	928	928
Number of time periods	16	16	16	16	16	16
Adjusted R-squared	0.043	0.043	0.043	0.043	0.041	0.041

Note: t-statistics in parentheses.

In figure 5.2, we provide an illustration of the relationship between overall pollution intensity and income during the sample period.[14] The figure is based on median values of overall intensity for each income group in the set of 2,210 observations. It suggests that sector-weighted average water pollution intensity declines from nearly 6 Kg to 4Kg per $US1 million per day, or about 30 percent, as income increases to around $5,000 per capita. Then it remains approximately stable over the higher-income range.

4.3 *End-of-pipe pollution intensity*

Tables 5.3 to 5.5 report cross-country regression results for equations (5) and (6). We use dummy variables to control for sectoral differences in average pollution intensity; dummy variable controls are also introduced for national differences in reporting procedures and measures of organic water pollution. The majority of environmental protection agencies (EPAs) have reported emissions of biological oxygen demand (BOD), which is a measure of oxygen removal from water by bacteria which are oxidizing organic materials. However, three EPAs—for China, Netherlands and Taiwan (China)—have reported COD (chemical oxygen demand). COD incorporates the effect of other pollutants on the rate of oxidization; it is systematically larger than BOD measures.

We have controlled for the measurement problem by introducing a dummy variable for COD-based emissions reports. As expected, the estimated COD dummy is positive, large and highly significant in all pollution intensity equations. Our sectoral dummy variable results are also in accord with prior expectations: Food and Paper have the highest average organic water pollution intensities; Metals and Mineral Products have the lowest. In the case of labor intensity, Textiles, Food and Wood Products are highest

Figure 5.2 Industrial BOD intensity vs. income per capita

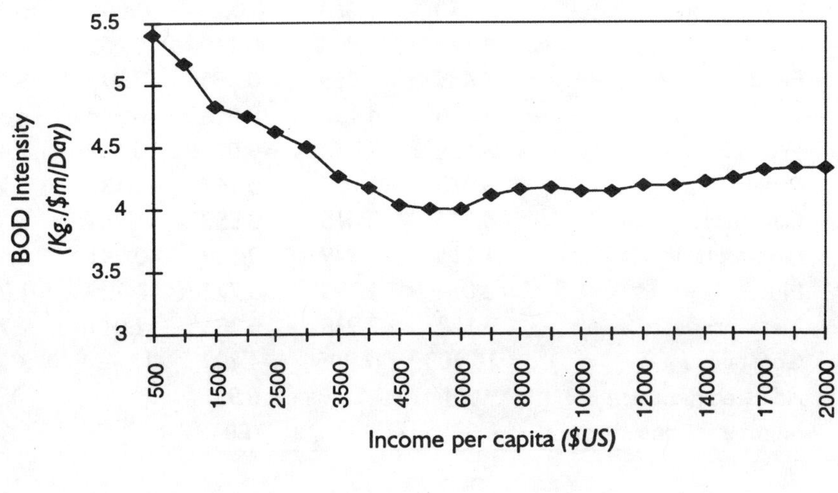

Table 5.3 Intensity equations for pollution and labor (in prices and regulation)

Dep. Var. – Log. of:	*Pollution/ Output*		*Pollution/ Output*		*Labor/ Output*		*Labor/ Output*	
Independent variables	*Coef.*	*t-stat.*	*Coef.*	*t-stat.*	*Coef.*	*t-stat.*	*Coef.*	*t-stat.*
Log wage	-1.714	-3.055**	-0.015	-0.044	-0.711	-8.473**	-0.379	-6.380**
Log brown index	2.459	0.958	-2.995	-1.601	0.164	0.422	-1.467	-4.657**
Log electricity price	6.123	3.684**	0.620	0.526	-0.098	-0.580	-0.564	-3.354**
Log real interest rate	0.455	1.903*			0.029	0.872		
Cod	4.308	4.829**	2.406	2.559**				
Food	5.658	5.044**	4.511	3.940**	-0.571	-3.817**	-0.813	-4.239**
Textiles	4.601	4.163**	3.932	3.449**	-0.018	-0.125	-0.168	-0.881
Wood products	3.717	2.775**	3.103	2.176**	-0.021	-0.140	0.053	0.280
Paper	6.864	6.102**	4.946	4.318**	-0.151	-1.006	-0.231	-1.205
Chemicals	4.614	3.916**	3.236	2.785**	-0.526	-3.320**	-0.715	-3.669**
Non-metallic minerals	1.290	1.118	1.023	0.879	-0.123	-0.823	-0.242	-1.263
Metals	2.312	1.910*	0.988	0.828	-0.697	-4.383**	-0.771	-3.903**
Metal products	3.538	3.063**	2.232	1.920*	-0.278	-1.842*	-0.502	-2.612**
Constant	-27.244	-2.466**	-0.702	-0.096	-5.253	-3.162**	1.933	1.479
Adjusted R-square		0.63		0.34		0.92		0.81
Number of observations		68		99		80		116

Notes: *** Significant at 1% confidence level.
** Significant at 5% confidence level.
* Significant at 10% confidence level.

Table 5.4 Intensity equations for pollution and labor (in prices and regulation)

Dep. Var. – Log of:	*Pollution/ output*		*Labor/ output*		*Pollution/ output*		*Labor/ output*	
Independent Variables	*Coef.*	*t-stat.*	*Coef.*	*t-stat.*	*Coef.*	*t-stat.*	*Coef.*	*t-stat.*
Log wage	-1.211	-6.153	-0.666	-22.600				
Log brown index					-4.885	-5.052	-2.872	-14.642
Log electricity price	5.634	3.565	-0.280	-1.223	3.765	2.384	-1.173	-3.871
Log real interest rate	0.370	1.668	0.025	0.807	0.234	0.957	-0.058	-1.27
cod	4.375	4.923	-0.110	-0.852	4.125	4.32	-0.197	-1.071
Food	5.485	4.959	-0.585	-3.979	5.073	4.278	-0.792	-3.767
Textiles	4.586	4.153	-0.018	-0.124	4.556	3.842	-0.016	-0.074
Wood Products	3.654	2.733	-0.028	-0.188	3.429	2.392	-0.131	-0.622
Paper	6.675	6.032	-0.167	-1.132	6.222	5.247	-0.396	-1.882
Chemicals	4.246	3.815	-0.558	-3.764	3.364	2.837	-1.023	-4.866
Non-metallic minerals	1.114	0.979	-0.138	-0.941	0.681	0.558	-0.362	-1.720
Metals	2.014	1.723	-0.722	-4.729	1.243	0.999	-1.094	-5.045
Metal products	3.323	2.935	-0.296	-2.011	2.784	2.299	-0.560	-2.661
Constant	-16.903	-7.208	-4.403	-13.734	3.324	0.661	7.522	7.83
Adjusted R-square	0.64		0.93		0.59		0.85	
Number of observations	68		80		68		80	

Table 5.5 Intensity equations for pollution and labor (in income per capita)

Dep. Var. – Log of:	*Pollution/output*		*Labor/output*		*Pollution/labor*	
Independent variables	*Coef.*	*t-stat.*	*Coef.*	*t-stat.*	*Coef.*	*t-stat.*
Log income	-0.875	-3.26**	-1.003	-17.041**	0.120	0.449
COD	1.908	2.542**			1.930	2.576**
Food	4.629	4.096**	-0.925	-4.085**	5.492	4.868**
Textiles	4.055	3.588**	-0.150	-0.662	4.143	3.673**
Wood products	3.315	2.350**	0.047	0.206	3.485	2.475**
Paper	5.064	4.481**	-0.350	-1.547	5.353	4.745**
Chemical	3.349	2.963**	-0.957	-4.225**	4.244	3.762**
Mineral	1.151	1.003	-0.361	-1.595	1.414	1.235
Metal	1.119	0.962	-0.964	-4.171**	2.038	1.786
Metal products	2.367	2.071**	-0.635	-2.803**	2.983	2.615**
Constant	-8.872	-3.615**	-1.497	-2.828**	-7.246	-2.972**
Adjusted R-square		0.35		0.74		0.39
Number of observations		99		116		100

(along with Other Manufacturing, the numeraire sector); Metals and Chemicals are the lowest.

We have also controlled for the possible impact of differences in emissions reporting procedures. In several cases (China, India, Indonesia, Netherlands, Philippines, Sri Lanka, Taiwan (China), Thailand) the plant-level information provided by the EPA's includes employment data. This has enabled us to estimate sectoral pollution/labor ratios directly from the EPA data. In the other cases (Brazil, Finland, Korea, Mexico and the United States), the EPA's have provided summary pollution data by sector. We have obtained summary employment data by sector from other national or regional sources, and have used the two summaries to calculate sectoral pollution/labor ratios.

We recognize the possibility of systematic differences in the results generated by these two approaches. EPA's in developing countries focus on large polluters, so the average pollution intensity of these facilities will be reflected in estimates based on plant samples. The situation is potentially quite different when EPA-reported sectoral emissions are divided by census-reported sectoral employment. Plants which ignore pollution regulations (and whose reported pollution is therefore zero) may nevertheless be registered in an employment census. This might impart a downward bias to summary-based intensities. In addition, all five countries for which we employ summary data (Brazil, Finland, Korea, Mexico, United States) are in the middle or high income category. Thus, failure to control for the sampling difference might also produce a downward bias in the estimated effect of income or wages on pollution intensity.

We have introduced a dummy variable to control for this difference, but it is not significant in our regressions. In fact, we are not overly surprised by this result because effective coverage of industrial facilities by both census-takers and regulators is a function of development.[15]

The Effects of Pollution Regulation and Relative Input Prices

As expected, the estimated wage-elasticity of labor intensity is large (around -0.70) and highly significant. The wage elasticity of pollution intensity is also negative, large (-1.71) and highly significant. In the pollution intensity equation, our results are consistent with the hypothesis that labor and pollution are complements in production. However, the converse is not true. Our index of regulatory strictness is not significant in the labor intensity equation.

While the latter result is not particularly surprising, we also find that our regulatory strictness index is not significant in pollution intensity regressions which control for wages. Does this imply that market forces alone drive pollution, and that regulation is irrelevant? Although our results are consistent with this interpretation, we reject it for several reasons. First, our wage and regulation variables are highly collinear because they are both correlated with per capita income. As table 5.4 shows, each variable is significant in equations which exclude the other. Second, a large body of empirical work suggests that industrial pollution is responsive to pressure from local communities (Pargal and Wheeler 1996; Hettige and others 1997; Hartman and others 1996), as well as formal regulation. Both forms of regulation are strongly affected by income, reflecting increasing preferences for environmental quality and higher valuation of pollution damage. We believe that the estimated wage elasticity in our pollution intensity regression is capturing cross-country income effects on formal and informal regulation, as well as the effect of complementarity with pollution in production. With currently-available information, we cannot distinguish clearly between these two effects. However, their joint effect clearly shows the impact of rising income on pollution intensity.

Our results for energy and capital prices are considerably weaker. Surprisingly, neither variable is significant in the labor intensity equation when both are included. In the pollution intensity regression, the estimated electricity price elasticity is positive, large and highly significant. The real interest rate elasticity is also positive, and close to significance at the 5 percent level. However, these results are not robust to changes in right-hand variables or sample composition. Dropping the real interest rate increases the sample size, because we do not have real interest rate data for Mexico, Brazil and Taiwan (China). However, with the larger sample the electricity price elasticity loses significance in the pollution intensity equation, while becoming large, *negative*, and highly 'significant' in the labor intensity equation. We conclude that our results for capital and energy prices are highly sensitive to outliers, and we see no reason to draw any clear conclusions from our results.

Economic Development and Pollution Intensity

We have also estimated reduced-form intensity equations which control for per capita income, sector and COD reporting. The results are summarized in table 5.4.5 for three intensities: labor/output, pollution/output and pollution/labor. In all three equations, the results for the sectoral dummies replicate the pattern of results in tables 5.3–5.4. As before, the dummy variable for COD is positive and significant in the pollution equations.

The results for per capita income suggest a striking regularity across countries. The income elasticities of pollution/output and labor/output are both negative, and not significantly different from one. In the third equation, we test for the equality of pollution and labor elasticities (w.r.t. income) by regressing pollution/labor on the same set of right-hand variables (this amounts to differencing the coefficients in the first two equations). *The resulting elasticity of pollution/labor with respect to income per capita is not significantly different from zero.* Of course, we cannot generalize from one sample for one pollutant to all industrial emissions. However, *for industrial water pollution, our results suggest that sectoral emissions/labor ratios are approximately constant across countries at all income levels.* Developing economies generate much more pollution per unit of output than developed economies, but they also employ much more labor per unit of output, and in the same proportion.

Figure 5.3 and table 5.6 portray the estimated relationship between pollution intensity (per unit of output) and income per capita. For ease of interpreta-

Figure 5.3. Water pollution intensity vs. income per capita

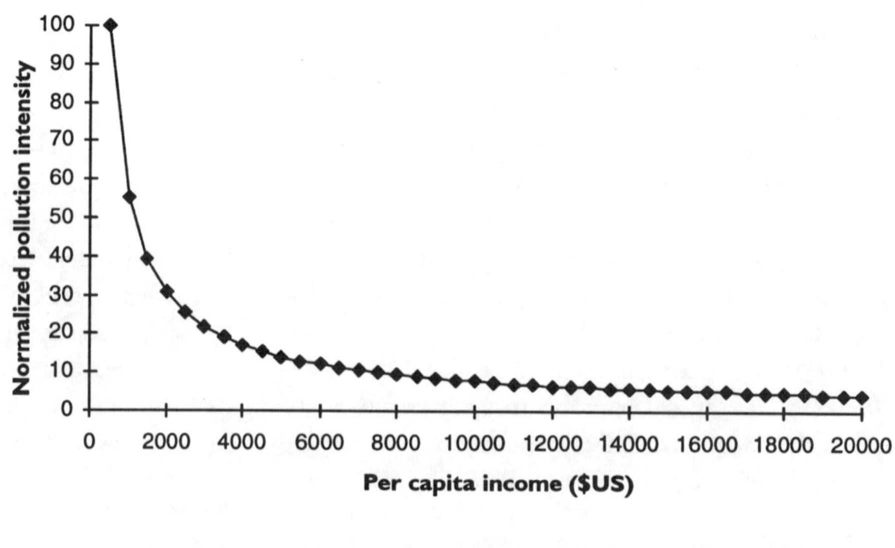

Table 5.6 Income and pollution abatement

Income per capita	*Percent abatement*
1,500	60
3,000	80
7,000	90
15,000	95

tion, we normalize to an intensity value of 100 for the poorest income category ($500 per capita). The cross-country evidence suggests a sharp drop in pollution intensity with income growth, as manufacturers respond to higher wages and regulatory pressures with end-of-pipe abatement and process change. From an emissions index value of 100 at $500 per capita, pollution abatement is about 60 percent at $1,500, 80 percent at $3,000, 90 percent at $7,000 and 95 percent at $15,000.

5. Implications of the Results

5.1 The Kuznets hypothesis

Our estimation exercises have suggested three distinct patterns of response to economic development. Industry's share of national output rises sharply through middle-income status and then slowly declines. Sectoral composition follows a 'clean' trend for low-income developing countries, but exhibits little or no trend beyond the middle income range. End-of-pipe pollution intensity, by contrast, declines continuously with income.

We use simulation to project the net result of changes in these three factors. Our four simulation variables are in columns 1-4 of table 5.7. Column 1 includes a broad range of incomes, from $US500 to $US20,000 per capita. Columns 2 and 3 replicate the information on manufacturing output shares and average pollution intensities in figures 4.1 and 4.2. Column 4 reproduces the pollution intensity index in figure 5.3, renormalized to one for the lowest income level.

We assume a unit population for convenience, so income per capita also serves as a measure of total output. We simulate the overall relationship between economic development and industrial pollution by multiplying the four column entries in each row. The result combines the effects of changes in total output, manufacturing share, sectoral composition, and end-of-pipe pollution intensity. Column 5 and figure 5.4 portray the total pollution estimate, which has been normalized to an index value of 100 at the lowest income level. Our result suggests that the inverted U-shaped story is only half right for industrial water pollution: Total emissions rise sharply in the range ($500–$7,000), but remain constant as income increases further.

To assess the contribution of each factor to the overall result, we perform three counterfactual simulations which are tabulated in columns 6-8 and illustrated in figure 5.5. Each simulation allows one of columns 2-4 to vary while holding the other two constant at the lowest-income level. The experiment in column 6 holds sectoral composition and end-of-pipe pollution intensity constant, while allowing the share of manufacturing to vary with income. The result is rapid growth of pollution over the whole income range, and an estimated pollution load at $20,000 which is eighty times the initial load. To produce column 7, we allow sectoral composition to vary while holding the other two factors constant. Pollution growth is considerably moderated by comparison with column 6, but the projected load at $20,000 is still 40 times the initial load. Finally, we test the effect of end-of-pipe change in column 8. This experiment clearly identifies the most important

Table 5.7 Industrial pollution and economic development: Simulation experiments

Income ($US)	*Manuf. share*	*BOD intens.*	*EOP intens.*	*Total BOD*	*Variable share*	*Variable BOD*	*Variable EOP*
500	11.0	5.4	1.00	100	100	100	100
1,500	13.4	4.8	0.39	128	366	268	118
2,500	16.9	4.6	0.25	167	771	428	127
3,500	18.5	4.3	0.19	177	1,179	553	133
4,500	21.0	4.0	0.15	197	1,726	670	138
6,000	24.3	4.0	0.12	237	2,663	888	144
8,000	23.5	4.2	0.09	247	3,424	1,230	150
10,000	23.3	4.1	0.08	253	4,256	1,531	155
12,000	22.6	4.2	0.07	255	4,953	1,859	160
14,000	21.2	4.2	0.06	246	5,399	2,188	163
17,000	20.3	4.3	0.05	248	6,298	2,709	168
20,000	19.5	4.3	0.04	249	7,904	3,559	175

Figure 5.4 Industrial pollution and economic development

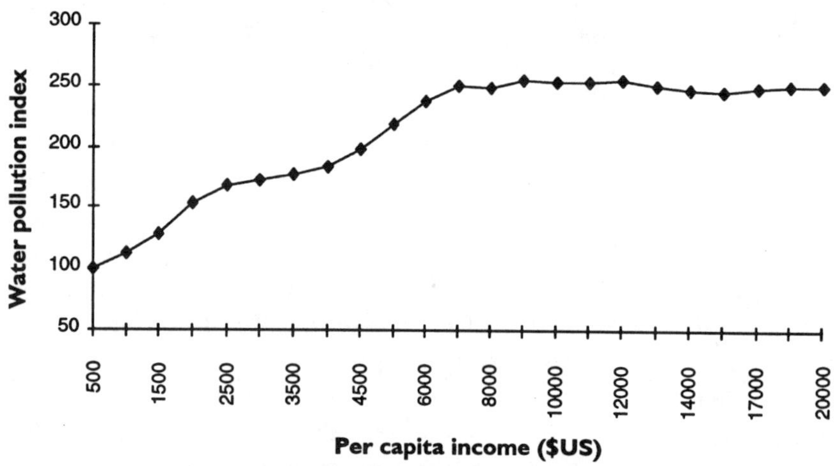

factor: Projected emissions at $20,000 are only 1.8 times the initial load, if manufacturing share and sectoral composition are held constant.

We conclude that pollution levels off in the middle income range because end-of-pipe pollution intensity responds to rising wages and stricter regulation. By comparison, the manufacturing share and sectoral composition are minor players. For industrial water pollution, the inverted-U pattern does not emerge because declining pollution intensity almost exactly balances output growth, while manufacturing share and sectoral composition remain constant beyond the middle income range.

5.2 Trends in international emissions

To explore the real-world implications of our results, we estimate pollution loads for a set of large industrial economies during the period 1977–1989. Powerful leverage is provided by our finding that sectoral pollution per unit of labor (P/L) remains approximately constant across the entire range of incomes. This allows us to use commonly-available sectoral labor/output (L/Q) ratios to predict international changes in industrial water pollution. As an illustration, we use the World Bank's BESD database to estimate sectoral L/Q ratios for fifteen countries during the period 1977–1989. To estimate BOD loads by sector, we multiply the L/Q ratios by sectoral P/L coefficients calculated from our regression results for P/L.[16]

We have chosen the fifteen countries to represent large industrial economies in four major groups: OECD (represented by the United States, Japan, France and Germany (former F.R.); the NIC's (Mexico, Brazil, Taiwan, Korea, South Africa, Turkey); Asian LDC's (China, India, Indonesia); and the ex-COMECON countries (Poland, former USSR). The results are tabulated in table 5.9 and summarized in table 5.8. Taken together, they illustrate the main implications of our empirical analysis.

In the OECD, despite modest continued economic growth, estimated BOD emissions remain almost constant. In our view, this reflects the countervailing effects of output growth and increases in wages and regulation; manufacturing shares and the 'clean' sector share change very little. The COMECON economies are in relative stagnation during the sample period, so there is little movement in their estimated emissions.

Figure 5.5 Counterfactual simulations

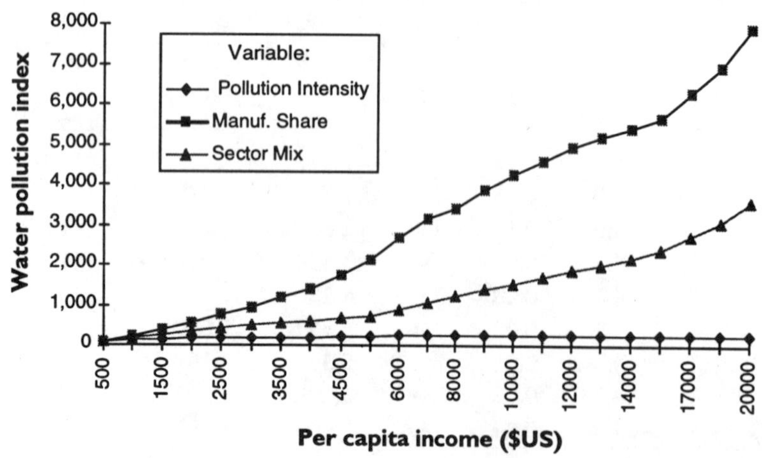

The story for the NIC's is quite different. Their estimated pollution increases by about 25 percent during the sample period—substantially less than their growth in per capita income. The increase is relatively moderate because rapid output growth is offset by three factors: the negative impact of increased wages and regulation on industrial pollution intensity; the first stage of the decline in manufacturing share; and the last stage of the 'clean' trend in sectoral composition.

Table 5.8 Trends in international emissions—Selected countries, 1977–1989

	BOD emissions ('000 Kg/Day)				
Region	*1977*	*1980*	*1983*	*1986*	*1989*
OECD	5,776	5,847	5,501	5,403	5,523
NIC's	1,565	1,917	1,848	2,197	2,188
Asian LDC'S	4,617	5,030	5,566	6,183	6,883
COMECON	4,127	4,218	4,302	4,228	4,039
Total	16,085	17,012	17,217	18,011	18,633
	Percent of sample total				
	1977	*1980*	*1983*	*1986*	*1989*
OECD	36	34	32	30	30
NIC's	10	11	11	12	12
Asian LDC'S	29	30	32	34	37
COMECON	26	25	25	23	22
Total	100	100	100	100	100

first effects of rising wages and regulation on pollution intensity. To a striking degree, BOD growth in our international sample is due to increased emissions in developing Asia.

The overall result of these changes is a significant shift in group shares of total pollution. Table 5.8 shows that the OECD and COMECON countries drop significantly in share; the NIC's increase marginally; and the Asian LDC's jump from 29 percent to 37 percent of the total. Equally impressive, however, is the apparently moderate growth in total BOD emissions during the period when world concern over environmental damage was reaching a peak. While economic development was sparking greater interest in pollution, is was also setting the stage for real improvements in environmental performance. From 1977 to 1989, we estimate that total industrial BOD emissions grew by only 16 percent in these fifteen major industrial countries.

The Asian LDC experience is also distinctive. Estimated BOD emissions grow by approximately 55 percent in these lower-income economies, because rapid output growth and increasing manufacturing share dominate the clean compositional trend and the

Table 5.9 Estimated industrial BOD emissions—Selected countries, 1977–1989 (*'000 Kg/day*)

Country	*1977*	*1980*	*1983*	*1986*	*1989*
United States	2,652	2,743	2,551	2,454	2,564
France	739	716	683	666	652
Germany (former FR)	929	932	800	789	800
Japan	1,456	1,456	1,467	1,493	1,507
OECD	5,776	5,847	5,501	5,403	5,523
Brazil	611	867	771	965	914
Mexico	109	131	130	179	174
Korea, Republic of	261	282	296	345	377
Taiwan, China	208	239	252	296	282
South Africa	226	238	245	245	262
Turkey	150	160	155	167	179
NICs	1,565	1,917	1,848	2,197	2,188
China	3,118	3,358	3,957	4,551	5,023
India	1,309	1,457	1,380	1,277	1,428
Indonesia	190	214	230	355	433
Developing Asia	4,617	5,030	5,566	6,183	6,883
Poland	578	581	546	484	459
U.S.S.R., former	3,549	3,638	3,756	3,744	3,580
Ex-COMECON	4,127	4,218	4,302	4,228	4,039
Total	16,085	17,012	17,217	18,011	18,633

6. Summary and Conclusions

In this paper, we have used new international data to investigate the relationship between industrial pollution and economic development. To test for a Kuznets effect, we measure the effect of income growth on three proximate determinants of pollution: The share of manufacturing in total output; the sectoral composition of manufacturing; and the intensity (per unit of output) of industrial pollution at the end-of-pipe. We find that the manufacturing share follows a Kuznets-type trajectory, but the other two determinants do not. Sectoral composition gets 'cleaner' through middle-income status and then stabilizes. At the end-of-pipe, pollution intensity declines strongly with income. We attribute part of this to stricter regulation as income increases, and partly to pollution-labor complementarity in production.

Our results suggest that income elasticities of both pollution- and labor-intensity are approximately minus one. The remarkable implication is that *a sector's pollution/labor ratio is constant across countries at all income levels.* Our findings motivate two illustrative simulation exercises. First, for a set of income benchmarks, we simulate total pollution by combining representative measures of manufacturing share in output, sectoral composition, and end-of-pipe pollution abatement. We do not see a Kuznets-type story in the result, since total pollution rises rapidly through middle-income status and remains approximately constant thereafter. In three counterfactual experiments, we assess the relative importance of the three proximate determinants. Our results highlight the dominance of end-of-pipe reductions as wages and regulation increase with development. The combined influence of changes in manufacturing share and sectoral composition is lower by almost two orders of magnitude.

Our second simulation uses international panel data to explore the implications of constant sectoral pollution/labor ratios. We estimate recent trends in water pollution for fifteen major industrial nations in the OECD, the NIC's, Asian LDC's and the ex-COMECON economies. We find approximately stable emissions in the OECD and ex-COMECON, moderate increases in the NIC's and rapidly-growing pollution in the Asian LDC's. During the 1980's, our estimates suggest that the latter group displaced the major OECD economies as the world's largest generator of organic water pollution. Overall, however, the negative feedback from economic development to pollution intensity was sufficient to hold total world pollution growth to around 15 percent during a twelve-year sample period.

In closing, it is worth asking whether these results are cause for optimism or pessimism. The appropriate answer seems to be 'both.' It is comforting to see that industrial water emissions level off in richer economies because pollution intensity has an elastic response to income growth. Unfortunately, unitary elasticity implies that total emissions remain constant unless other factors intervene. Of course, industry tends to deconcentrate over time as infrastructure improves and prosperity spreads. Constant total emissions may therefore be consistent with improving water quality in at least some areas. However, the continued existence of many seriously-polluted waterways, even in the most prosperous countries, suggests that economic development remains far short of a Kuznets-style happy ending in the water sector.

Appendix—Data Sources

Brazil: The water pollution data for the Sao Paulo Metropolitan region of Brazil were collected by CETESB, the environmental agency for Sao Paulo State. Our pollution estimates are based on CETESB's 1250-plant database, which includes measures of BOD loads in kg/day. The corresponding employment data came from the Sao Paulo State Ministry of Labor, which provided 2-digit sectoral information from 1991 on nearly 41,000 plants and 2.15 million workers.

China: Water pollution data for China were obtained from the National Environmental Protection Agency (NEPA), which maintains a comprehensive database on major sources of industrial pollution in China. Our estimates are based on NEPA's 1993 emissions data for 269 factories scattered throughout China.

Finland: The Finnish economic data, aggregated at the 3-digit ISIC level, were provided by the Central Statistical Office, covering both white and blue collar workers for 1989. The pollution data were provided by the Industrial Waste Water Office of the National Board of Waters and the Environment. They cover water emissions in 1992 from 193 large water-polluting factories.

India: The India data are from the state of Tamil Nadu. Plant-level pollution data and employment data for 1993-94 were provided by the Tamil Nadu Pollution Control Board, which monitors air and water pollution for all the manufacturing units in the state.

Indonesia: The Indonesia data came from two different sources. The plant-level emissions data were provided by BAPEDAL, Indonesia's National Pollution Control Agency in the Ministry of Environment. The economic data are from Indonesia's Central Statistics Bureau (BPS).

Korea: Korean pollution data were provided by the National Pollution Control Agency. They cover water emissions by 13,504 facilities in 1991. Complementary employment data have been drawn from Korea's National Statistical Yearbooks and the ILO's **International Labor Statistics**, 1991.

Mexico: Data for water emissions in the Monterrey Metropolitan Area were provided by the State Water Monitoring Authority. The data cover emissions from 7,500 facilities in 1994. Complementary employment data were provided by Mexico's Census Bureau (INEGI).

Netherlands: Water emissions and employment data for approximately 700 regularly-monitored facilities in 1990 were provided by the Emissions Inventory System maintained by the Ministry of Housing, Spatial Planning and the Environment (VROM).

Philippines: Water emissions and employment data for factories in the Metro Manila Area (MMA) were provided the Philippines Department of Natural Resources (DENR) and the Laguna Lake Development Authority.

Taiwan (China): Water emissions and employment data for 1,800 plants were provided by the Water Quality Protection division of the Taiwan Environment Protection Agency.

Thailand: Seatec International, a private-sector environmental consulting firm in Bangkok, provided plant-level data from two industrial estates in Rangsit and Suksawat. The dataset contained information on water emissions and employment for approximately 450 facilities in 1992.

Sri Lanka: Water pollution and employment data for Sri Lanka were obtained from a study of waste water treatment options for the Ekala/Ja-ela Industrial Estate, which includes 143 industrial establishments with 21,000 employees. The data were collected by a joint project of the World Bank's Metropolitan Environment Improvement Program and the Sri Lankan Board of Investment. Ekala/Ja-Ela industrial estate is one of the two major industrial estates in Sri Lanka.

U.S.A.: The information for the United States were drawn from two main sources. The water emissions data have been collected from regional databases which monitor industrial water discharges as part of the U.S. Environmental Protection Agency's NPDES system. Employment data are from the U.S. Census Bureau's Longitudinal Research Database.

Notes

Our thanks to the many Bank staff members, consultants, and officials of national environmental protection institutions who made the data for this study available to us. We gratefully accept responsibility for any errors of transcription or interpretation.

1. A partial exception is the work of Selden and Song (1994), whose regressions employ air emissions instead of ambient air quality measures. The lack of monitoring information forces the authors to estimate air emissions from secondary sources: National fuel use data and fuel-based pollution parameters which are adjusted for conditions in countries at varying income levels. Data scarcity in developing countries is clearly a problem for this exercise. Of thirty countries in the estimation sample only four (China, India, Thailand, Turkey) are LDC's.

2. For a discussion of structural change in development, see Syrquin (1989).

3. See Mani and Wheeler (1997) for further discussion.

4. "Influent" refers to emissions from industrial processes before treatment (or abatement); 'effluent' refers to emissions to air, water or land after treatment; 'concentration' refers to the quantity of pollutant per unit volume of the waste stream.

5. For recent empirical evidence, see Hartman and others (1997) and Dasgupta and others (1996).

6. These may, according to the circumstances, include local administrators, pressure groups, national regulators, stockholders, and "green consumers." Each group is in a position to impose some cost on a firm or plant if its emissions exceed the norms adopted by that group. Thus, even where pollution charges are in effect, there is no single "price" of pollution. For a detailed discussion, see Afsah and others (1996).

7. For recent evidence, see Pargal and Wheeler (1996), Wang and Wheeler (1996), and Hettige and others (1997).

8. Data-gathering in this context is not a simple task. Even assembly of the relatively sparse dataset used for this exercise has required a massive canvass of World Bank project files, consultants' reports, and emissions reports from many national environmental protection institutions. The data are briefly surveyed in the following section, with a more detailed description in the Appendix.

9. See the Appendix for a description of data sources in each country.

10. Marginal abatement costs decline with treatment scale for most pollutants, because abatement capital is lumpy. Thus, the estimated output elasticity of emissions in a plant-level equation is generally less than one. For evidence from Asia, see Pargal and Wheeler (1996). At the sectoral level, however, the constant-returns assumption seems appropriate for cross-country work. It is possible that characteristic plant scale is larger in countries with greater sectoral output, but we have no way to test this proposition with the available data.

11. See Christensen and others 1973.

12. See for example Levinson (1996) and Beede and others (1992).

13. We have smoothed the series with a three-interval moving average: Each share observation on the graph is the average for the previous, corresponding, and succeeding income groups.

14. We have also used three-interval smoothing for figure 5.4.2. See footnote 13.

15. Both approaches may underestimate 'true' sectoral pollution intensities in developing countries, because existing research suggests that medium and large plants have lower pollution per unit of output than smaller facilities (ceteris paribus). Since smaller plants are covered by regulators in developed economies, our econometric result may actually *understate* the effect of income on pollution intensity. We accept the plausibility of this hypothesis, but we have no way to test it at present.

16. For this application, we regress log (P/L) on dummy variables for COD and the industry sectors. Since income is insignificant, we impose a parameter value of zero by dropping it from the equation. To calculate sectoral P/L ratios, we assume the BOD case (COD=0), add the constant term to the estimated parameters for the sector dummies, and calculate the antilogs of the results.

References

Afsah, S., B. Laplante, and D. Wheeler. 1996. "Controlling Industrial Pollution: A New Paradigm." World Bank, Policy Research Department Working Paper.

Beede, D., D. Bloom, and D. Wheeler. 1992. "Measuring and Explaining Cross-Establishment Variation in the Generation and Management of Industrial Waste." World Bank (mimeo.)

Birdsall, N., and D. Wheeler. 1993. "Trade Policy and Industrial Pollution in Latin America: Where are the Pollution Havens?" *Journal of Environment and Development* 2(1): 137–44.

Christensen, L., D. Jorgensen, and L. Lau. 1973. "Transcendental Logarithmic Production Frontiers." *Review of Economics and Statistics* 55: 28–45

Dasgupta, S., and D. Wheeler. 1996. "Citizen Complaints as Environmental Indicators: Evidence from China." World Bank, Policy Research Department Working Paper, December.

Dasgupta, S., A. Mody, S. Roy, and D. Wheeler. 1995. "Environmental Regulation and Development: A Cross-Country Empirical Analysis." World Bank, Policy Research Department Working Paper no. 1448, April.

Dasgupta, S., M. Huq, D. Wheeler, and C.H. Zhang. 1996. "Water Pollution Abatement by Chinese Industry: Cost Estimates and Policy Implications." World Bank, Policy Research Department Working Paper.

Grossman, G., and A. Krueger. 1995. "Economic Growth and the Environment." *Quarterly Journal of Economics* May: 353–377.

Gruver, G.W. 1976. "Optimal Investment in Pollution Control Capital in a Neoclassical Growth Context." *Journal of Environmental Economics and Management* 5: 165–177.

Hartman, R., M. Huq, and D. Wheeler. 1997. "Why Paper Mills Clean Up: Determinants of Pollution Abatement in Four Asian Countries." World Bank, Policy Research Department Working Paper, Number 1710.

Hartman, R., M. Singh, and D. Wheeler. 1997. "The Cost of Air Pollution Abatement." *Applied Economics* 29(6): 759–74.

Hettige, H., R.E.B. Lucas, and D. Wheeler. 1992. "The Toxic Intensity of Industrial Production: Global Patterns, Trends and Trade Policy." *American Economic Review Papers and Proceedings* 82: 478–481.

Hettige, H., P. Martin, M. Singh, and David Wheeler. 1995. "IPPS: The Industrial Pollution Projection System." World Bank, Policy Research Department Working Paper, February.

Hettige, H., M. Huq, S. Pargal, and D. Wheeler. 1996. "Determinants of Pollution Abatement in Developing Countries: Evidence from South and Southeast Asia." *World Development* December.

Hettige, H., M. Singh, S. Pargal, and David Wheeler. 1997. "Formal and Informal Regulation of Industrial Pollution: Evidence from the U.S. and Indonesia." *World Bank Economic Review* Fall.

John, A., and R. Pecchenino. 1992. "An Overlapping Generations Model of Growth and the Environment." Department of Economics, Michigan State University (mimeo).

Levinson, A. 1996. "Environmental Regulations and Manufacturers' Location Choices: Evidence from the Census of Manufactures." *Journal of Public Economics* 62: 5–29.

Mani, M.S., and D. Wheeler. 1997. "In Search of Pollution Havens? Dirty Industry in the World Economy, 1960-1995." World Bank, Policy Research Department Working Paper.

Mani, M.S. 1996. "Environmental Tariffs on Polluting Imports: An Empirical Study." *Environmental and Resource Economics* 7: 391–411.

Mody, A., and D. Wheeler. 1990. *Automation and World Competition: New Technologies, Industrial Location, and Trade.* London: Macmillan Press.

Pargal, S., and D. Wheeler. 1996. "Informal Regulation in Developing Countries: Evidence from Indonesia." *Journal of Political Economy* (December).

Robison, D.H. 1988. "Industrial Pollution Abatement: The Impact on the Balance of Trade." *Canadian Journal of Economics* 21: 702–706.

Selden, T., and D. Song. 1994. "Environmental Quality and Development: Is There a Kuznets Curve for Air Pollution Emissions?" *Journal of Environmental Economics and Management* 27: 147–162.

______. 1995. "Neoclassical Growth, the J Curve for Abatement, and the Inverted U Curve for Pollution." *Journal of Environmental Economics and Management* 29: 162–168.

Shafik, N. 1994. "Economic Development and Environmental Quality: An Econometric Analysis." *Oxford Economic Papers* 46: 757–773.

Syrquin, M. 1989. "Patterns of Structural Change." In H. Chenery and T.N. Srinivasan, eds., *Handbook of Development Economics* Vol. 1. Amsterdam: North-Holland.

Tobey, J.A. 1990. "The Effects of Domestic Environmental Policies on Patterns of World Trade: An Empirical Test." *Kyklos* (Fasc.): 191–209.

Wang, H., and D. Wheeler. 1996. "Pricing Industrial Pollution in China: An Econometric Analysis of the Levy System." World Bank, Policy Research Department Working Paper, No. 1644.

Wheeler, D., and A. Mody. 1992. "International Investment Location Decisions: The Case of U.S. Firms." *Journal of International Economics* 33: 57–76.

Wheeler, D. 1991. "The Economics of Industrial Pollution Control: An International Perspective." World Bank, Industry and Energy Department Working Paper, No. 60, January.

Chapter 6

Preferential Trading Arrangements between Kenya and the EU

A case study of the environmental effects of the horticulture sector

Anil Markandya, Lucy Emerton, and Sam Mwale

1. Introduction

As part of the effort to promote development, developed countries and regions such as the European Union (EU) offer preferential access to producers from developing countries. The rationale is obvious: preferential access promotes employment through exports by the affected sectors; provides an impetus to industrialization; and helps to create the conditions for export-led growth. At the same time, however, the privileged sectors can cause harm to the environment and forestall advances toward sustainable development.

An evaluation of preferential trading arrangements must examine both the economic and environmental consequences of these arrangements. Until recently the environmental dimension was largely ignored, although attention was drawn to the environmental consequences of liberalizing trade in Anderson (1992), Grossman and Kruger (1993), Markandya (1994), Munasinghe and Cruz (1995), and other works. It is difficult to assess whether a change in trade regime is beneficial if the change has significant environmental impacts. The same may be said of preferential trading arrangements, which change the structure of production in both countries and thereby alter the use of natural resources and provoke changes in employment, output, and possibly growth.

The study of such impacts is complex, because intersectoral effects have to be taken into account. General equilibrium models have been used for this purpose in some cases (Unemo 1993; Tyler 1996). Others have used sectoral and macroeconomic models for the same purpose (Cruz and Repetto 1993; Markandya and others 1997). Although arguments can be made for and against each type of model, use is often dictated by data considerations. The present study was undertaken in the spirit of these intersectoral studies. It looks at one sector, horticulture, and estimates the environmental costs of growing several different crops. These costs are then compared with those of other crops, especially those for which horticulture may substitute. The paper then analyzes the impact of preferential trading policies on land use, the environment, and overall employment. We do not take a full general equilibrium approach (the data would not permit such an analysis), but rather examine the relationships between major competing agricultural uses. The "novel" features are: (a) a detailed assessment of the environmental costs of different crops, and (b) the use of a relatively simple "profitability" rule to allocate land between crops when costs are changed either by internalizing environmental costs, or by giving different preferential access to certain products.

Section two provides background on the horticultural sector in the general context of agriculture in Kenya. Section three reviews preferential trading arrangements for horticulture. Section four discusses the environmental impacts of different crops, and section five provides monetary estimates of the damages in Ksh (Kenyan shillings) and U.S. dollars per hectare.

Section six develops a model for estimating changes in land use when the prices received for the different crops are altered and applies it to assess the effects of preferential trading arrangements and the impact of internalizing environmental costs. Section seven offers a conclusion, noting the limitations of the present analysis and the implications of its results for preferential trading policy.

2. The Horticultural Sector in Kenya

The horticultural sector is one of Kenya's most profitable and rapidly expanding export sectors. Its main products are cut flowers, Asian vegetables (mainly brinjals, karella, chillies, and okra), and French beans. The growing globalization of markets brings European consumers a year-round supply of fresh fruits, vegetables, and flowers, many of which come from African Caribbean Pacific (ACP) countries. Kenya and Zimbabwe are two of the most important ACP horticultural producers. Although this sector is relatively new in Kenya, by 1993 horticulture had displaced coffee as the third most important national foreign exchange earner, after tourism and tea.

The rapid growth of export horticulture can be attributed to several factors. First, preferential treatment under the Lomé Convention between ACP and the EU provides concessionary access for Kenyan flowers and vegetables to the European market. Second, the sustained demand for horticultural products as a result of high—and growing—incomes in Europe provides a stable and growing market for Kenyan producers. Third, Nairobi's location as a hub of air transport between Europe and the East and Southern Africa region, and Kenya's role as a major tourist destination, ensure that there is sufficient northbound air cargo to transport exports. Finally, the presence of ample local and international investors, particularly in the cut-flower business, provides Kenya with an added advantage.

Although large-scale producers dominate the horticultural sector, smallholder production is increasing rapidly. The growth of smallholder production is largely a result of land pressure arising from rapid population growth, outgrower schemes by large producers and exporters, and long-term declining returns from alternative cash crops. As land size decreases, households shift to higher-value crops to ensure income security. Income from horticulture is used to purchase food from markets. Horticultural production by smallholders is most pronounced in areas where the commercialization of agriculture has had the strongest impact.

Another source of growth in horticulture is the structural adjustment policies (SAPs) in the agricultural sector that the Kenyan government has pursued over the last decade. Such policies have resulted in real increases in input prices (for example, fertilizer and pesticides), while output prices for food commodities have been declining in nominal and real terms. The result has been declining net profits in traditional cash crops, encouraging the shift to horticulture. Land intensification, application of better husbandry practices, and the introduction of higher-yielding varieties have also contributed to growth in the horticultural sector. The amount of land shifted over to horticulture has been relatively small at the national level, but highly significant in particular regions of the country (Richardson 1996).

Trends in horticulture

The main trends in horticultural production and exports are given below. Table 6.1 provides data on production, area under production, and exports for Asian vegetables. Table 6.2 gives the same data for French beans. Unfortunately data on cut flowers are more fragmented, as described below.

Production volumes for Asian vegetables and French beans vary considerably by year for reasons that are not yet known. Trends, however, have been upward for Asian vegetables and static for French beans.

Export volumes of Asian vegetables remained mostly static from 1988 to 1993. The South Asian pop-

Table 6.1 Indicators for Asian vegetables

Indicator	*1989*	*1990*	*1991*	*1992*	*1993*	*1994*	*1995*
Production (tons)	21,773	28,557	46,682	80,662	22,695	70,040	72,357
Area under production (ha)	3,102	2,392	3,675	2,618	1,766	5,162	5,365
Exports (tons)*	5,078	7,260	7,240	7,649	5,173		

Note: Asian vegetables counted in exports here are dudhi, okra, karella, chillies, and others. There were no data for brinjals.
Sources: HCDA, Ministry of Agriculture.

ulation in the United Kingdom is the largest consumer of these commodities. Prospects for future growth are limited, as that market is declining and competition from other suppliers is increasing. Kenya's French beans have been more or less constant in terms of exports, but the area under production has increased. They continue to hold their own against stiff competition from North African countries such as Morocco, and new entrants such as The Gambia and Burkina Faso (See table 6.2).

Table 6.2 Indicators for French beans

Indicator	*1989*	*1990*	*1991*	*1992*	*1993*	*1994*	*1995*
Production (tons)	17,832	13,565	24,265	22,265	19,624	18,271	17,400
Area under production (ha)	3,082	3,707	5,939	6,190	5,807	4,792	4,524
Exports (tons)	15,227	16,329	14,852	15,197	14,476		

Sources: HCDA, Ministry of Agriculture.

Cut flowers have performed well as a cash crop, largely as a result of high-quality production by large-scale, vertically integrated, local and international producers with access to new planting materials. Kenyan cut flowers have maintained a large market share in Dutch flower auctions, which serve as the principal distributors for Europe and the Middle East. Despite stiff competition Kenya has managed to retain its market share over the past four years.

Kenya's total horticultural exports have grown rapidly since 1972, from just under 8,000 tons to over 65,000 tons in 1994, as shown in table 6.3. Acreage has increased correspondingly, and is currently around 1,445 hectares. As discussed above and elsewhere, the diversity of commodities may indicate that Kenya's horticultural sector has internal robustness. Yet analysis of the composition of exports, not only by volume but also by value, shows significant commodity and market concentration. The principal horticultural exports in 1991 were cut flowers (33 percent), French beans (30 percent), and Asian vegetables (19 percent), which together constituted 82 percent of all horticultural exports (Harris 1992). Principal markets include France, Germany, the Netherlands, and the United Kingdom, all of which are EU-member countries.

Relatively few importers dominate horticultural markets. As noted earlier, Asian vegetables are primarily exported to the United Kingdom, French beans to France, and cut flowers to Germany and the Netherlands. The leading importing countries of Kenyan horticultural produce in 1991 were the United Kingdom (34 percent), the Netherlands (22 percent), France (20 percent), and Germany (13 percent), which together accounted for 89 percent of all exported fresh produce. When other EU-member countries are included, the European Union imported over 93 percent of Kenya's fresh produce exports. The European continent imported over 95 percent of Kenya's horticultural exports in 1991, when non EU-member countries such as Switzerland are included (Harris 1992).

Table 6.3 Exports of fresh horticultural products: 1985–1993

Year	*Volume (tons)*	*Change (percent)*
1985	30,000	-
1986	36,210	20.7
1987	36,550	0.9
1988	59,119	61.8
1989	49,503	-19.4
1990	49,147	- 0.7
1991	49,848	1.4
1992	57,363	15.1
1993	62,129	8.3
1994	65,176	4.9

Source: HCDA.

Market participants

Smallholders and large farms produce both French beans and Asian vegetables; small-scale producers predominate throughout Kenya, except in Kibwezi and Embu. Although some producers are landowners, land is commonly leased to smallholders for two to three years and to largeholders for five to ten years. Tenure arrangements vary by region. In Loitokitok, for example, most producers lease land for short periods, and production is predominantly by smallholders. In Kibwezi, in contrast, there is a significant presence of large-scale farmers, some of whom are tenants on five- to ten-year leases. However the majority of producers are smallholders, many of whom have two- to three-year tenancy arrangements. In Machakos and Makueni most horticultural producers are landowners, while in Embu and Meru a mix of tenancy and land ownership prevails.

Land-tenure arrangements have an important impact on the environment. In order to minimize risk and maximize output, it is rational for landowners to invest in the sustainable use of land resources to safeguard their resource base. Conversely, evidence suggests that short-term tenants are unwilling to make investments in land maintenance and improvements over which they have no long-term security or ownership. The evidence on this issue is mixed. In Loitokitok landowners are predominantly pastoral Maasai who have recently turned to agriculture. In the case of the Maasai, landowners and tenants differ little in regard to soil and water conservation practices. In other parts of the country, however, landowners exhibit conventional behavior by investing in soil and water conservation, such as sprinkler irrigation, which has lower wastewater runoff. Tenants tend to use furrow or flood irrigation, a more environmentally damaging practice.

In the Aberdares and Limuru regions the bulk of cut flowers (carnations and roses) are produced by largeholders, although some smallholders produce statice and alstromelia, because of the capital-intensive and more technical nature of production. Most rose operations rely heavily on Israeli and Dutch expatriates for technical assistance and production management. In 1994 just over 50 flower operations existed in Kenya, mostly around Nairobi.

Unlike many of the French bean and Asian vegetable producers, cut-flower producers tend to be vertically integrated and to manage their own overseas marketing. French bean and Asian vegetable producers rely mainly on nongrower exporters as middlemen between the producer and European markets, while flower producers tend to market directly to Europe. Cut-flower producer-exporters dominate the market. One Kenyan cut-flower producer-exporter is responsible for more than one-quarter of all horticultural produce earnings, and three-quarters of all cut-flower exports come from two firms. Much the same situation holds for French beans and Asian vegetable markets. Three large firms and a handful of medium-scale exporters dominate the market. Despite the evidence of market power, the share not dominated by large firms is highly dynamic, comprising many so-called "briefcase exporters," who opportunistically buy fresh produce from smallholders.

Inputs and returns for horticultural production and alternative cash crops

Horticultural production is generally quite profitable (table 6.4). In 1995 profits per hectare ranged from Ksh 9,262,400 for roses (largeholder) to Ksh 17,500 for okra (smallholder). This compares favorably with profits from coffee of Ksh 250,502 (largeholder) to Ksh 35,775 (smallholder) per hectare and for tea from Ksh 139,748 (largeholder) to Ksh 43,699 (smallholder). The exchange rate in 1995 was Ksh56 to US$1. This rate will be used throughout this paper.

Horticulture is labor intensive. Alstromelia, for example, requires 803 person days per hectare, compared to 442 for pyrethrum, 318 for tea, and 294 for coffee (Egerton and others 1995). Moreover, capital outlay and costs are high. For vegetables (French beans, karella, okra, chillies, and snow peas) the average capital outlay covering all costs ranges from Ksh 204,809 for chillies to Ksh 49,533 for French beans, an average of Ksh 106,535 per hectare. In comparison total costs in coffee range from Ksh 26,239 to Ksh 71,215 per hectare. The average for various produc-

Table 6.4 Returns from horticultural crops

Crop	*Yield/ha*	*Total Revenue (Ksh)*	*Total Cost (Ksh)*	*Profits (Ksh)*
Roses	1,800,000 stems	14,400,000	5,137,600	9,262,400
Statice	435,708 stems	435,708	137,169	298,539
Alstromelia	700,245 stems	854,299	123,411	730,888
French beans	1,606 kgs	96,330	49,533	46,797
Karella	2,149 kgs	214,890	137,789	77,101
Okra	711 kgs	85,363	67,858	17,505
Chillies	3,557 kgs	426,816	204,809	222,007
Snow peas	3,522 kgs	316,911	72,685	244,226

Source: Egerton and others (1995).

tion systems across the country is Ksh 48,424 per hectare. Tea costs are lower on average than those for horticulture or coffee, ranging from Ksh 23,284 (smallholder) to Ksh 74,935 (largeholder) per hectare (Egerton and others 1995).

Only a limited amount of Kenya's land is suitable for tea and coffee production. Horticulture (including domestic production) is suited to a wider range of land classes. Land suitable for horticulture is classified into three classes, taking all production factors into consideration. The amount of land under cultivation in each class zone is listed in table 6.5.

Table 6.5 Land potential and environmental sensitivity of selected crops

	Land in class 1	*Land in class 2*	*Land in class 3*	*Land in classes 1&2*
Horticulture	8.6	29.4	62.0	38
Coffee	21.7	27.9	50.4	49.6
Tea	21.4	16.4	62.2	37.8
Maize	3.4	38.5	58.1	41.9
Beans	6.5	46.4	47.1	52.9

Suitability class one is the best land for horticultural crops. Major alternative crops are tea, dairy, and food-crops . This land consists of deep, medium-textured soils with moderate natural fertility that is well drained, slightly saline, and nonsodic. Examples include the French bean and snow pea growing areas around Mt. Kenya and the Aberdares, as well as western Kenya. Most production is rainfed.

Suitability class two land has medium potential for horticulture. Major alternative crops are coffee, dairy, and food-crops. Suitability class two horticultural land is characterized by heavy or light textured soils with low natural fertility that are moderately deep, slightly saline, nonsodic, and well drained. Examples include the cut-flower growing areas around Aberdares, Mt. Kenya, and Limuru. These areas are largely rainfed, but with some irrigation.

Suitability class three land has low potential. These lands are characterized by strongly sodic, light or heavy, moderately well-drained soil, with low natural fertility and moderate salinity. Unlike for class one or two lands, horticulture has few competing arable activities. Marginal food-crop production, livestock, and wildlife are the major alternative land uses. Examples include French bean and Asian vegetable production in Loitokitok, Makueni, Machakos, and Mwea and cut-flower production in the Aberdares. Other agro-ecological zones with significant horticultural production are Naivasha and parts of Loitokitok, where extensive irrigation facilitates production of horticultural crops.

In terms of susceptibility to environmental degradation, suitability class one land is least susceptible; class two is moderately susceptible, and class three is the most susceptible. Suitability class one areas are least susceptible to damage from either rainfed or irrigated agriculture. Due to the steepness of the land, however, surface runoff and soil erosion are potential sources of degradation, particularly once groundcover has been lost. The impact of pesticides and fertilizer depends on production techniques.

Suitability class two areas are more susceptible to environmental degradation, particularly as a result of the impact of irrigation and rising water tables on the soil. Light soils are easily erodible and heavy soils are easily waterlogged. Rising water tables cause salinity, and impeded drainage increases sodicity. Fertilizer and pesticide residues are retained longer in heavy soil, since leaching occurs more slowly in heavy soil. Most smallholder horticultural production takes place in these areas, using some form of irrigation. As will be shown later, the environmental impact on this class of land is considerable.

Suitability class three lands are the most susceptible to environmental degradation. The environmental impacts are similar to those on class two land, but more are severe, largely as a result of the production systems and climatic conditions. Most vegetables, particularly Asian vegetables, are grown in this zone, largely by smallholders. The combination of arid climate and water from furrow irrigation makes fungus and pest attacks particularly common for Asian vegetables in Machakos and Makueni. Increasing pest attacks have led to intensive pesticide use. Yet the greatest volume and value of horticultural production is from this zone, particularly when the Lake Naivasha region is included. This zone has the greatest irrigation potential in the country, and more land is available for short- and long-term leasing in class three areas than in class one or two zones.

3. Tariff Structure for Horticultural and Related Products

Kenya currently has tariff-free access to the EU market for horticultural products. This puts the country in a preferential position, for example, with respect to non-EU Mediterranean basin countries that face tariff rates of 4.2 percent for cut flowers and 5.3 percent for vegetables. The tariffs for other countries' (non-Mediterranean basin or ACP) horticultural products entering the EU are 15 percent for cut flowers and 13 percent for vegetables.

In the analysis that follows we examine the consequences of a change in tariff rates that would: (a) impose the non-EU tariff on Kenyan products, or (b) impose a "tariff" that internalizes environmental costs. The latter need not, of course, be a tariff, but could be an internal tax, imposed by the government to internalize environmental costs. Estimates of the environmental costs are provided in the next section.

Table 6.6 Impact of removing preferential tariffs on profitability (Ksh/ha)

Crop	*Average private profitability*	*Tariff at Medit. Basin level*	*Tariff at third-country level*
French beans	46,797	5,105	12,523
Asian vegetable (karella)	77,101	11,389	27,936
Statice (large producers)	298,539	18,300	65,356
Alstromelia (small producers)	730,888	35,881	128,145

Source: Emerton and others (1997).

The consequences of the preferential tariff are demonstrated in table 6.6. If one of the tariffs suggested above were imposed, profitability would decline as detailed in the table.

The impacts of the changes in profitability are discussed further in section five. At this point we simply note that the strongest impact would be on marginal producers, many of which will be small enterprises.

4. Environmental Costs of Different Crops in Kenya

Agricultural production affects the environment through its use of natural, chemical, mechanical, and human inputs to produce, process, store, and transport output. These environmental impacts are felt both on- and off-farm. This section presents a general outline of the environmental hazards of crop production in Kenya's major horticultural areas. The two major levels upon which agricultural production may impact on the environment are:

- *Agricultural land-use practices*: environmental impacts arising from the use of land, vegetation, water, chemicals, and other inputs to generate farm output.
- *Intermediary goods and final products*: environmental impacts arising from the use of inputs in producing, processing, storing, using, and transporting the intermediary goods necessary to support agricultural production and final agricultural products.

Environmental impact of agricultural land-use practices

The use of land, vegetation, water, and chemicals in agricultural production can have a number of overlapping impacts on the environment. Agricultural land-use replaces natural vegetation systems. Crops introduced may be environmentally inferior to the vegetation they replace, especially when they are poorly managed or grown in unsuitable or vulnerable areas. The major land-use and vegetation-based hazards of crop production are soil erosion and exhaustion, watershed change, and loss of biological resources.

Soil erosion, runoff, and sedimentation. Most of the areas where horticulture is practised in Kenya lie either in mountainous or semiarid areas. Much cultivation takes place on steep slopes and unsuitable, marginal lands where the risk of soil erosion is high. Pockets of saline soil have been found in a number of irrigated horticultural areas, including Mwea (NES 1981). The combination of soil salinity, overintensive land-use, and soil exhaustion has resulted in a loss of soil fertility and depth.

When ground protection is lost and soil erosion occurs, local runoff increases and greater volumes of soil are carried off-site. Sediment loads in rivers can increase significantly, and higher levels of silt are transported downstream. The rivers located downstream from horticultural areas, most notably the Tana, Athi, and Ewaso Ngiro, as well as smaller streams and watercourses, carry extremely high suspended sediment loads (UNEP 1987). Clearance of natural vegetation for agriculture and poor subsequent land management are major factors contributing to these high sediment loads.

Increased runoff and sedimentation can lead to changed waterflow characteristics in downstream watercourses and exacerbate dry-season water shortage and wet-season flooding. The diversion of surface water for irrigation may also alter waterflow. Local water tables can fall when groundwater recharge levels decrease, as a result of lower soil moisture, and when pumping groundwater for irrigation exhausts aquifers. Overuse of local water supplies is a major concern in the flower-growing areas around Lake Naivasha (Naitore 1995). Changed waterflow results in downstream production losses and increased damage by seasonal water shortages, floods, and reductions in groundwater resources.

Within the horticultural sector vegetable crops generally provide poorer ground cover than flower crops, and are more likely to give rise to the above effects. Nonhorticultural perennial products such as tea, coffee, and dairy products, however, provide excellent ground protection and cause little soil erosion; maize and beans provide poor groundcover and increase rates of soil erosion. The transfer of land from perennial to horticultural or nonhorticultural annual crops is likely to contribute to increased soil erosion, loss of soil fertility and depth, and associated downstream effects. These effects will be especially intense on erodible soils in major watersheds, such as the Mount Kenya and the Aberdares regions.

Biodiversity. Exotic agricultural crops replace natural vegetation and indigenous landraces. Clearance of vegetation for agriculture creates a loss of diverse plant species and natural habitats. Natural vegetation also provides a range of goods and services, including direct uses, ecological benefits, and option and existence values, which effectively represent the opportunity cost of agricultural land.

Multiple varieties of indigenous crops exist; replacing these crops with exotic varieties creates the risk that indigenous landraces will no longer be planted and thus lost over time. The destruction of landraces is important primarily because it narrows the genetic base of agriculture and increases the risk of crop failure. Moreover, undisturbed vegetation around horticultural areas, especially within the Mount Kenya, Aberdares, and Naivasha regions, provides habitat for a range of animals and birds, including rare and endangered species. In addition many households rely on natural vegetation to supply subsistence and income needs including timber, charcoal fuelwood, polewood, medicines, grazing, and wild foods (Emerton 1994b).

Chemical pollution. The increasing use of chemicals is also having significant effects. Kenya imports chemicals, so the environmental costs of their production accrue outside the country. Many of the agrochemicals in general circulation in Kenya have been banned or designated as restricted-use chemicals in the developed world because of adverse health effects or environmental hazards (Matteson and Meltzer 1995). About one-half of the pesticides used for vegetable production in Kenya fall into this category (Kibata 1993).

Agrochemicals, especially herbicides and soil sterilants, can contaminate surface water and groundwater resources. As a result of chemical pollution water may become unfit for human consumption and unable to support plant and animal populations. Pollutants may accumulate in living organisms and, over time, reach toxic levels. Regions with intense horticultural production, especially lake wetlands and watersheds, are of particular concern. Around Lake Naivasha pyrethroid insecticides have been found in runoff and streams; soil sterilants have also been detected (Matteson and Meltzer 1995). The British Broadcasting Corporation has reported livestock poisoning from Aldrin runoff in the area around the lake (BBC 1995). There is also apprehension about horticultural pesticide residues found in Lake Nakuru and their effect on the lake's flamingo population. Evidence suggests that fish populations are also affected by agrochemical water pollution. Studies carried out in Lake Naivasha and the Tana and Athi Rivers, all of which are located downstream from major horticultural and irrigation areas, have found a wide array of pesticide residues in fish, some of which make them unfit for human consumption (Matteson and Meltzer 1995). A number of water bodies downstream from horticultural areas are displaying signs of eutrophication (NES 1981).

On-site human health risks arise from the ingestion of agrochemicals through contaminated containers and other water and airborne transfers that can cause skin, eye, gastrointestinal, and respiratory illnesses. Long-term health effects include pathogenesis of childhood aplastic anaemia, chronic mercury poisoning, and impotence (Matteson and Meltzer 1995). Commonly applied pesticides that are reasonably safe for human applicators may be acutely toxic to fish, birds, bees, beneficial insects, and other desirable nontarget species.

Most on-site human health hazards arise because of unsafe chemical application practices. In the Kenyan small farms sector most pesticides are hand-mixed and applied by hand, twig brooms, or backpack sprayers (KNFU 1987). Protective measures are rarely taken, and farmers are generally ignorant of pesticide safety practices (Matteson and Meltzer 1995). Surveys in major horticultural areas have found that most farmers experience occasional poisoning symptoms after applying agrochemicals (Partow 1992). It has been estimated that pesticides poison 7 percent of the people in Kenya's agricultural sector every year (Matteson and Meltzer 1995), and that one-quarter of the farmers in major horticultural areas regularly suffer from pesticide-related ill health (KNFU 1987). Organophosphate pesticides constitute the most acute danger because of their relatively high toxicity. About 90 percent of the agrochemical poisoning cases treated between 1987 and 1990 at Kiambu District Hospital, which is located in a growth area for coffee, vegetable, and flower production, involved organophosphates (Mwanthi and Kimani 1990), and one-tenth of all illnesses treated at Lake Naivasha North Clinic involved pesticide poisoning of flower-farm workers□mainly rashes, sores and gastrointestinal problems (BBC 1995). High organochlorine residues, especially DDT and Dieldrin, have been found in human milk samples taken from mothers in horticultural and coffee-growing areas (Matteson and Meltzer 1995; KNFU 1987).

Irrigation heightens the risk of waterborne disease and increases the health risk from contaminated wastewater. In Mwea, a major area of irrigated horticulture, the incidence of waterborne diseases among farmers is well above the norm. Thirty one percent of the residents show signs of bilharzia, 15 percent have ascaris, 15 percent hookworms, and up to one-half show signs of malaria (NES 1981).

Most of the cash crops grown in horticultural areas rely on chemical fertilizers. As soil fertility declines as a result of intensive production, causing soil erosion and exhaustion, increasing quantities of fertilizer are applied to maintain soil fertility. This can lead to agrochemical pollution, as discussed above. Heavy fertilizer use also contributes to greenhouse gas emissions. Nitrous oxide (N_20), a major greenhouse gas, is produced from soils through the process of denitrification and nitrification, both of which are associated with the application of agricultural fertilizers. Synthetic fertilizers are more harmful because they are comprised of extra nitrogenous elements and lose up to 4 percent of their nitrogen when applied (Adger and Brown 1994). Finally, some evidence indicates that a range of agricultural pests have become resistant to commonly used pesticides, which could lead to a vicious circle of increased pesticide use to cope with increased resistance.

Environmental impact of intermediary goods and final products

Agricultural production relies on a range of intermediary goods and services to generate output. Producing final products for the market involves processing, storage, packaging materials, and transportation. These stages of the production process use inputs that involve environmental risk

Most horticulture consists of exotic varieties, such as French beans, Asian vegetables, and cut flowers. These crops are produced from exotic seeds and seedlings originally imported from overseas. Imported pests and viruses may accompany the introduction of exotic planting materials. Pests from the United States and Europe may already have been introduced into central Kenya via imported flower seeds. Once pests are imported with seed, they can quickly spread within exotic crops, and may be transferred to indigenous crops and vegetation.

Some horticultural crops are propagated using plastic trays, containers, sheeting, and pots. Most of these items are made from plastics produced from petroleum products. They are usually nonrecyclable, and their production and disposal entail negative environmental impacts.

Environmental impact of different crops

The environmental impact of different crops depends partly on their natural characteristics and suitability to the region in which they are being grown, as well as on their production technology and input use. Certain crops are more likely to cause particular types of environmental damage than others.

Tea. Tea is grown without pesticides, except for herbicides such as paraquat and glyophosphate (Matteson and Meltzer 1995). Although it is frequently grown on steep slopes, tea provides good groundcover and soil-holding capacity. Its production therefore entails little environmental risk.

After harvest green leaves are transported by road to local factories for processing. Many of these tea roads are in poor condition and lie in ecologically fragile areas. Green leaf is processed by means of indoor drying, using a combination of electric fans and wood-fed dryers, which consume fossil fuel and fuelwood from tea estates and the Forest Department's exotic plantations.

Coffee. Coffee producers use high levels of pesticides including insecticides, fungicides, and herbicides that cause a high incidence of pesticide poisoning (KNFU 1987). Although it is frequently grown on steep slopes, much coffee production takes place on bench terraces. The coffee bush provides relatively good groundcover and soil-holding capacity. The main environmental risk of coffee production is agrochemical pollution.

After harvest coffee berries are transported by road to local drying centers, where they are fermented and cleaned in water and then sun-dried in the open air. The cleaning process leaves husk residues and wastage, which is rarely disposed of properly and flows into nearby rivers and streams.

Vegetables. Tomatoes and export vegetables rely on high levels of fertilizers and are usually treated with fungicides and insecticides, creating a high risk of applicator poisoning. Vegetables are normally grown using flood and furrow irrigation. Wastewater from such irrigation transports agrochemical pollutants from farms into local rivers and watercourses. Soil-to-water chemical transfer is exacerbated by high rates of soil erosion and runoff caused by inferior land management practices and irrigation techniques. Vegetable crops provide poor groundcover and soil-holding capacity, and much cultivation takes place on erodible or marginal soils. The environmental risks of vegetable production are therefore high. Production of exotic vegetables relies on introduced seed, raising concerns about the introduction of new pests and viruses via imported planting materials. Most production takes place from seed, and there is little off-site propagation.

Cut Flowers. Fifteen percent of all pesticides used in Kenya are applied in cut-flower production (Matteson and Meltzer 1995). Flowers use soil sterilants, fungicides, insecticides, and fumigants, creating a high risk of applicator poisoning. Cut flowers are normally grown under drip, sprinkler, and furrow irrigation, which contributes to polluted wastewater off-site. Most flowers are perennial and provide adequate groundcover, although poor land-management practices can contribute to soil erosion. The environmental risks of cut-flower production are high. Because production of cut flowers relies on introduced seed, there is concern about the introduction of new pests and viruses via imported planting materials.

Maize and Beans. Maize and bean production is rarely irrigated and provides poor groundcover and soil-holding capacity.

Dairy. The main environmental hazards from dairy production are chemical-related risks and methane production. Cattle are regularly dipped in, or sprayed with, acaricides (the most common organophosphates) to control tick-borne disease (Matteson and Meltzer 1995). These solutions are highly toxic, but more rapidly biodegradable than many other dipping chemicals. Cattle-dip solution is added to the natural drainage system without any treatment, and applicators may be at risk if cattle are sprayed. Methane is produced directly by the enteric fermentation in the intestines of ruminants and from methanogenesis of stored manure. Dairy cattle in milk produce almost one-third more methane than dairy cattle out of milk (Adger and Brown 1994). Apart from their contribution to global warming, methane emissions are also of concern because the capability of the atmospheric sink and soil sink to absorb increased concentrations of the gas is reduced over time.

5. An Economic Analysis of Environmental Impacts

Having examined the physical and environmental impacts of different crops in the previous section, we provide here an analysis of the monetary valuation of these impacts. The analysis is carried out primarily by estimating the production losses caused by environmental impacts, including the cost of replacing lost environmental functions and averting environmental damage. The choice of valuation technique depends on the kind of data available. Ideally, the estimate of changes of environmental values should be made in terms of willingness to pay. However, given the scarcity of primary studies of environmental values for the agricultural sector in Kenya, we have had to limit this estimation to the method noted above. In most cases this means that the estimated cost of damages is the *lower boundary* of the true cost. Nevertheless, the estimates are useful and important for analyzing the effects of policy changes, as will be seen below. Techniques for valuing specific environmental impacts are outlined in table 6.7.

A certain level of soil erosion can be tolerated without significant effects on productivity. Beyond this level yields decline as a result of falling soil fertility and nutrient levels. Crop yield losses are related to topsoil loss, soil susceptibility and the level of input use. Yield losses resulting from soil erosion for different crops and areas have been estimated as part of this study.

Sedimentation and changed waterflow

It is possible to cost downstream sedimentation and changed waterflow in terms of the expenditure necessary to prevent these circumstances from occurring. An effective way of minimizing soil erosion, loss of vegetation cover, and resulting downstream effects is to employ on-site conservation measures. Data are available on the soil conservation measures required for different regions and crops (Kassam and others 1992) and the cost of carrying them out. These preventive costs are used here as a proxy for the environmental cost of downstream sedimentation and changed waterflow.

Table 6.7 Techniques for valuing major environmental impacts of agricultural production in Kenya

Environmental effect	*Technique*	*Method of calculation*
Decline in soil fertility and depth	Effect on production	Value of yield losses
Sedimentation, water pollution	Preventive cost	Cost of on-site soil conservation
Loss of biological resources	Effect on production	Value of lost resource uses
Health hazards	Human capital	Cost of therapy and lost earnings

Decline in soil fertility and depth

The best-known predictor of surface erosion is the Universal Soil Loss Equation (USLE). The USLE links soil loss per unit area with the erosive power of rain, runoff, soil erodibility, vegetation cover, and cultivation methods. The USLE is used to estimate on-site losses in productivity resulting from declines in soil fertility and depth caused by erosion.

A modified USLE has been developed for Kenya (Kassam and others 1992). The model specifies that the annual soil loss A is a function

$$A(R,K,LS,C,M,P), \qquad (1)$$

where R is the rainfall erodibility factor, K is the soil erodibility factor, LS is the length and steepness of slope factor, C is the vegetation cover factor, M is the management factor, and P is the physical protection factor.

Loss of biological resources

The cost of losing biological resources can be calculated by looking at the values foregone by agricultural land-use. Although data exist regarding the indirect, option, and existence value of biological resources in Kenya (Brown 1989; Emerton 1992, 1994a; Moran 1994; Norton-Griffiths 1995), most refer to nonagricultural areas (national parks and forest reserves). Information is available, however, on the direct use values of natural vegetation obtained by local households surrounded by areas of montane forest and dry, bushy scrub (Emerton 1994b) the main regions where horticulture is carried out. The value of this foregone use forms one part of the cost of biological resource loss. Estimates of such losses have been made as part of this study.

Water pollution

Agrochemicals pollute surface and groundwater sources. Most of the chemicals used in horticultural areas have limited mobility in soil and are transferred into surface water via soil particles through agricultural runoff. There is less leaching of agrochemical residues into groundwater in horticultural areas (Edwards 1970; FAO 1972, 1979). Although data are available concerning levels of chemical use in agriculture, their residue and delivery rates, and guidelines for acceptable levels in water, it is difficult to link chemical pollution in water to given levels of health or ecosystem damage. Most chemicals are transferred from soils to surface water. Limiting runoff and soil erosion through soil conservation measures minimizes downstream water pollution. Data are available on required soil-conservation measures for different regions and crops (Kassam and others 1992), as well as the cost of implementing them. These preventive expenditures are used as a proxy for the environmental cost of agrochemical production. The cost of soil conservation measures for different crops and areas have been estimated as part of this study.

On-site health hazards

Aside from water pollution, the most negative on-site effect of chemical use is health hazards to agricultural workers and local residents. The cost of on-site health hazards can be calculated by using a human-capital approach, which takes into account days of labor lost due to illness and medical expenditure. Although little quantitative information is available linking irrigated agriculture and increased incidence of waterborne diseases, data describing the effects of pesticide use on human health are available.

The presence of high levels of pesticide residues in blood is one indicator of human exposure to unsafe levels of chemicals. Surveys in central and eastern Kenya (major horticultural areas) have shown that 25 percent of farmers have levels of pesticide concentration in their blood above those considered safe (KNFU 1987). Most pesticide poisoning takes place after spraying, the frequency of which varies by crop and area. Data are available concerning the frequency and type of pesticide application for different crops and regions, medical charges for diagnosing and treating different types of pesticide poisoning, and for the number of work days lost as a result of pesticide-related ill health (HDCA). The cost of medical treatment and labor lost as a result of pesticide-related ill health was estimated as part of this study.

The environmental impacts of crop production

The level of environmental damage arising from agricultural production depends on the natural characteristics of different crops, the nature of the areas in which they are grown, and the method of cultivation. Details of the environmental costs of producing different crops in different areas are available in Emerton and others (1997). With other factors held constant, an increase in the production of a particular agricultural commodity is likely to imply an increase in environmental cost. Some of these impacts are quantifiable. For quantifiable effects, the net environmental cost (NEC) per hectare of crop x is calculated as: NEC(x) = yield losses from soil erosion + cost of soil conservation + loss of natural resource use + cost of medical treatment for on-site health hazards. The estimates are summarized in table 6.8.

These figures have been used in the next section to estimate the effect of tariffs on land use and total environmental damage.

Table 6.8 Summary of net environmental costs of agricultural production ('000 Ksh/Ha)

	Tomatoes	*Coffee*	*Tea*	*Dairy*	*Maize & beans*	*Statice*	*Alstromeria*	*Karella*	*French beans*	*Average*
Loitokitok	2.4			3.0	1.7			2.5	2.5	2.4
Mt. Kenya	7.0	2.0	1.4	3.4	6.4	8.5	8.5	7.1	7.1	5.7
Aberares	7.0	2.0	1.4	3.4	6.4	8.5	8.5	7.1	7.1	5.7
Juja	2.4	2.6		3.0	1.7	11.1	11.1	2.5	2.5	4.6
Limuru	2.0	2.1		3.0	1.4	16.2	16.2	2.1	2.1	5.6
Mwea	2.4		2.0	3.0	1.7	3.8	3.8	2.5	2.5	2.7
Machakos	5.4			3.3	4.7	6.9	6.9	5.5	5.5	5.5
Naivasha	2.4			3.0	1.7	3.8	3.8	2.5	2.5	2.8
Average	3.8	2.2	1.6	3.2	3.2	8.4	8.4	4.0	4.0	

6. Estimating the Impact of Preferential Trading on Land Use, the Environment, and other Indicators

Data in the previous section include average rates of profitability for each crop and zone in Kenya. Also provided are some data on the amount of land in each zone devoted to each crop. The methodology for assessing the impact of a change in tariff rates on profitability is described below.

Methodology for estimating changes in land use

It is assumed that the average profitability for each crop is obtained from a range which is linear, with the *marginal profitability being zero in each case.* Hence the marginal profitability for crop *i* in zone *j* is given by P_{ij} where

$$\Pi_{ij} = \alpha_{ij} - \beta_{ij} X_{ij} \quad (2)$$

$$\alpha_{ij} > 0,\ \beta_{ij} > 0 \quad (3)$$

Profitability varies with the amount of land X_{ij} allocated to crop *i* in zone *j*. α_{ij} and β_{ij} are coefficients of the profitability function that need to be estimated. This is carried out as shown below.

Given that the actual amount allocated is $\bar{X}_{ij}$, it is further assumed that the marginal profitability for the last unit is zero. This allows for any returns that are necessary to recover a return on capital. Hence one equation to determine α and β is given by:

$$0 = \alpha_{ij} - \beta_{ij} \bar{X}_{ij} \quad (4)$$

The second equation to determine a and b is given by the fact that average profitability from crop *i* in zone *j* is $\bar{\Pi}_{ij}$. Hence integrating the marginal profitability curve gives:

$$\bar{\Pi}_{ij} \bar{X}_{ij} = \int_0^{\bar{x}} (\alpha_{ij} - \beta_{ij} X_{ij}) dX, \quad (5)$$

or,

$$\bar{\Pi}_{ij} = \alpha_{ij} - \beta_{ij} X_{ij} / 2 \quad (6)$$

Equations (4) and (6) allow us to determine the values of α_{ij} and β_{ij}. The impact of changes in profitability is assessed by assuming that a change in profitability of DP causes marginal profitability to decline by that amount. The new equation for profitability is then given by:

$$\Pi_{ij} = \{\alpha_{ij} - \Delta\Pi\} - \beta_{ij} X_{ij} \quad (7)$$

The new value of the intercept in the linear equation allows us to compute the new land area allocated to the crop. The shift in profitability is shown in figure 6.1.

The above analysis makes a number of assumptions that could be questioned. First, it assumes that land is used in a way that ensures that private profitability is equalized at the margin; that is, that there is no benefit for the marginal farmer in turning from the present crop to a different crop. This may be disputed if farmers are operating under conditions of poor knowledge or are constrained in some way from changing their use of land. But as a first approximation it is likely to be satisfactory. Second, the assumption of linearity may be questioned, but in the absence of data it is often taken as a first approximation. Third, it is also being assumed that land can be removed from, or brought into, use according to the economic parameters.[3] In some areas land is limited and it may not be possible to expand production. In other cases decreasing production may not be feasible; for example, when no other sources of income are available. Some sensitivity analysis was carried out using the above model, under the constraint that the total amount of land area be held constant. Shifts in production are then based on relative profitability. As noted below, however, the broad conclusions of this analysis remain unchanged even with that constraint.

Figure 6.1 Marginal profitability

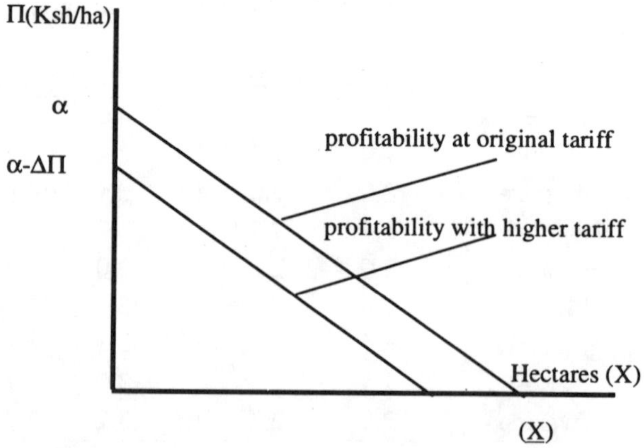

Estimating the impact of environmental cost internalization

The model described above has been applied to data for the following crops: Asian vegetables, French beans, cut flowers, maize, coffee, and tea. Emerton and others (1997) report average profitability data for each of these crops; table 6.4 summarizes this data for horticultural crops. Data on land areas for the main crops by region are also available for 1995, and are summarized in table 6.9, along with the implied values of α_{ij} and β_{ij}.[4] Analysis has been carried out for three zones only, Central, Eastern, and Rift, since these are the only zones where horticultural products are produced in significant quantities.

Table 6.9 Average profitability, land areas, and implied values of α_{ij} and β_{ij}

Crop	*Profit (000 Ksh/ha)**	*Land used (000 ha)****				*Implied value*	*Implied value*
		Central	*Eastern*	*Rift*	*Total*		
Asian Vegetables**	94.6	0.086	1.320	1.454	2.86	189.2	-66.23
French beans	46.8	0.174	3.191	2.335	5.81	154.2	-73.12
Cut flowers	10,291.8	0.040	0.649	0.616	1.33	20,583.6	-15,488.08
Maize	24.8	8.712	534.528	248.644	1,250.0	49.6	-0.04
Coffee	164.2	4.820	54.099	39.584	156.0	328.4	-2.11
Tea	107.3	2.875	28.672	27.215	97.0	214.6	-2.21

Notes: * Profitability is the average for all zones. Separate profitability figures were not available for each zone.
** Asian vegetables include only okra and karella.
*** Total land used is taken from Emerton and others (1997) and Kenya Horticultural Industry Association data.

Table 6.10 Impacts of full environmental cost internalization on land use

Region/crop	*Area at present (000ha)*	*Environmental cost (000Ksh/ha)*	*Area with full internalization (000ha)*	*Change in area (000ha)*	*Reduction in damage (000Ksh)*
CENTRAL					
Asian veg.	0.086	9.80	0.081	-0.0045	44.35
French beans	0.174	6.90	0.161	-0.0129	89.32
Cut flowers	0.040	3.44	0.040	0.0000	0.15
Coffee	4.820	2.07	4.779	-0.0414	85.79
Tea	2.875	1.50	2.858	-0.0176	26.36
Maize	8.712	3.28	8.065	-0.6464	2,120.27
TOTAL	16.707		15.984	-0.7230	2,366.20
EASTERN					
Asian veg.	1.320	3.63	1.294	-0.0267	96.84
French beans	3.191	3.30	3.076	-0.1147	378.58
Cut flowers	0.649	3.80	0.648	0.0007	2.76
Coffee	54.099	2.60	53.547	-0.5522	1435.80
Tea	28.672	1.50	28.497	-0.1752	262.82
Maize	534.53	4.70	479.685	-54.8426	257,760.00
TOTAL	622.46		566.747	-55.7120	259,936.00
RIFT					
Asian veg.	1.454	3.25	1.428	-0.0265	86.27
French beans	2.335	3.05	2.257	-0.0777	237.01
Cut flowers	0.616	3.80	0.615	-0.0007	2.62
Coffee	39.584	2.40	39.204	-0.3800	912.03
Tea	27.215	1.50	27.049	-0.1663	249.47
Maize	248.644	1.75	237.803	-10.8409	18,971.54
TOTAL	319.848		308.356	-11.4920	20,458.50
GRAND TOTAL	959.015		891.087	-67.927	282,730.70

The results of applying the model are shown in table 6.10. Note that in table 6.8 the environmental costs were at the district level. In tables 6.10 and 6.11 we have summarized them into three regions, using agricultural and district maps of Kenya.

Table 6.9 shows that if estimated internal costs were internalized, about 68,000 hectares would become unprofitable, mostly in maize production. Altogether this amounts to about 7 percent of the land area in the three regions that cultivate these crops. The decrease in production of horticultural crops would be very small—about 500 hectares total—mostly French beans. The production of cut flowers would hardly be affected, as profitability is high enough to absorb most additional costs.

The impact of changes in environmental damage is shown in the last column of table 6.10: a reduction in damages of Ksh. 282 million, or about US$5 million per annum. Most of the reduction would result from using less land for maize. Internalizing the environmental costs of the horticultural sector has a small impact in terms of damages avoided. However, it is important to note that this analysis does not reflect the effect of changes in *practices* on the level of environmental damages. Such effects could be important, but to achieve them would require a tax capable of distinguishing among practices rather than crops.

Regionally the effects are likely to be most pronounced in areas where profitability has been most reduced. Since separate profitability figures were not available for the regions, this impact could not be evaluated fully, although environmental costs appear to be highest in the Eastern region, where production of horticultural crops is minimal.

The employment effects of internalization are difficult to gauge. Horticulture loses about 265 hectares, amounting to about 210,000 person days, or about 1,000 employees. The biggest impacts are in maize, where the employment effects are not quantified.

Estimating the Impact of Changes in Preferences

Tables 6.11 and 6.12 provide material from which to analyze the impact of changes in tariffs. Table 6.11 imposes tariffs based on those applying to Mediterranean Basin countries; table 6.12 shows the impact of introducing third-country tariffs as indicated in table 6.6 . The impact of such tariffs is not strong. Total land cultivated declines by 530 hectares, with the biggest reductions being French beans and Asian vegetables. Export revenues are affected to the extent of Ksh 48 million (US$0.9 million). At the same time, however, reduction in environmental damages is also small (about Ksh 2 million, or US$40,000). The main

Table 6.11 Impacts of introducing Mediterranean basin tariffs

Region/ Crop	*Area at Present 000HA.*	*Tariff*	*New Area*	*Change in Area 000ha.*	*Reduction in Export Revenues 000Ksh*	*Reduction in Damages 000Ksh*
CENTRAL						
Asian vegetables	0.09	11.39	0.08	0.01	539.21	51.39
French beans	0.17	5.11	0.16	0.01	925.67	66.30
Cut flowers	0.04	27090.50	0.04	0.00	10.25	4.45
Total	0.30		0.28	0.02	1475.13	122.15
EASTERN						
Asian vegetables	1.32	11.39	1.24	0.08	8311.27	293.01
French beans	3.19	5.11	3.01	0.18	16975.00	581.52
Cut flowers	0.65	27090.50	0.63	0.02	167.01	80.13
Total	5.16		4.88	0.28	25453.29	954.65
RIFT						
Asian vegetables	1.45	11.39	1.37	0.09	9153.79	289.33
French beans	2.33	5.11	2.21	0.13	12420.53	393.26
Cut flowers	0.62	27090.50	0.60	0.02	158.52	76.06
Total	4.40		4.17	0.24	21732.85	758.64
GRAND TOTAL	9.86		9.33	0.53	48661.27	1835.45

Table 6.12 Impacts of introducing third country tariffs

Region/ Crop	Area at Present 000HA.	Tariff 000Ksh/ha	New Area	Change in Area 000ha.	Reduction in Export Revenues 000Ksh	Reduction in Damages 000Ksh
CENTRAL						
Asian vegetables	0.09	27.94	0.07	0.01	1308.59	124.72
French beans	0.17	12.52	0.15	0.02	2253.27	161.40
Cut flowers	0.04	1186.89	0.04	0.00	36.43	15.82
Total	0.30		0.26	0.04	3598.29	301.94
EASTERN						
Asian vegetables	1.32	27.94	1.12	0.20	20170.29	711.10
French beans	3.19	12.52	2.76	0.43	41320.65	1415.53
Cut flowers	0.65	1186.89	0.57	0.07	593.46	284.73
Total	5.16		4.46	0.70	62084.41	2411.36
RIFT						
Asian vegetables	1.45	27.94	1.24	0.22	22214.97	702.16
French beans	2.33	12.52	2.02	0.31	30234.14	957.27
Cut flowers	0.62	1186.89	0.54	0.07	563.30	270.26
Total	4.40		3.80	0.60	53012.41	1929.70
Grand Total	9.86		8.52	1.34	118695.11	4643.00

reason is that producers take the cut in profits rather than reduce output. Consequently, employment effects would also be small, around 1,800 persons.

The impact of a shift to third-country tariffs is more pronounced, but still not large. The area under horticulture would decline by 1,340ha, and export revenues would fall by Ksh 118 million (US$2 million). About 4,800 jobs would be affected.

7. Conclusions

This paper has analyzed the impacts of horticultural production in Kenya, focusing on how preferential trading arrangements affect the environment. Horticulture is an important and growing sector of the economy, contributing significantly to exports and employment. Although there is some concentration of activity in terms of ownership, much production is by smallholders, contributing notably to incomes among the poor.

At the same time, horticultural activities are environmentally damaging. The paper provides an analysis of the impact on the environment, quantifying it to the maximum extent possible in monetary terms. The figures show that, per hectare, damages to the environment are higher for horticulture than for tea, coffee, maize, or beans. The damages arise from various sources, however, and cannot all be monetized, and thus the analysis is partial. The estimates of environmental damages are lower bounds because they are not based on willingness to pay for reduced damages, but rather on loss of earnings or output.

The economic analysis of preferential trading was carried out on the assumption that land use is adjusted so that marginal rates of return are equalized across crops. Average rates vary since productivity, technology, and other factors are also variable. Given the average profitability of different crops, a linear function can be estimated for marginal profitability. Using this function we can estimate changes in land use following the removal of preferential tariffs or the introduction of measures to internalize environmental costs. The analysis shows horticulture to be largely insensitive to such measures. The main impact of internalizing environmental costs across all crops would be to reduce maize production. As a whole, horticultural production would drop by only about 500 hectares; French bean production would decrease the most. The impact on the environment would also be minimal; environmental damages would be reduced only slightly. The main explanation for these phenomena is the high profitability of most horticultural production. Given this situation, the government could take measures to internalize the cost of environmental damages, and thereby generate revenue that could be used for environmental protection in agriculture.

Similar results emerge from the removal of preferential tariffs. If Kenya were to be allotted Mediterranean Basin tariff rates, horticulture would be affected similarly to the impact of environmental cost internalization. French beans and Asian vegetables would be the most affected. The imposition of third-country tariffs would produce roughly double the impact of Mediterranean Basin tariffs.

This analysis has not modeled the impact on more vulnerable producers. It is almost certain that, should tariff preferences be removed, these groups would be the most heavily affected. All the adjustments are being made *at the margin*. Consequently, the impact on producers who are barely surviving would be strongest, and measures to protect these producers would be needed if trade preferences were to be altered.

Notes

This paper draws extensively on "EU Trade Policy, the Lomé Convention, The Horticultural Sector and the Environment in Kenya." This study was carried out with financial support from the European Commission, DG8, under contract B-7-5040/94. In addition to the above, the following have contributed to the earlier study: Cuthbert Idawo, Daniel, Karanja, Gem Kodhek, James Nyoroat , Francis Oguya and Nicholas Dale.

1. Asian vegetables counted in exports here are dudhi, okra, karella, chillies and others. There were no data for brinjals.

2. In Kenya, there is little slack land in areas with high potential . Increasing the total agricultural land area implies expansion on to virgin land or into drier and more marginal areas. Much of the settled agricultural land around Mount Kenya, the Aberdares and Limuru has been excised from protected forest areas, which contain a diverse range of plant and animal species. Further encroachments will continue to erode natural forest areas. Hence the marginal environmental cost may be much higher than the average costs. This is a factor we have not allowed for. It adds to the fact that the environmental costs are underestimated for much of this exercise.

3. The regional data are constructed from (a) data on land classes in each region (I- III), (b) data on how much of each crop is grown on each type of land class and (c) the amount of overall production for each crop. Inevitably there are some approximations involved, as we do not have exact data for each crop in each zone, but the figures should provide a reasonable approximation for the purposes of this analysis.

References

Adger, N., and K. Brown. 1994. *Land Use and the Causes of Global Warming*. London: J. Wiley Press.

Anderson, K. 1992. "The Standard Welfare Economics of Policies Affecting Trade and Environment." In K. Anderson and R. Blackhurst, eds., *The Greening of World Trade Issues*. London: Harvester Wheatsheaf.

BBC (British Broadcasting Corporation). 1995. "Flower from Lake Naivasha." *Today Programme* (September 1). London.

Brown, G. 1989. "The Economic Value of Elephants." LEEC Paper 89-12. International Institute for Environment and Development and London Environmental Economics Centre.

Cruz, W., and R. Repetto. 1993. *The Environmental Effects of Stabilization and Structural Adjustment Programs: The Philippine Case*. Washington D.C.: World Resources Institute.

Edwards, G. 1970. *Persistent Pesticides in the Environment*. New York: Butterworths.

Egerton and others. 1995. "Liberalization of Processing and Marketing of Industrial Crops and Export Diversification." Egerton Policy Analysis Matrix (PAM) Team. Report by Task Force 2 of the Agricultural Sector Review.

Emerton, L. 1992. "An Economic Valuation of the Environmental Benefits of the Mau Forest Complex." Mimeo. KIFCON, Overseas Development Agency (UK), Forests Department, Nairobi.

_____. 1994a. "An Environmental Impact Assessment and Environmental Valuation of the Proposed Aberdares Natural Resources Development Project." Consultancy report. FAO Investment Centre, Rome.

_____. 1994b. "Summary of Current National Value of Use of Kenya's Indigenous Forests to Local Households." KIFCON, Overseas Development Agency (UK), Forests Department, Nairobi.

Emerton, L. and others. 1997. "EU Trade Policy, the Lomé Convention, the Horticultural Sector and the Environment in Kenya." Report produced for EC DGVIII. Metroeconomica Ltd., Bath.

FAO (U.N. Food and Agriculture Organization). 1972. *Effects of Intensive Fertilizer Use on the Human Environment*. FAO Soils Bulletin 16. FAO Soil Resources Development and Conservation Service, Land and Water Development Division; with the cooperation of the Swedish International Development Authority.

_____.1979. *Ground Water Pollution.* Rome: FAO.

_____.1992. *Fertilizer Handbook*. Rome: FAO.

Grossman, G.M., and A.B. Krueger. 1992. "Environmental Impacts of a North American Free Trade Agreement." In P. Gaber, ed., *The US-Mexico Free Trade Agreement*. Cambridge: MIT Press.

Harris, S. S. 1992. "Kenya Horticultural Subsector Survey." Report by Development Alternatives Inc. for USAID Kenya Exports Development Supports (KEDS) Project. Nairobi: U.S. Agency for International Development.

Jaffee, S. 1991. "Marketing Africa's Horticultural Exports: A Transaction Cost Perspective." Paper presented at Workshop of Fresh Fruit and Vegetables System, University of California, Santa Cruz.

Kassam, A., and others. 1992. "Agro-Ecological Land Resources Assessment for Agricultural Development Planning: A Case Study of Kenya." Mimeo. FAO/IIASA.

Kenya, Horticultural Development Crops Authority (HCDA). n.d. Various production and export data.

_____, Ministry of Agriculture. 1983. *Farm Management Handbook*. Nairobi: Ministry of Agriculture, GTZ.

_____, Various years. *Economic Survey*. Nairobi.

_____, National Environmental Secretariat. n.d. Various ecological, soil, water, agrochemical, and environmental data.

Kibata, G. 1993. "Implementation of Integrated Pest Management in Kenya." Background paper for the IPM Working Group East/Central/Southern Africa. IPM Implementation Workshop, Harare, Zimbabwe.

KNFU (Kenya National Farmers Union). 1987. "Pesticide Distribution and Use in Kiambu and Nakuru." Report prepared by KAMFOR for KNFU. Nairobi: KNFU.

Koning, A. 1993. "The Impact of European Union Policies on Sub-Saharan Fruit and Vegetable Exports." Paper presented at Conference on Financial and Market Strategies for African Exporters of Horticultural Products in Harare, Zimbabwe.

Markandya, A. 1994. "Is Free Trade Compatible with Sustainable Development?" *UNCTAD Review* (9): 22.

Markandya, A. and others. 1997. "EU Trade Policy, The Lomé Convention, and The Third World Environment: A Study of Economy-Environment Linkages Through Trade." Metroeconomica, Ltd., Bath.

Matteson, P., and M. Meltzer. 1995. *Environmental and Economic Implications of Agricultural Trade and Promotion Policies in Kenya: Pest and Pesticide Management*. EPAT Project working paper. Arlington, Va.: Winrock International Environmental Alliance.

Moran, D. 1994. "Contingent Valuation and Biodiversity: Measuring the User Surplus of Kenyan Protected Areas." Working Paper GEC 94-00. CSERGE, University College London and University of East Anglia.

Munansinghe, M., and W. Cruz. 1995. *Economywide Policies and the Environment: Lessons from Experience*. World Bank Environmental Paper 10. Washington, D.C.: World Bank.

Mwanthi, M., and V. Kimani. n.d. "Agro-chemicals: A Potential Hazard to Kenyan Smallholder Farmers." Paper presented to the IDRC Pesticides Symposium. Ottawa, Ontario: International Development Research Council.

Naitore, J. 1995. "Lake is Choking to Death." *Sunday Standard* (July 23).

National Environmental Secretariat. 1981. *Kenya: Report on Environment and Development*. Nairobi: United Nations Environment Programme.

Norton-Griffiths, M. 1995. "The Opportunity Cost of Biodiversity Conservation in Kenya." *Ecological Economics* 12: 125–39.

Partow, H. 1992. "Pesticides: Agents of Exploitation, the Case of Kenya." Mimeo. Environmental Liaison Centre International, Nairobi.

Reed, D., ed. 1992. *Structural Adjustment and the Environment*. Oxford: Westview Press.

_____. 1996. *Structural Adjustment, the Environment, and Sustainable Development*. London: Earthscan.

Repetto, R. 1993. "Trade and Environment Policies: Achieving Complementarities and Avoiding Conflicts." WRI *Issues and Ideas*. World Resources Institute, Washington, D.C.

Tyler, G.J. 1996. "The Contribution of Community Based Wildlife to Tourism in Botswana." Mimeo. University of Oxford.

Unemo, L. 1993. "Botswana, Environmental Impact of Government Policies and External Shocks in Botswana—A CGE Approach." Working Paper 26, Beijer Institute, Stockholm.

UNEP (United Nations Environment Programme). 1987. *Kenya: State of the Environment Report.* Nairobi: UNEP.

Chapter 7

Fuel Prices, Woodlands and Woodfuel Markets in the Sahel

An integrated economic-ecological model

Kenneth M. Chomitz,
Charles Griffiths, and Jyotsna Puri

1. Introduction

In the Sahel as in many parts of the world, there has long been concern that overexploitation of woodlands for woodfuels leads to a vicious circle of environmental degradation, rising fuel prices, and increasing poverty (Schreiber and Cleaver 1994). In this stylized story, urban demand for charcoal and fuelwood leads to ever-widening circles of periurban deforestation, as open-access areas are 'mined' for energy. Urban fuel costs increase as the supplies must be brought in from ever more distant areas.

In principle, this dynamic is influenced by trade and fiscal policies related to modern fuels. Kerosene and LPG can substitute for woodfuels. If cheap enough and reliably distributed, they could act as a backstop technology, limiting price rises of woodfuels and therefore arresting the expansion of deforestation. On the other hand, higher motor fuel prices could accelerate the transition away from woodfuels. Because the urban wholesale price of woodfuels depends mostly on transport cost, higher motor fuel prices restrict the exploitable radius around cities, boosting woodfuel prices and increasing the likelihood of a transition to a backstop fuel.

Prices of kerosene, gasoline, and other fuels vary considerably between countries. This variation is partly due to geography but mostly due to policy. Some countries subsidize kerosene with the explicit goal of reducing pressures on forests and woodlands. In others, though, modern fuels are well above world prices as a result of policies affecting petroleum product trade, manufacture, procurement, distribution, and taxation. Trade liberalization could therefore result in substantial price changes.

Other policies could also modulate the relationship between fuel markets and the environment by affecting supply or demand. Niger has encouraged conversion of open access areas to community management while taxing woodfuels produced from unmanaged areas. In many places, attempts have been made to promote or subsidize high-efficiency woodstoves, and kerosene stoves, as means of reducing energy demand. Finally, policies affecting the cost and competitiveness of transport could have a large effect on the supply price of woodfuels, and on the distribution of benefits from wood production.

While these policies all have plausible impacts on fuel prices and land degradation, the actual magnitude of the impacts depends on the interaction of woodland ecology with the behavior of consumers, producers, and transporters. How quick are consumers to substitute kerosene for charcoal? When do producers switch from wood to charcoal? How fast does the frontier of exploitation expand as prices go up? How fast do exploited woodlands regrow? Are woodlands being cleared for agricultural expansion in any case? Policy impacts depend on the interaction of a complex system of actors, and it is difficult to make *a priori* impact predictions.

This paper demonstrates a simulation model for analyzing the interrelations between urban fuel markets and rural land cover, building on an earlier effort (Chomitz and Griffiths 1997) and similar in spirit to Hofstad (1997). Like those models, the one presented here uses a von Thünen-style supply function for woodfuels. Unlike those models, the present one links the supply function to a demand function which allows substitution among fuels, and between fuel and other goods. The model presented here consists of an urban fuel demand module; a spatially disaggregate woodfuel supply module employing GIS data on land cover and biomass; and a module describing woodland regrowth in response to extraction. The modules, which can be elaborated to any desired degree of detail, are integrated through a mechanism which solves for equilibrium prices across the landscape.

The model is used to simulate the ecological and economic consequences of alternative fuel pricing situations in a generic Sahelian setting. The principal question is the extent to which policy or market-driven changes in the relative prices of modern and traditional fuels can affect woodland degradation, rural incomes, and urban fuel consumption. The model also serves to illustrate an approach for linking plot-based land use models with sectoral or macroeconomic models, which may be useful for examining deforestation and land use change dynamics in a variety of settings.

A benefit of constructing such a model is that the need to specify parameters highlights areas of uncertainty. Those areas are many, despite years of attention to these issues. An underlying theme of the paper is that our understanding of policy-environment-poverty linkages depends a great deal on understanding those basic parameters. Nonetheless, sensitivity analysis allows some conclusions to be drawn.

The plan of the paper is as follows. The next section reviews background material on the nature of the fuel market–woodland degradation linkage, the relation between policies and fuel prices, and the impact of fuel prices on woodfuel consumption. The third section describes the model and data. Results and conclusions follow.

2. Background

Fuelwood demand and woodland degradation – an environmental and economic problem of uncertain dimensions

Concern about the fuelwood-woodland degradation linkage – especially in the Sahel – is long-standing. Studies in the early 1980's, for instance, warned that woodlands were being rapidly depleted, with serious consequences (de Montalembert and Clément 1983). Loss of woodlands would result in high fuel prices in urban areas. It could also increase fuel-gathering time in rural areas, and reduce soil fertility as rural dwellers turned to dung as a fuel source (Schreiber and Cleaver 1994). Cattle would lose crucial sources of browse during the long dry season. Loss of woodland cover, on some types of soils, can lead to biological processes which seal the soil and result in perhaps irreversible desertization (Le Houérou 1989, p. 94).

More recently, a number of authors have questioned the degree to which this "conventional wisdom" describes the Sahel and other areas (Nichol 1988; Leach and Mearns 1988; Benjaminsen 1993; Leach and Fairhead 1994; Dewees 1995; RPTES 1995; Wilton 1996; Foley and others 1997). At issue are such things as:

- The rate at which periurban deforestation is taking place
- The standing stock of biomass
- The relative roles of agricultural expansion, woodfuel exploitation, and climatic fluctuations in causing deforestation
- The price-elasticity of demand for fuels
- The degree to which woodland degradation is irreversible
- The degree to which woodfuels are supplied from dead trees, agricultural land clearing, or as a coproduct of farming.

The newer view suggests that agricultural land clearing, rather than woodfuel exploitation, plays a major role in loss of woodlands, that stocks and growth rates might be higher than had been supposed, and that land-clearing might be slower. This is essentially an empirical debate about the magnitudes of various processes and their impacts. To a large extent it can be resolved empirically. Large scale time-series studies of land use change, such as those currently being undertaken in Senegal[1] and Nigeria[2], will help to resolve some of the questions. Simulation models such as the one presented here can use these studies' findings to better describe the complex interactions of agricultural, transport, and fuel markets. In particular, they can disentangle the effects of woodfuel-driven degradation from other causes of land cover change.

Fuel price policies

Barnes (1992) documents wide variation in kerosene prices between countries, ranging from about $0.16/gallon in Mexico, Peru, and Burma to more than $2.00 in Malawi and Burundi (mean data for late 70s and early 80s). Similarly, gasoline prices vary widely. A 1997 survey found that gasoline pump prices in Sub-Saharan Africa ranged from $0.13/liter in Nigeria to about $0.70 in Niger, Burkina Faso, Chad, and Mali, to $1.14 in Uganda.[3]

Fiscal policy drives some of this variation. Indonesia and Nigeria subsidize kerosene, in part with the rationale of reducing pressure on forest resources. Though shortages at the official rate are common in some subsidizing countries, these subsidies can have an impact on price. ESMAP (1993a) for instance reports that kerosene prices in northern Nigeria are only one-quarter of economic prices. Other countries, such as Burkina Faso and Mauritania, have taxed kerosene. Many countries tax motor fuels as a means of cross-subsidizing household fuels, raising general revenues, or conserving foreign exchange (Gately and Streifel 1997). Petroleum products in general account for 40 percent of fiscal revenues in sub-Saharan Africa and absorb 20 percent to 35 percent of foreign exchange earnings (Schloss 1993).

In many African countries, the prices of petroleum products are driven up by a variety of policies beside taxation. A comprehensive study of sub-Saharan Africa (Cuneo e Associati 1993; Mayorga-Alba 1993) found three sources of inefficiency. Procurement practices are hampered by high costs, poor bidding practices, and distorted pricing policies. Refining costs are high because protected local refiners operate small, antiquated, underutilized equipment. Inland distribution costs are high because of lack of competition, poor infrastructure, and distribution systems which do not take advantage of opportunities for cross-national economies of scope and scale. On average, rectification of these inefficiencies could realize savings of 13 percent of the cost of petroleum products (Mayorga-Alba 1993). The savings would be higher in some countries, with potential savings of about 25 percent in Chad and Niger, for example (Cuneo e Associati 1992, p. 15).

Woodfuel supply and demand policies

There has long been interest in reducing woodfuel demand by promoting the diffusion of high-efficiency woodstoves. The underlying assumption has been that energy demand is inelastic, so that decreasing the effective price of energy (by providing more cooking services per kilogram of wood) results in lower, not higher, wood consumption. In practice, the stoves have often proved unattractive to consumers, and where adopted yielded at most modest fuel savings[4] (Barnes, Openshaw, Smith and van der Plas 1993; Wilton 1996).

On the supply side, taxes on fuelwood and charcoal have often been levied both for revenue and in order to conserve the resource. However, collection rates have generally been low. More recently, attention has focused on the dual approach of securing community tenure over woodlands while levying a tax on woodfuels coming from remaining open-access areas (see Foley and others 1997, for a detailed description). As demonstrated in the Niger Household Energy Project, this involves setting up approved rural markets linked to communities that are granted woodland tenure rights, and agree to harvest quotas and approved harvesting techniques. Management is thought to increase the sustainable yield of wood, though it involves forgoing the profits of 'mining' all salable wood. Purchasers from these markets pay a small levy which supports community development. Those who gather woodfuel from unmanaged areas, and therefore do not have proof of purchase from an approved market, must pay a higher tax, enforced at roadside checkpoints. This tax is Pigouvian in intent, correcting for the dynamic costs of woodcutting (Wiedenmann 1991)—that is, the open-access woodcutter's lack of concern for his impact on future harvests. It is also intended to encourage transporters to buy from rural markets rather than harvest from open-access areas or steal from managed areas. Its effectiveness in doing so will depend on the spatial distribution (and hence locational rents) of managed and unmanaged producers, on their relative production levels, and on the demand elasticity for woodfuels (Chomitz and Griffiths 1997).

Price elasticities and subsitution

Policies that affect fuel prices will affect the fuel market-deforestation nexus only if consumers are price-sensitive in their choice of fuels or their overall consumption of energy. Own-price and cross-price elasticities have been difficult to measure in cross-sectional household data due to lack of variation (Barnes and others 1998). There are relatively few large-sample household studies. Kidane (1991) finds relatively inelastic demand for fuelwood in urban Ethiopia (own-price elasticity = -.37), and no cross-price effects with agricultural residues or modern fuels. However, experience shows that large changes in the price ratio of alternative fuels can bring about rapid, massive shifts between fuels. Barnes and others (1998, p. 46–7) describe how such shifts occurred in relatively short periods in Thailand, due to the imposition of a ban on logging, and in Zambia, due to a temporary interruption of charcoal supply. They suggest that cross-national analysis of prices, market availability, and consumption patterns can take advantage of considerable cross-variation in relative fuel prices and give a more accurate picture of consumer price-responsiveness and fuel substitution behavior. Barnes and others report energy choice and conditional energy demand estimates using a data set with observations on each of five income classes for 45 cities. They find substantial own-price and cross-price fuel elasticities, as well as strong access effects.

3. Model

A spatial price equilibrium model

The model assumes that all fuel consumption takes place at a single urban market. There are four fuels—wood, charcoal, kerosene, and LPG—used primarily for cooking. Kerosene and LPG are imported, and their prices are set exogenously. Wood and charcoal are supplied from surrounding woodland areas. Supply of these fuels does not compete with the supply of biomass to rural consumers, who are assumed to obtain energy from crop residues and unmarketable wood sources.

Market equilibrium is determined annually through aggregate demand and supply equations. With time subscripts suppressed:

$$QD_i = QD_i(p_{0c}, p_{0w}, p_{0k}, p_{0l})\ [i=w,c,k,l];$$
$$QS_i = QS_i(p_{0c}, p_{0w})\ [i=w,c];$$
$$QS_i = QD_i \qquad [i=w,c,k,l],$$

where:

i indexes the four fuels (wood, charcoal, kerosene, LPG)

p_{0i} is the price at the market center, expressed in terms of end-use energy units.

The model is implemented as a GAUSS program, which integrates supply, demand, regrowth, and accounting procedures and uses a grid search to solve for the market-clearing values of p_{0c} and p_{0w}. The program is available from the authors on request.

Supply and change in biomass

Using data in a GIS (geographic information system), the landscape is gridded into 1 square kilometer (100 hectare) cells, and supply is modeled at each cell. Cells are classified according to four land cover types: grassland, bushland, woodland, and other (including agriculture, scrubland, inundated grasslands, and settlements). The first three types may be in two tenure categories: unmanaged (open-access) and managed. The land use types differ in maximum biomass and in biomass growth rates.

Each cell has an associated transport cost for supplying the market. GIS methods were used to calculate the cheapest path to the market, allowing for relative differences in travel cost on and off roads (see figure). The terrain-adjusted distance $_j$ to market for cell j was scaled by a unit cost per ton-mile of transport to yield the cost per ton of transporting fuel from cell j to the market. The 'farmgate' price p_{ji} of fuel i at cell j is therefore:

$$p_{ji} = max[0,\ p_{0i}\text{-}retail\ markup_i - (unit\ cost\ of\ transport) \cdot distance_j]$$

Suppliers in cell j may be resident (if the cell is managed), or not (if it is open-access). Supply is offered from the cell if at least one woodfuel has a positive 'farmgate' price. Charcoal is offered if $p_{cj} > p_{wj}$, and $p_{cj} >$ *production cost*$_c$; wood is offered if $p_{wj} > p_{cj}$ and $p_{wj} >$ *production cost*$_w$, where production cost includes the costs of cutting and charcoaling. Although charcoal's price is generally higher (because it has a higher energy content per gram), a kilogram of wood yields only 120 to 200 grams of charcoal. The result is a von Thünen landscape in which areas near the market supply wood, because avoidance of the charcoal conversion losses outweighs the higher transport cost per unit of useful energy; areas further out supply charcoal; and those beyond the economic frontier supply nothing to the central market.

The amount of biomass cut, converted, and sold depends on the land cover type and tenure in the cell. Managed areas are assumed to be bound by a management plan, and market only the cell's sustainable yield. Exploiters of open-access areas are arbitrarily assumed to cut a fixed fraction of available biomass each year in economically exploitable cells.

These assumptions define the cell-specific supply of woodfuels *i*:

$$qs_{ji} = qs(p_{ji}, biomass_j, land\ cover_j, tenure_j)$$

Biomass in the cell is decremented by the amount supplied. A growth function then increments the biomass by an amount which depends on the land cover and tenure, with more rapid regrowth in managed areas.[5] Introducing time subscripts:

$$biomass_{jt} = biomass_{j,t-1} - qs_{jw,t-1} - e^{-1} qs_{jc,t-1} + growth\ (land\ cover\ type,\ tenure\ type)$$

where *e* is the charcoaling efficiency (charcoal yield as a proportion of wood input).

The aggregate supply is the sum over all cells *j*:

$$QS_i(p_{0c}, p_{0w}; unit\ cost\ of\ transport) = S_j\ qs_{ji}$$

The unit transport cost depends on the cost of motor fuel, which is exogenously given.

Data and parameters for the supply model were drawn from information on Chad (ESMAP 1993a; van der Plas and Gutierrez 1996). (There is however no intent to analyze the Chadian situation, since the scenarios to be examined deliberately impose simplifying assumptions in order to sharpen the results.)

The biomass data are based on a land-cover classification of 20-meter resolution remote sensing data for an area of approximately 20,000 square kilometers, representing the woodfuel catchment area for N'Djamena, the capital of Chad (see Quarmby and others 1996). The classification distinguishes several types of woodland and savanna. Applying biomass density factors, we aggregated this information into a 1 km grid of biomass density. Information on road and village locations was used to impute relative travel costs from each cell to the central market, allowing for differential on and off road travel costs. Further details on parameters are described in Chomitz and Griffiths (1997).

Demand

A pragmatic two-stage aggregate demand function models first the share of end-use energy demand (expressed in joules) allocated to each of the three fuels; and then the total quantity of energy demanded, given the fuel-share-weighted effective price of energy.

The shares equations use a multinomial logit-like specification which ensures that shares are bounded between 0 and 1, and sum to 1; captures the intuition that shares may change rapidly, in a logistic fashion, as two fuels approach the same effective price per joule; and yet allows for asymptotic non-zero shares for 'expensive' forms of energy, reflecting specialized, less-substitutable uses of each energy form. The shares of energy consumed in the forms of wood, charcoal, kerosene, and LPG are given as:

$$s_i = exp(x_i)/\Sigma_j exp(x_j), \qquad (1)$$

where

$$x_i = \alpha_i + \beta_i ln\ y + \Sigma_{j \neq kerosene}\ \gamma_{ij}\ ln(p_{0j}/p_{0k}), \qquad (2)$$

(with the coefficients normalized to zero for *i=kerosene*)

y is mean income per capita

and prices are expressed per unit of effective energy (end-use, allowing for stove efficiency).

In the simulations reported here, total demand for end-use energy is taken as price-inelastic. However, the model allows total demand for end-use energy QED to be determined as:

$$QED(y,p) = ky\theta^1 \bullet (price\ index)\theta^2,$$

where

$k\ \theta_1$ and θ_2 are parameters

p is the vector of fuel prices

$$price\ index = \Sigma_i\ s_i \bullet p_{0i}$$

The shares function was constructed using estimates based on the 45-city cross-national data described in Barnes and others (1998). The source data were derived from surveys of 20,000 households in 12 countries in 1988. We used city-level aggregate data. The sample was restricted to cities where all four fuels were consumed.[6] From (1) and (2),

$$ln\ (q_i/q_{kerosene}) = x_i$$

where $q_i/q_{kerosene}$ is the ratio of consumption of fuel *i* to the reference fuel, kerosene. This equation was estimated for each fuel, and measuring quantity in joules. The coefficients were then used to construct

(1), after correcting the constants so that predicted ratios were in terms of end-use energy. The estimated equations are shown in table 7.1.

The table shows negative own-price elasticities as expected. For instance, equation 2 shows an elasticity of substitution of charcoal with respect to kerosene of –4, significant at the 1 percent level. The cross price elasticities have to interpreted in light of the system as a whole and these are best seen graphically.

Figure 7.1 shows the actual versus predicted share of kerosene in end-use energy (among kerosene, LPG, wood, and charcoal), based on equation 1, showing that this somewhat convoluted function represents the data reasonably well. Figure 7.2 shows the predicted shares of end-use energy implied by equation 1, as a function of changes in the price of kerosene.[7] As kerosene prices decrease, the graph shows a strong shift into kerosene from wood, and to a lesser extent from charcoal. The shift takes place somewhat below the point where kerosene is price-equivalent (in terms of end-use energy), meaning that some disutility is attached to the use of wood caused by for instance, the emission of smoke and the awkwardness of handling and storing wood. Figure 7.3 shows how energy shares react to changes in charcoal price. Holding other prices constant, there is a strong shift from charcoal towards wood as charcoal prices increase, but relatively little substitution into kerosene.

4. Results

A baseline scenario was run for 10 years. Kerosene and LPG start with a negligible share; charcoal is the predominant fuel, but wood is still widely used. To focus attention on the mutual impact of prices and resource depletion, income is held constant over the simulation period, and there is no allowance for conversion of land to agriculture (which may increase short term supply but decrease long term supply of woodfuels). The model also assumes that all woodlands are open-access rather than managed resources. Population grows at 4 percent annually. The

Table 7.1 Estimated relative fuel demands

Equation	*Obs*	*R-sq*	*F*	*P*
lnQ_wk	23	0.8369	23.08369	0
lnQ_ck	23	0.7304	12.19028	0.0001
lnQ_lk	23	0.7602	14.26686	0

Equation 1 *ln (wood/kerosene) Quantity (joules)*	*Coefficient*	*t-statistic*	*P>|t|*
ln (charcoal/kerosene)price	-2.36684	-4.381	0
ln (lpg/kerosene) price	-2.090107	-2.824	0.011
ln (wood/kerosene) price	-0.754981	-1.648	0.117
ln (income per capita)	1.875554	4.099	0.001
constant	-5.298216	-3.07	0.007

Equation 2 *ln (charcoal/Kerosene) Quantity (joules)*	*Coefficient*	*t-statistic*	*P>|t|*
ln (charcoal/kerosene)price	-4.024249	-4.51	0
ln (lpg/kerosene) price	-2.561514	-2.096	0.051
ln (wood/kerosene) price	1.636667	2.163	0.044
ln (income per capita)	3.492979	4.622	0
constant	-10.36086	-3.634	0.002

Equation 3 *ln (LPG/Kerosene) Quantity (joules)*	*Coefficient*	*t-statistic*	*P>|t|*
ln (charcoal/kerosene)price	-0.626344	-0.807	0.43
ln (lpg/kerosene) price	-4.032859	-3.795	0.001
ln (wood/kerosene) price	0.4145364	0.63	0.536
ln (income per capita)	3.65188	5.558	0
constant	-10.93914	-4.414	0

Note: Price and quantity ratios are based on energy content of fuels and are not adjusted for end-use efficiency.

Figure 7.1 Actual vs. predicted kerosene share

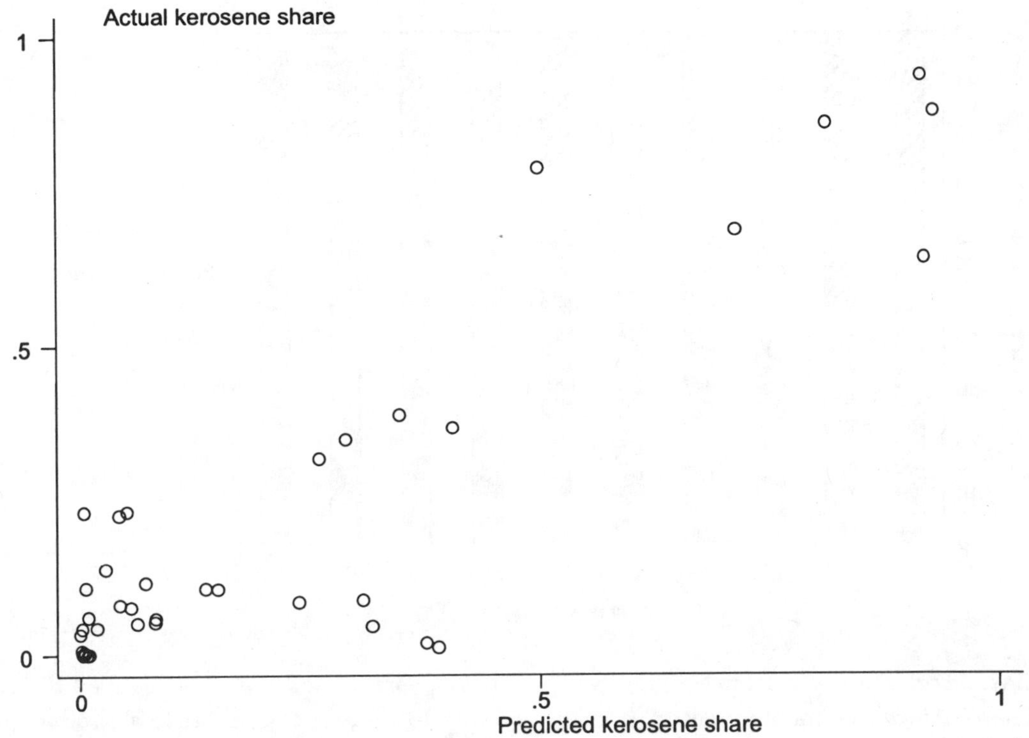

Figure 7.2 End-use energy shares as a function of kerosene price

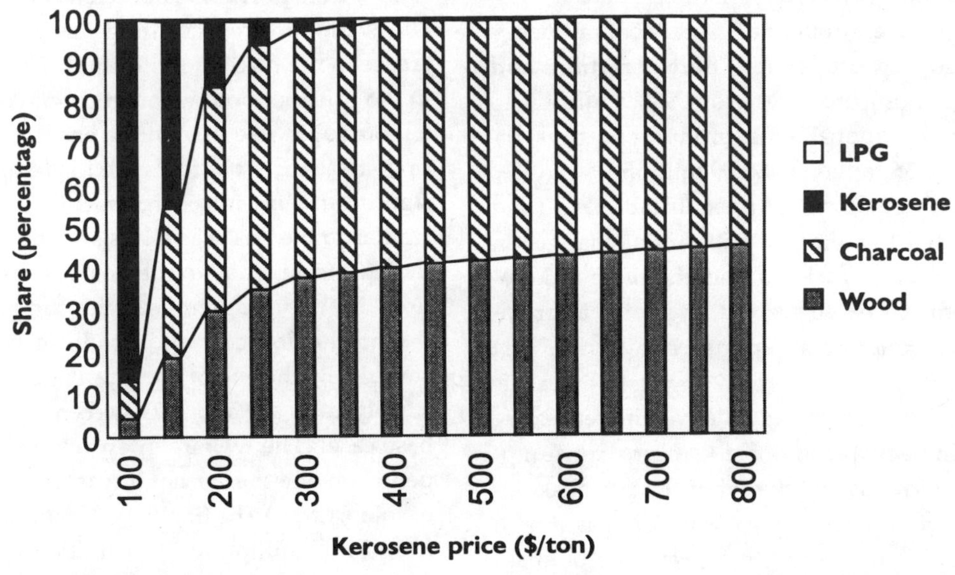

overall demand for end-use energy is taken to be perfectly inelastic.

The baseline run shows a nearly constant rate of depletion of biomass (see Appendix table A7.1). Stocks in the study area are run down from 7.9 million tons to 5.6 million tons over a decade. The frontier of fuelwood production, initially 76 kilometers from the market, moves out to 130 kilometers. The charcoal frontier moves from 106 to 178 kilometers. The environmental impact is evident from a comparison of the panels of the maps at the end of this section, showing the virtual elimination of close-in biomass.

Figure 7.3 End-use energy shares as a function of charcoal prices

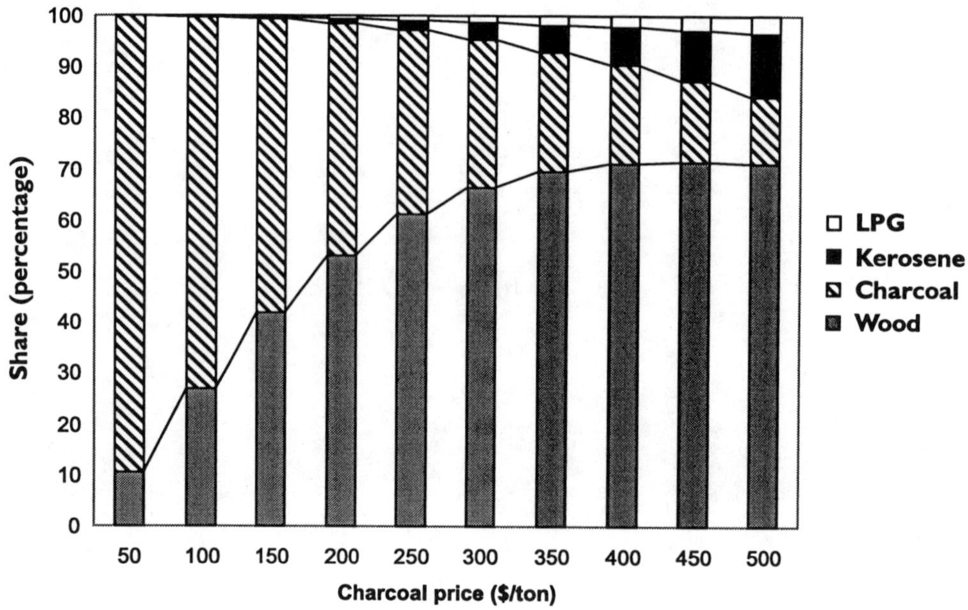

The retail wood price increases from US $45/ton to $55, while charcoal increases more modestly, from $146/ton to $159.[8] These price increases are not enough to induce much substitution into kerosene or LPG; while absolute consumption increases faster than population growth, the share of modern fuels remains negligible throughout. Total cost of energy supply (including production, transportation, and retail distribution) increases from $10.7 million to $17.5 million. Locational rents (producer surplus) increase from $0.56 million to $1.09 million.

Two comparison runs (Appendix tables A7.2 and A7.3) examined the effect of substantial changes in the costs of modern fuels. In one, the price of kerosene was reduced by 40 percent, to a level approximating the current lowest reported retail prices (net of tax) in the world. As figure 7.2 suggests, even this was not sufficient to make a qualitative difference. The immediate impact was to boost kerosene consumption twelve-fold, but by the end of the period kerosene's share of end-use energy was still less than 6 percent. Relative to the base case, retained biomass was just 2 percent higher and the charcoal frontier just 3 kilometers closer-in. Part of the reason for the lack of impact, though, is that the shift into kerosene has come from wood, rather than charcoal (which uses more biomass). At the end of the simulation period, wood consumption is 12 percent lower than the base case, while charcoal consumption is only 2 percent lower. Charcoal and wood prices are little changed relative to the base case, as are total production costs. Total supply costs, and producer rents, are about the same as in the base case.

In the second comparison run, the cost per ton-mile of transport was doubled from its initial value of $0.18/ton-km, representing an extremely large increase in the price of motor fuel. The effect is a jump in the prices of both wood and charcoal, followed by a more rapid rise than in the base case. However the price rises for woodfuels are inadequate to induce a significant shift into kerosene. Thus biomass loss is similar to the base case. It is slightly greater because the shift from wood to charcoal results in more depletion. The main difference with the base case is that the production cost and producer surplus increase sharply. By the end of the supply period, the total fuel supply costs are about 21 percent higher than in the base case. (The welfare interpretation of this rise depends on whether or not it was due to an increase in gasoline taxes.) The final-year locational rents increase from $1.09 million to $1.97 million, as closer-in harvesters benefit from higher prices. This is a transfer from consumers, who in the final year spend 25 percent more than in the base case.

5. Discussion and Conclusions

In sum, gross perturbations of kerosene and gasoline prices had almost no impact on the rate of woodland degradation. This is not surprising in light of the demand functions, which imply that significant transitions take place only at substantially subsidized kerosene prices or when woodfuels are brought in from much greater distances than shown here. It suggests that reductions in policy distortions, while desirable on many grounds, may often have less environmental impact than might be hoped. Reductions in gasoline taxes will have distributional effects, shifting rents away from harvesters—who could be urban-based transporters, or rural villagers—to urban consumers.

These conclusions need to be qualified with an admission of the tentative nature of many of the underlying parameters. The demand function is constructed from cross-country data and does not yet incorporate any degree of price elasticity for overall energy demand. Other important unknowns include the impact of agricultural conversion on short and long term woodfuel supply, and the rate at which unmanaged woodlands regenerate. We also lack information on the extent to which open-access harvesters secure locational rents, rather than incurring increasing search and harvest costs as woodland densities decline.

However, we have provided a framework into which this information can be incorporated, and which allows sensitivity analysis for parameters which are difficult to gather. The framework also provides an example of how macro and sectoral economic processes can be linked to spatially explicit environmental conditions. The full potential of this framework will be realized in applications which require spatial analysis, including impacts of fuel markets on carbon emissions, and impacts of alternative geographical patterns of establishing managed woodlands.

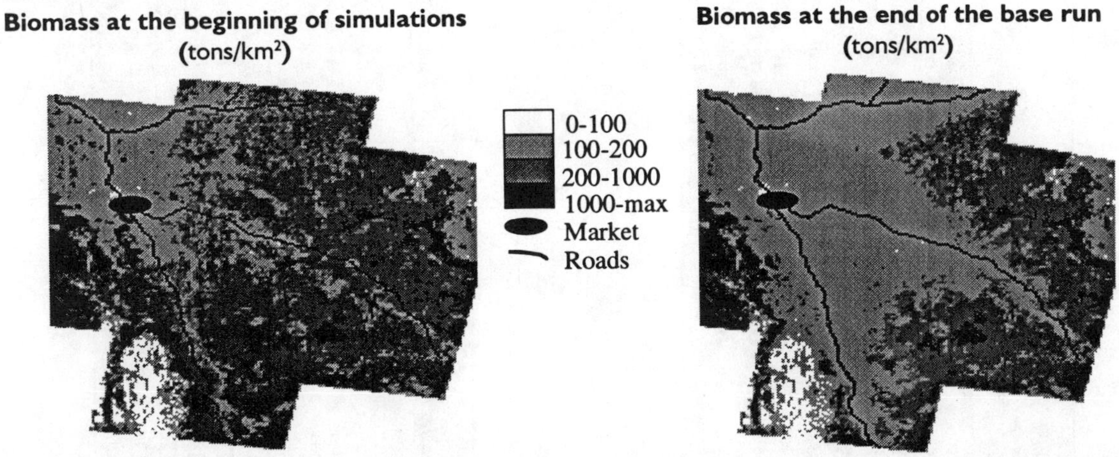

Appendix Table A7.1 Base run

Year	Total biomass	Wood price	Charcoal price	Quantity wood	Quantity charcoal	Quantity kerosene	Quantity LPG	Locational rents	Total supply cost	Wood frontier	Charcoal frontier
	Tons	$/Ton	$/Ton	Tons	Tons	Tons	Tons	$	$	Kms	Kms
1	7921152.	44.80	146.22	88,759	45,711	136	44	559,260	10,214,746	76.18	106.32
2	7652906.	46.32	147.96	89,022	48,713	144	47	609,382	10,843,023	84.67	115.97
3	7386834.	47.78	149.64	89,517	51,755	152	50	659,503	11,490,205	92.73	125.31
4	7122593.	49.01	151.05	90,502	54,751	161	53	691,545	12,149,373	99.57	133.14
5	6862033.	50.16	152.34	91,685	57,810	169	56	731,286	12,817,601	105.97	140.34
6	6601790.	51.18	153.61	93,261	60,867	178	59	777,982	13,495,979	111.65	147.39
7	6341789.	52.12	155.03	95,205	63,933	188	63	843,772	14,189,699	116.89	155.24
8	6082824.	52.99	156.45	97,436	67,045	199	66	918,489	14,902,830	121.71	163.12
9	5824806.	53.79	157.87	99,936	70,216	211	70	1,001,255	15,638,587	126.16	171.02
10	5563478.	54.55	159.30	102,661	73,467	224	75	1,092,535	16,400,328	130.35	178.96

Note: Kerosene price - $432.50/ton; LPG price - $1,250/ton.

Appendix Table A7.2 Reduced kerosene price run

Year	Total Biomass	Wood price	Charcoal price	Quantity wood	Quantity charcoal	Quantity kerosene	Quantity LPG	Locational rents	Total supply cost	Wood frontier	Charcoal frontier
	Tons	$/Ton	$/Ton	Tons	Tons	Tons	Tons	$	$	Kms	Kms
1	7,932,459	44.32	146.02	79,148	45,548	1,723	64	509,235	10,175,872	73.54	105.18
2	7,672,860	45.84	147.72	79,164	48,442	1,817	68	557,679	10,783,045	81.98	114.66
3	7,417,216	47.24	149.35	79,513	51,330	1,916	72	600,753	11,407,767	89.73	123.71
4	7,162,684	48.47	150.76	80,203	54,225	2,015	76	633,560	12,046,243	96.60	131.53
5	6,911,731	49.57	152.00	81,196	57,142	2,115	80	665,996	12,693,503	102.72	138.45
6	6,662,235	50.54	153.23	82,553	60,050	2,224	84	704,938	13,350,908	108.11	145.24
7	6,413,085	51.45	154.54	84,172	62,980	2,345	89	761,075	14,021,629	113.12	152.52
8	6,165,290	52.26	155.89	86,101	65,924	2,478	94	825,741	14,710,839	117.63	160.02
9	5,917,597	52.99	157.24	88,298	68,905	2,621	99	896,797	15,421,240	121.71	167.54
10	5,669,309	53.68	158.62	90,703	71,948	2,775	105	976,518	16,156,170	125.52	175.18

Note: Kerosene price - $259.50/ton; LPG price - $1250/ton.

Appendix Table A7.3 Increased transport cost

Year	Total Biomass	Wood price	Charcoal price	Quantity wood	Quantity charcoal	Quantity kerosene	Quantity LPG	Locational rents	Total supply cost	Wood frontier	Charcoal frontier
	Tons	$/Ton	$/Ton	Tons	Tons	Tons	Tons	$	$	Kms	Kms
1	7,908,985	57.03	165.87	70,184	52,258	174	58	1,028,287	11,790,228	72.09	107.75
2	7,629,641	59.75	169.51	69,305	55,651	188	62	1,111,523	12,622,209	79.64	117.84
3	7,353,213	62.44	172.94	68,535	59,129	201	67	1,196,807	13,479,003	87.09	127.37
4	7,078,935	64.83	175.70	68,106	62,618	214	72	1,251,248	14,348,559	93.74	135.06
5	6,807,147	66.89	178.41	68,325	66,005	228	77	1,314,908	15,225,198	99.46	142.56
6	6,536,209	68.81	181.15	68,863	69,412	243	82	1,406,996	16,112,870	104.79	150.17
7	6,265,604	70.56	184.09	69,851	72,795	261	88	1,529,994	17,022,935	109.66	158.36
8	5,995,891	72.08	187.03	71,285	76,162	281	95	1,662,525	17,960,492	113.89	166.51
9	5,726,809	73.54	190.01	72,921	79,608	303	102	1,817,683	18,929,779	117.93	174.79
10	5,456,404	74.83	192.85	74,854	83,107	326	110	1,971,609	19,935,177	121.50	182.70

Note: Kerosene price - $432.50; LPG price - $1250/ton.

Notes

This work was supported by the project on the Social and Environmental Consequences of Growth-oriented Policies. We are grateful to Douglas Barnes for sharing data on household fuel consumption, Neil Quarmby of IS Ltd for providing the GIS data used in this report and to Robert van der Plas and Luis Gutierrez for a variety of parameters and data.

1. The United States Geological Survey and Senegal's Centre de Suivi Ecologique (CSE) are monitoring long-term changes in land cover at 150 sites in Senegal, complemented by the use of aerial videography and remote sensing to monitor land cover change over wider areas. See G. Tappan, E. Wood, A. Hadj, and A. Bodian 1994, "Monitoring Natural Resource Changes in Senegal: Preliminary Evidence from Field Sites," EROS Data Center, Sioux Falls, SD.
2. "The Assessment of Vegetation and Land Use Changes in Nigeria between 1976/78 and 1993/95." Report submitted by Geomatics International Inc. to The Forestry Management, Evaluation and Co-ordinating Unit and the Environmental Management Projection (EMP) for Nigeria, 1998.
3. Data from a June 1997 tabulation by TWUTD, World Bank.
4. Other benefits, such as the health benefits of reduced smoke, may be substantial, however.
5. Not utilized in the simulations reported here.
6. The equations were also run excluding cities with low reported availabilities of any of the fuels. The coefficients were robust save for the own-price elasticity of LPG, which became statistically insignificant and close to zero. Since it is possible that low availability of LPG reflected high price, we used the more intuitive results of table 7.1, which shows a strong substitution between LPG and kerosene.
7. The model was calibrated for the simulations of part 4. Constant terms for each of the ln ratio equations were chosen so as to generate the starting share values; these in turn were based on estimated levels for Chad in 1995.
8. The retail markup is held constant in absolute terms. To the extent that retailing costs include capital costs, they might increase proportionately to the wholesale price, yielding a more rapid run-up in retail prices.

References

Barnes, Douglas F., Jeffrey Dowd, Liu Quan, Kerry Krutilla, and William Hyde. 1998. *The Urban Energy Transition: Energy, Poverty, and the Environment in the Developing World.* World Bank. Processed.

Barnes, Douglas F., Keith Openshaw, Kirk R. Smith and Robert van der Plas. 1993. "The Design and Diffusion of Improved Cooking Stoves." *The World Bank Research Observer* 8(3): 119–141.

Benjaminsen, Tor A. 1993. "Fuelwood and Desertification: Sahel Orthodoxies Discussed on the Basis of Field Data from the Gourma Region of Mali." *Geoforum* 24(4): 397–409.

Chomitz, Kenneth M., and Charles Griffiths. 1997. *An Economic Analysis of Woodfuel Management in the Sahel: The Case of Chad.* World Bank, Policy Research Department: Policy Research Working Paper no. 1788.

Cleaver, Kevin M., and Götz Schreiber. 1994. *Reversing the Spiral: the Population, Agriculture, and Environment Nexus in Sub-Saharan Africa.* Washington DC: World Bank.

Cuneo e Associati. 1992. *Petroleum Products Supply and Distribution in Sub-Saharan Africa: Report on Nigeria and Landlocked Countries.* World Bank. Processed.

Cuneo e Associati. 1993. *Petroleum Products Supply and Distribution in Sub-Saharan Africa: Executive Summary.* World Bank. Processed.

de Montalembert, M.R., and J. Clement. 1983. *Fuelwood Supplies in the Developing Countries.* Rome: FAO. Forestry Paper no. 42.

Dewees, Peter A. 1995. "Fuelwood responses to tree scarcity: The case of woodfuel." In J.E. Michael Arnold and Peter A. Dewees, eds., *Tree Management in Farmer Strategies: Responses to Agricultural Intensification.* Oxford: Oxford University Press.

ESMAP. 1993a *Tchad: Eléments de stratégie pour l'énergie domestique urbaine: Le cas de N'djaména.* Report no. 160/94.

_____. 1993b. *Nigeria: Issues and Options in the Energy Sector.*

Foley and others. 1995. *The Niger Household Energy Project: Promoting Rural Fuelwood Markets and Village Management of Natural Woodlands.* World Bank Technical Paper no. 362, Energy Series.

Gately, Dermot and Shane Streifel. 1997. *The Demand for Oil Products in Developing Countries.* World Bank Discussion paper no. 359.

Hofstad, Ole. 1997. "Woodland Deforestation by Charcoal Supply to Dar es Salaam." *Journal of Environmental Economics and Management* 33(17): 17–32.

Jensen, Axel Martin. 1995. *Examen des Politiques, Strategies, et Programmes du secteur des Energies Traditionelles.* World Bank: AFTPS, January 1995. Processed.

Kidane, Asmerom. 1991. "Demand for energy in rural and urban centres of Ethiopia: an econometric analysis." *Energy Economics* 13: 130–34.

Leach, Gerald, and Robin Mearns. 1988. *Beyond the Woodfuel Crisis: People, Land and Trees in Africa.* London: Earthscan.

Leach, Melissa and James Fairhead. 1994. *The Forest Islands of Kissidougou: Social dynamics of environmental change in West Africa's forest-savanna mosaic.* Report to ESCOR of the Overseas Development Administration.

Le Houérou, Henry N. 1989. *The Grazing Land Ecosystems of the African Sahel.* New York: Springer-Verlag.

Mayorga-Alba, Eleodoro. 1993. "Rationalization of imports, refineries and distribution of petroleum in Sub-Saharan Africa." *Natural Resources Forum* 17(May): 109–16.

Nichol, J.E. 1989. Ecology of fuelwood production in Kano Region, Northern Nigeria. *Journal of Arid Environments* 16: 347–60.

Quarmby, Neil, Andrew Millington and Hugh Vaughn Williams. 1996. Domestic Energy Project: Fuelwood Inventory in the region around N'Djamena. Final report, January 1996. Manchester, U.K.: I.S. Ltd.

RPTES (Review of Policies in the Traditional Energy Sector). 1995. *Regional Report: Senegal-Gambia-Burkina Faso-Mali-Niger.* Maastricht, Netherlands, May: 15–17.

Schloss, Miguel. 1993. "Does Petroleum Procurement and Trade Matter?: The Case of sub-Saharan Africa." *Finance and Development* 30(March): 44–46.

Van der Plas, Robert, and Luis Gutierrez. 1996. Personal communication.

Wiedenmann, Ralf. 1991. "Deforestation from the overexploitation of wood resources as a cooking fuel. A comment on the optimal control model of Hassan and Hertzler." *Energy Economics* 13(2): 81–85.

Wilton, Max. 1996. "Traditional Energy—the West African Experience." World Bank. RPTES Discussion Paper no. 12.

Chapter 8

In Search of Pollution Havens?

Dirty industry in the world economy, 1960-1995

Muthukumara Mani and David Wheeler

1. Introduction

During the past three decades, many poor countries have experienced rapid economic development after adopting liberal economic policies. In manufacturing sectors such as apparel assembly, a "cascading" pattern of growth has accompanied this global movement toward openness. Production has accelerated in progressively poorer countries, as wage increases in rapidly-developing open economies have changed the pattern of comparative advantage. Downward migration of garment assembly has reflected its continuing labor-intensity: Low unit labor costs in poor economies have been sufficient to offset the potential for automated production in higher-wage countries.[1] We might therefore characterize the world garment story as a continuous (and self-defeating) search for "low wage havens" by apparel manufacturers. From the perspective of development economics, this has been salutary: Exports of garments and other light assembly goods have provided the first rung on the ladder of rapid income growth and skills development for millions of poor workers.

Although they are critical factors, relative wages and labor skills are not the only determinants of locational advantage. Other long-recognized factors include the quality and local price of available energy and raw materials, agglomeration economies, and so forth.[2] More recently, attention has turned to the possible impact of differences in environmental regulation. In the OECD economies, stricter regulation means polluters pay more - for pollution control equipment, conversion to cleaner processes, or penalties for unacceptable emissions. This regulatory gap between developed and developing countries could, in principle, produce "pollution havens" analogous to "low wage havens." Pollution-intensive industries (that is, those with low elasticities of substitution between use of the environment and other productive factors) might join labor-intensive industries in the migration from the OECD countries to open developing economies, if the latter remained unregulated and environmental pricing were a significant determinant of comparative advantage.

Have "pollution havens" in fact emerged? In this paper, we examine the record using international information on industrial production, trade and environmental regulation for the period 1960–1995. The paper is organized as follows. In Section 2, we use recent results on the relationship between regulation and development to argue that "pollution havens" must be as transient as "low wage havens:" In the worst case, we would expect to see pollution-intensive sectors follow the "cascading" international growth pattern of garment production. Section 3 draws on several empirical approaches to identify industry sectors which are clearly among the most pollution-intensive. Focusing on these sectors, the rest of the paper examines the evidence on shifts in pollution-intensive production from the OECD to developing economies. Section 4 focuses on the OECD, giving particular attention to the Japanese case. Section 5 considers the experience of developing Asia and Latin America, while Section 6 provides a summary and conclusions.

2. Development, Regulation, and "Pollution Havens"

"Low wage havens" are transient because incomes and wages increase continuously with development. Similarly, recent evidence suggests that "pollution havens," if they exist, may be transient because environmental regulation also increases with development. Dasgupta and others (1996) document the striking correlation between national income per capita and the strictness of environmental regulation. Recent studies of regional income and regulation in China (Wang and Wheeler 1996; Dasgupta and Wheeler 1997) and Indonesia (Pargal and Wheeler 1996) find similar relationships.

Regulation of industrial pollution increases with economic development for two main reasons. First, the demand for environmental quality rises with income, both for aesthetic reasons and because the valuation of pollution damage increases. Secondly, more developed economies have (on average) more highly-developed public institutions and are more capable of enforcing desirable environmental norms.[3] If the income elasticity of regulation is greater than one, then developing countries will not retain a comparative advantage in dirty production. However, the interplay of relative prices and agglomeration economies might lead to a garment-style "cascading" pattern of growth, in which rapid growth of dirty sectors is visible during transitional periods when regulation lags behind the growth of output and income.

3. Defining Dirty Industries

To test for pollution havens, we need a clearly-defined set of "dirty" industries. A conventional approach in the literature has been to identify pollution-intensive sectors as those which have incurred high levels of abatement expenditure per unit of output in the United States and other OECD economies (Robison 1988; Tobey 1990; Mani 1996). By this criterion, five sectors emerge as leading candidates for "dirty industry" status: Iron and Steel, Non-Ferrous Metals, Industrial Chemicals, Pulp and Paper, and Non-Metallic Mineral Products.[4] Another, more direct, approach is to select sectors which rank high on actual emissions intensity (emissions per unit of output). To determine high-ranking sectors by this criterion, we have used detailed emissions intensities by medium for U.S. manufacturing at the 3-digit Standard Industrial Classification (SIC) level, computed by the World Bank in collaboration with the U.S. EPA and the U.S. Census Bureau (Hettige and others 1995). We have computed average sectoral rankings for conventional air pollutants, water pollutants, and heavy metals, with results displayed in table 8.1.

Again, five of the six sectors with highest overall ranks are Iron and Steel, Non-Ferrous Metals, Industrial Chemicals, Pulp and Paper, and Non-Metallic Mineral Products. We have therefore selected them as the "dirty sectors" for this analysis. If there is a significant pollution havens story, it should emerge in their international development history since 1960. However, since this is a comparative advantage story, we need to be sure that it is not confounded by changes in relative prices of factors other than "environment" in which dirty industries may also be intensive.

In fact, it is quite reasonable to suppose that pollution-intensive industries *are* intensive in other inputs, particularly bulk raw materials, energy and land. Pollutants are waste residuals—harmful byproducts of industrial processes which are not profitable to recycle or resell at existing prices (including the price

Table 8.1 Ranking of pollution-intensive industries

Rank	*Air*	*Water*	*Metals*	*Overall*
1	371 Iron and Steel	371 Iron and Steel	372 Non-Ferrous Metals	371 Iron and Steel
2	372 Non-Ferrous Metals	372 Non-Ferrous Metals	371 Iron and Steel	372 Non-Ferrous Metals
3	369 Non-Metallic Min. Prd.	341 Pulp and Paper	351 Industrial Chemicals	351 Industrial Chemicals
4	354 Misc. Petroleum, Coal Prd.	390 Misc. Manufacturing	323 Leather Products	353 Petroleum Refineries
5	341 Pulp and Paper	351 Industrial Chemicals	361 Pottery	369 Non-Metallic Min Prd.
6	353 Petroleum Refineries	352 Other Chemicals	381 Metal Products	341 Pulp and Paper
7	351 Industrial Chemicals	313 Beverages	355 Rubber Products	352 Other Chemicals
8	352 Other Chemicals	311 Food Products	383 Electrical Products	355 Rubber Products
9	331 Wood Products	355 Rubber Products	382 Machinery	323 Leather Products
10	362 Glass Products	353 Petroleum Refineries	369 Non-Metallic Min. Prd.	381 Metal Products

of pollution). The volume of such residuals is, almost tautologically, largest in weight-reducing industries which transform bulk raw materials into primary inputs for industrial production. Such industries should be land intensive, because some bulk material inventories must be stored on-site. They should also be energy-intensive, because transformation processes generally involve the application of high temperature, pressure, and/or mechanical force to raw material inputs. We are agnostic about their capital- and labor-intensity, but these factors are also clearly important for the comparative advantage story.

To test for differential intensities, we have identified the five "cleanest" sectors using the same pollution-intensity rankings employed for table 8.1. They are SIC sectors 321 (Textiles), 382 (Non-Electrical Machinery), 383 (Electrical Machinery), 384 (Transport Equipment), and 385 (Instruments). Using available data from Japan, we have computed energy, land and labor intensities for the five cleanest and dirtiest sectors and compared the results.

The results for energy intensity, displayed in figure 8.1, are very clear: The five dirty sectors are about three times more energy intensive than the five clean sectors, and there is striking uniformity within the two groups. Although there is more within-group variation, the result is basically the same for land intensity (figure 8.2): It is about three times higher in the dirty sectors. Capital intensity is also substantially higher in the dirty sectors, with an average ratio around 2:1 for capital/output (figure 8.3) and investment/output (figure 8.4). Labor intensity shows considerable variation within groups, but the clean sectors are about 40 percent more labor intensive on average (figure 8.5).

Figure 8.1 Energy intensity in Japanese manufacturing

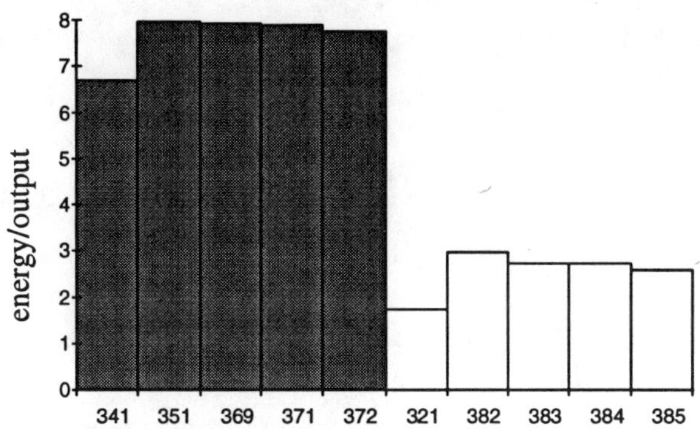

Figure 8.2 Land intensity in Japanese manufacturing

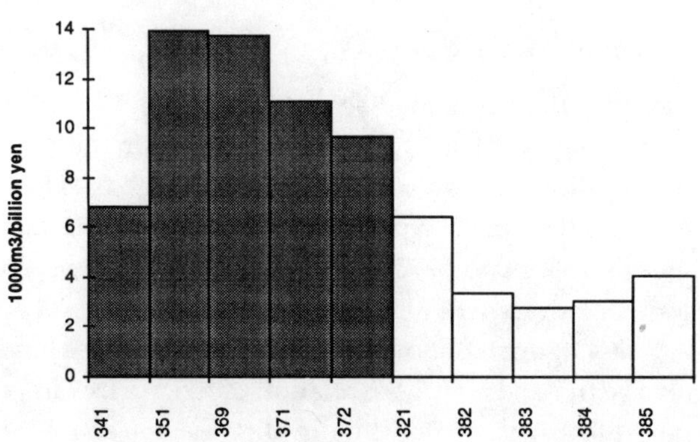

Figure 8.3 Investment/output ratios in Japanese manufacturing, 1972–1991

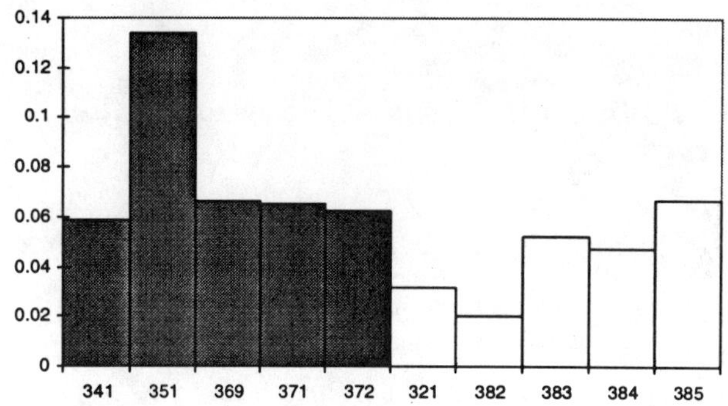

Figure 8.4 Capital/output ratios in Japanese manufacturing, 1985–1989

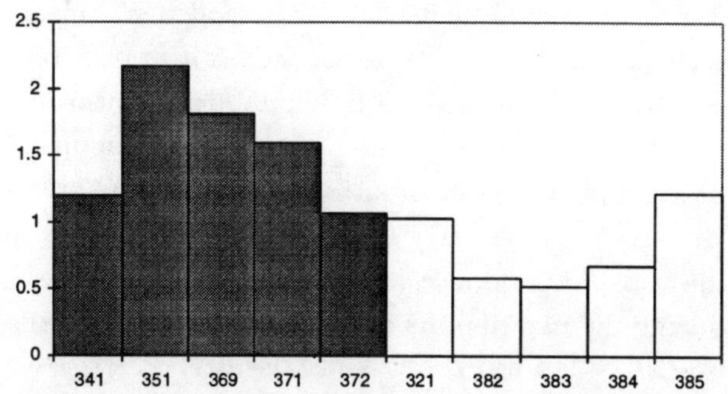

Figure 8.5 Labor intensity in Japanese manufacturing

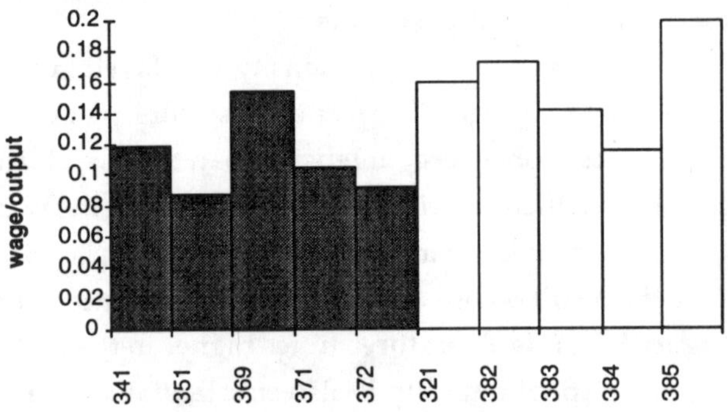

To summarize, our evidence suggests that dirty industries are relatively intensive in capital, energy and land; their clean counterparts are relatively intensive in labor, although the difference is not as striking. Clearly, the pollution havens hypothesis cannot be tested using information on environmental regulation alone. Shifts in pollution-intensive production might also be explained by differences in the relative prices of these other inputs. In the following section, we take a careful look at the relative price story for Japan.

4. Pollution-Intensive Production in the OECD

The Japanese story

The Relative Decline of Pollution-Intensive Sectors

During the past three and one-half decades, Japan has gone through major changes in economic and environmental conditions. As figures 8.6 and 8.7 suggest, these changes have had significant consequences for pollution-intensive industry in Japan. Whether compared to the five cleanest sectors (figure 8.6) or Japanese manufacturing as a whole (figure 8.7), the share of our five dirtiest sectors trended strongly downward during the period 1963-1993. As a proportion of clean-sector production, dirty-sector output dropped from nearly 70 percent in 1963 to about 30 percent in the mid-1990s. As a proportion of total manufacturing production, dirty-sector output dropped from about 25 percent in the early 1960s to about 15 percent in the mid-1990s. Both series show clear breaks in trend during the two periods of rapid energy price escalation, 1973-74 and 1978-80. Since the dirty sectors have relatively high energy intensity, the short-run response to the energy price increases was a "pass-through" to customers and temporary escalation of output value relative to the value of sectors with lower energy intensity. After each break, however, the downward trend quickly reasserted itself. What explains this decline? Obvious candidates are price changes for factors in which the pollution-intensive

Figure 8.6 Japanese production ratio (*polluting/non-polluting*)

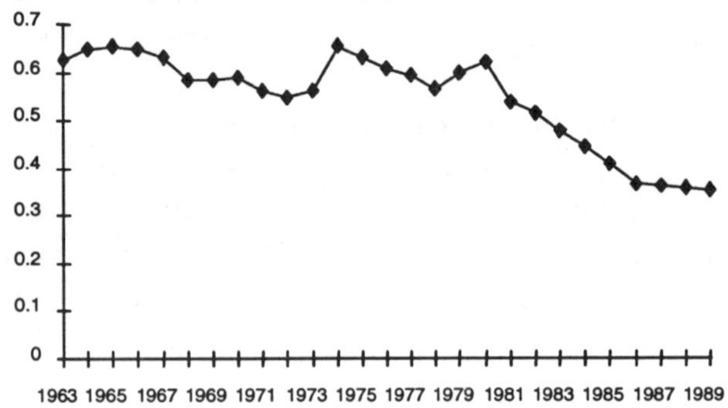

Figure 8.7 Japan's production of polluting products (*as a percentage of total manufacturing*)

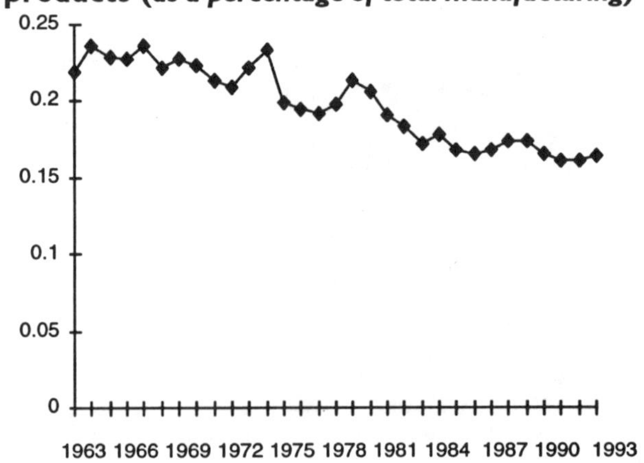

sectors are highly intensive: Energy, land and environment.

Energy and Land Prices

Energy prices escalated sharply in 1973, and this increase may well explain part of the decline in the share of pollution-intensive production in the 1970s. However, relative energy prices were not increasing during the 1960s and 1980s—periods when Japan's dirty industry share was also declining.

As figure 8.8 shows, the past three decades have also witnessed a rapid escalation of land prices in Japan. However, the decline in dirty-sector share began slackening in the 1980s, at precisely the time when

Figure 8.8 Urban commercial land price index (*1990 prices*)

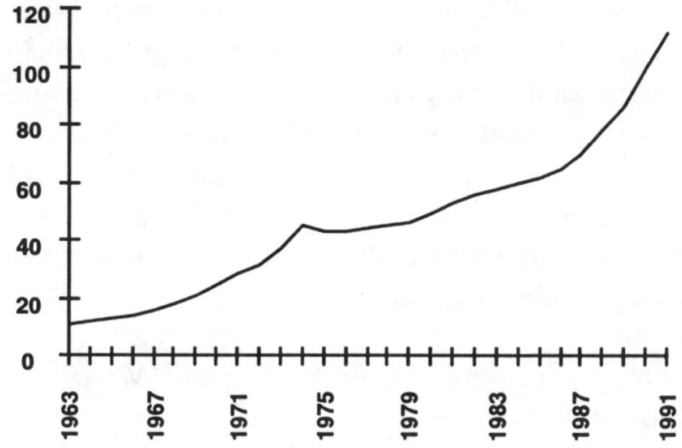

Figure 8.10 Pollution control investment by big enterprises

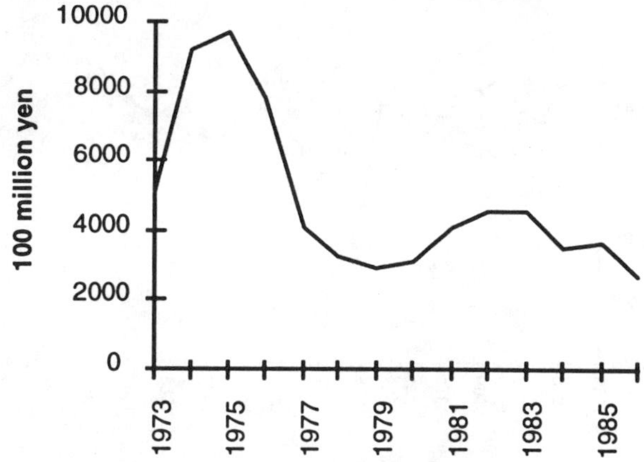

land prices began escalating sharply. Land price increases may therefore have played some role, but it seems unlikely that they were a decisive factor.

The Timing and Impact of Environmental Regulation

Does the timing of stricter environmental regulation in Japan jibe with the pattern of relative decline in pollution-intensive production? Cities like Tokyo, Osaka, and Kyoto enacted some pollution control measures by the mid-1950s, and Japan's first water quality preservation law was enacted in 1958. However, strong opposition from growth- and industry-oriented national ministries hampered the national movement toward stricter regulation until the late 1960s. From 1967 to 1970, regulations covering industrial air and water emissions were enacted in rapid succession. The Japanese Environmental Agency (JEA) was set up in 1971 and, as figure 8.9 shows, its activities grew very rapidly during the 1970s.

Figure 8.9 Japanese Environmental Agency budget

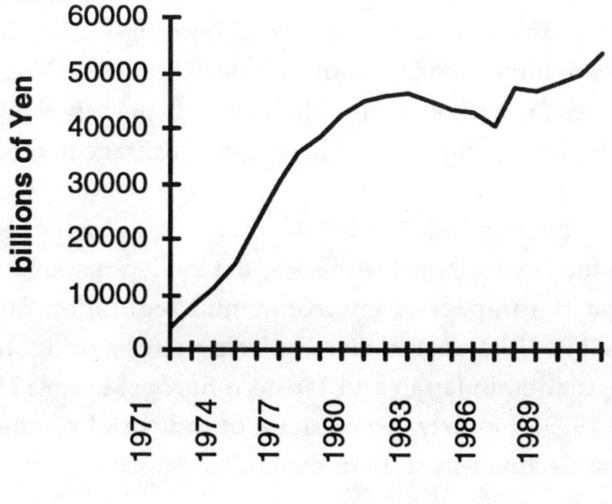

As JEA's regulatory activity increased, Japanese industry went through a period of rapid adjustment to new environmental norms. Figure 8.10 shows that the mid-1970s witnessed a surge of investment in pollution control by Japanese industry. Thus, it is plausible to suppose that tightened regulation had an impact on the relative fortune of pollution-intensive production in Japan during in the 1970s and early '80s. However, tightened regulation cannot explain the decline of pollution-intensive production in the 1960s.

Income growth

Figures 8.6 and 8.7 suggest a consistent pattern of decline in the share of dirty industry from the sixties to the nineties, despite large interim changes in the prices of energy, land and environment. During this entire period, of course, Japanese income per capita increased rapidly. Our five dirty sectors are "basic" industries, whose domestic demand elasticity falls as income increases. Thus, income growth alone may explain a significant part of their relative decline.

Figures 8.11 and 8.12 tell an intriguing story in this context. During the "pre-environmental" period of rapid growth, from 1963 to the mid-1970s, declining trends in both consumption/production and import/export ratios are consistent with the income-elasticity hypothesis. However, in the mid-1970s both ratios reversed course: Production of polluting products slowed relative to consumption, and imports increased much more rapidly than exports. Thus, although relative domestic demand for pollution-

Figure 8.11 Consumption-production ratio of polluting products in Japan

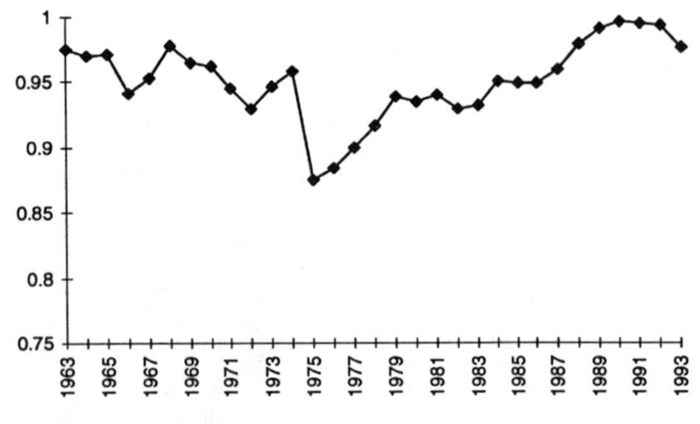

Figure 8.12 Import-export ratio of polluting products in Japan

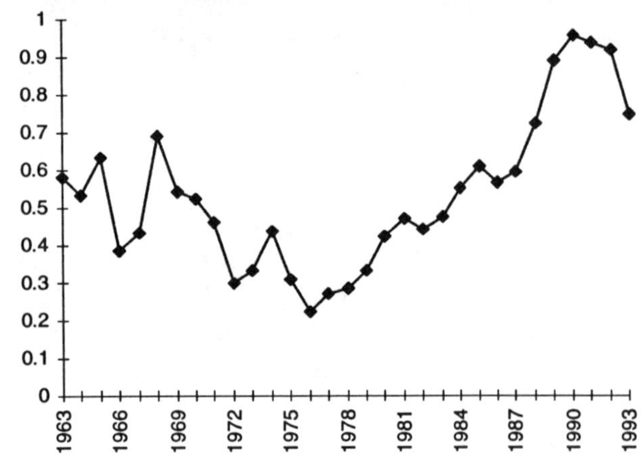

intensive products undoubtedly continued to decline with income growth after 1975, the evidence suggests that the pure "income effect" was outweighed by another factor which suddenly retarded the growth of domestic production and exports. In light of the regression results, the most plausible candidate for this role is increased environmental regulation.

Dirty Industry's "Retreat" from Japan: A Summary Perspective

Many factors can be invoked to explain the relative decline of pollution-intensive industry in Japan since 1963. Although energy and land prices are plausible culprits, our regression analysis suggests that they have not played dominant roles in the story. Lower income elasticities for dirty-sector products have undoubtedly played a role. Indeed, the evidence suggests that they played a dominant role in the 1960s. However, the most striking part of Japan's dirty-sector story is the rapid increase in consumption/production and import/export ratios since 1976, coupled with rapid growth of the JEA and sharp increases in industrial pollution control investments. A plausible inference is that stricter environmental regulation had a significant impact on Japan's comparative advantage in pollution-intensive products. We conclude that regulation probably led to both significant abatement by pollution-intensive industries in Japan, and displacement of some pollution-intensive production to Japan's trading partners.

Dirty production in North America and Western Europe

Although we have used the Japanese case to examine the "environmental transition" in detail, regulation was also increasing rapidly in North America and Western Europe during the same period. Rapidly-rising real wages in the 1960s and energy price hikes in the 1970s were common to all three OECD regions. As in the case of Japan, the growth of environmental regulation imposed substantial abatement costs on industry in North America and Western Europe during the 1970s. However, other conditions were different. Slower income growth after 1970 should have dampened the domestic income elasticity effect and kept the escalation of land prices well below Japanese rates. In the case of North America, three additional factors were operative: Relative to Japan and Western Europe, North America has low settlement density (and land prices), a much greater supply of bulk raw materials, and substantially lower energy prices—all factors which would enhance comparative advantage in pollution-intensive products. North America also has a skilled labor force capable of rapid adjustment toward cleaner production processes. It is therefore at least possible that the environmental era witnessed displacement of pollution-intensive production from Japan and Western Europe to North America, whose higher abatement expenses would have been compensated by a cost advantage in other factors.

Figures 8.13–8.16 tell us what actually happened. In the case of North America, the evidence suggests that the impact of environmental regulation outweighed the potentially-displacing effects of tighter regulation in Japan and Western Europe. From 1963 to 1993, the dirty-sector share of industrial production declined steadily in the United States and, more

Figure 8.13 Production of polluting products in the United States and Canada

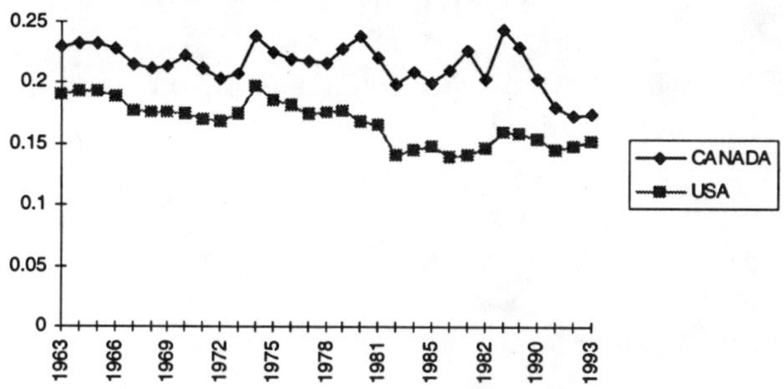

Figure 8.14 Production of polluting products in Europe

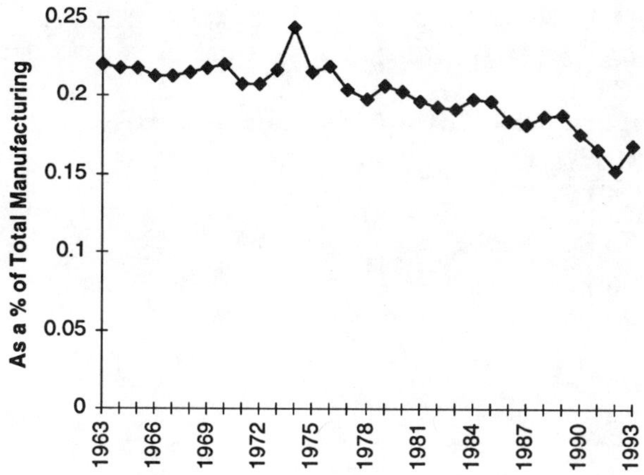

Figure 8.15 North America's import/export ratio

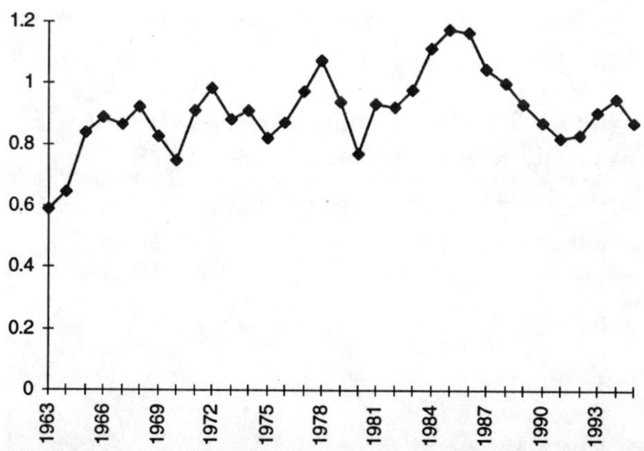

modestly, in Canada. North America's dirty-sector consumption/production ratio shows no trend and fluctuates within a very narrow range; its import/ex-

Figure 8.16 Europe's import/export ratio

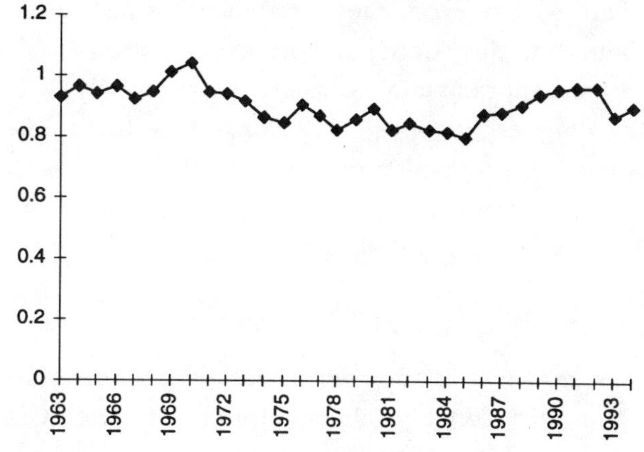

Figure 8.17 United States-Canada consumption-production ratio

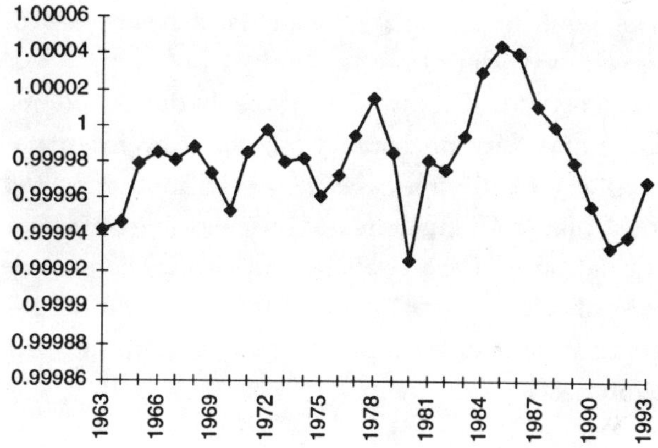

Figure 8.18 Euorpe's consumption-production ratio

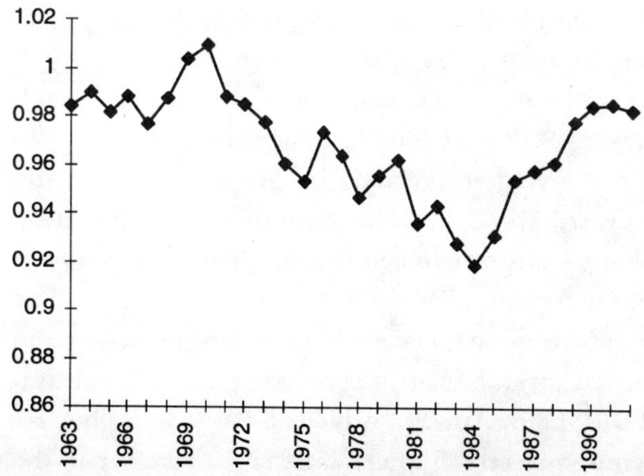

port ratio increases steadily. Thus, despite several possible countervailing factors, the North American experience was actually quite similar to that of Japan.

Western Europe also displays a declining share of dirty-sector production throughout the period, although its dirty-sector import/export ratio has remained approximately constant. Paradoxically, it is the Western European, not North American, consumption/production ratio which exhibits a downward trend well into the 1980s before returning to its 1960s level in the 1990s.

Summarizing the OECD experience

To summarize briefly, two general patterns are visible in dirty-sector production trends for the OECD economies since 1960. In all three regions, the share of pollution-intensive industries has significantly declined. In two of the regions—Japan and North America—this decline has been accompanied by net displacement of polluting production to trading partners, while approximate trade balance has been preserved in Western Europe.

Part of the decline was probably due to low income elasticity of demand for pollution-intensive products. In all three cases, however, another part is most plausibly attributed to stricter environmental regulation and rising abatement costs. The energy price shock may also have had an impact, but our regression results for Japan cast some doubt on this hypothesis.

5. Pollution-Intensive Production in Developing Asia and Latin America

The general story

The international impact of regulation, income growth and (perhaps) energy price changes are strikingly illustrated by the juxtaposition of OECD trends with figures 8.19–8.22 for Latin America and Asia.[5] For these developing regions, the graphs show a steady upward trend in pollution-intensive production share—a mirror image of the downward trends in North America, Europe and Japan. Superposed on this steady increase are pronounced turning points in Latin American and Asian import/export ratios in the mid-1970s. Latin America exhibits a rising trend beforehand, a steep fall afterwards, and a leveling in the 1980s. The Asian series also exhibits a sudden shift downward in the mid-1970s, but approximate constancy otherwise.

Although other interpretations are doubtless possible, these data are consistent with the following argument: During the 1960s, rapid growth in all regions coincided with relatively weak environmental

Figure 8.19 Latin America's production of polluting products

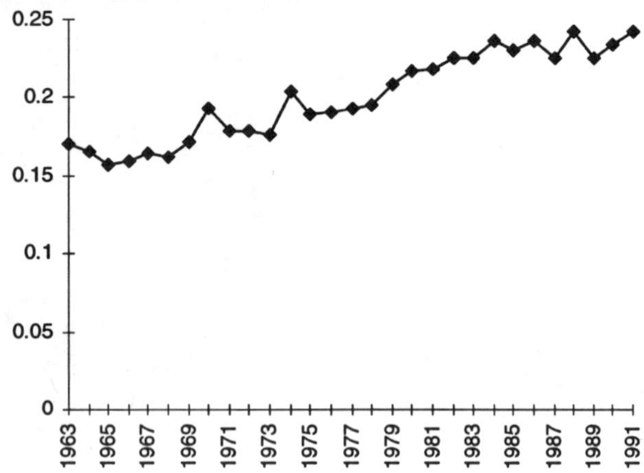

Figure 8.20 Latin America's import/export ratio

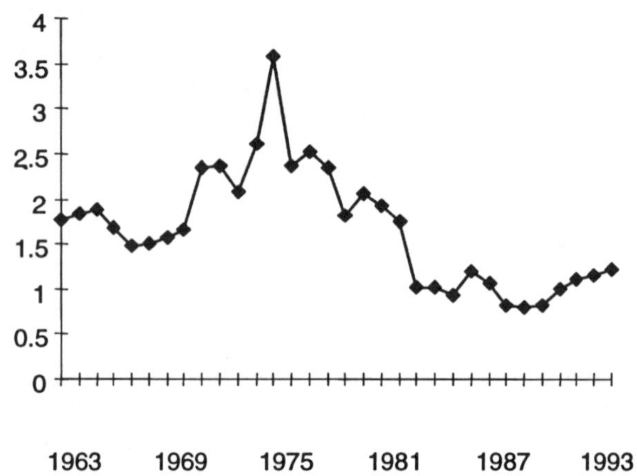

Figure 8.21 Asia (*excluding Japan*): Polluting sector production share, 1964–1998

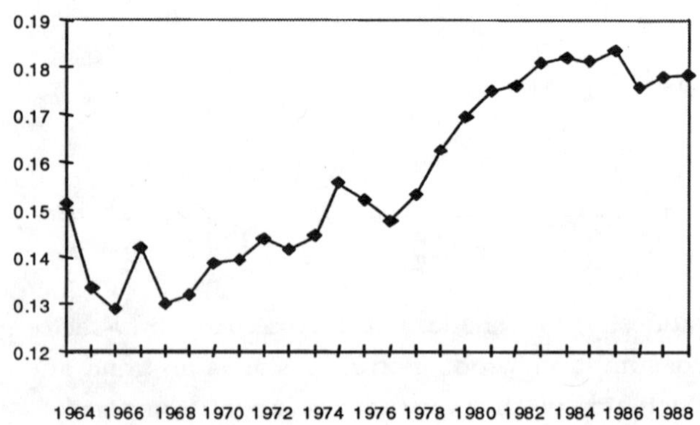

Figure 8.22 Asia (*excluding Japan*): Import/export ratio for polluting products, 1964–1994

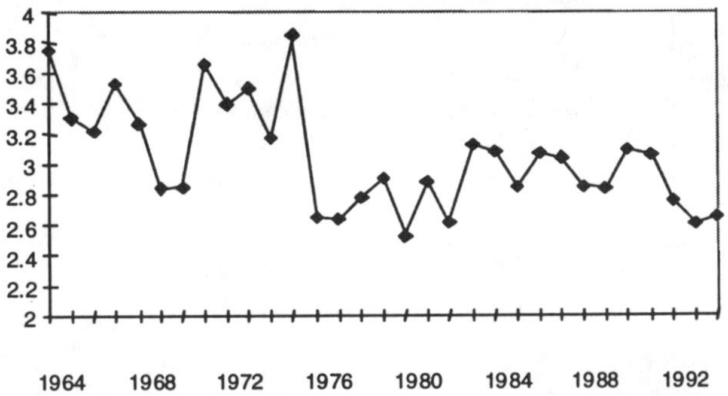

regulation in the OECD economies and low, stable energy prices worldwide. During this period, domestic income elasticity effects were dominant: Relative demand for pollution-intensive basic products such as metals, chemicals, paper and cement fell in the OECD economies and grew at least as rapidly as domestic production in the poorer nations of Asia and Latin America (apparently more rapidly in the latter).

When the environment/energy shock hit in the mid-1970s, the sudden shift in relative prices changed conditions very significantly at the margin. From a position as net importers of pollution-intensive goods (with imports at three times the level of exports), Latin America and Asia experienced a rapid decline in import/export ratios as weaker regulation and, possibly, lower energy prices altered comparative advantage in dirty-sector production. During this period, changes in relative costs augmented the income elasticity effect: Pollution-intensive production grew faster in the developing regions, and receded more quickly in the industrial economies, than could have been predicted from income change alone.

By the mid-1980s, three mitigating factors had again changed the picture significantly. First, as income growth continued, the more industrialized (and polluted) economies of Latin America and Asia probably experienced some decline in the income elasticity of demand for dirty-sector production. Second, rising consciousness of environmental problems led to enactment and enforcement of stricter environmental regulations in both Latin America and Asia.[6] Third, the energy price gap narrowed as world petroleum prices stabilized and developing countries began abandoning energy subsidies. As a result of these three changes, the share of dirty-sector production stopped increasing and import/export ratios stopped decreasing in both regions. Latin America's import/export ratio stabilized near unity (balanced trade), while Asia remaining a significant net importer of pollution-intensive products.

Asian sub-regions

We turn to Asia for a more detailed analysis of historical trends because its recent growth experience has included rapid transitions in income and economic structure for a number of countries. These raise the possibility of rapid change in locational advantage for pollution-intensive sectors, and in fact the data suggest that such transitions actually occurred. For our analysis, it is convenient to group the Asian economies into three categories (see table 8.3):[7] the Newly Industrializing Economies (NIEs—Hong Kong, Singapore, Korea, Taiwan); Developing East Asia (DEA—Malaysia, Indonesia, Thailand, Philippines and China); and South Asia (SA—India, Pakistan, Bangladesh, Sri Lanka).

Tables 8.2–8.3 and figure 8.23 provide comparative evidence on economic growth, degree of openness (by the Summers-Heston measure[8]) and the timing of environmental regulation during the past three decades. The NIEs were relatively open in 1970, at the beginning of the environmental era and were already experiencing rapid growth; DEA began liberalizing significantly and growing rapidly in the 1970s.

Figure 8.23 Openness in Asia

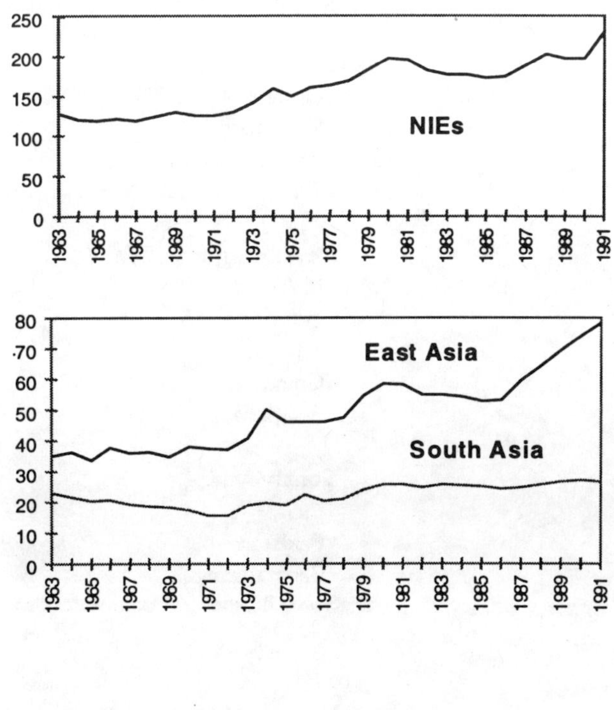

Table 8.2 Openness and economic progress in selected developing countries in Asia and Latin America

	Openness	*Economic Progress*		
	Degree of openness 1990[a]	*Average annual growth of GNP per capita (percent) 1970-1995*	*People living on less than $1 a day (percent) 1981-95*	*Average annual growth of exports (percent) 1980-95*
East Asia				
China	25.4	6.9	29.4	12.5
Indonesia	52.6	4.7	14.5	10.6
Korea, Rep. of	62.5	10.0	--	11.6
Malaysia	154.20	4.0	5.6	13.6
Philippines	61.5	0.6	27.5	5.3
Thailand	75.8	5.2	0.1	16.7
South Asia				
Bangladesh	26.9	1.5	--	10.1
India	18.8	2.4	52.5	6.5
Pakistan	35.0	2.9	11.6	9.1
Sri Lanka	67.4	3.2	4.0	11.5
Latin America				
Brazil	12.6	--	28.7	6.3
Chile	65.5	1.8	15.0	7.3
Colombia	35.4	1.9	7.4	8.1
Mexico	32.7	0.9	14.9	13.0
Peru	26.8	1.1	49.4	2.4
Venezuela	59.6	1.1	11.8	1.0

Notes: -- Not available.

a. Summers-Heston openness index defined as (exports+imports)/nominal GDP.

Source: World Bank 1997.

Table 8.3 Initial national environmental legislation in Asia

Country	*Air*	*Water*	*Toxics*
Japan	1967	1958	1958
NICs			
Hong Kong			
Singapore	1978	-----	-----
Korea, Rep. of			
Taiwan (China)	1975	-----	
Developing East Asia			
Malaysia	1977	1977	1979
Indonesia	1988	1988	-----
Thailand	1975	1975	1989
China	1985	1985	1989
Philippines			
South Asia			
India	1974	1981	1986
Pakistan	1983	1983	-----
Bangladesh	-----	-----	-----

Source: Brandon and Ramankutty (1993).

Figure 8.24 Republic of Korea: Pollution-intensive industry share, 1963–1993

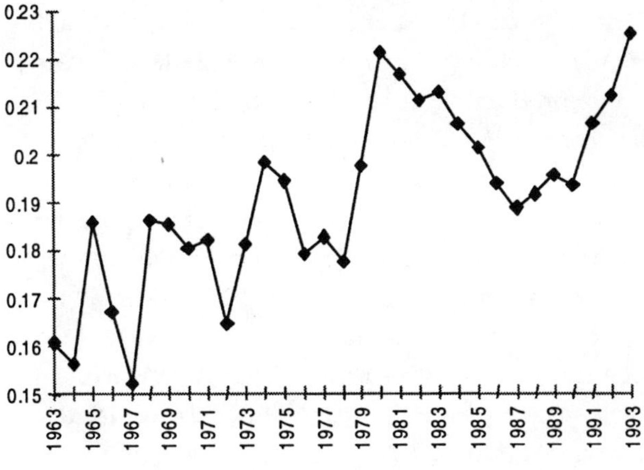

Figure 8.27 Developing East Asia's production of polluting products

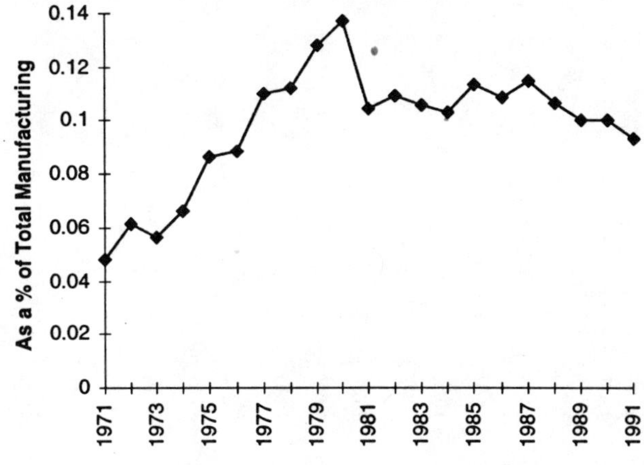

Figure 8.25 NIEs' production of pollution products

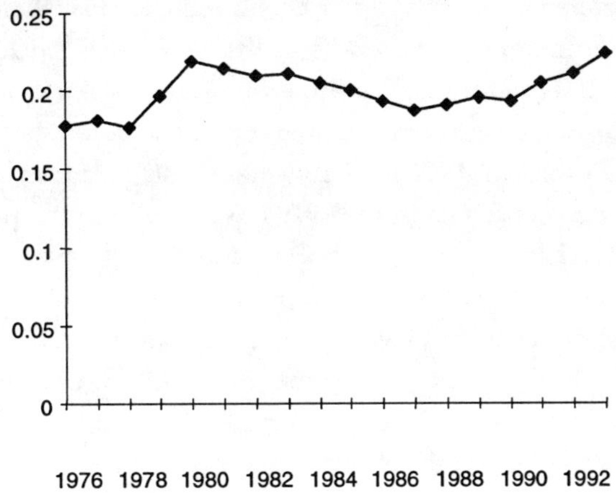

Figure 8.28 Developing East Asia's import/export ratio

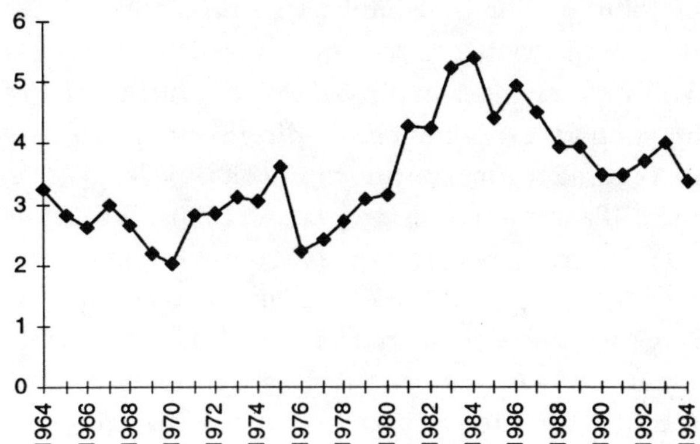

Figure 8.26 NIEs' import/export ratio

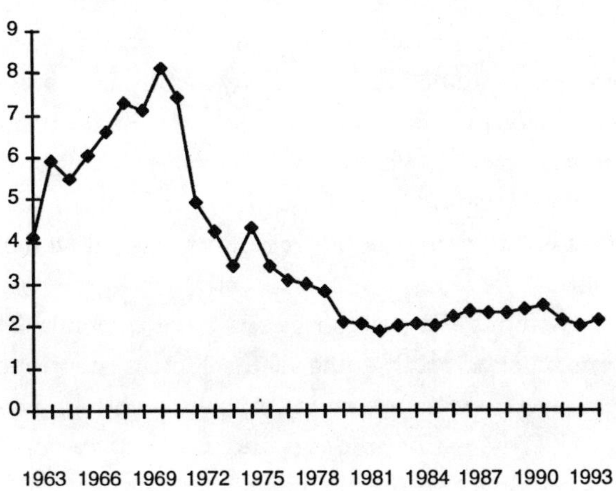

Figure 8.29 South Asia's production of polluting products

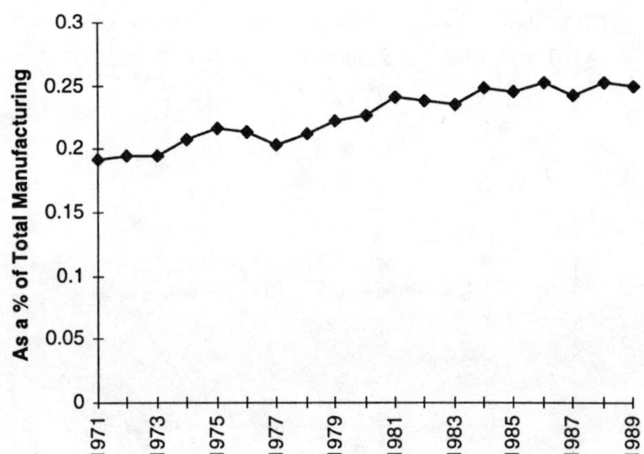

Figure 8.30 South Asia's production of polluting products

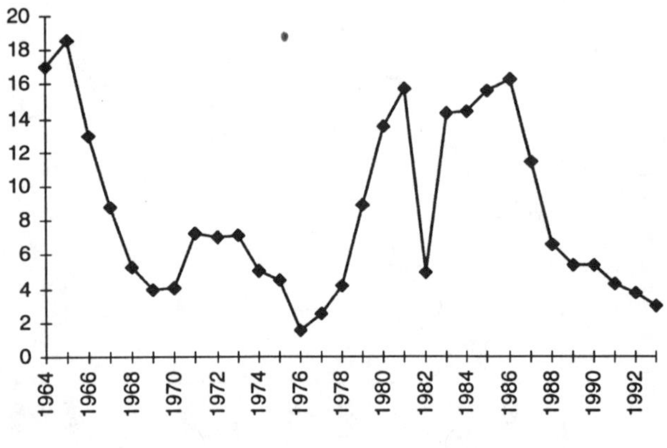

Stricter enforcement of environmental regulation began in the 1970s in the NIEs and the 1980s in DEA. SA began more rapid growth in the 1980s, but stricter environmental regulation was delayed until the 1990s.

Across the three regions, the growth experience of pollution-intensive industry seems to reflect these developments in a "cascading" pattern. Figures 8.24–8.30 show changes in dirty-sector production shares and import/export ratios. The dirty-sector share grew in all three regions during the 1970s; it leveled off in the NIEs and DEA, but continued rising in SA. The NIEs' dirty-sector import/export ratio fell sharply during the 1970s. When regulation tightened and the NIEs' ratio leveled off in the early 1980s, it began falling in DEA. As regulation tightened in DEA during the late 1980s, the import/export ratio began falling in SA.

To summarize, for dirty-sector production in Asia we see an adjustment pattern which looks like a "cascading pollution havens" story. It begins in Japan in the early 1970s, and continues for two decades

Figure 8.31 Consumption-production ratio in Asia (*excluding Japan*)

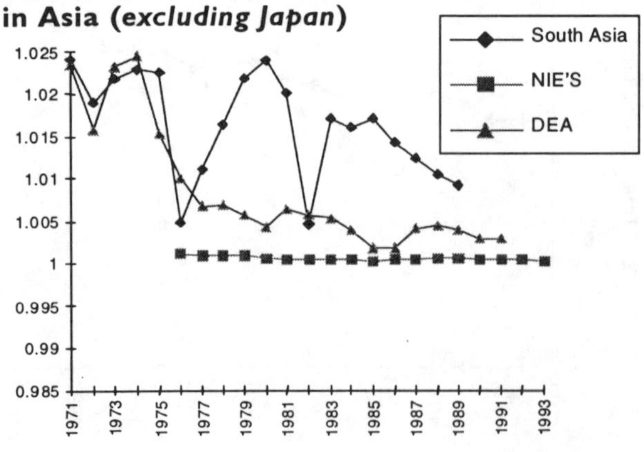

in the NIEs, DEA and SA. However, in each region it has remained a markedly short story. In the NIEs and DEA, the combined effect of regulation and falling demand elasticity has apparently stabilized the dirty-sector production share, leaving both regions (and SA) as *net importers* of pollution-intensive products.

The same story is reflected in the historical pattern of consumption/production ratios (figure 8.31). Although they have declined for over two decades in both DEA and SA, they remain above one in all three regions. In fact, all the ratios have been very close to one during the entire period. Thus, our "cascading" dirty-sector production story has been a decidedly marginal affair.

6. Conclusions and Implications

The last three decades have witnessed rapid economic development, particularly in countries which have pursued relatively open economic policies. Rising environmental awareness in the 1960s also led to a rapid tightening of pollution regulation in the industrial economies. This created an international gap in environmental pricing between industrial and developing economies in the 1970s. According to the pollution havens hypothesis, the result should have been more rapid growth of dirty industries in unregulated economies which were open to international trade.

In this paper, we argue that a full understanding of the pollution havens problem requires good evidence about the interactions linking economic development to regulation, industrial location, sectoral pollution intensity, energy and other input prices. Most of the previous studies have focused on the location issue, typically suppressing the other factors by lumping countries into simple "developed/developing" categories and basing conclusions on sectoral changes evaluated at constant (generally U.S.-based) abatement expenditures. In addition, the locational analyses have typically not considered many of the standard location factors in drawing inferences about the impact of differential regulation and abatement costs.

Although data restrictions have prevented us from incorporating some of the factors mentioned here, our(as we have shown for Japan) results do point to some interesting findings and implications for future research and policy analysis.

Our cross-country analysis has found a pattern of evidence which does seem consistent with the pollution havens story: Pollution-intensive output as a percentage of total manufacturing has fallen consistently in the OECD and risen steadily in the developing world. Moreover, the periods of rapid increase in net exports of pollution-intensive products from developing countries coincided with periods of rapid increase in the cost of pollution abatement in the OECD economies.

However, our evidence also shows that pollution haven effects have not had major significance, for several reasons. First, consumption/production ratios for dirty-sector products in the developing world have remained close to unity throughout the period; most of the dirty-sector development story is strictly domestic. Second, a significant part of the increase in dirty-sector production share in the developing regions seems due to a highly income-elastic demand for basic industrial products. With continued income growth, this elasticity has declined.[9] Third, some portion of the international adjustment has probably been due to the energy price shock and the persistence of energy subsidies in many developing countries. These subsidies have been on the wane for a decade. Finally, environmental regulation increases continuously with income and seems to have played a role in the shift from dirty to cleaner sectors.

Thus, any tendency toward formation of a pollution havens seems to have been self-limiting, because economic growth brings countervailing pressure to bear on polluters through increased regulation, technical expertise, and "clean sector" production. In practice, pollution havens have apparently been as transient as low-wage havens.

In closing, it is worth asking whether these results are a cause for optimism or pessimism about the relationship between economic development and environmental quality. The appropriate answer seems to be "both." It is conforting to see that industrial pollution levels off or declines in richer countries, because pollution intensity has an elastic response to income growth. In addition, our results suggest that pollution haven effects have been transient and relatively unimportant. It is clear that no feasible trade policy could "neutralize" this effect. Cross-country differences in environmental regulation reflect a broad continuum of experience, and the domestic impacts of regulation dwarf international displacement impacts.

However, the evidence suggests that something like a pollution havens effect is real, even if it has been transient for many countries. The results, however, also suggest there will be some countries that lag behind in their efforts to control pollution now and may even take years to catch-up with the rest of the world. This also rises serious issues about continued existence of polluted waterways and lands left behind by itinerant dirty industries, and their legacy will remain for generations.

What, if anything, then should the industrial countries or rest of the world do about this disparity? Our results cast strong doubt on the wisdom of intervention through trade-related measures. The continuous, smooth relationship between income growth and environmental performance shows that developing countries are already making social choices which reflect the calculus of benefits and costs. Countries become less polluted as rising incomes makes a cleaner environment more desirable and affordable. Fortunately, there are progressive alternatives to heavy-handed intervention: The positive alternative to heavy-handed intervention lies in aiding activities to finance pollution control training; the transfer of cost-effective pollution control technologies; and appropriate information systems for regulation and public dissemination of environmental information. At each level of development, such assistance can help developing countries move closer to locally-appropriate levels of pollution control. Ultimately, income growth will be the answer. As developing economies prosper and tighten their regulations, we are confident that the shadow of pollution havens will recede to insignificance.

Notes

Funding for this study has been provided by the World Bank"s Research Support Budget and the Netherlands Trust Fund for "Social and Environmental Consequences of Growth-Oriented Policies." The findings, interpretations, and conclusions expressed in this paper are entirely those of the authors. They do not necessarily reflect the views of the World Bank, its Executive Directors, or the countries they represent. For useful comments, we would like to thank Judy Dean, Per Fredriksson and other participants in the workshop on Social and Environmental Consequences of Growth-Oriented Policies, World Bank, Washington, DC, May 1997 and the Conference on Trade, Global Policy and the Environment, World Bank, Washington, DC, April 1998. This chapter is published with permission from Sage Publications, Inc. It has been published in *Journal of Environment and Development*, Vol. 7, No. 3, September 1998, pp. 215-247.

1. For a detailed discussion, see Mody and Wheeler (1990).
2. See Wheeler and Mody (1992).
3. This is confirmed in a recent study by Hettige, Mani, and Wheeler (1998).
4. Petroleum has been excluded because a very few countries are actually involved in its production.
5. We do not have complete data series for all Asian countries for the entire period. Our Asia series in figure 16 includes data for Korea, Singapore, Pakistan, Philippines and India.
6. For a detailed analysis, see Wheeler and Mody (1992).
7. Data were not available for the other Asian developing economies.
8. Summers-Heston openness index is defined as (exports+imports)/nominal GDP.
9. Dasgupta and others (1995) also find a very strong, monotone increasing relationship between national income per capita and the strictness of environmental regulation.

References

Birdsall, N., and D.R. Wheeler. 1993. "Trade Policy and Industrial Pollution in Latin America: Where Are the Pollution Havens." *Journal of Environment and Development* 2(1): 137–49.

Brandon, C., and R. Ramankutty. 1993. Toward an Environmental Strategy for Asia. *World Bank Discussion Paper Number 224*. Washington, DC: World Bank.

Dasgupta, S., and D.R. Wheeler. 1997. "Citizen Complaints as Environmental Indicators: Evidence from China." Policy Research Department Working Paper 1704, Washington, DC: World Bank.

Dasgupta, S., A. Mody, S. Roy, and D.R. Wheeler. 1995. "Environmental Regulation and Development: A Cross-Country Empirical Analysis." Policy Research Department, Working Paper No. 1448, Washington, DC: World Bank.

Hettige, H., P. Martin, M. Singh, and D.R. Wheeler. 1995. "IPPS: The Industrial Pollution Projection System." Policy Research Department Working Paper 1431, Washington, DC: World Bank.

Hettige, H., M. Mani, and D.R. Wheeler. 1998. "Industrial Pollution in Economic Development: Kuznets Revisited." Policy Research Working Paper 1876. Washington, DC: World Bank.

Mani, M. 1996. "Environmental Tariffs on Polluting Imports: An Empirical Study." *Environmental and Resource Economics* 7: 391–411

Mody, A., and D.R. Wheeler. 1990. *Automation and World Competition: New Technologies, Industrial Location, and Trade.* London: Macmillan Press.

Pargal, S., and D.R. Wheeler. 1996. "Informal Regulation in Developing Countries: Evidence from Indonesia." *Journal of Political Economy* 104: 1314–27.

Robison, D.H. 1988. "Industrial Pollution Abatement: The Impact on the Balance of Trade." *Canadian Journal of Economics* 21: 702–706.

Tobey, J.A. 1990. "The Effects of Domestic Environmental Policies on Patterns of World Trade: An Empirical Test." *Kyklos* 43(2): 191–209.

Wang, H., and D.R. Wheeler. 1996. "Pricing Industrial Pollution in China: An Econometric Analysis of the Levy System." Policy Research Department Working Paper No. 1644. Washington, DC: The World Bank.

Wheeler, D.R., and A. Mody. 1992. "International Investment Location Decisions: The Case of U.S. Firms." *Journal of International Economics* 33: 57–76.

World Bank. 1997. *World Development Indicators 1997*. Washington, DC: World Bank.

Chapter 9

The Political Economy of Environmental Regulations, Government Assistance, and Foreign Trade

Paavo Eliste and Per G. Fredriksson

1. Introduction

This paper attempts to explain the political determinants of environmental regulations and assistance programs for agriculture. The international trading system is heavily influenced by a variety of subsidy schemes in effect in many countries. We seek to analyze the relationship between such transfers and environmental policies, which, in turn, should yield new insights into the potential joint effect of these factors on patterns of international trade.[1]

We argue that producer-support schemes may be intimately connected with environmental policies. Increased demand for environmental quality (observed in many countries during recent decades) may stimulate simultaneous increases in both environmental regulations and transfers. This would occur if polluters received compensation, via transfers, for expenditures incurred as a result of environmental regulations.[2] This is a political economy explanation for why observed increases in the stringency of environmental regulations have been found to have small, insignificant, or even reverse effects on trade patterns.[3, 4]

This study also examines whether government assistance serves as a "carrot" in environmental policymaking. Can distortionary trade and subsidy policies be justified on the basis that they improve welfare by enabling policymakers to set more stringent environmental regulations?

The following two hypotheses are tested empirically: (i) Are more stringent environmental regulations associated with greater government assistance to agricultural producers? (ii) Do greater government support to polluters lead to more stringent environmental regulations? To our knowledge this study is the first attempt at explaining the empirical relationship between environmental regulations and transfer policies.

We also incorporate the impact of farm lobbying on environmental regulations and assistance policies, the deadweight loss of transfers, and the environmental pressures caused by agriculture. Such variables address the question of whether the policies selected tend toward efficiency. Moreover, we investigate the effects of freedom of information and political freedoms on environmental and assistance policies.

The empirical results support the first hypothesis: the stringency of environmental policies appear to be positively associated with the size of transfers in the agricultural sector. This, in turn, suggests that trade patterns may have been influenced by such compensatory transfers, meaning that the transfers may have mitigated the effects of regulations on trade flows. Many forms of support given to producers to compensate for environmental protection costs imply inefficient environmental protection and trade patterns, since producers are not facing the true social cost of the damage caused, that is, the polluter pays principle is violated.[5]

The results do not, however, indicate that government assistance programs have a significant impact on the stringency of environmental regulations.[6] Thus in the aggregate, support programs designed to facilitate the strengthening of environmental protection are hardly justifiable. In particular, programs that have a negative effect on environmental quality should be targeted for a quick phaseout (see OECD 1998a).

The results also indicate that the political power of the farm lobby is positively related to the relative economic importance of the agricultural sector, but negatively related to its members' share of the population. Another finding is that land-use pressures result in more stringent environmental policies, indicating that a concern for efficiency is present. Finally, we find no significant impacts of freedom of information and freedom of civil rights on environmental regulations and government transfers, respectively.

The next section describes the data and empirical specification, while section three examines the results, and section four offers a conclusion.

2. Empirical Analysis

Our research was aimed at testing whether more stringent environmental regulations are positively associated with government assistance to agricultural producers, and whether government support to these producers enables policymakers to set more stringent environmental regulations. The potentially simultaneous nature of the relationship between environmental regulations and transfers implies that environmental regulations may have an effect on transfers, which may in turn influence regulations. The two effects are isolated by simultaneously estimating two equations. We estimate one equation for the stringency of environmental regulations and another for the level of government assistance. We provide both ordinary- and two-stage least squares estimation results.

Data on environmental regulations

The empirical analysis uses cross-country data from 49 countries for the year 1990. Our measure of the stringency of environmental regulations is a newly designed index based on individual country reports on the status and extent of environmental regulations in the agricultural sector. The index was initially constructed by Dasgupta and others (1995) based on reports compiled for the 1992 United Nations Conference on Environment and Development (UNCED) in Rio de Janeiro. Each country report is based on identical survey questions and was prepared under clearly defined UNCED guidelines, facilitating cross-country comparison (Dasgupta and others 1995). The country reports provide sector specific information about the state of the environment and natural-resource utilization by the agricultural sector, with a focus on existing environmental policies, legislation, control mechanisms, and enforcement. Using the information gathered, a quantitative index of the stringency of environmental regulations was developed by Dasgupta and others for an initial set of 31 countries. The answers to each of 25 questions were assigned a score of zero, one, or two for each of four different forms of environmental degradation (air, water, land, and living resources or biodiversity) and the scores were added to yield the index.[7]

The pool of countries was extended further by our own work using the same methodology as Dasgupta and others. We believe this to be the largest available cross-country measure of environmental policies. It has the advantage of measuring the stringency of environmental regulations in one sector (agriculture) alone, instead of the broad, aggregate measures used in many other studies. The remaining data sources are provided in the appendix, table A.9.1.

Endogenous variables

The index of environmental regulations described in the previous section is used as a measure of the stringency of environmental policy (*STRING*). Compensation channeled to farmers in return for increased expenditures on environmental protection is delivered through a variety of policy interventions. Governments may use production subsidies, pollution abatement subsidies, or land set-aside schemes, as well as import restrictions, tax concessions, or waste-management assistance for this purpose.

The Producer Subsidy Equivalent (*PSE*) is used here as a measure of aggregate government assistance in the agricultural sector. The *PSE* measures the monetary value of all transfers to the agricultural sector, including tariffs, nontariff barriers, and various explicit compensation schemes for environmental regulations resulting from agricultural regulatory policies.[8] To reduce the effects of random volatility between years (resulting, for example, from large exchange-rate fluctuations), we use the average *PSE* for the three years 1988 to 1990.

The equation for the stringency of environmental regulations

This section examines the exogenous determinants of the stringency of environmental policy (*STRING*). We used the *PSE* to determine the effect of transfers on the level of environmental regulations. We had no strong prior expectations regarding the effect of the *PSE* on *STRING*.

We expected per capita income (*GDPpc*) to have a positive effect on *STRING*. If environmental quality is a normal good, demand should increase along with income, so that per capita income can be viewed as a proxy for the political pressure from environmental interests.

The total cost of environmental regulations to producers should depend on the relative size of the agricultural sector. Thus the larger the output level of the agricultural sector relative to the rest of the economy, the more influential the farm lobby since more is at stake. In an extensive survey of the empirical interest-group literature, Potters and Sloof (1996) find that the greater a lobby group's stake in the policy outcome, the greater its success. Moreover, the larger the relative size of the sector, the stronger the effect of regulations on social welfare. We therefore hypothesized that the larger the share of value-added of agriculture to total GDP (*AGDPsh*), the lower the *STRING*.

A substantial share of soil erosion and loss of marginal ecosystems, biodiversity, and carbon sinks comes from the conversion of land to agricultural production. This has been labeled an "extensive pressure" in the literature (Goklany 1996). Another form of pressure on the environment comes from more intensive cultivation or grazing of existing farmland; for example, farm run-off of nutrients and sediments or "intensive pressure." In sum existing pressures on environmental resources are important variables determining the demand for environmental regulations. We use the share of agricultural land (defined as the sum of arable and pasture land) from total land area (*AGLANDsh*) as an indicator of "extensive" pressure on the environment, and fertilizer use per hectare (*FERTph*) as an indicator of "intensive" environmental pressure. Both can be expected to have a positive impact on *STRING*.

Political attention to environmental problems can be expected to increase as objective information about environmental damage becomes more publicly available (see Pargal and Wheeler 1996). Thus we expected that variations in the stringency of environmental regulation could be explained by the availability of information. Moreover, Potters and Sloof report that the presence of a well-informed electorate implies a reduction in the influence of lobby groups. Gastil (1987) developed an index of freedom of information. The original indicator is an integer: 1 represents the most free information and 5 the least free information. Freedom of information may not be measurable on a nominal scale, as assumed in Gastil's index, however. We therefore defined a dummy variable (*FOIdummy*), following Murdoch and Sandler (1997). Our variable has a value of 1 when Gastil's index is 2 or less (unrestricted diffusion of information) and 0 otherwise (restricted diffusion of information). We expected that *FOIdummy* would have a positive impact on *STRING*.

The producer subsidy equivalent equation

Considering the many empirical studies that have found minimal or no effects of environmental regulations on trade flows, we anticipated that *STRING* would have a positive effect on the *PSE*.

Transfer levels are partly determined by the economic and political incentives of lobby groups (Becker 1983; Grossman and Helpman 1994; Aidt 1998; Fredriksson 1998). An interest group's political influence is enhanced by a common, concentrated, and sufficiently large economic interest because free-riding is reduced (Olson 1965). We use the share of agricultural sector labor in the total labor force as a proxy for the political power of the farm lobby group (*AGLABORsh*). The expected effect of an increase in *AGLABORsh* is ambiguous because of the considerations noted below.

First, a small change in the *PSE* has a larger aggregate effect on the farm lobby's welfare as *AGLABORsh* increases, because of the relatively larger number of transfer recipients. This translates into greater lobbying pressure and voting power (Potters and Sloof 1996). Thus pressure for support increases with *AGLABORsh*. Yet the farm lobby suffers from increased free-riding, so the pressure for assistance decreases as the number of farmers increases (Olson 1965). Third, as the share of agricultural producers in the total labor force increases, it becomes more difficult and costly to transfer income to farmers. This is the case because as farmers increase their share of the population, the share of the remaining population necessarily falls. Each unit of income extracted yields a smaller marginal benefit to each farmer and a greater marginal cost to the remaining population. If the first effect is greater (smaller) than the sum of the second and third effects, *AGLABORsh* has a positive (negative) impact on *PSE*.

The ability of producers to obtain transfers through the political process is greater the lower the deadweight loss associated with the redistribution of public funds (Becker 1983; Gardner 1987; Grossman and Helpman 1994; OECD 1998b). The greater the elasticity of output supply the more costly it becomes to redistribute through production subsidies, because the supply price is more negatively affected, other things being equal. Thus the greater the elasticity of supply, the lower the level of government assistance. Since cross-country supply elasticity estimates are not available, the estimation relies on a proxy variable (*SUPPLYelasticity*). We hypothesized that the difference in the elasticity of supply across countries is reflected by the value-added per hectare of agricultural land. High per-hectare value-added should correspond to low elasticity of supply, because available resources are allocated in a way that maximizes value-added. A further increase in the subsidy should yield a lower marginal output response and a greater positive effect on the producer's net price. Therefore, *SUPPLYelasticity* can be expected to have a positive impact on the *PSE*.

The political economy approach to trade policy pioneered by Grossman and Helpman (1994) views lobbying activities as more influential the lower the priority that a government puts on aggregate social welfare (that is, the welfare maximizing policy package) relative to political support. Since this should be true for both farm and environmental lobby groups (who should push in opposite directions), an increase in the relative weight of social welfare will bring the *PSE* closer to zero (from either a negative or positive value), so that the expected sign is ambiguous. We use Gastil's Freedom of Civil Rights as a proxy for the weight on social welfare relative to political contributions. Again, Gastil's index uses integers: 1 represents the most secure rights, and 6 the least secure rights. We define a dummy variable (*DEMOCRACYdummy*), which takes a value of 1 when Gastil's index is 2 or less (politically free country) and 0 otherwise (not free) (see also Murdoch and Sandler 1997). If the influence of the farm lobby falls relatively faster as the level of democracy increases, *DEMOCRACYdummy* will have a negative sign; if the environmental lobby's influence falls faster, the sign will be positive.

The discussion above implies that the equations for the stringency of environmental regulations and for government assistance are given by the following two specifications, respectively, where subscript *i* denotes individual country *i*, *i* = 1,...*N*:

$$STRING_i = \beta_{11} + \gamma_2 PSE_i + \beta_{12} GDPpc_i + \beta_{13} AGDPsh_i + \beta_{14} AGLANDsh_i + \beta_{15} FOIdummy_i + e_{1i} \quad (1.1)$$

$$PSE_i = \beta_{21} + \gamma_1 STRING_i + \beta_{22} AGLABORsh_i + \beta_{23} SUPPLYelasticity_i + \beta_{24} DEMOCRACYdummy_i + e_{2i} \quad (1.2)$$

3. Empirical Results

Our empirical work yields a number of results. For the *STRING* equation (1.1) the OLS results in table 9.1 are discussed since this is our preferred specification, and for the *PSE* equation (1.2) we discuss the heteroscedasticity-robust 2SLS results.[9]

The STRING equation

The coefficient estimate for government assistance (*PSE*) in the equation for *STRING* is highly insignificant. This suggests that government-support policies may have no effect on the stringency of environmental regulations in agriculture. One explanation may be that increased government assistance may yield higher political pressures on environmental regulations from several directions, and the total effect may be negligible because individual effects neutralize each other (see also Fredriksson 1999). This result has implications for environmental policymaking. Our finding does not support the argument that assistance policies are justified because they serve to increase the stringency of environmental regulations.

Table 9.1 Regression results for the stringency of environmental regulations (*STRING*)[§]

	OLS	*Robust OLS*	*Robust 2SLS*
Dependent Variable: STRING			
CONSTANT	79.884***	79.884***	79.996***
	(8.746)	(12.070)	(12.753)
PSE	0.020	0.020	0.067
	(0.263)	(0.325)	(0.485)
GDPpc	0.004***	0.004***	0.004***
	(7.248)	(6.659)	(5.791)
AGDPsh	-0.562*	-0.562**	-0.529**
	(-1.880)	(-2.123)	(-2.444)
FERTph	0.002	0.002	0.021
	(1.261)	(1.418)	(1.123)
AGLANDsh	0.251**	0.251**	0.249***
	(2.131)	(2.528)	(2.645)
FOIdummy	4.656	4.656	4.887
	(0.655)	(0.757)	(0.882)
Adjusted R^2	0.83	0.83	0.83
No. of observations	49	49	49

§* significant at the 10 percent level; ** significant at the 5 percent level; *** significant at the 1 percent level.

Table 9.1 Regression results for government assistance (PSE)

	OLS	*Robust OLS*	*Robust 2SLS*
Dependent Variable: PSE			
CONSTANT	-1.937	-1.937	-17.564
	(-0.074)	(-0.073)	(-0.691)
STRING	0.236	0.236	0.370*
	(1.205)	(1.280)	(1.947)
AGLABORsh	-0.682**	-0.682*	-0.596**
	(-2.351)	(-1.918)	(-2.050)
SUPPLYelasticity	0.004*	0.004**	0.003***
	(1.679)	(2.261)	(2.964)
DEMOCRACYdummy	8.707	8.707	3.650
	(0.605)	(0.665)	(0.294)
Adjusted R^2	0.46	0.46	0.46
No. of observations	49	49	49

§* significant at the 10 percent level; ** significant at the 5 percent level; *** significant at the 1 percent level.

GDPpc, on the other hand, is highly significant with the expected positive sign. This finding is consistent with those of other studies, such as Antle and Heidebrink (1995) and Pargal and Wheeler (1996). *AGDPsh* has the expected negative sign, and is statistically significant. Thus an increase in the relative economic importance of the agricultural sector translates into greater political influence, which has a negative effect on the stringency of environmental regulations.[10]

The coefficient for *AGLANDsh* has the expected positive sign and is significant. The coefficient for *FERTph* is insignificant, although it takes the expected positive sign. Using the Wald test to estimate the combined effect of the two environmental pressure variables, we found a (chi-squared) test statistic of 7.18 indicating that *AGLANDsh* and *FERTph* are jointly significant at the 5 percent level. This implies that political pressure for more stringent regulations increases with the degree of environmental degradation (caused by agricultural activities). The policymaker sets more stringent regulations when the negative externalities are greater, suggesting that efficiency considerations play a role in environmental policy determination.

Finally, *FOIdummy* has the expected positive sign, but is insignificant. The insignificant result could be explained by the following factors. First, the non-point nature of some forms of pollution from agriculture (as opposed, for example, to point-source air and water pollution) makes this form of environmental degradation more difficult to detect for the average citizen, and the absence of information reduces political pressure for action. Second, pollution from agriculture has a lagged effect on environmental quality and human health, sometimes requiring years of accumulation to result in damage. This particular type of information may not be readily available in rural areas in many countries. Third, the result may reflect the fact that many governments attach a relatively low weight to the health of the rural population relative to urban dwellers, so that less funds may be directed to monitoring activities in rural areas. The variable may also be imprecisely measured.

The PSE equation

We now turn to the equation for the *PSE* in table 9.1.2, where we discuss the 2SLS results.[11] First, *STRING* is positively associated with the *PSE*. The farm lobby group appears to become relatively more powerful as the stringency of regulations increases. The coefficient is significant at the 10 percent level (p-value 0.06); thus we reject the hypothesis that *STRING* has no effect on *PSE*. This lends some support to the hypothesis that polluters receive compensation for environmental protection costs. Although we cannot infer that the same phenomena has taken place in other sectors, this finding appears to provide initial evidence that support policies may have neutralized the effects of environmental regulations on trade flows.

The coefficient for *AGLABORsh* has a negative sign and is significant at the 5 percent level. It appears that the effects of free-riding and increased redistribution costs outweigh the effects of increased membership numbers on political pressure from the farm lobby as its membership increases. We are, however, not able to separate the former two individual effects.

The *SUPPLYelasticity* variable has the expected positive sign, and is statistically significant. Finally, *DEMOCRACYdummy* is found to be positive but insignificant. This may reflect the ambiguity associated with this variable. Increased democracy may have a similarly negative effect on the ability of all interest groups to buy influence.

4. Conclusion

Economic theory predicts that an increase in the stringency of environmental regulations will reduce exports and increase imports. This paper offered an explanation for the fact that previous empirical research has largely found no, or only weak, effects of environmental regulations on trade patterns (see Jaffe and others 1995). We presented empirical evidence from the agricultural sector that support the hypothesis that producers who face more stringent environmental regulations also receive compensation for the expenditures associated with environmental protection. This implies that future tests of the effects of environmental regulations on trade flows should include measures of transfers.

We found no support, however, for the hypothesis that higher levels of assistance to agriculture increase the stringency of environmental regulations in this sector. It appears that, in aggregate, transfers tend to be ineffective as a "carrot" to encourage polluters to accept more stringent environmental policies. One explanation may be that assistance programs have implications for the long-run influence of lobby groups. Government support policies may increase the relative political pressure of the farm lobby, for example, because these measures increase the value of total agricultural output. This, in turn, increases the lobby's incentive to spend further resources on seeking political influence.

This study also demonstrated the importance of other political factors and deadweight loss in the determination of cross-country differences in both environmental and assistance policies in the agricultural sector. We found that the relative economic influence of farmers, free-riding, and supply elasticity play significant roles. Finally, we found that greater environmental pressures result in stricter regulations.

This paper does not address the effect of the combination of environmental policies and assistance programs on aggregate pollution levels. The environmental effects of commodity programs are relatively well-known, see Just and Bockstael (1991). Since agricultural production is a significant contributor to environmental problems such as soil erosion, water pollution, wetland losses, and reductions of wildlife populations (through stimulating excessive use of pesticides and fertilizers, encouraging conversion of land to agricultural production, and reducing crop diversity), the results have implications for environmental policy (see, for example, Lewandrowski and others 1997). One possible implication of our results is that the combination of environmental policies and associated transfer policies *may*, in the aggregate, worsen environmental quality, even compared to a laissez-faire approach.

Appendix Table A9.1 Variable definition and data sources

Variable	*Definition and source*
STRING	Index of stringency of environmental regulations. *Source*: Dasgupta *et al.* (1995) and authors' calculations based on UNCED (1992).
PSE	Producer Subsidy Equivalent as a percentage of the total value of production.[a] *Sources*: OECD (1997) for OECD countries; unpublished OECD data files for Czech Republic, Hungary, and Poland; Valdés (1996) for Latin American countries; USDA (1990, 1994a). PSE for Morocco was computed using unpublished USDA data files.
GDPpc	Gross domestic product per capita (1987 U.S. dollars). *Source*: World Bank (1992).[b]
AGDPsh	Agriculture value-added as a share of GDP (percent). *Source*: World Bank (1997a).
FERTph	Fertilizer consumption per hectare of arable land (kilograms) *Source*: World Bank (1997a).
AGLANDsh	Agricultural land as a share of total land (percent). *Source*: World Bank (1997b).
FOIdummy	Dummy variable for the Freedom of Information. *Source*: Scully (1992).
AGLABORsh	Share of labor force in agriculture (percent). *Source*: World Bank (1997a).
SUPPLYelasticity	Agricultural value-added per ha of agricultural land (1987 US dollars). *Source*: USDA (1994b).
DEMOCRACYdummy	Dummy variable for the Freedom of Civil Rights. *Source*: Scully (1992).

a. Data for Thailand and Venezuela is from 1987.
b. 1987 local currency GDP was converted to 1987 US$ using average exchange rates for 1987.

Notes

We thank Torbjörn Becker, Cees van Beers, Peter Christoffersen, Stratford Douglas, Jerry Fletcher, Bruce Gardner, Leo Maier, Lisa Segnestam, Ronald Steenblik, David Wheeler, the participants at the *Trade, Global Policy, and the Environment* conference and West Virginia University Departments of Natural Resource Economics and Economics, respectively, for helpful discussions and comments on earlier versions of this paper, and USDA for making data sources available for this project. Funding from the Swedish International Development Cooperation Agency (Sida), within the project "Trade, Macroeconomic Reform, and the Environment" is gratefully acknowledged.

1. Jaffe and others (1995) provide a survey of the literature on the effects of environmental regulations on trade and investment.

2. Eliste and Fredriksson (1998) develop a theoretical model which shows that an increase in the demand for environmental quality, which results in a higher equilibrium pollution tax, also affects special interest groups' marginal incentive to influence the government's subsidy policy. The subsidy may increase simultaneously with the tax as a result of changing relative political pressures from environmental and farmer lobby groups, given taxpayers' political pressure. The subsidy enables the government to respond to an increase in the demand for environmental quality without a large drop in producer support.

3. Recent empirical evidence from the manufacturing sectors indicates that more stringent environmental policies may have counter-intuitive effects on trade patterns (van Beers and van den Bergh 1997). Their results suggest that more stringent environmental regulations may have given rise to reduced imports, which is opposite to what is predicted by conventional models of comparative advantage. Moreover, Grossman and Krueger (1993) find that tariff-free exports to the United States from the Mexican maquiladora sector were *higher* in sectors with relatively high abatement costs in the United States. Kalt (1988) and Tobey (1990) found insignificant effects of environmental regulations. However, Low and Yeats (1992) and Hettige and others (1992) found evidence of a migration of polluting industries from OECD to developing countries.

4. Other explanations include that of Porter and van den Linde (1995) who argue that environmental regulations encourage innovations that enhance firms' long-run competitiveness. Alternatively, small abatement costs relative to labor costs, low intercountry differences in regulatory stringency, or the lack of enforcement, could explain the results (see Jaffe and others 1995).

5. Environmental quality is thus likely to be negatively affected (see Just and Bockstael 1991 for a discussion of the environmental effects of commodity programs). Many subsidy schemes have a positive output effect and cause problems such as soil erosion and water pollution from fertilizer and pesticide leakage. This implies that increased attention should be paid to the effects on the environment of the comprehensive policy package in place. Compensation policies aimed at reducing trade effects may have important implications for environmental quality. However, we abstract from an explicit analysis of this issue in the present paper.

6. OECD (1995, p. 29) reports that Austria, Finland, and Sweden have introduced fertilizer and pesticide taxes and levies, and the revenues have been used to subsidize crops and exports. In the United States, the 1985 and 1990 Farm Bills and the Conservation Reserve Program (CRP) are primary forms of environmental programs in agriculture. Unless farmers refrain from cultivating highly erosive areas, all farm program payments are lost by the farm. Gardner (1996) reports that CRP has idled 36.5 million acres, approximately 10 percent of U.S. cropland acreage. In the United Kingdom farmers receive direct compensation for adopting suboptimal agricultural practices in "nitrate sensitive" areas (Blom 1996). OECD (1998a, p. 55) reports that in Denmark, Germany, and Sweden payments to prevent farmers from adopting harmful practices often have not led to significant changes in farming practices. See also Bower and others (1981) and Jenkins and Lamech (1994) for industrial subsidy policies.

7. Our analysis is limited to a single cross-section because we have not been able to find or construct an index of environmental regulations for multiple time-periods, precluding a more extensive analysis of the dynamic interactions between regulations and transfers in agriculture.

8. The *PSE* is calculated by adding indirect transfers from the government (for example, budget and tax expenditures) to implicit transfers from consumers to producers. The sum is measured by multiplying the volume of domestic production by the gap between the domestic producer price and the border price.

9. We employed the Breusch-Pagan Lagrange Multiplier test for heteroscedasticity applied to the structural residuals. The test statistic was equal to 18.91 for equation (1.2) which implies that we reject the null hypothesis of homoscedasticity at the 5 percent level of significance (p-value 0.015). The test did not indicate a heteroscedasticity problem in equation (1.1). We also report the White heteroscedasticity-adjusted estimates for this equation (White 1980). Using a Hausman test, we could not reject the null hypothesis of exogeneity of the *PSE* variable in equation (1.1). Therefore, the OLS results in table 9.1.1 are our preferred estimates. The Hausman test rejected the exogeneity hypothesis for *STRING* in equation (1.2), however (the chi-square test statistic equals 7.95), and therefore the heteroscedasticity-robust 2SLS results are the preferred estimates in table 9.1.2.

10. Lobbying on pollution taxes also appears to be important in the industrial sector; see for example, the discussion in OECD (1998b, p. 30) on tax breaks for energy-intensive sectors in Sweden.

11. Collinearity diagnostics was performed on the reduced form equations, and our test shows that the linear specification does not suffer from multicollinearity (the eigenvalue and condition index are 0.03 and 12.78, respectively). See Belsley (1982).

References

Aidt, T.S. 1998. "Political Internalization of Economic Externalities and Environmental Policy." *Journal of Public Economics* 69(1): 1–16.

Antle, J.H., and G. Heidebrink. 1995. "Environment and Development: Theory and International Evidence." *Economic Development and Cultural Change* 43(1): 603–25.

Becker, G. 1993. "A Theory of Competition Among Pressure Groups for Political Influence." *Quarterly Journal of Political Economy* 98: 371–400.

Belsley, D.A. 1992. "Assessing the Presence of Harmful Collinearity and other Forms of Weak Data through a Test for Signal-to-Noise." *Journal of Econometrics* 20(2): 211–53.

Blom, J.C. 1996. "Environmental Policies in Europe and the Effect on the Balance of Trade." In M.E. Bredahl and others, eds., *Agriculture, Trade, and the Environment: Discovering and Measuring the Critical Linkages*. Boulder, Colo.: Westview Press.

Bower, B.D., R. Barré, J. Kühner, C.S. Russell, and A.J. Price. 1981. *Incentives in Water Quality Management: France and the Ruhr Area*. Washington, D.C.: Resources for the Future.

Dasgupta, S., A. Mody, S. Roy, and D. Wheeler. 1995. "Environmental Regulation and Development: A Cross-Country Empirical Analysis." Policy Research Working Paper 1448, Policy Research Department, World Bank, Washington, D.C.

Eliste, P., and P.G. Fredriksson. 1998. "Environmental Regulations, Transfers, Institutions, and Trade: Theory and Evidence." Mimeo, Environment Department, World Bank, Washington, DC.

Fredriksson, P.G. 1997. "The Political Economy of Pollution Taxes in a Small Open Economy." *Journal of Environmental Economics and Management* 33(1): 44–58.

_____. 1998. "Environmental Policy Choice: Pollution Abatement Subsidies." *Resource and Energy Economics* 20(1): 51–63.

_____. 1999."The Political Economy of Trade Liberalization and Environmental Policy." *Southern Economic Journal* 65(3): 513–25.

Gardner, B.L. 1987. "Causes of U.S. Farm Commodity Programs." *Journal of Political Economy* 95: 290–310.

_____. 1996. "Environmental Regulation and the Competitiveness of U.S. Agriculture." In M.E. Bredahl, N. Ballanger, J.C. Dunmore, and T.L. Roe, eds., *Agriculture, Trade, and the Environment: Discovering and Measuring the Critical Linkages*. Boulder, Colo.: Westview Press.

Gastil, R.D. 1987. *Freedom in the World*. Westport, Conn.: Greenwood Press.

Goklany, I.H. 1996. "Factors Affecting Environmental Impacts: The Effect of Technology on Long-term Trends in Cropland, Air Pollution, and Water Related Diseases." *Ambio* 25(8): 497–503.

Grossman, G.E., and E. Helpman. 1994. "Protection for Sale." *American Economic Review* 84(4): 833–50.

Grossman, G.M. and A.B. Krueger. 1993. "Environmental Impacts of North American Free Trade Agreement." In P. Garber, ed., *The U.S.-Mexico Free Trade Agreement*. Cambridge, Mass: MIT Press.

Hettige, H., R.E.B. Lucas, and D. Wheeler. 1992. "The Toxic Intensity of Industrial Production: Global Patterns, Trends, and Trade Policy." *American Economic Review Papers and Proceedings* 82: 478–81.

Jaffe, A.B., S.R. Peterson, P.R. Portney, and R. Stavins. 1995. "Environmental Regulation and the Competitiveness of U.S. Manufacturing." *Journal of Economic Literature* 33(1): 132–63.

Jenkins, G.P., and R. Lamech. 1992. "Fiscal Policies to Control Pollution: International Experience." Harvard Institute for International Development, Development Discussion Paper 439. Cambridge, Mass: HIID.

Just, R.E., and N. Bockstael, eds. 1991. *Commodity and Resource Policies in Agricultural Systems.* Berlin and New York: Springer-Verlag.

Kalt, J.P. 1988. "The Impact of Domestic Environmental Regulatory Policies on U.S. International Competitiveness." In A.M. Spence and H.A. Hazard, eds., *International Competitiveness.* Cambridge, Mass: Harper and Row, Ballinger.

Lewandrowski, J., J. Tobey, and Z. Cook. 1997. "The Interface between Agricultural Assistance and the Environment: Chemical Fertilizer Consumption and Area Expansion." *Land Economics* 73(3): 404–27.

Low, P., and A. Yeats. 1992. "Do 'Dirty' Industries Migrate?" In P. Low, ed., *International Trade and the Environment.* World Bank Discussion Paper 159. Washington, D.C.

Murdoch, J. C., and T. Sandler. 1997. "The Voluntary Provision of a Pure Public Good: The Case of Reduced CFC Emissions and the Montreal Protocol." *Journal of Public Economics* 63: 331–49.

OECD. 1995. *Environmental Taxes in OECD Countries.* Paris: Organisation for Economic Co-operation and Development.

_____. 1997. *Producer Subsidy Equivalents and Consumer Subsidy Equivalents Database, 1979–1996.* Paris: Organisation for Economic Co-operation and Development.

_____. 1998a. *The Environmental Effects of Reforming Agricultural Policies.* Paris: Organisation for Economic Co-operation and Development.

_____. 1998b. *Improving the Environment Through Reducing Subsidies, Part II.* Paris: Organisation for Economic Co-operation and Development.

Olson, M. 1965. *The Logic of Collective Action.* Cambridge: Harvard University Press.

Opschoor, J.B., and H.B. Vos. 1989. *Economic Instruments for Environmental Protection.* Paris: Organisation for Economic Co-operation and Development.

Pargal, S., and D. Wheeler. 1996. "Informal Regulation in Developing Countries: Evidence from Indonesia." *Journal of Political Economy* 104: 1314–27.

Porter, M., and C. van den Linde. 1995. "Toward a New Conception of the Environment-Competitiveness Relationship." *Journal of Economic Perspectives* 9(4): 119–32.

Potters, J., and R. Sloof. 1996. "Interest Groups: A Survey of Empirical Models That Try to Assess Their Influence." *European Journal of Political Economy* 12: 403–42.

Scully, G. W. 1992. *Constitutional Environments and Economic Growth.* Princeton, New Jersey: Princeton University Press.

Tobey, J.A. 1990. "The Effects of Domestic Environmental Policies on Patterns of World Trade: An Empirical Test." *Kyklos* 43: 191–209.

UNCED. 1992. *Nations of the Earth Report,* Vol. I–III. Geneva: United Nations.

USDA. 1990. "Estimates of Producer and Consumer Subsidy Equivalents: Government Intervention in Agriculture 1982–87." *Statistical Bulletin* 803. Economic Research Service. Washington, D.C.: U.S. Department of Agriculture.

_____. 1994a. "Government Intervention in Agriculture 1982–92." *Statistical Bulletin* 913. Economic Research Service. Washington, D.C.: U.S. Department of Agriculture.

_____. 1994b. *World Agriculture: Trends & Indicators, 1961–91.* CD-ROM. Department of Economics and Statistics. Washington, D.C.: U.S. Department of Agriculture.

Valdés, A. 1996. "Surveillance of Agricultural Price and Trade Policy in Latin America During Major Policy Reforms." World Bank Discussion Paper 349. Washington, D.C.: World Bank.

van Beers, C., and J.C.J.M. van den Bergh. 1997. "An Empirical Multi-Country Analysis of the Impact of Environmental Policy on Foreign Trade Flows." *Kyklos* 50(1): 29–46.

White, H. 1980. "A Heteroscedasticity-Consistent Covariance Matrix Estimator and a Direct Test for Heteroscedasticity." *Econometrica* 48: 817–38.

World Bank. 1992. *World Tables.* Washington, D.C.: World Bank.

_____. 1997a. *World Development Indicators 1997.* Washington, D.C.: World Bank.

_____. 1997b. *Economic and Social Database.* Washington, D.C.: World Bank.

Chapter 10

Pollution and Capital Markets in Developing Countries

Susmita Dasgupta, Benoit Laplante, and Nlandu Mamingi

1. Introduction

Though environmental regulations have now been in use for more than 20 years, it is increasingly recognized that their efficacy in controlling pollution emissions has been dampened by a lack of appropriate monitoring and enforcement. Resources devoted by various regulatory agencies to the monitoring of emission standards have typically been characterized as insufficient.[1] Moreover, when compliance with the standards is found to be lacking, it is generally acknowledged that fines and penalties are too low (compared to pollution abatement costs) to act as effective deterrents. In a recent study of environmental regulations in East Asian countries, O'Connor (1994, p.94) writes:

> In several of the countries studied here,[2] the monitoring problem is compounded by weak enforcement. In short, when violators of standards are detected, if penalized at all they often face only weak sanctions. (...) polluters are exempted from fines either on grounds of financial hardship or because the violators wield undue political influence. Perhaps the most pervasive problem is that, even when fines are levied, they are frequently so low in real terms that they have little if any deterrent value. In virtually all the countries studied, there remains considerable room for improvement on the enforcement front.

It is indeed generally said that firms in developing countries do not have incentives to invest in pollution control effort because of weak monitoring and enforcement of the environmental regulations. This argument however assumes that the environmental regulator is the only agent that can penalize the firm lacking pollution control effort, or reward the firm for good environmental performance or innovation in environmental technologies. It ignores that capital markets may react *negatively* to the announcement of adverse environmental incidents (such as violation of permits, spills, court actions, complaints, and so forth) or *positively* to the announcement of greater pollution control effort such as the adoption of cleaner technologies.

The impact of firm-specific environmental news on market value may work its way through various channels: a high level of pollution intensity may signal to investors the inefficiency of the firm's production process; it may invite stricter scrutiny by environmental groups and/or facility neighbors; it may result in the loss of reputation, goodwill, and so forth. On the other hand, the announcement of a good environmental performance or of the investment in cleaner technologies may have the opposite effect: lesser scrutiny by regulators and communities (including the financial community), greater access to international markets, and so forth.[3]

Hence, the inability of institutions in developing countries to provide incentives for pollution control effort via the traditional channel of fines and penalties may not be as serious an impediment to pollution control as is generally argued. Capital markets, if properly informed, may provide the appropriate reputational and financial incentives.

A limited number of papers have analyzed the reaction of capital markets to environmental news in Canada and the United States. These studies have generally shown that firms suffer from a decline in market values upon announcement of adverse environmental news.[4] In this paper, we assess whether or not capital markets in Mexico, Chile, Argentina, and the Philippines react to the announcement of firm-specific environmental news. To our knowledge, the current analysis is the first of this nature performed in developing countries. Even in those countries where it is generally argued that the environmental regulations suffer from poor implementation, we show that capital markets react negatively (decrease in firms' value) to citizens' complaints targeted at specific firms. We also show that markets react positively (increase in firms' market value) to the announcement of rewards and explicit recognition of superior environmental performance. An immediate policy implication from the current analysis is that environmental regulators in developing countries may explicitly harness those market forces by introducing structured programs of information release on firms' environmental performance, and empower communities and stakeholders through environmental education programs.[5]

These results may also shed some new light on the pollution haven hypothesis. A large number of studies have examined the potential impact of environmental regulations on international competitiveness.[6] Many of these have concluded that pollution intensive firms have *not* invested or relocated in developing countries to benefit from lower environmental standards and/or poor enforcement of environmental regulations. Hettige and others (1992, p. 480) observe that "one possibility is that the expected profitability of investment in pollution-intensive sectors has also been affected by growing concern over legal liability or reputational damage." Where traditional tools and actions may have been unable to create incentives for pollution control, our results give some support to this point of view to the extent that capital markets may reward firms with good environmental performance and penalize firms with poor environmental performance.

In the next section, we describe our dataset. In section 3, we briefly describe the event-study methodology used in this analysis to measure the reaction of capital markets to environmental news (both positive and negative news). Results are presented in section 4. We briefly conclude in section 5.

2. Dataset

The countries retained in this study—Argentina, Chile, Mexico, and the Philippines—are countries where stock markets are believed to work reasonably well, where market capitalization is relatively high and increasing over time (table 10.1), and where market concentration is not an impediment to conducting event-study analyses (table 10.2).[7]

For each country, we selected a newspaper which has a large circulation and is of particular interest to the business community.[8] Environmental news were collected in each of the countries over the period 1990-94 inclusively. Once these news were collected, we identified those articles involving firms traded in local capital markets. As shown in table 10.3, the amount of environmental news (that is, newsclips) collected in each country is relatively large (a total of 7,354 environmental news were collected over the period 1990-94), with Mexico alone representing 47.5 percent of the total number of news. The number of environmental news is also relatively constant over

Table 10.1 Capitalization of the stock market of Argentina, Chile, Mexico, and the Philippines, 1990–1994 *(in millions of U.S. dollars)*

Market	*1990*	*1991*	*1992*	*1993*	*1994*
Argentina	3 268	18 509	18 633	43 967	36 864
Chile	13 645	27 984	29 644	44 622	68 195
Mexico	32 725	98 178	139 061	200 671	130 246
Philippines	5 927	10 197	13 794	40 327	55 519

Source: International Finance Corporation, *Emerging stock markets factbook*, 1995.

Table 10.2 Market concentration in the IFC general indexes, end–1994

Market	*IFCG Index share of total market capitalization*	*10 largest stocks' share of total market capitalization*
Argentina	50.9	41.7
Chile	66.1	46.4
Mexico	63.9	33.8
Philippines	54.4	44.3

Source: International Finance Corporation, *Emerging stock markets factbook*, 1995.

the period of analysis. Approximately 20 percent of the news involve specific firms, traded and non-traded. As expected, the number of news involving publicly traded companies is relatively small in all countries. However, publicly traded companies represent a much larger share of the number of companies cited in environmental news than their relative numbers in the economy. This may be explained by their generally larger size, thus being of greater scrutiny.

Environmental news were divided into two groups: positive (for example rewards, investment in pollution control, and so forth), and negative (spills, complaints, warnings, and so forth). The sample set is described in table 10.4. As can be observed, Chile registered 53 events (environmental news) involving 17 publicly traded firms over the period 1990-94; 20 of those events were positive while 33 were negative. Argentina registered 20 events (5 positive and 15 negative) involving 11 firms. The Manila Bulletin reported 18 events (10 positive and 8 negative) with 10 firms. Finally, the Mexican sample consists of 35 events (of which only 4 were positive) involving 10 publicly-traded firms. Observe that the number of events in table 10.4 is smaller than the number of news (with name of publicly traded companies) in table 10.3. This is the case since a significant number of newsclips is simply a repetition or follow-up on an initial event and does not provide any additional information to what is already known. In most cases, we have included in our dataset only the announcement of the initial event.

3. Event-Study Methodology

The event-study methodology is used in this study to examine the reaction of investors to positive and negative news (also called events).[9] The methodology is based on the assumption that capital markets are sufficiently efficient to evaluate the impact of new information (events) on expected future profits of the firms.

Table 10.3 Number of news, 1990–1994

	1990	*1991*	*1992*	*1993*	*1994*
Argentina					
Total number of environmental news	201	189	168	198	170
With name of non-traded companies	28	32	48	33	27
With name of publicly traded companies	0	0	2	13	15
Chile					
Total number of environmental news	309	285	293	282	272
With name of non-traded companies	29	48	43	22	32
With name of publicly traded companies	4	25	34	36	16
Mexico					
Total number of environmental news	625	707	759	613	618
With name of non-traded companies	161	143	118	73	88
With name of publicly traded companies	14	25	7	10	8
Philippines					
Total number of environmental news	317	309	334	265	266
With name of non-traded companies	54	47	44	47	55
With name of publicly traded companies	8	8	4	9	12

Table 10.4 Description of data set

Country	*Name of firm**	*Sector of activity*	*Nature and number of events* Positive	Negative
Argentina	Astra	Oil	1	1
	Ipako	Oil	1	2
	Perez	Oil	0	2
	YPF	Oil	1	4
	Celulosa	Pulp and paper	1	0
	Telefonica	Telephone	0	1
	Colorin	Chemical	0	2
	Indupa	Chemical	1	0
	Molinos Rio	Food	0	1
	Sevel	Metal	0	1
	Siderca	Metal	0	1
Total	*11 firms*	*6 sectors*	*5*	*15*
Chile	Endesa	Electric	3	4
	Chilgener	Electric	4	4
	CMPC	Pulp and paper	2	1
	CAP	Metal	3	4
	Volcan	Building material	0	1
	Minera	Investment	0	1
	Vapores	Transportation	0	1
	Emos	Water	3	1
	Puerto	Water	0	1
	Victoria	Fabric	0	1
	Iansa	Food	1	1
	Molymet	Metal	1	1
	Coloso	Fishery	0	5
	Iquique	Fishery	1	5
	Lirquien	Building material	0	1
	Chilectra	Electric	1	1
	Eperva	Fishery	1	0
Total	*17 firms*	*10 sectors*	*20*	*33*
Mexico	Cydsasa	Pulp and paper, oil	1	3
	Grupo Maya (A)	Cement	0	6
	Grupo Maya (B)	Cement	0	4
	Tolteca (Tolmex)	Cement	0	2
	Met-Mex Penoles (A)	Mining	1	6
	Met-Mex Penoles (B)	Mining	0	3
	Femsa	Food	1	0
	Grupo Vitro	Manufacture	1	0
	GC3	Cement	0	1
	Kimberly y Clark	Pulp and paper	0	2
	Grupo Bimbo	Food	0	2
	Telefonos de Mexico	Communication	0	2
Total	*10 firms*	*8 sectors*	*4*	*31*
Philippines	Apex Mining	Mining	0	1
	Atlas C. Mining	Mining	1	0
	Ayala Land, Inc.	Property	0	1
	Benguet	Mining	3	2
	Jolibee	Food	1	0
	Lepanto	Mining	0	1
	Manila Mining	Mining	1	0
	Mondragon	Trading	0	1
	San Miguel	Food	4	1
	Robinson Land	Property	1	0
Total	*10 firms*	*5 sectors*	*10*	*8*

* Complete names of firms appear in the Appendix.

It involves the following steps: (1) identification of the events of interest and definition of the event window;[10] (2) selection of the sample set of firms to include in the analysis;[11] (3) prediction of a "normal" return during the event window in the absence of the event; (4) estimation of the abnormal return within the event window, where the abnormal return is defined as the difference between the actual and predicted returns; and (5) testing whether the abnormal return is statistically different from zero. Several methods may be used to obtain to estimate abnormal returns: the single-index model (constant mean return model), the market model and the capital asset price model (CAPM) are the most widely used.

The market model assumes a linear relationship between the return of any security to the return of the market portfolio:

$$R_{it} = \alpha_i + \beta_i R_{mt} + e_{it}$$
$$with \;\; E(e_{it}) = 0 \qquad and \quad Var(e_{it}) = \sigma^2_{e_i} \tag{1}$$

where t is the time index, $i = 1,2,...,N$, stands for security, R_{it} and R_{mt} are the returns on security i and the market portfolio respectively during period t, and e_{it} is the error term for security i.

Equation (1) is generally estimated over a period which runs between 120 and 210 days prior to the event up to 10 days prior to the event. The event window is defined as the period from 10 days prior to the event to 10 days after the event. With the estimates of α_i and β_i from equation (1), one can predict a "normal" return during the days covered by the event window. The prediction error (the difference between the actual return and the predicted normal return), commonly referred to as the abnormal return (AR), is then calculated as:

$$AR_{it} = R_{it} - \hat{\alpha}_i - \hat{\beta}_i R_{mt} \tag{2}$$

Under the null hypothesis, the abnormal returns will be jointly normally determined with a zero conditional mean and conditional variance $\sigma^2(AR_{it})$:

$$\sigma^2(AR_{it}) = \sigma^2_{e_i} + \frac{1}{L}[\,1 + \frac{(R_{mt} - \overline{R}_m)^2}{\sigma^2_m}] \tag{3}$$

where L is the estimation period length (that is, number of days used for estimation) and $\overline{R}_m$ is the mean of the market portfolio. With L large, $\sigma^2(AR_{it}) \to \sigma^2_{e_i}$.

For each individual event, one can estimate the abnormal return and relevant test statistics at each instant in time within the event window. However, in order to draw overall inference on the abnormal return observations for the event(s) of interest, one can also aggregate the abnormal returns. For any given subset of N events (or securities), the sampled aggregated abnormal returns (AAR_t) at each instant t within the event window is computed as

$$AAR_t = \frac{1}{N}\sum_{i=1}^{N} AR_{it} \tag{4}$$

For large L, the variance is

$$VAR(AAR_t) = \frac{1}{N^2}\sum_{i=1}^{N} \sigma^2_{e_i} \tag{5}$$

To test for the significance of AAR_t a Z (or t) test can be derived.

In order to test for the persistence of the impact of the event during a period $(T_2 - T_1)$, the abnormal return can be added to obtain the cumulated abnormal returns $(CAR_i(T_1,T_2))$ for security i over the period $(T_2 - T_1)$:

$$CAR_i(T_1,T_2) = \sum_{t=T_1}^{T_2} AR_{it} \tag{6}$$

where $T_a \le T_1 < t < T_2 \le T_b \in$ event window, and T_a and T_b are the lower and upper limits of the event window, respectively. Asymptotically (as L increases) the variance of the cumulative abnormal return for security i is

$$\sigma^2_i(T_1,T_2) = (T_2 - T_1 + 1)\,\sigma^2_{e_i}. \tag{7}$$

To test the null hypothesis of zero cumulative abnormal return, one can formulate a Z test as $CAR_i(T_i,T_2) \sim N(0, \sigma^2_i(T_i,T_2))$:

$$Z = \frac{CAR}{(\sigma^2_i(T_1,T_2))^{1/2}} \sim N(0,1) \tag{8}$$

An aggregation of interest can also be performed across both time and events. In that scenario, the average cumulative abnormal return is defined as:

$$CAAR(T_1,T_2)=\frac{1}{N}\sum_{i=1}^{N}CAR_i(T_1,T_2) \qquad (9)$$

where N is the number of events. The variance of *CAAR* is

$$\text{var}(CAAR(T_1,T_2))=\frac{1}{N^2}\sum_{i=1}^{N}\sigma_i^2(T_1,T_2) \qquad (10)$$

Under the null hypotheses that the abnormal returns are zero,

$$Z=\frac{CAAR(T_1,T_2)}{(\text{var}(CAAR(T_1,T_2)))^{1/2}} \sim N(0,1) \qquad (11)$$

As pointed by MacKinlay (1997, p. 24), this distributional result is asymptotic with respect to the number of securities N and the length of estimation window L.

In the next section, we present results obtained from using the single-index model (constant mean return model).[12]

4. Empirical Results

We apply the event-study methodology to the environmental events collected in each of the country over the period 1990–94. While various subsets of firms can be presented (for example by countries, by industrial sectors, and so forth), each of those subsets contains a relatively small number of firms, and results in each subset are typically driven by changes in the market values of a limited number of firms. Hence, for the purpose of the analysis, we first present the results obtained at the most disaggregated level, that is, the firm level. This is more likely to indicate the nature of the events to which capital markets appear to be more sensitive. In tables 5 and 7, we indicate the nature of events for which statistically significant increases or reductions in market values are observed.[13]

With respect to positive news, it is of extreme interest to note in table 10.5 (and the Appendix) that out of the 13 events for which statistically significant increases in market values are obtained, 8 of them involve the report of an agreement with the regulator or the explicit recognition by the regulator of a superior environmental performance. That a firm reports an investment in pollution control (or compliance with standards) does not appear to impact capital markets. Markets appear to react to the recognition of such investment or performance by the authorities. For those events, market values increase by more than 20 percent over the entire event window.

As indicated in section 3, it is possible to pool together events and test for the statistical significance of the average abnormal return for the events thus pooled. Given the nature of the results on individual stock markets, it is of interest to test if government actions (for example agreements and awards) as a whole are statistically significant. In table 10.6, we have grouped together these government actions and treated them as a single set of events. As can be observed, government actions as a whole are mildly statistically significant on day +1. However, the difference between government actions and other positive events fail to be statistically significant. This may be explained by noting in table 10.5 that three individual government actions failed to be statistically significant.[14]

These results give some support to public information programs whereby the regulator rates and releases not only bad environmental performance but also superior performance. The results indicate that such recognition does not solely limit itself to an increase in reputation but also has a positive financial impact on the firm (through an expected increase in demand brought about by the enhanced reputation, or reduction in expected costs, for example lesser scrutiny by environmental groups, communities, and regulators).

With respect to negative events (table 10.7), we obtain statistically significant decreases in market values especially when it is reported that governments or citizens have complained about the pollution record of the firm, and not when court actions or fines are reported.

Given the nature of these results, we have pooled together government and citizens' complaints and tested whether or not they had a statistically significant differential impact on market values when compared to all other negative events. Results in table 10.8 indicate that they strongly do.

We may interpret this result by noting that the filing of a complaint can provide *unanticipated* news to markets leading them to expect further actions, yet unknown, to be undertaken. Reductions in market values range on average from 4 percent to 15 percent. These losses are much greater in magnitude than any of our possibilities to comprehensively address this losses observed in previous studies conducted in developed countries.[15]

Table 10.5 Positive events

Name of Company	Date	Nature of Event
ARGENTINA		
Astra	3/15/94	Investment in environmental protection.
Ipako	2/7/93	Investment in environmental protection.
YPF	12/24/94	Investment to save birds.
Celulosa	8/3/92	Investment in manufacturing recyclable papers.
Indupa	2/7/93	Company action : agreement with government for environmental performance improvement.
CHILE		
Endesa	1/31/92	Investment in pollution abatement.
	9/6/93	Court verdict: positive for the company.
	8/8/94	Investment in environmental protection.
Chilgener	1/9/90 *	Pollution abatement: agreement between company and government.
	8/5/90	Pollution abatement announcement.
	11/9/93 *	Government action: agreement approved by the President of Chile.
	6/23/94	Company action: declaration of technical aspects of the agreement.
CMPC	2/26/92	Investment in water pollution abatement.
	1/7/94 *	Investment realization: recycling plant to be inaugurated by the president of Chile.
CAP	8/15/92*	Court verdict: investment in pollution abatement.
	10/2/92	Investment action: use of equipment for pollution control.
	11/8/92 *	Government action: recognition of the company's investment in pollution control equipment.
Emos	4/16/92	Investment in construction of a waste water treatment plant.
	2/24/93	The treatment plant will start working from March 15.
	8/11/93	President of Chile will officially inaugurate the plant.
Iansa	9/26/93 *	Investment in water pollution abatement.
Molymet	10/11/93	Pollution treatment plant inaugurated by the President of Chile.
Iquique	8/11/92	Investment in pollution abatement.
Chilectra	5/29/93	Company reward for environmental performance.
Eperva	7/1/94	Self impact assessment of environment.
MEXICO		
Cydsasa	5/11/92	Investment in improvement of environment.
Apenol	7/10/93 *	Announcement: existence of pollution control equipment.
Femsa	9/14/91	Agreement with government on pollution abatement.
Vitro	4/18/91*	Investment in environmental projects.
PHILIPPINES		
Atlas	10/20/90	The company has a representation project since 1970.
Benguet	12/28/92	Government action: mandatory environmental guarantee fund for the company.
	7/19/93 *	Government action: Reward (trophy) for reforestation program.
	2/6/94	Investment in environmental protection.
Jolibee	6/28/94*	Investment in recyclable paper.
Manila Mining	4/17/92 *	Compliance certified by the Environmental Regulatory authority of Philippines.
San Miguel	11/5/90 *	Investment in waste water treatment plant.
	2/10/91 *	Government action: praise company for having environmental concern.
	9/14/91	Company action: implementation of reforestation project.
	6/8/93	Announcement: new waste water treatment plant.

***** *indicates a statistically significant increase in market value*

Table 10.6 Government actions vs. other positive events

Day -1		*Day 0*		*Day +1*		*Window*
Government actions						
AAR	*CAAR*	*AAR*	*CAAR*	*AAR*	*CAAR*	*CAAR*
5.080	23.805	-10.627	13.177	14.420•	27.615	9.574
(0.650)	(0.904)	(-1.360)	(0.509)	(1.846)	(1.020)	(0.267)
All other positive events						
-2.156	-10.583	-0.846	-11.457	-1.625	-15.488	17.245
(0.176)	(-0.247)	(-0.069)	(-0.255)	(-0.133)	(-0.330)	(0.308)
Government actions vs. all other positive events						
7.236	34.387	-9.781	24.634	16.045	43.103	-7.670
(0.499)	(0.696)	(-0.674)	(0.475)	(1.106)	(0.796)	(-0.115)

Notes: For government actions and All other positive events, the sampled aggregate abnormal return (AAR) is computed for day -1, 0, and +1. The average cumulative abnormal return (CAAR) is computed for day -10 up to the day. For the event window, the average cumulative abnormal return is calculated over the period -10 to +10. Within brackets is the value of the Z statistics. For Government actions Vs All other positive events, the AAR is here defined as the difference between the AAR for Government actions and the AAR for All other positive events. The Z statistics is defined accordingly. "•", "*", and "**" mean significant at the 10 percent, 5 percent and 1 percent level respectively (one tailed-test).

5. Conclusion

In this paper, we have shown that despite a generally acknowledged poor enforcement of environmental regulations, capital markets in Argentina, Chile, Mexico and the Philippines appear to react to the announcement of environmental events involving publicly traded companies. While fines and penalties used by the environmental agencies of these countries may have fallen short of creating incentives for pollution control, capital markets have penalized firms suffering from adverse environmental events, and rewarded firms with positive environmental news. While we are certainly not arguing that strong enforcement of regulations should be abandoned and that markets (firms, consumers, communities) be left to themselves to negotiate and induce pollution abatement from polluters (not all firms may be responsive to public release of their environmental performance), these results suggest that in numerous circumstances market forces (even in developing countries) have not remained idle upon receiving signals of the environmental performance of firms. These results indicate that at the margin, environmental regulators should devote less resources to the enforcement of regulations, and more to the collection, analysis, and dissemination of appropriate, reliable, and timely information. Further research in this area will indicate whether or not our findings can be generalized, as well as providing a greater understanding of the mechanisms which underpin the reaction of capital markets.

Moreover, whether or not firms have "voluntarily" undertaken pollution abatement activities seeking the obtention of the reward, and whether or not adverse market reaction has lead firms to subsequently invest in pollution control is a further issue of investigation.[16] It is indeed currently beyond the realm issue as it requires a vast amount of firm-level data that is not currently available for the countries studied here. From an anecdotal point of view however, it is interesting to note, among others, that after Chilgener (Chile) had released a cloud of toxic air pollution over Santiago and suffered a loss of 5 percent of its market value in April 1992, it announced on September 25, 1992, an investment of 115 million dollars to control air pollution.

Table 10.7 Negative events

Name of company	Date	Nature of event
ARGENTINA		
Ipako	10/16/92*	Government action: warning about pollution problem.
	9/9/93	Accident.
Perez	5/2/93	Government action: warning for oil spill.
	12/12/94	Accidental oil spill.
YPF	11/7/93*	Environmental problem (birds killed).
	11/30/93 *	Citizens complaint.
	1/24/94	Government action: warning.
	8/10/94	Oil spill to river.
Colorin	8/2/93	Suspicious transfer of solid waste.
	11/2/94 *	Government deadline to company.
Molinos	9/30/93	Government action: fine.
Sevel	8/2/93	Government Court action against co.
Siderca	11/2/94	Government action: warning.
CHILE		
Endesa	1/19/92 *	Government complaint.
	9/29/92 *	Warning from environment ministry.
	2/7/93	President's advice on pollution improvement.
	4/21/93 *	Citizens protests against company.
Chilgener	7/13/90	Government complaint.
	1/19/92	Government complains on bad environmental performance of the company.
	4/8/92 *	Environmental accident.
	4/16/92	Court action by citizens.
CMPC	9/30/92 *	Citizens complain about solid waste pollution.
CAPC	4/2/91	Air polluter.
	6/27/92	Court action by citizens.
	8/8/92	Grace period granted to curb water pollution.
	8/12/92	Government supports court action.
Volcan	12/2/93	Government black list of polluters.
Minera	9/2/91	Court action.
Vapores	6/6/92	Company is fined by government.
Emos	10/17/93	Accident: drinking water contamination.
Puerto	7/23/92 *	Government complains about health hazard in the vicinity of the company.
Victoria	12/2/93	Government black list of air polluter.
Iansa	5/29/93	One of the plants ordered to shutdown.
Coloso	4/1/92	Government action: fine.
	12/2/93	Government action: company shutdown for few hours.
	2/5/94	Court action:fine.
	3/11/94	Government action: company shutdown.
	3/18/94	Citizens complaint: accident.
Iquique	4/1/92 *	Government action: fine.
	12/21/93	Government action: fine.
	2/5/94	Court action: fine.
	3/10/94	Government action (Company closed for 72 hours).
	3/11/94	Court action for bad smell problem.
Lirquien	7/15/92	Government black list of air polluter.
Chilectra	7/11/92	Citizens complain against company expansion.
Molymet	1/19/92	Government complaint: company major air polluter.
PHILIPPINES		
Apex	4/24/91 *	Government action.
Ayala	12/8/94 *	Government warning.
Benguet	3/21/90	Government action: penalty.
	3/23/90	Workers dismissals.
Lepanto	10/22/90	Pollution problem resulting in death and illness.
Mondragon	10/11/94	Complaint by citizens about tree cutting.
Robinson Land	6/15/94	Government action: company shutdown.
San Miguel	10/7/94	Oil spill.

***** *indicates a statistically significant reduction in market value*

Table 10.7 Negative events (*continued*)

		MEXICO
Cydsasa	2/16/90	Spill causing death and injury.
	3/19/92	Black list of air polluter for company's subsidiary.
	10/9/92	Government action: environmental audit.
Grupo Maya (A)	10/4/90	NGO's black list of air polluter.
	3/12/91	Company relocation requested by Citizens.
	3/15/91	Government action: warning.
	9/20/91 *	Citizens complaint.
	11/27/91*	(11/25/94): Citizens and ecologists complaint.
	7/29/92 *	Citizens complaints.
Grupo Maya (B)	3/12/91	Company relocation requested by Citizens.
	3/15/91	Government action: warning.
	9/20/91 *	Citizens complaint.
	11/27/91*	(11/25/94): Citizens and ecologists complaint.
Tolteca	10/14/90	NGO's black list of air polluter.
	2/13/92	Temporary and partial shutdown.
Met-Mex Penoles (A)	3/22/91	Citizens complaints.
	6/4/91	Company pollution bad record pointed by a Senator.
	8/9/91 *	Government action: company temporarily shutdown.
	3/2/94	Accident: citizens complaint.
	3/4/94	Pollution control equipment investigation.
	8/27/94	Relocation of 300 families living in the vicinity of the co.
Met-Mex Penoles (B)	3/22/91	Citizens complaints.
	6/4/91 *	Company pollution bad record pointed by a Senator.
	3/4/94	Pollution control equipment investigation.
Cementos de Chiguagua (GC3)	5/25/92	Government action: warning about environmental performance.
Kimberly Clark	5/21/92 *	Government action: fine for water pollution.
Grupo Bimbo	3/19/92 *	Black list of air polluter.
	2/14/93	Government action: initiate court action.
Telefonos de Mexico	5/21/93	Government action: warning about tree cutting.
	6/9/94	Government action: fine.

* *indicates a statistically significant reduction in market value*

Table 10.8 Complaints vs. all other negative events

DAY -1		Day 0		Day +1		Window
Complaints (Government and citizens)						
AAR	CAAR	AAR	CAAR	AAR	CAAR	CAAR
-1.405	-30.209*	3.137	-27.331*	-1.244	-24.473•	-36.014•
(-0.343)	(-2.335)	(0.767)	(-2.014)	(-0.304)	(-1.727)	(-1.921)
All other negative events						
-2.751	-1.274	0.524	-1.489	2.889	2.680	1.1687
(-0.988)	(-0.146)	(0.190)	(-0.162)	(1.047)	(0.280)	(0.092)
Complaints vs. all other negative events						
1.347	-28.934•	2.613	-25.842•	-4.133	-27.152•	-37.182•
(0.273)	(-1.853)	(0.530)	(-1.578)	(-0.838)	(-1.587)	(-1.643)

Note: See *Note* in table 6 for details of computation.

Appendix Table A10.1 Complete name of companies in sample set

ARGENTINA	
Astra	Astra Compania Argentina de Petroleo
Ipako	Ipako Industria Petroquimica
Perez	Perez Compane
YPF	Yacimientos Petroliferos Fiscales
Celulosa	Empresa Celulosa Argentina
Telefonica	Empresa Telefonica de Argentina
Colorin	Colorin Industrial de Material Sintetico
Indupa	Indupa
Molinos Rio	Molinos Rio de la Plata
Sevel	Sevel Argentina
Siderca	Siderca
CHILE	
Endesa	Empresa Nacional de Electricidad
Chilgener	Chilgener
CMPC	Compania Manufacturera de Papetes y Cartones
CAP	Compania de Acero del Pacifico
Volcan	Compania Industrial el Volcan
Minera	Compania Minera Tamaya
Vapores	Compania Sud Americana de Vapores
Emos	Empresa Metropolitana de Obras Sanitarias
Puerto	Empresa Portuaria Puchoco
Victoria	Fabrica Victoria de Puente Alto
Iansa	Industria Azucarara Nacional
Molymet	Molibdenos y Metales
Coloso	Empresa Pesquera Coloso
Iquique	Pesquera Iquique
Lirquien	Vidrios y Planos Lirquien
Chilectra	Chilectra
Eperva	Empresa Pesquera Eperva
MEXICO	
Cydsasa	Celulosa y Derivados
Grupo Maya	Grupo Empresarial Maya
Tolteca (Tolmex)	Cementos Tolteca
Met-Mex Penoles	Empresa Metalurgica Met-Mex Penoles
Femsa	Fomento Economico Mexicano
Vitro	Grupo Vitro
GC3	Cementos de Chiguagua
Kimberly Clark	Kimberly y Clark de Mexico
Bimbo	Grupo Bimbo
Telmex	Telefonos de Mexico
PHILIPPINES	
Apex Mining	Apex Mining Company
Atlas C. Mining	Atlas Consolidated Mining & Development Corporation
Ayala Land	Ayala Land
Benguet	Benguet Corporation
Jolibee	Jolibee Corporation
Lepanto	Lepanto Consolidated Mining Company
Manila Mining	Manila Mining
Mondragon	Mondragon International Philippines
San Miguel	San Miguel Corporation
Robinson Land	Robinson Land Corporation

Appendix Table A10.2 Reaction of market to positive news

ARGENTINA								
		Day -1		*Day 0*		*Day + 1*		*Event window*
Astra	3/15/94	2.651	2.705	-0.476	2.229	-1.355	0.874	-7.626
		(1.017)	(0.328)	(-0.183)	(0.258)	(-0.520)	(0.097)	(-0.639)
Ipako	2/7/93	-4.107	2.266	-2.819	-0.553	-0.825	-1.378	19.965
		(-0.534)	(0.093)	(-0.366)	(-0.054)	(-0.107)	(-0.052)	(0.566)
YPF	12/24/94	-4.573	-4.714	-2.279	-6.933	-0.346	-7.339	-7.695
		(-0.169)	(-0.123)	(-0.084)	(-0.149)	(-0.013)	(-0.136)	(-0.127)
Celulosa	8/3/92	-2.462	-10.117	0.696	-9.421	0.696	-8.725	-9.984
		(-0.425)	(-0.546)	(0.119)	(-0.485)	(0.119)	(-0.430)	(-0.372)
Indupa	2/7/93	-1.106	11.735	-5.145	6.589	0.855	7.444	18.187
		(-0.157)	(0.528)	(-0.732)	(0.283)	(0.122)	(0.306)	(0.565)
CHILE								
Firms	*Date*	AR_i	CAR_i	AR_i	CAR_i	AR_i	CAR_i	CAR_i
Endesa	1/31/92	0.873	2.428	1.029	3.457	-0.861	2.596	8.568
		(0.327)	(0.288)	(0.386)	(0.391)	(-0.323)	(0.281)	(0.700)
	9/6/93	-0.426	-0.367	-0.031	-0.397	-0.096	-0.493	0.530
		(-0.318)	(-0.087)	(-0.023)	(-0.090)	(-0.072)	(-0.106)	(0.086)
	8/8/94	-0.019	0.839	-0.486	0.353	-1.497	-1.145	-2.388
		(-0.015)	(0.213)	(-0.391)	(0.085)	(-1.203)	(-0.265)	(-0.419)
Chilgener	1/9/90	0.347	6.899	0.596	7.495	1.588	9.083	21.290*
		(0.146)	(0.917)	(0.251)	(0.950)	(0.668)	(1.102)	(1.953)
	8/5/90	-3.626	-12.180	-4.386	-16.566	-2.500	-19.066	-21.697
		(-1.350)	(-1.434)	(-1.633)	(-1.860)	(-0.931)	(-2.049)	(-1.863)
	11/9/93	2.746 *	7.624•	0.943	8.567*	0.250	8.817*	25.443**
		(1.780)	(1.563)	(0.611)	(1.674)	(0.162)	(1.650)	(3.599)
	6/23/94	-1.510	-8.549	-1.711	-9.843	-1.343	-8.753	-23.820
		(-0.654)	(-0.943)	(-0.746)	(-1.124)	(-0.586)	(-1.245)	(-2.267)
CMPC	2/26/92	1.401	3.346	2.560	5.906	-0.604	5.302	0.755
		(0.699)	(0.505)	(1.222)	(0.850)	(-0.288)	(0.731)	(0.144)
	1/7/94	-2.523	4.475	1.957*	6.431*	2.980**	9.412**	25.915**
		(-2.188)	(1.227)	(1.697)	(1.681)	(2.584)	(2.356)	(4.903)
CAP	8/15/92	-3.077	-5.639	3.597•	-2.042	0.260	-1.783	0.094
		(-1.387)	(-0.803)	(1.621)	(-0.277)	(0.117)	(-0.232)	(0.009)
	10/2/92	0.448	(-2.033)	1.430	-0.603	-0.745	-1.344	0.808
		(0.261)	(-0.375)	(0.833)	(-0.106)	(-0.433)	(-0.277)	(0.103)
	11/8/92	-0.105	2.095	1.544	3.640	2.850*	6.489•	21.613**
		(-0.095)	(0.420)	(0.979)	(0.730)	(1.807)	(1.301)	(2.991)
Emos	4/16/92	-9.544	-13.429	-0.453	-13.884	-2.58	-27.684	-27.684
		(-1.797)	(-0.799)	(-0.085)	(-0.788)	(-1.215)	(-1.137)	(-1.137)
	2/24/93	1.131	-1.194	-0.385	-1.578	-1.137	-2.175	-12.693
		(0.257)	(-0.086)	(-0.087)	(-0.108)	(-0.258)	(-0.178)	(-0.629)

CHILE (*continued*)								
		Day -1		Day 0		Day +1		Event window
	8/11/93	-0.024	-0.169	-0.024	-0.193	-0.024	-0.217	0.919
		(-0.006)	(-0.012)	(-0.06)	(-0.015)	(-0.006)	(-0.227)	(0.051)
Iansa	9/26/93	-0.727	9.881 •	-1.626	8.255	0.170	8.425	21.265**
		(-0.345)	(1.483)	(-0.772)	(1.182)	(0.081)	(1.155)	(2.203)
Molymet	10/11/93	-5.500	-15.168	-1.409	-16.577	-1.409	-17.986	-35.849
		(-0.704)	(-0.614)	(-0.180)	(-0.634)	(-0.180)	(-0.664)	(-1.000)
Iquique	8/11/92	-5.947	-4.452	-0.437	-4.889	-4.603	-9.492	-13.421
		(-1.293)	(-0.306)	(-0.095)	(-0.320)	(-1.001)	(-0.596)	(-0.638)
Chilectra	5/29/93	-1.026	4.499	-1.039	3.460	-0.822	2.368	8.440
		(-0.500)	(0.533)	(-0.506)	(0.387)	(-0.401)	(0.371)	(0.897)
Eperva	7/1/94	-2.284	3.093	-4.802	-1.709	-7.642	-9.352	11.877
		(-0.491)	(0.210)	(-1.031)	(-0.111)	(-1.642)	(-0.580)	(0.557)
MEXICO								
Cydsasa	5/11/92	-0.361	-10.654	-0.3975	-10.783	-1.729	-10.912	-12.558
		(-0.129)	(-1.363)	(-0.052)	(-1.299)	(-0.052)	(-1.259)	(-1.109)
Apenol	7/10/93	1.603	0.927	9.979**	10.905*	-1.997	8.909•	11.397
		(0.806)	(0.147)	(5.018)	(1.653)	(-1.004)	(1.293)	(1.241)
Femsa	9/14/91	-0.872	-3.102	-2.967	-6.068	1.254	-4.814	-13.125
		(-0.247)	(-0.278)	(-0.840)	(-0.518)	(0.355)	(-0.393)	(-0.817)
Vitro	4/18/91	4.863**	11.703*	-4.213	7.490	-1.922	5.498	-8.386
		(2.533)	(1.943)	(-2.212)	(1.186)	(-1.046)	(0.833)	(-0.936)
PHILIPPINES								
Atlas	10/20/90	0.142	0.419	-1.078	-0.658	0.142	-0.517	-10.746
		(0.045)	(0.042)	(-0.342)	(-0.063)	(0.045)	(-0.047)	(-0.945)
Benguet	12/28/92	-0.071	0.049	-8.404	-8.356	-0.071	-8.426	-16.287
		(0.015)	(0.003)	(-1.773)	(-0.531)	(-0.015)	(-0.513)	(-0.750)
	7/19/93	-0.111	7.769	-0.111	7.657	7.581 •	15.238	42.271*
		(-0.020)	(0.441)	(-0.020)	(0.415)	(1.303)	(0.790)	(1.656)
	2/6/94	-0.107	-3.926	-0.107	-4.033	-0.107	-4.141	-9.660
		(-0.019)	(-0.224)	(-0.019)	(-0.219)	(-0.019)	(-0.216)	(-0.389)
Jolibee	6/28/94	0.032	-9.049	0.032	-9.017	4.032•	-4.985	-14.616
		(0.010)	(-0.910)	(0.010)	(-0.868)	(1.282)	(-0.458)	(-1.014)
Manila Mining	4/17/92	29.086**	20.201	-8.606	11.595	40.753**	52.347**	107.786**
		(5.211)	(1.145)	(-1.542)	(0.526)	(7.302)	(2.708)	(4.214)
San Miguel	11/5/90	1.843	18.210*	0.353	18.563**	-1.097	17.466*	20.663*
		(0.696)	(2.199)	(0.135)	(2.138)	(-0.419)	(1.926)	(1.722)
	2/10/91	3.688	33.578**	4.651*	38.234**	-2.738	35.496**	48.323**
		(1.244)	(3.582)	(1.571)	(3.889)	(-0.924)	(3.457)	(3.557)
	9/4/91	-0.342	-7.808	-0.342	-8.150	-1.268	-9.418	-12.389
		(-0.120)	(-0.867)	(-0.120)	(-0.862)	(-0.445)	(-0.954)	(-0.949)
	6/8/93	-4.008	-43.761	-5.875	-49.636	-5.262	-54.894	-97.839
		(-0.059)	(-0.204)	(-0.087)	(-0.211)	(-0.078)	(-0.234)	(-0.315)

Note: The cumulative abnormal return for day -1, 0 and +1 is computed for day -10 up to the specified day. For the event window, the cumulative abnormal return is calculated over the period -10 to +10. Within brackets is the value of the Z statistics. "•", "*", and "**" means significant at the 10 percent, 5 percent and 1 percent level respectively (one tailed-test).

Appendix Table A10.3 Reaction of market to negative news

		Day -1		Day 0		Day + 1		Event window
Firms	Date	AR_i	CAR_i	AR_i	CAR_i	AR_i	CAR_i	CAR_i
ARGENTINA								
Astra	9/10/93	-1.057	8.415	-1.969	6.447	-0.864	5.583	4.333
		(-0.385)	(0.743)	(-0.717)	(0.708)	(-0.315)	(0.587)	(0.344)
Ipako	10/16/92	-21.038**	-20.897	0.664	-20.143	28.381	8.238	50.549
		(-3.902)	(-0.967)	(0.098)	(-0.893)	(4.171)	(0.350)	(1.621)
	9/9/93	3.037	-13.871	-0.167	-14.038	0.180	-13.858	-20.347
		(0.646)	(-0.889)	(-0.035)	(-0.944)	(0.038)	(-0.850)	(-0.944)
Perez	5/2/93	-1.706	1.876	-0.003	1.873	2.491	4.364	18.290
		(-0.374)	(0.130)	(-0.001)	(0.124)	(0.547)	(0.277)	(0.876)
	12/12/94	-0.053	0.255	1.439	1.694	0.580	2.274	-14.778
		(-0.021)	(0.031)	(0.556)	(0.197)	(0.224)	(0.254)	(-1.245)
YPF	11/7/93	1.057	-10.942*	2.224	-8.718 •	1.978	-6.740	-8.499
		(0.600)	(-1.963)	(1.262)	(-1.491)	(1.122)	(-1.104)	(-1.052)
	11/30/93	-0.306	-10.723*	1.519	-9.204•	-1.102	-10.305*	-14.820*
		(-0.171)	(-1.890)	(0.847)	(-1.547)	(-0.614)	(-1.658)	(-1.803)
	1/24/94	-1.631	-0.973	-0.710	-1.683	1.564	-0.119	7.406
		(-0.964)	(-0.182)	(-0.420)	(-0.300)	(0.924)	(-0.020)	(0.955)
	8/10/94	-0.052	-0.522	-0.250	-0.773	-0.647	-1.420	-1.477
		(-0.028)	(-0.090)	(-0.136)	(-0.300)	(-0.352)	(-0.223)	(-0.175)
	5/15/94	2.692	7.326	2.924	10.250	5.306	15.556	15.461
		(0.948)	(0.816)	(1.030)	(1.089)	(1.343)	(1.582)	(1.189)
Color	8/2/93	-5.761	5.786	0.211	5.977	0.211	6.208	15.708
		(-0.744)	(0.240)	(0.028)	(0.237)	(0.028)	(0.235)	(0.450)
	11/2/94	-0.261	-16.840	-3.039	-19.880•	-0.261	-20.141	-37.418*
		(-0.056)	(-1.146)	(-0.654)	(-1.290)	(-0.056)	(-1.251)	(-1.757)
Molymos	9/30/93	2.852	7.673	6.798	14.471	-2.159	12.311	34.425
		(0.926)	(0.788)	(2.208)	(1.417)	(-0.701)	(1.154)	(2.440)
Sevel	8/2/93	-3.061	-6.476	-1.092	-7.568	-0.061	-7.628	-5.440
		(-1.107)	(-0.741)	(-0.395)	(-0.825)	(-0.022)	(-0.796)	(-0.429)
Siderca	11/2/94	2.997	-5.423	1.236	-4.186	-0.167	-4.353	-5.854
		(1.394)	(-0.790)	(0.575)	(-0.587)	(-0.078)	(-0.585)	(-0.594)
CHILE								
Endesa	1/19/92	-2.112	-13.831*	-2.326	-16.157*	-2.362	-18.519*	-9.370
		(-0.794)	(-1.920)	(-0.870)	(1.831)	(-0.888)	(-2.009)	(-0.768)
	9/29/92	-4.603**	-12.720	1.0401	-11.680	-2.356•	-14.035	-4.419
		(-2.612)	(-0.793)	(0.590)	(-0.756)	(-1.337)	(-0.724)	(-0.547)
	2/7/93	-1.139	2.971	-0.817	2.154	-0.315	1.893	5.112
		(-0.698)	(0.575)	(-0.500)	(0.398)	(-0.193)	(0.325)	(0.683)
	4/21/93	1.505	-1.635	1.837	0.201	-2.000•	-1.799	-12.281**
		(0.980)	(-0.337)	(1.196)	(0.040)	(-1.302)	(-0.338)	(-1.745)

CHILE *(continued)*								
		Day -1		Day 0		Day + 1		Event window
Firms	Date	AR_i	CAR_i	AR_i	CAR_i	AR_i	CAR_i	CAR_i
Chilgener	7/13/90	1.305 (0.479)	-1.052 (-0.122)	0.294 (0.108)	- 0.759 (-0.084)	4.524 (1.663)	3.765 (0.399)	1.667 (0.134)
	1/19/92	-1.556 (-0.507)	-9.914 (-1.022)	-0.306 (-0.100)	-10.220 (-1.004)	-0.306 (-0.100)	-10.525 (-0.990)	-7.082 (-0.504)
	4/8/92	-8.325** (-2.841)	-7.054 (-0.761)	5.689 (1.941)	-1.365 (-0.140)	-5.316* (-1.814)	-6.681 (-0.658)	-6.534 (-0.487)
	4/16/92	1.285 (0.432)	-12.290• (-1.373)	2.612 (0.878)	-10.308 (-1.045)	0.712 (0.239)	-9.595 (-0.931)	12.009 (-0.881)
CMPC	9/30/92	-0.041 (-0.026)	-9.023* (-1.805)	-2.891* (-1.833)	-11.921* (-2.274)	0.018 (0.012)	-11.903* (-2.174)	-1.349 (-0.186)
CAPC	4/2/91	4.021 (1.682)	5.704 (0.754)	-1.145 (-0.479)	4.559 (0.575)	-2.165 (-0.906)	2.394 (0.289)	-7.426 (-0.678)
	6/27/92	0.025 (0.009)	-0.668 (-0.074)	0.025 (0.009)	-0.644 (-0.068)	1.087 (0.378)	0.444 (0.045)	-1.021 (-0.078)
	8/8/92	0.472 (0.209)	1.946 (0.272)	-0.384 (-0.170)	1.562 (0.258)	-0.925 (-0.408)	0.637 (0.081)	2.716 (0.262)
	8/12/92	-0.944 (-0.419)	-0.284 (-0.040)	-1.825 (-0.810)	-2.109 (-0.282)	-0.201 (-0.089)	-2.310 (-0.296)	2.973 (0.288)
Volcan	12/2/93	-2.862 (-0.357)	-28.589 (-1.128)	2.138 (0.267)	-26.451 (-0.995)	1.900 (0.237)	-24.551 (-0.884)	-33.202 (-0.904)
Minera	9/2/91	-0.477 (-0.171)	-2.374 (-0.270)	-0.477 (-0.171)	-2.850 (-0.309)	-0.477 (-0.171)	-3.327 (-0.345)	-3.942 (-0.309)
Vapores	6/6/92	-1.498 (-0.593)	-3.135 (-0.393)	0.926 (0.367)	-2.209 (-0.115)	0.911 (0.361)	-1.298 (-0.148)	0.807 (0.070)
Emos	10/17/93	-0.148 (-0.038)	-1.471 (-0.119)	-0.148 (-0.038)	-1.619 (-0.125)	-0.148 (0.038)	-1.767 (-0.131)	-5.799 (-0.324)
Puerto	7/23/92	-0.374 (-0.208)	-5.464• (-1.473)	-2.160 (-1.203)	-7.624• (-1.343)	-0.738 (-0.411)	-8.362 (-0.963)	-16.892* (-2.054)
Victoria	12/2/93	-9.895 (-0.502)	-42.389 (-0.680)	-13.272 (-0.673)	-55.661 (-0.851)	-10.848 (-0.550)	-66.508 (-0.974)	-86.081 (-0.953)
Iansa	5/29/93	0.500 (0.242)	0.015 (0.002)	0.498 (0.241)	0.513 (0.081)	0.042 (0.020)	0.555 (0.072)	3.279 (0.346)
Coloso	4/1/92	6.961 (2.165)	35.171 (3.459)	-2.988 (-0.932)	35.174 (3.017)	-0085 (-0.026)	32.089 (2.881)	32.052 (2.243)
	12/2/93	0.256 (0.087)	16.630 (1.777)	4.359 (1.472)	20.989 (2.138)	0.256 (0.087)	21.245 (2.072)	44.995 (3.317)
	2/5/94	0.086 (0.028)	-3.492 (-0.357)	-4.460• (-1.440)	-7.952 (-0.774)	-4.914• (-1.510)	-12.628 (-1.177)	-15.746 (-1.109)
	3/11/94	-4.860• (-1.545)	1.273 (0.128)	0.140 (0.045)	1.413 (0.135)	0.140 (0.045)	1.533 (0.143)	-12.670 (-0.879)
	3/18/94	0.139 (0.044)	0.741 (0.074)	0.139 (0.044)	0.880 (0.084)	-3.808 (-1.211)	-2.928 (-0.269)	-13.210 (-0.916)

CHILE (*continued*)								
		Day -1		Day 0		Day + 1		Event window
Firms	Date	AR_i	CAR_i	AR_i	CAR_i	AR_i	CAR_i	CAR_i
Iquique	4/1/92	-0.032	13.750	21.632	35.382	-17.838**	17.543	19.676
		(-0.07)	(0.955)	(4.753)	(2.344)	(-3.919)	(1.113)	(0.943)
	12/21/93	3.895	15.384	0.124	15.507	11.151	26.659	35.137
		(0.779)	(0.996)	(0.025)	(0.957)	(2.283)	(0.916)	(1.569)
	2/5/94	0.086	25.987	-0.017	25.971	-0.017	25.954	16.726
		(0.028)	(1.666)	(-0.003)	(1.587)	(-0.003)	(1.519)	(0.740)
	3/10/94	-0.032	18.820	-0.094	18.725	-0.032	18.694	52.526
		(-0.006)	(1.177)	(-0.019)	(1.123)	(-0.006)	(1.073)	(2.279)
	3/11/94	-0.147	7.126	-0.085	7.042	-3.209	3.832	40.314
		(-0.029)	(0.443)	(-0.017)	(0.417)	(-0.631)	(0.217)	(1.729)
Lirquien	7/15/92	-2.509	-23.458	27.491	4.033	0.600	4.633	6.302
		(-0.121)	(-0.358)	(1.325)	(0.059)	(0.029)	(0.064)	(0.066)
Chilectra	7/11/92	-0.207	-7.201 •	1.065	-6.136	1.133	-5.003	-1.204
		(-0.132)	(-1.391)	(0.651)	(-1.130)	(0.693)	(-0.882)	(-0.160)
Molymet	1/19/92	-3.140	-40.617•	-9.390	-50.007*	-4.029	-54.036*	-111.943**
		(-0.378)	(-1.545)	(-1.130)	(-1.814)	(-0.485)	(-1.877)	(-2.939)
MEXICO								
Cydsasa	2/6/90	-1.661	4.582	0.254	4.448	-0.134	3.928	-1.842
		(-0.733)	(0.605)	(0.112)	(0.610)	(-0.059)	(0.567)	(-0.178)
	3/19/92	1.591	3.058	1.565	4.623	1.146	5.768	6.671
		(0.676)	(0.411)	(0.665)	(0.392)	(0.487)	(0.707)	(0.618)
	10/9/92	0.104	11.788	0.104	11.892	-0.396	11.146	13.082
		(0.040)	(1.414)	(0.040)	(1.394)	(-0.154)	(1.290)	(1.110)
Grupo Maya (A)	10/4/90	-0.176	6.264	-0.176	6.088	-0.176	5.912	7.347
		(-0.045)	(0.505)	(-0.045)	(0.468)	(-0.045)	(0.435)	(0.409)
	3/12/91	-0.209	3.875	1.220	5.095	0.073	5.168	29.874
		(-0.053)	(0.308)	(0.307)	(0.387)	(0.018)	(0.376)	(1.641)
	3/15/91	1.222	5.624	0.075	5.699	-0.207	5.492	30.213
		(0.308)	(0.448)	(0.019)	(0.432)	(-0.052)	(0.399)	(1.660)
	9/20/91	-1.269	-11.604*	-1.269	-12.873*	-1.269	-14.141*	-24.845**
		(-0.675)	(-1.953)	(-0.675)	(-2.066)	(-0.675)	(-2.173)	(-2.885)
	11/27/91	-1.041	-14.545**	-1.041	-15.586**	-0.295	-15.881**	-27.475**
		(-0.566)	(-2.500)	(-0.566)	(-2.554)	(-0.160)	(-2.492)	(-3.259)
	7/29/92	-1.170	-26.986*	-1.171	-28.409*	-1.423	-31.854 *	-52.891**
		(-0.297)	(-2.069)	(-0.297)	(-2.063)	(-0.361)	(-2.079)	(-2.926)
Grupo Maya (B)	3/12/91	2.737	14.242	1.268	15.511	-0.121	15.390	59.367
		(0.954)	(1.569)	(0.442)	(1.630)	(-0.042)	(1.548)	(4.514)
	3/15/91	1.257	13.579	-0.132	13.448	-0.132	13.316	63.416
		(0.438)	(1.480)	(-0.046)	(1.412)	(-0.046)	(1.338)	(4.818)
	9/20/91	-1.386	-12.392•	-1.748	-14.140•	0.069	-14.410•	-30.332**
		(-0.525)	(-1.484)	(-0.662)	(-1.615)	(0.026)	(-1.539)	(-2.507)
	11/27/91	-2.688	-16.099*	-1.591	-16.193*	-0.094	-16.632*	-29.371**
		(-1.075)	(-1.835)	(-0.636)	(-1.942)	(-0.038)	(-1.870)	(-2.564)
Tolmex	10/14/90	4.594	6.162	9.798	15.961	0.417	16.378	30.047
		(1.658)	(0.703)	(3.536)	(1.737)	(0.151)	(1.706)	(2.366)

MEXICO (*continued*)								
		Day -1		Day 0		Day + 1		Event window
Firms	Date	AR_i	CAR_i	AR_i	CAR_i	AR_i	CAR_i	CAR_i
MetMEx (A)	3/22/91	4.142 (1.992)	20.674 (2.789)	0.119 (0.057)	20.793 (3.104)	-0.710 (-0.341)	20.084 (3.143)	37.335 (3.917)
	6/4/91	-0.008 (-0.004)	23.669 (3.370)	-0.521 (-0.240)	23.149 (3.213)	10.044 (4.623)	33.193 (4.411)	29.115 (2.925)
	8/9/91	-9.677** (-4.237)	-3.142 (-0.445)	-5.239** (-2.343)	-8.388 (-1.131)	-0.088 (-0.039)	-8.476 (-1.094)	-15.193• (-1.482)
	3/2/94	-0.765 (-0.105)	1.088 (0.047)	-0.113 (-0.016)	0.975 (0.040)	0.107 (0.015)	1.081 (0.043)	0.812 (0.024)
	3/4/94	-0.134 (-0.018)	0.882 (0.038)	0.086 (0.012)	0.968 (0.040)	-0.795 (-0.110)	0.173 (0.007)	0.599 (0.018)
	8/27/94	0.141 (0.020)	6.067 (0.268)	-0.923 (-0.129)	5.144 (0.217)	-0.289 (-0.040)	4.854 (0.196)	7.850 (0.239)
MetMEx (B)	3/22/91	-2.662 (-0.284)	-8.572 (-0.289)	3.480 (0.371)	-5.092 (-0.164)	9.577 (1.022)	4.485 (0.138)	-16.531 (-0.385)
	6/4/91	-8.985 (-0.936)	-28.811 (-0.949)	-13.064• (-1.361)	-41.875• (-1.316)	-0.161 (-0.017)	-42.036 (-1.264)	-43.385 (-0.986)
	3/4/94	-0.187 (-0.021)	18.743 (0.655)	0.279 (0.031)	18.556 (0.618)	0.046 (0.005)	18.835 (0.601)	25.107 (0.605)
GCG	5/25/92	-3.168 (-0.937)	-12.765 (-1.193)	9.937 (2.938)	-2.828 (-0.252)	-1.820 (-0.538)	-4.648 (-0.397)	-8.458 (-0.546)
Kimber	5/21/92	0.560 (0.308)	-6.951 (-1.210)	-0.565 (-0.311)	-7.516 (-1.217)	-0.192 (-0.106)	-7.708 (-1.225)	-55.103** (-6.618)
Bimbo	3/19/92	1.630 (0.942)	-8.763 • (-1.603)	1.972 (1.140)	-6.792 (-1.184)	-0.301 (-0.174)	-7.092 (-1.184)	-22.521** (-2.842)
	2/14/93	-0.655 (-0.761)	4.452 (0.141)	0.861 (0.086)	5.313 (0.160)	-4.139 (-0.414)	1.174 (0.034)	-89.247* (-1.950)
Telmex	5/21/93	-0.761 (-0.455)	-1.361 (-0.257)	-0.436 (-0.261)	-1.797 (-0.324)	0.883 (0.527)	-0.915 (-0.158)	-10.272• (-1.339)
	6/9/94	-0.953 (-0.508)	-3.065 (-0.340)	1.044 (0.556)	-2.021 (-0.324)	-1.148 (-0.611)	-3.169 (-0.487)	-9.840• (-1.453)
PHILIPPINES								
Apex	4/24/91	0.263 (0.035)	-9.810 (-0.408)	-14.023* (-1.844)	-23.832 (-0.935)	0.263 (0.035)	-23.564 (-0.895)	-40.704 (-1.168)
Ayala	12/8/94	0.024 (0.008)	1.752 (0.187)	-4.201* (-1.415)	-2.449 (-0.249)	4.436 (1.494)	1.986 (0.193)	9.238 (0.679)
Benguet	3/21/90	-2.217 (-0.451)	1.752 (0.113)	-2.275 (-0.463)	-0.524 (-0.032)	2.664 (0.542)	2.140 (0.126)	3.615 (0.161)
	3/23/90	2.634 (0.538)	-1.119 (-0.072)	0.134 (0.027)	1.515 (0.102)	0.134 (0.024)	1.649 (0.105)	2.990 (0.133)
Lepanto	10/22/90	3.388 (1.412)	-3.298 (-0.435)	3.273 (1.364)	-0.025 (-0.003)	6.391 (2.664)	6.366 (0.766)	5.917 (0.538)
Mondragon	10/11/94	-0.284 (-0.087)	-5.824 (-0.564)	2.841 (0.870)	-2.983 (-0.275)	-0.284 (-0.087)	-3.268 (-0.289)	3.057 (0.204)
San Miguel	10/7/94	0.342 (0.129)	3.589 (0.427)	0.342 (0.129)	3.931 (0.446)	0.342 (0.129)	4.273 (0.461)	-4.810 (-0.395)
Robinson Land	6/15/94	-1.389 (-0.373)	-2.605 (-0.221)	1.127 (0.303)	-1.417 (-0.120)	-0.139 (-0.037)	-1.617 (-0.125)	-5.332 (-0.397)

Note: The cumulative abnormal return for day -1, 0 and +1 is computed for day -10 up to the specified day. For the event window, the cumulative abnormal return is calculated over the period -10 to +10. Within brackets is the value of the Z statistics. "•", "*", and "**" means significant at the 10 percent, 5 percent and 1 percent level respectively (one tailed-test).

Notes

Our most sincere thanks to Mrs. Maria Teresa Correa who for a period of 8 months relentlessly collected the vast amount of information necessary to conduct the current analysis. We would also like to thank the following individuals for their collaboration and support: in Argentina, Mssrs. Hugo Medina and Osvaldo Mignini; in Chile, Mr. Carlos Parra; in Mexico, Mssrs. Alejandro Ritch and Ricardo Rivera; in the Philippines, Mr. Sergio Marquez and Mrs Socorro Clemente for allowing us access to the appropriate stock market data and answering our numerous questions. We also thank Mr. Miodrag Deric and Mr. Craig Meisner for their research assistance. Finally, we thank the participants at the Canadian Environmental and Resource Economists Workshop (October 1997), Mr. Randy Wigle, and Mr. David Wheeler, for their generous comments.

1. See Russell (1990).
2. Those being Japan, Korea, Taiwan, Thailand, and Indonesia.
3. See Porter and Van Linde (1995) and Klassen and McLaughlin (1996) for more details.
4. In the United States, these studies include, among others, analysis of the reaction of markets to releases of the *Toxics Release Inventory* (Hamilton 1995; and Konar and Cohen 1997). Lanoie and Laplante (1994) analyze the reaction of capital markets to environmental news in Canada. For a survey of these studies, see Lanoie, Laplante and Roy (1997).
5. We know of at least two such programs currently in place in developing countries: in Indonesia (PROPER Prokasih) and the Philippines (Ecowatch). Similar programs are currently being developed in Mexico and Colombia. For further details, see Afsah and others (1996).
6. See for example, Jaffe and others (1995), Kolstad and Xing (1994), Levinson (1992), Low and Yeats (1992), Stewart (1993), Tobey (1990), Walter (1992), and Wheeler and Mody (1992).
7. Although market concentration may appear to be high, note that the IFC General Indexes represent only a fraction of total market capitalization. Actual market concentration is lower than suggested in table 2.
8. In the United States, the Wall Street Journal is generally the preferred source of information for conducting event-study analyses. In Argentina, environmental news were collected from the newspaper *La Nacion* (daily circulation of approximately 250,000; ranks 3rd in Buenos Aires); in Chile, we used *El Mercurio* (daily circulation of approximately 200,000; ranks 3rd in Santiago); in Mexico City, we used *Excelsior* (daily circulation of 200,000; ranks 7th in Mexico City); finally, in the Philippines, news were collected from the *Manila Bulletin* (daily circulation of 300, 000; ranks 3rd in Manila). All newspapers were available from the Library of Congress for most of the period 1990-94. Information from missing issues was obtained directly from the publishers of the papers in the respective countries.
9. For more details, see MacKinlay (1997).
10. The event window consists of the day where the event occurred (day 0) and some days before and after the event.
11. Firms may be excluded if simultaneous events are occurring within the event window.
12. The single-index model is a particular case of the market model described above. Where market returns were available, we also obtained results using the market model. Results were similar to those presented here. In fact, Henderson (1990) points out that the three estimating methodologies yield results of similar nature.
13. Complete statistical results are presented in Appendices 2 and 3. Where the length of estimation period is too short, we combine days prior to the event window with post event period starting 30 days after the event window.
14. In Argentina: Indupa (2/7/93). In Chile: Emos (8/11/93) and Molymet (10/11/93). In these last two events, it was announced that the President of Chile would inaugurate a plant (as opposed to approving an investment or agreement).
15. See Lanoie and others (1997) for more details.
16. Konar and Cohen (1997) have shown that firms that have suffered the largest reduction in market value following the release of the TRI in 1989 have subsequently invested most in pollution abatement.

References

Afsah, S., B. Laplante, and D. Wheeler. 1996. *Controlling Industrial Pollution: A New Paradigm*. Policy Research Working Paper 1672, The World Bank.

Fama, E.F. 1976. *Foundations of Finance*. New York, Basic Books Inc.

Hamilton, T. 1995. "Pollution as news: Media and stock market reaction to the Toxics Release Inventory data." *Journal of Environmental Economics and Management* 28: 98–113.

Henderson, G. V. 1990. "Problems and solutions in conducting events studies." *Journal of Risk and Insurance* 42: 282–306.

Hettige, H., R.E. Lucas, and D. Wheeler. 1992. "The toxic intensity of industrial production: Global patterns, trends, and trade policy." *American Economic Review* 82(2): 478–81.

Jaffe, A.B., S.R. Peterson, P.R. Portney, and R. Stavins. 1995. "Environmental regulation and the competitiveness of U.S. Manufacturing." *Journal of Economic Literature* 33(1): 132–63.

Kolstad, C.D., and Y. Xing. 1994. *Do Lax Environmental Regulations Attract Foreign Investment?* Working Paper, Department of Economics, University of Illinois, Urbana, Illinois.

Konar, S., and M.A. Cohen. 1997. "Information as regulation: The effect of community right to know laws on toxic emissions." *Journal of Environmental Economics and Management* 32: 109–24.

Lanoie, P., and B. Laplante. 1994. "The market response to environmental incidents in Canada: A theoretical and empirical analysis." *Southern Economic Journal* 60: 657–72.

Lanoie, P., B. Laplante, and M. Roy. 1997. *Can Capital Markets Create Incentives for Pollution Control?* Working Paper 1753, Development Research Group, The World Bank. Forthcoming in *Ecological Economics.*

Levinson, A. 1992. *Environmental Regulations and Manufacturers' location choices: Evidence from the Census of Manufacturers.* Columbia University, New York.

Low, P., and A. Yeats. 1992. "Do dirty industries migrate?" In *International Trade and the Environment.* World Bank, Washington, D.C.

MacKinlay, A.C. 1997. "Event studies in economics and finance." *Journal of Economic Literature* 35 (1): 13–39.

O'Connor, D. 1995. *Managing the Environment with Rapid Industrialisation: Lessons from the East Asian Experience.* OECD, Paris.

Porter, M. E., and van der Linde, C. 1995. "Toward a new conception of the Environment-Competitiveness Relationship." *Journal of Economic Perspectives* 9(4): 97–118.

Russell, C.S. 1990. "Monitoring and Enforcement." *Public Policies for Environmental Protection.* In P. R. Portney, ed., Washington D.C.: Resources for the Future, p. 243–74.

Stewart, R.B. 1993. "Environmental regulation and international competitiveness." *Yale Law Journal* 102: 2039–106.

Tobey, J.A. 1990. "The effects of domestic environmental policies on patterns of world trade: An empirical test." *Kyklos* 43: 191–209.

Walter, I. 1982. "Environmentally induced industrial relocation to developing countries." In *Environment and Trade: the Relation of International Trade and Environmental Policy.* J. Seymour and T.R. Graham, eds. Totowa, NJ: Allanheld.

Wheeler, D.W., and A. Mody. 1992. "International investment location decisions: The case of U.S. firms." *Journal of International Economics* 33: 57–76.

Chapter 11

The Credibility of Trade Sanctions in International Environmental Agreements

Scott Barrett

1. Introduction

Global environmental protection is a game in the sense that the state of affairs realized by each country depends on the actions of all countries. Protection of the stratospheric ozone layer, for example, depends on global emissions of ozone-depleting chemicals. But, while the benefits of abatement are shared by all countries, the costs of abatement are borne only by the countries that undertake the abatement. So there exist incentives to free-ride. If these incentives are strong enough, the global environment may not be protected by any country, even though every country may be better off if the environment were protected by all countries.

The provision of public goods and the correction of externalities are common problems that are routinely resolved at the level of the nation state. But global environmental protection is special because agreements between countries cannot be enforced by a third party. They must be self-enforcing (Barrett, 1990).

It is well known that parties caught in a prisoners'-dilemma-like situation can nonetheless sustain cooperation by employing a strategy of reciprocity—that is, by punishing any party that fails to cooperate. Indeed, the folk theorems for repeated games tell us that cooperation can be sustained by any number of players provided none discounts the future too heavily. However, the folk theorems only obey the individual rationality constraint, and cooperative agreements between countries must also be collectively rational, meaning—in the context of repeated games—that they should not be vulnerable to renegotiation. This is because countries cannot commit to carry out just any punishment. Since they will only carry out a punishment if doing so does not make them worse off, only these punishments can be used to enforce an equilibrium agreement. I have shown elsewhere (Barrett 1994a, 1998) that a large number of countries may still be able to sustain the full cooperative outcome as an equilibrium, but only if the aggregate gains to cooperation are small. If these gains are large, full cooperation cannot be sustained by a strategy of reciprocity.

However, this assumes that the strategy space available to countries is limited to the provision of the public good. So a deviant state can only be punished if the cooperating countries reduce their provision of the public good. This is a problem, however, because curtailing provison of the public good harms the countries that are called upon to impose the punishment as well as the countries that the punishment is intended to harm. Naturally, signatories to an international environmental agreement (IEA) will want to find alternative punishments that are relatively more damaging to free-riding states. A prime candidate is a restriction on trade.[1]

Indeed, arguably the most successful IEA ever negotiated—the Montreal Protocol on Substances that Deplete the Ozone Layer—relies on trade sanctions as a means of enforcement. Since this agreement is held up to be a prototype for future agreements, it is important to know whether the trade sanctions in this treaty really have proved important to its success, and whether the use of trade sanctions in different situations would prove just as successful.

In this paper I show that the trade sanctions in the Montreal Protocol are important to its success, but that the circumstances that allow for this are special. Trade sanctions are not a quick-fix for sustaining international cooperation.

In an earlier paper (Barrett 1997), I developed a stylized model of international trade and environmental cooperation in which the threat to impose trade sanctions emerges as an equilibrium. It turns out that countries would only choose to include the threat in an IEA if the agreement also made use of a minimum participation clause, and so this model also obtains another important feature of the Montreal Protocol as an equilibrium. Importantly, the model shows that, in equilibrium, trade is never restricted. But if the threat to impose sanctions were prohibited by the rules of the game, international cooperation could only sustain a collectively inferior outcome.

In this paper I present a different model of international cooperation and international trade. As in Barrett (1997), I find that, if the signatories to the IEA impose trade sanctions, no country would free-ride. But if a country withdrew from the agreement, the signatories would be collectively better off by not carrying out the threat to restrict trade. The threat to impose sanctions is not credible. This is reminiscent of the result noted earlier concerning collective rationality in repeated games.

Two basic requirements must be satisfied if free-riding is to be deterred by trade sanctions. First, it must be the case that the trade ban harms free riders; there must exist gains from trade that nonsignatories would lose if sanctions were imposed. Second, it must be the case that the countries called upon to impose the trade ban are collectively better off if they do so than if they do not restrict trade. The problem is that, if the first requirement is satisfied, then countries imposing the trade ban will also suffer a loss in the gains from trade, and the threat to impose the ban will not be credible. So for trade sanctions to be effective in deterring free riding, something else must make the cost to signatories of free riding greater under a regime of free trade than a trade ban. The essential ingredient, I argue, is trade "leakage." Paradoxically, leakage improves the prospects for sustaining cooperation.

2. Trade Leakage and Trade Linkage

In the model developed later, trade and environmental protection are linked deliberately, but it is as well to note that these issues are typically linked *automatically*. If signatories to an IEA reduce their pollution emissions, for example, comparative advantage in the pollution-intensive industries is likely to shift to nonsignatories, with the consequence that global emissions fall by less than the reduction undertaken by signatories—a phenomenon known as "leakage." In the case of an incomplete climate change treaty, this shift in comparative advantage would be compounded by the workings of the international energy market. A reduction in carbon dioxide emissions by signatories would depress the world price of traded, carbon-intensive fuels, and so have the effect of increasing consumption of these fuels by nonsignatories. Estimates of the magnitude of leakage vary widely. In the case of a unilateral reduction in carbon emissions by the European Union, estimated leakage rates range from 2 to 80 percent (see Fisher and others 1996). That is, for every 100 tons of carbon abated by the EU, global emissions could fall by from 20 to 98 tons. If the 2 percent estimate is right, leakage will not matter. If the 80 percent figure is right, however, unilateral abatement will be virtually impotent.

Trade leakage and free-riding are independent but closely associated phenomena. Trade leakage is transmitted by the market mechanism, by the effect of unilateral abatement on relative prices. Free-riding is a consequence of the public good aspect of environmental protection. Both phenomena undermine cooperation but they are otherwise very different. If free-riding is morally repugnant, trade leakage is morally innocent. The countries that increase their emissions via the trade mechanism may not have any interest in the environmental problem and may not be seeking to gain from the abatement undertaken by others. Punishment of these countries, therefore, cannot be justified on moral grounds in the way that punishment of free-riders can be.

However, leakage may be transmitted by a channel other than trade. For suppose that the marginal benefit of abatement is decreasing in global abatement. Then nonsignatories can be expected to increase their emissions as a consequence of signatories reducing theirs (see Barrett 1994a). This "atmospheric" leakage is a product of the nonexcludable nature of the abatement and is inseparable from the free-riding problem.

In principle, signatories can correct for trade leakage by adjusting their border taxes. A simple example explains the logic.[2] Suppose that signatories and nonsignatories can be treated as separate monoliths and suppose also that pollution arises from one sector only. Then, if the signatories are net importers of carbon-intensive products, a carbon tax imposed by signatories should be supplemented by a tariff on imports from nonsignatories. The tariff shifts production toward the domestic industry and therefore reverses the leakage. If, however, signatories are net exporters of carbon-intensive products, then an export subsidy is required to shift production toward the countries that abate their pollution.[3] Granted, this is a second-best policy; it would be better if participation in the treaty were full. But under the rules of international law, countries cannot be forced to participate in a treaty, and so parties to an IEA may have no alternative but to use second-best instruments.

This much is obvious. In a more realistic setting, however, calculation of the optimal adjustment would strain the computing capabilities of even a well-funded secretariat. Where production of goods in two or more sectors causes pollution, for example, the analysis must take account of distortions between and not simply within the sectors. Hoel (1996) shows that in these more realistic settings even the sign of the border tax adjustment cannot be determined without a detailed analysis of the workings of the domestic and international economies.

Even ignoring these practical difficulties, border tax adjustments may clash with the multilateral trading rules of the World Trade Organization (WTO), incorporating the General Agreement on Tariffs and Trade (GATT). There are two main problems.

The first is that, if some parties to the WTO are not also parties to the IEA, then the adjustments may violate the non-discrimination principle of the WTO; some WTO members would be subject to different tariff arrangements than others. It is possible that differentiated tariffs may be allowed; Article XX of the GATT allows parties to take measures "necessary to protect human, animal or plant life or health" or "relating to the conservation of exhaustible natural resources," and a legal expert from the GATT Secretariat advised negotiators to the Montreal Protocol that these exemptions would apply to this treaty (Benedick, 1991). However, the Secretariat later criticized the discriminatory nature of the Montreal Protocol trade restrictions, on the basis that they were not "necessary," that other, less GATT-inconsistent measures could have been taken. I shall return to this criticism later in this paper, but it is as well to point out now that, whatever a legal interpretation may recommend, no member of the GATT has challenged the trade restrictions in the Montreal Protocol. The parties to this agreement have thus voted with their feet, as it were, and endorsed the discriminatory trade restrictions in the Montreal Protocol.

The second problem is that, if the adjustment were based on the pollution associated with the manufacture of the traded good (in the trade jargon, with the "production or processing methods" or PPMs), rather than on the characteristics of the good itself, then otherwise identical products would be subject to different border taxes. Such a differentiation is currently prohibited by the trading rules. Of course, the parties to the WTO could always renegotiate this agreement to allow for differentiation of this kind. But implementation will inevitably be difficult.

Indeed, though Article 4 of the Montreal Protocol allows parties to restrict trade in products made using ozone depleting substances, such as electronics components made using CFCs as a solvent, the ozone secretariat was advised in 1993 that such a restriction couldn't be implemented (Van Slooten 1994). It is technically impossible to detect trace residues for all uses, especially where CFCs have been used as solvents. Moreover, since ozone-depleting substances are bound to be used indirectly, if not directly, in the manufacture of most traded goods, a wide interpretation of the clause would need to include nearly all trade. Brack (1996) claims that the costs to signatories of a blanket import ban would exceed the environmental benefits. Application of such restrictions in the case of a climate change agreement would be at least as difficult; virtually all production is directly associated with the emission of greenhouse gases.

Could a cruder but easier-to-calculate instrument work nearly as well as the appropriate border tax adjustment? Probably not. Hoel (1996) shows that a carbon tax differentiated by sector would be even harder to calculate than the optimal border tax adjustment. For example, Hoel finds that there is no simple relationship between fossil fuel intensity and the optimal sector-specific carbon tax. Moreover, the available empirical evidence suggests that crude sectoral differentiation may not be effective. Oliveira-Martins, Burniaux, and Martin (1992) find that, if energy-intensive industry in Europe were exempted from a carbon tax, then leakage would be unaffected and the predicted output losses for the energy-intensive sector would be virtually unchanged.

It would seem that we have reached a dead end. The policies needed to correct for trade leakage may well be impractical, illegal (in the sense of violating the existing multilateral trade agreements), or ineffective. In most instances (there may be exceptions), leakage cannot be corrected using second-best policies.

However, recall that leakage is only a problem if participation in an agreement is less than full. If every country is a party to an agreement that endeavors to provide a global public good, then leakage will be zero. So, if leakage cannot be corrected directly by the use of tariffs, differentiated taxes and the like, perhaps it can be fixed indirectly by policies that punish non-participation (reward participation) and that at the same stroke deter free-riding. As we shall now see, this is how the Montreal Protocol plugged the trade leak.

3. Free-Rider Deterrence in Linked Games

The Montreal Protocol bans trade between signatories and nonsignatories in the substances controlled by the treaty, and it also bans imports from nonsignatories of goods containing these substances. The treaty leaves open the possibility that signatories may also ban imports from nonsignatories of products made using the listed substances, but as noted previously implementation of this ban would pose a number of practical problems and trade in these products has not been restricted. Signatories have, however, retained the option to restrict trade in these products in the future, and according to van Slooten (1994) the threat to do so has provided some incentive for countries to participate in the Protocol (see also Brack 1996).

Of course, a trade ban is a blunt instrument for controlling leakage—blunter, certainly, than the appropriate border tax adjustment. But, as noted earlier, leakage can be controlled indirectly by deterring non-participation, and this is what the negotiators intended the trade ban to do. According to the chief U.S. negotiator at the Montreal Protocol talks (Benedick 1991, p. 91), the sanctions were expected "to stimulate as many nations as possible to participate in the protocol, by preventing nonparticipating countries from enjoying competitive advantages and by discouraging the movement of CFC production facilities to such countries." Moreover, in deterring non-participation, the trade ban would simultaneously deter free-riding and thus do what a strategy of reciprocity could perhaps not do: sustain full cooperation as a self-enforcing agreement. In Benedick's (1991, p. 91) words, the sanctions were "critical, since they constituted the only enforcement mechanism in the protocol." Though a counterfactual is lacking, and so the effectiveness of the trade sanctions cannot be measured, it is remarkable that participation in the agreement is virtually full, and that leakage is accordingly non-existent, even though the agreement demands that signatories undertake very substantial abatement. The blunt instrument of a trade sanction thus appears to have sustained a first-best outcome.

Precisely because a counterfactual is missing, theory is especially useful here. It should tell us something about the conditions that must hold for the threat to restrict trade to be credible. It should also tell us how such a threat would affect participation in an IEA. It is to these matters that I now turn.

4. The Strategy of Trade Sanctions in a Self-Enforcing International Environmental Agreement

In the Appendix to this paper I present a model of international cooperation and international trade, in which parties to an IEA may impose trade sanctions. In this section I describe this model and discuss the results.

As noted previously, the Montreal Protocol restricts trade in ozone depleting substances and products containing these substances. Ozone depleting substances are commodities, and in an earlier paper (Barrett 1997) I analyzed the use of trade restrictions in these products as a means of enforcing a cooperative agreement. The essential feature of this model is that the industry manufacturing bulk CFCs is imperfectly competitive. Firms choose a quantity of CFCs to produce and ship to each country, taking as given the output and shipment choices of other countries. In equilibrium there is trade in identical products. The gains from trade result from the increase in competition associated with having more firms competing (Cournot-style) in any given market.

This ignores an important feature of the Montreal Protocol, which is the ban on trade in products containing ozone-depleting substances—products like aerosols, refrigerators, air conditioners, automobiles (with air conditioning or safety foam), furniture (with foam cushioning), and fire extinguishers. In this paper I consider international trade in products of this kind—that is, differentiated products.

In particular, I take every country to be specialized in the production of a single good that is an imperfect substitute for the products of other countries. Countries are identical in the sense that they are of the same economic size, have the same tastes and the same costs and benefits of public good provision. The production side of the model can be looked at in two different ways. It can reflect perfect competition, in which a large number of firms make the same product, price at marginal cost, and break even. Or it can reflect increasing returns, in which a small number of firms charge a markup over marginal cost but make zero profits because of free entry.

Provision of the public good by each country is a binary decision: the good is either provided or it isn't. Every country gains the same from the provision of the public good, and this gain is independent of the quantity of private goods consumed by each country. Only the countries that provide the public good pay the cost of provision, and this cost is measured as a reduction in the output of the private good.

Preferences for private goods have the property that every pair of goods is equally well substitutable for each other and the degree of substitutability of a given pair of goods doesn't depend on the quantities of these or other goods being consumed.

There are four parameters in this model: N, the number of countries; ϕ, production of the private good by a country that provides the public good; σ, the elasticity of substitution between any pair of private goods in consumption; and b, the gain to each country from the provision of the public good by any country.

I consider four games, and since the model is so special, illustrate them for a simple example, shown in figure 11.1. The values of the parameters for this example are shown under the title of this figure. These values were chosen to obtain the qualitative results described below. These qualitative results are intended to show how the trade regime affects the ability of the countries to sustain cooperation in provision of the public good by means of a self-enforcing agreement.

The four diagrams shown in this figure collapse an entire game into a single binary choice problem. The horizontal axis specifies the choices made by all the *other* countries. The vertical axis shows the payoffs to any one country of making the binary choice (since the countries are by assumption symmetric, each faces precisely the same problem). You can think of this payoff as being a monetary estimate of net benefits. In general, the payoffs that a particular country gets depends not only on its own choice, but also on how all the other countries have chosen. In the diagrams, this will be true whenever the payoff curves are not horizontal.

The four diagrams correspond to four different regimes. Countries may either choose to provide the public good unilaterally or by international agreement, and they may do so either under a regime of free trade or a trade ban. The superscripts for the payoffs shown in the figure label the trade regime (with F denoting free trade and B a trade ban). The subscripts denote whether the public good is provided in a unilateral or multilateral context. If the choice is made unilaterally, countries may either play Pollute (P) or Abate (A). If the choice is made in a multilateral setting, countries choose either to be a signatory (S) or a nonsignatory (N).

Unilateral provision of public goods with free trade

Game 1 considers the provision of the public good when countries behave unilaterally and trade is unrestricted. The game is in two stages. In stage 1, the governments of every country simultaneously choose whether or not to supply the public good under a regime of free trade. In stage 2, firms choose their production plans and consumers their consumption plans. The details of the production decision are unimportant. I normalize such that each firm produces one unit of the private good if the public good is not provided and ϕ units otherwise (in the figure, $\phi = 0.5$, meaning that the cost of providing the public good is a 50 percent drop in the output of the private good). The assumption about preferences implies that (in a symmetric outcome) every consumer will consume

Figure 11.1 Provision of the public good

Figure 11.1a
Free trade/No IEA

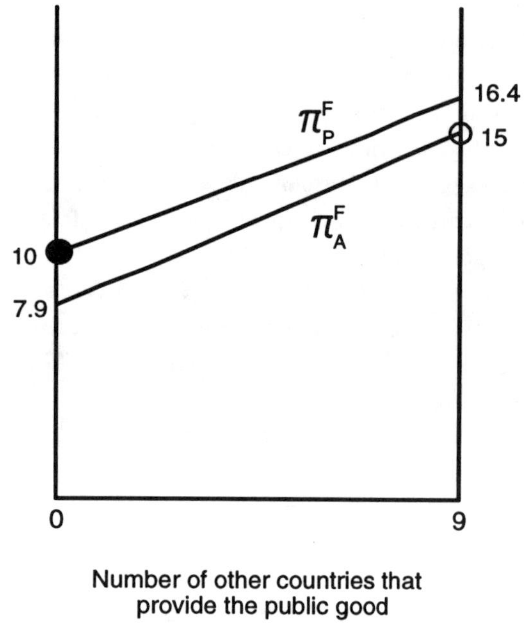

Figure 11.1b
Trade ban/No IEA

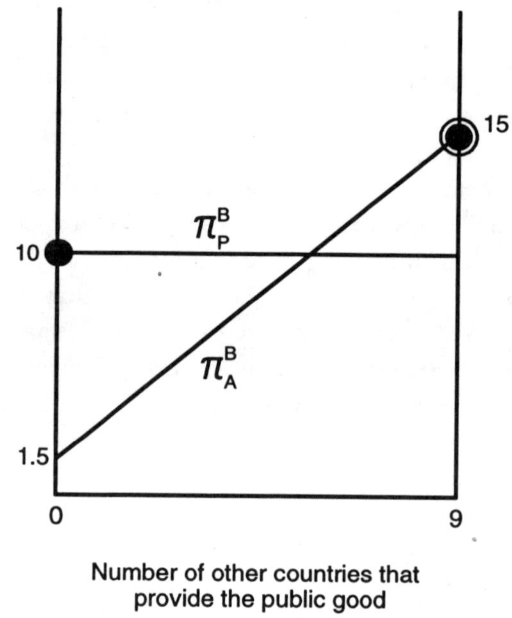

Figure 11.1c
Free trade/IEA

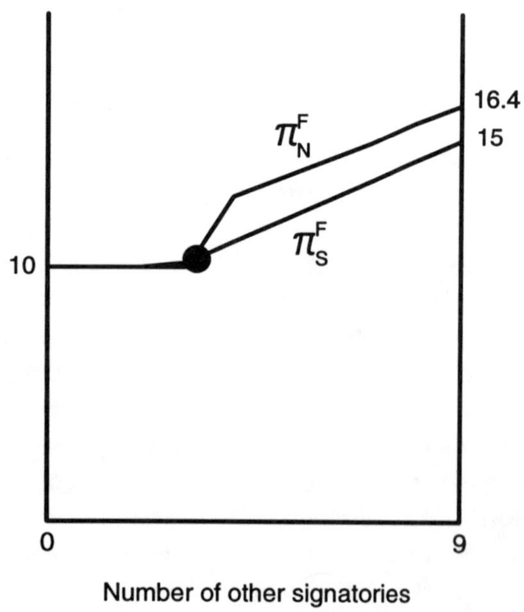

Figure 11.1d
Trade ban/IEA

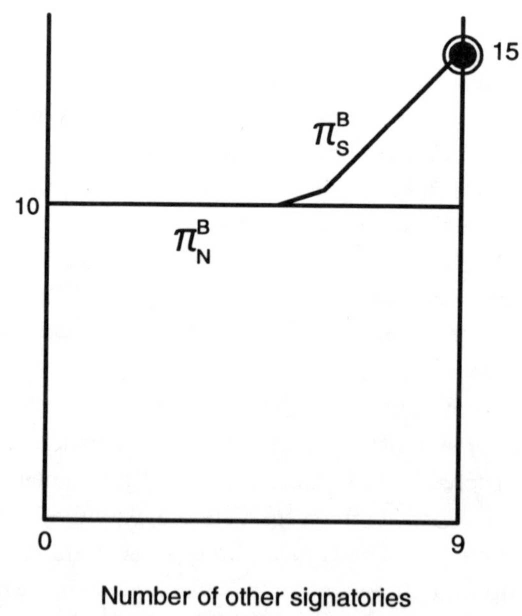

Note: IEA = International Environmental Agreement.

every pair of private goods in the same proportion. My choice of parameter values ensures that this game is a prisoners' dilemma. So in the first stage, every government chooses not to provide the public good, irrespective of the number of countries which do provide the public good. In equilibrium, therefore, no country provides the public good, every country produces one unit of the traded private good, and each country consumes *1/Nth* of the output of every country.

This game is important only as a benchmark. It tells us the outcome that is likely if there is no cooperation. Because the parameters are assumed to yield a prisoners' dilemma, one feature of the noncooperative outcome is that it is inefficient; every country would be better off if all countries provided the public good. To see this, notice that the payoff to playing Pollute always exceeds the payoff to playing Abate, and so every country will choose to play Pollute. However, the consequence is that each country gets a payoff of 10 in equilibrium. Were every country to play Abate instead, each would get a payoff of 15.

Unilateral provision of public good with trade ban

Game 2, illustrated in figure 11.1b, provides another benchmark. It is the same as game 1 with the exception that the stage 1 game is solved under the assumption of a trade ban between the countries that provide the public good and those that don't.

The chosen parameter values ensure that this game has two equilibria: one in which no country provides the public good and one in which every country does so. Notice in the figure that when only one country provides the public good, this country suffers a huge penalty, as compared with figure 11.1a (its payoff falls from 7.9 to 1.5). Not only does this country lose by having to incur the cost of providing the public good (the drop in the output of the private good), but it also loses the gains from trade. On the other hand, when all countries but one provide the public good, the one that doesn't now loses—it gains from free-riding (as in figure 11.1a) but it loses more in terms of the foregone gains from trade (so its payoff falls from 16.4 to 10).

Game 1 illustrates why countries will want to cooperate in providing the public good and game 2 illustrates why a trade ban may be instrumentally useful in supporting cooperation as an equilibrium. But would signatories to an IEA choose to behave as specified in these benchmark games? Games 3 and 4 model these cooperation problems.

Multilateral provision of the public good with free trade

Game 3 is similar to game 1 but allows countries to change the rules of the game such that (partial) cooperation can be sustained in equilibrium. The game is in 4 stages. In stage 1, every country chooses to be a signatory or a nonsignatory; in stage 2, signatories choose whether or not to provide the public good; in stage 3, nonsignatories make the same choice; and in stage 4 firms and consumers solve their optimization problems. In solving this game I make an explicit and an implicit assumption. The explicit assumption is that signatories make their stage 2 choice with the objective of maximizing their collective payoff (collective rationality). The implicit assumption is that signatories will comply with the agreement they negotiate in stage 2. This last assumption is needed because the game does not model punishment for non-compliance. However, I have shown elsewhere (Barrett 1998) that this assumption is innocuous; in a repeated game framework, under certain plausible assumptions, the equilibria will be the same. The reason is that the game 3 model *does* allow for free-riding to be punished (abatement by signatories is a non-linear function of the number of signatories), and it turns out that if free-riding can be deterred then so can non-compliance.

As shown in figure 11.1c, the equilibrium to game 3 is unique and consists of an IEA with 4 signatories, each of which provides the public good, and 6 nonsignatories, none of which provides the public good. The IEA is an equilibrium in the sense that each signatory could not do better by withdrawing from the agreement, and each nonsignatory could not do better by acceding to the agreement, taking as given the choices made by the other countries. Moreover, signatories do better than in game 1. However, nonsignatories do better still. Nonsignatories free ride. In total, however, the aggregate payoff is only slightly larger in this situation as compared with the equilibrium shown in figure 11.1a. Against the background of free trade, an international environmental agreement is only able to improve marginally on the outcome in unilateral policies.

Multilateral provision of the public good with a trade ban

Game 4 is the same as game 3 with the exception that signatories in stage 2 now decide whether they are to impose trade sanctions and, if so, under what circumstances, as well as deciding whether they are to provide the public good or not. We can see from figure 11.1b that trade sanctions are instrumentally useful to the signatories, for they can allow full cooperation in the provision of the public good to be sustained by a self-enforcing IEA. However, the figure also shows that this will only be the case if enough countries are signatories. So the signatories will not want to provide the public good in the trade ban regime unless at least a minimum number of countries are signatories.

The game is illustrated in figure 11.1d. Provided the IEA contains a minimum participation clause of 6 countries, there is a unique equilibrium, and this now sustains full cooperation. However, this equilibrium is not very compelling.

To see this, suppose that all countries were signatories to the agreement. Then, if a signatory withdrew unilaterally, taking as given the trade ban, its payoff would fall from 15 to 10. So given the trade ban, free riding would be deterred. But if a signatory withdrew from the agreement—by accident, say—the remaining 9 signatories would not want to impose the trade ban. They each get a payoff of 13.5 if they restrict trade but 14.2 if they don't. The treat to ban trade with nonsignatories isn't credible.

Indeed, it turns out that for this game a trade ban is never credible, even though it would be effective in deterring free-riding if signatories could commit to imposing the trade ban. Trade sanctions are thus not an easy solution to the free-riding problem.

What really distinguishes this model from Barrett (1997) isn't the source of the gains from trade but rather the presence of trade leakage. In the model developed here, there is no leakage, and so, given that a defection has occurred, signatories can only be made worse off by restricting trade. But suppose that leakage were severe. Suppose, in particular, that if a country were to withdraw from an IEA, output in the pollution-intensive industry would increase substantially in this free-riding country—but only if there were free trade. Then the remaining signatories would have an incentive to restrict trade. Trade sanctions would be credible.

5. Conclusions

Trade sanctions harm free-riders by reducing the gains from trade available to these countries. To be effective, this loss in the gains from trade must exceed the net costs to each country of providing the public good.

However, trade sanctions—like all free-rider punishments—harm the countries that impose them as well as those on the receiving end. To be credible, signatories to an IEA must be better off when they impose sanctions than when they do not, given that some countries choose to free-ride. Though I have not offered a formal proof, I believe that this last condition is most likely to be met when leakage is substantial. For then the sanctions increase provision of the public good, to the benefit of the signatories to the IEA. Provided this benefit exceeds the loss in the gains from trade from a restriction on trade with nonsignatories, sanctions will be credible. And provided both of the above conditions are met, the threat of imposing trade sanctions will be sufficient to ensure that the public good is provided—that free-riding is deterred—and that sanctions are never imposed.

It seems that both of these conditions were satisfied in the case of the Montreal Protocol. And, yet, the GATT Secretariat has argued that the trade restrictions against non-parties was unnecessary (GATT 1992, p. 25):

> "...the parties to the Montreal Protocol...could have structured the Protocol in such a way that it reduced consumption of CFCs in the participating countries by the target amount, without the necessity of including provisions for special restrictions on trade with non-parties. Since, however, the drafters had other goals as well, including that of providing compensation to CFC producers in the participating countries (by allowing them to receive extra profits from selling the diminishing quantity of CFCs), trade provisions which discriminate against non-participants were included in the Protocol."

The Secretariat is mistaken here on two counts. The first is to assume that signatories would want only to limit consumption at home. As noted earlier, signatories will want to reduce trade leakage not only in consumption but also in production. They will also want to reduce emissions abroad by altering the terms of trade (see Uimonen and Whalley 1997). Finally, they will want to deter free-riding. The Secretariat's criticism does not address the question of how free-riding could be deterred without the use of sanctions.

The Secretariat is also wrong in concluding that the sanctions were aimed at filling the pockets of the CFC producers in signatory countries. The proposal to restrict trade between parties and non-parties was first tabled by the United States. It is true that the U.S. realized that the Montreal Protocol would increase the profits of its CFC manufacturers by restricting the quantity of CFCs that could be traded. But the U.S. did not allow these manufacturers to reap the surplus sown by the treaty; instead, it taxed the windfall.

A GATT panel ruling from 1994 raises an additional concern, and that is whether trade restrictions should be allowed when their purpose is to change the environmental policies of other states (non-parties, in the context of the Montreal Protocol restrictions). According to this ruling (Uimonen and Whalley 1997, p. 77):

> "If Article XX were interpreted to permit Contracting Parties [to the GATT] to take trade measures so as to force other Contracting Parties to change their policies within their jurisdiction, including their conservation policies, the balance of rights and obligations among Contracting Parties, in particular the right of access to markets, would be seriously impaired. Under such an interpretation the General Agreement could no longer serve as a multilateral framework for trade among Contracting Parties."

The claim that trade restrictions should not be used to alter the environmental policies of other countries may be valid where there are no cross-border externalities.[4] But where there are such externalities, and where trade restrictions can be used to correct them, a prohibition on their use can be welfare-reducing. It is wrong to assume that the multilateral trading rules must take precedence over all other international affairs, including environmental protection, just as it is wrong to assume that environmental protection is more deserving than other claims on the international system.

But the number of cases in which trade sanctions will be both effective and credible is probably very small. The Montreal Protocol appears to be a special case.

Appendix

A.1 The Model

There are N symmetric countries. Following Krugman (1991) I assume that each country specializes in the production of a single good, which is an imperfect substitute for the goods produced by the other countries. If the public good is *not* provided by country i, units are chosen such that i's output is equal to one. If i *does* provide the public good, i's output is equal to ϕ, $0 < \phi < 1$.

The goods produced by every country enter symmetrically in each country's payoff function:

$$\Pi_i = \left[\sum_{j=1}^{N} c_{ij}^{\theta}\right]^{1/\theta} + b\sum_{j=1}^{N} z_j \qquad \text{(A.1)}$$

where c_{ij} is country i's consumption of the good of country j and z_j is j's provision of the public good. Supply of the public good is a binary choice, and units are chosen such that $z_j \in \{0,1\}$.

Notice that the elasticity of substitution between any two private goods is $\sigma = 1/(1-\theta)$.

Notice, too, that production in this model can be looked at in two different ways: as arising in a perfectly competitive environment or in a monopolistically competitive market, characterized by increasing returns and free entry.

Let v denote the number of countries that provide the public good—that is, the number that play Abate—and consider two extreme outcomes, $v = 0$ and $v = N$. Given the symmetry of the model, in equilibrium the price of all products will be identical in each of these outcomes; and when $v = 0$, $c_{ij} = 1/N$ in equilibrium, while when $v = N$, $c_{ij} = \phi/N$ in equilibrium. The payoffs in these extreme outcomes are then $\Pi_i(0) = N^{1/(\sigma-1)}$ and $\Pi_i(N) = \phi N^{1/(\sigma-1)} + bN$.

Solving for intermediate outcomes where some countries play Abate and some play Pollute is more complicated and depends on the trade regime. I consider two cases: free trade and a trade ban.

A.2 Free Trade

Optimization by consumers yields

$$\left(\frac{c_{ij}}{c_{il}}\right)^{1/\sigma} = \frac{P_l}{P_j} \quad \forall i, j, l; j \neq l.$$

Since utility is homothetic in the private goods, changes in income will not change the proportions by which consumers will consume any pair of goods.

All goods produced by countries that play Abate will therefore trade at the same price. So will all goods produced by countries that play Pollute. However, the price of the former goods will exceed the price of the latter for the simple reason that the quantity of a good produced by a country that plays Abate will be less than the quantity of a good produced by a country that plays Pollute.

Since countries are symmetric, we need only distinguish between those that play Abate and those that play Pollute. Denote these countries by the subscripts A and P. Then we know that $c_{AP}/c_{AA} = c_{PP}/c_{PA} = 1/\phi$ or that $P_A/P_P = \phi^{-1/\sigma}$.

Using this price normalization, the following must hold in equilibrium

$$1 = (N-v)c_{PP} + v\phi^{-1/\sigma}c_{PA} \qquad \text{(A.2a)}$$

$$\phi^{1-1/\sigma} = (N-v)c_{AP} + v\phi^{-1/\sigma}c_{AA} \qquad \text{(A.2b)}$$

$$1 = (N-v)c_{PP} + v \quad c_{AP} \qquad \text{(A.2c)}$$

$$\phi = (N-v)c_{PA} + vc_{AA} \qquad \text{(A.2d)}$$

Eqs. (A.2a)-(A.2b) says that the value of i's consumption must equal the value of i's production, while (A.2c) and (A.2d) say that supply must equal demand.

Solving (A.2a)-(A.2b) yields

$$c_{PP} = \frac{1}{N - v(1-\phi^{1-1/\sigma})}, c_{PA} = \frac{\phi}{N - v(1-\phi^{1-1/\sigma})} \qquad \text{(A.3a)}$$

$$c_{AP} = \frac{1}{(N-v)\phi^{1/\sigma-1} + v}, c_{AA} = \frac{\phi}{(N-v)\phi^{1/\sigma-1} + v} \qquad \text{(A.3b)}$$

Substituting (A.3a) and (A.3b) into A.1 yields

$$\Pi_A^F(v) = \left[vc_{AA}^{\theta} + (N-v)c_{AP}^{\theta}\right]^{1/\theta} + bv$$

$$\Pi_P^F(v) = \left[vc_{PA}^{\theta} + (N-v)c_{PP}^{\theta}\right]^{1/\theta} + bv$$

or

$$\Pi_A^F(v) = \frac{[N - v(1-\phi^{1-1/\sigma})]^{\sigma/(\sigma-1)}}{(N-v)\phi^{1/\sigma-1} + v} + bv \qquad \text{(A.4a)}$$

$$\Pi_P^F(v) = \frac{[N - v(1-\phi^{1-1/\sigma})]^{\sigma/(\sigma-1)}}{N - v(1-\phi^{1-1/\sigma})} + bv \qquad \text{(A.4b)}$$

where the superscript F denotes free trade.

It is easy to confirm that $\Pi_P^F(v) > \Pi_A^F(v)$ for $1 < v < N-1$; free-riders do better than the countries that supply the public good. However, eqs. (A.4) are cumbersome and further analytical results are hard to obtain. Since the model is so special anyway, I consider simulations in the main text of the paper.

A.3 Trade Ban

If trade between the countries that play Abate and Pollute is banned, then each of the former countries will consume $c_{AA} = \phi/v$ and each of the latter $c_{PP} = 1/(N-v)$. Upon substituting into (A.1) we get

$$\Pi_A^B(v) = v^{1/(\sigma-1)}\phi + bv \tag{A.5a}$$

$$\Pi_P^B(v) = (N-v)^{1/(\sigma-1)} + bv \tag{A.5b}$$

where the superscript B denotes a trade ban. By appropriate choice of parameter values, the loss in the gains from trade will be large relative to the cost of providing the public good. So (A.5b) will exceed (A.5a) when v is "small" and (A.5a) will exceed (A.5b) when v is "large."

Notes

I am grateful to Per Fredriksson, David Roland-Holst, and other participants at the World Bank's Conference on Trade, Global Policy, and the Environment, April 1998, for helpful comments. This paper was also presented at the NBER-Yale Global Change Snowmass Workshop, August 1998, and I am also grateful to Jagdish Bhagwati and other participants at this workshop for their comments.

1. This is an issue-specific linkage. Carraro and Siniscalco (1997) consider linking R&D cooperation in an international environmental agreement. See also Cesar and de Zeeuw (1994) and Folmer, van Mouche, and Ragland (1993) for alternative analyses of linkage.
2. I consider here only trade leakage in goods markets. For an analysis of trade leakage in the market for traded fuels, see Hoel (1994).
3. I am ignoring here the optimal tariff that would accompany these adjustments. See Markusen (1975).
4. It is often claimed that weaker environmental standards confer a competititive advantage and that fair trade demands countervailing remedies that level the playing field of international competition. In Barrett (1994b), I identify instances in which a country may want to weaken its environmental policy for reasons of competitiveness, but I argue that these cases are special and that countervailing measures are more likely to be welfare-reducing than welfare-enhancing. See also Bhagwati and Srinivasan (1996), Esty (1994), and Uimonen and Whalley (1997).

References

Barrett, S. 1990. "The Problem of Global Environmental Protection." *Oxford Review of Economic Policy* 6: 68–79.

Barrett, S. 1994a. "Self-Enforcing International Environmental Agreements." *Oxford Economic Papers* 46: 878–94.

Barrett, S. 1994b. "Strategic Environmental Policy and International Trade." *Journal of Public Economics* 54: 325–38.

Barrett, S. 1997. "The Strategy of Trade Sanctions in International Environmental Agreements." *Resource and Energy Economics* 19: 345–61.

Barrett, S. 1998. "A Theory of International Cooperation." mimeo, London Business School.

Benedick, R.E. 1991. *Ozone Diplomacy.* Cambridge, MA: Harvard University Press.

Bhagwati, J., and T.N. Srinivasan. 1996. "Trade and the Environment: Does Environmental Diversity Detract form the Case for Free Trade?" In J. Bhagwati and R.E. Hudec, eds., *Fair Trade and Harmonization: Prerequisites for Free Trade? Volume 1: Economic Analysis* p. 159–223. Cambridge, MA: MIT Press.

Brack. 1996. *International Trade and the Montreal Protocol.* London: Chatham House.

Carraro, C., and D. Siniscalco. 1997. "R&D Cooperation and the Stability of International Environmental Agreements." In C. Carraro, ed., *International Environmental Negotiations* p. 71–96. Cheltenham: Edward Elgar.

Cesar, H., and A. de Zeeuw. 1994. "Issue Linkage in Global Environmental Problems." Nota ke Lavoro 56.94, Fondazione Eni Enrico Mattei, Milano.

Esty, D. C. 1994. *Greening the GATT: Trade, Environment, and the Future.* Washington, DC: Institute for International Economics.

Fisher, B. S., S. Barrett, P. Bohm, M. Kuroda, J.K.E. Mubazi, A. Shaw, and R.N. Stavins. 1996. "An Economic Assessment of Policy Instruments for Combatting Climate Change." In J.P. Bruce, H. Lee, and E.F. Haites, eds., *Climate Change 1995* p. 397–439. Cambridge: Cambridge University Press.

Folmer, H., P.V. van Mouche, and S. Ragland. 1993. "Interconnected Games and International Environmental Problems." *Environmental and Resource Economics* 3: 313–36.

GATT Secretariat. 1992. *International Trade 90–91.* Geneva: GATT.

Hoel, M. 1994. "Efficient Climate Policy in the Presence of Free Riders." *Journal of Environmental Economics and Management* 27: 259–74.

Hoel, M. 1996. "Should a Carbon Tax be Differentiated Across Sectors?" *Journal of Public Economics* 59: 17–32.

Krugman, P. 1991. "Is Bilateralism Bad?" In E. Helpman and A. Razin, eds., *International Trade and Trade Policy* p. 9–23. Cambridge, MA: MIT Press.

Markusen, J.R. 1975. "International Externalities and Optimal Tax Structures." *Journal of International Economics* 5: 15–29.

Oliveira-Martins, J., J.-M. Burniaux, and J.P. Martin. 1992. "Trade and the Effectiveness of Unilateral CO2 Abatement Policies: Evidence from GREEN." *OECD Economic Studies* 19: 123–40.

Uimonen, P., and J.Whalley. 1997. *Environmental Issues in the New World Trading System.* New York: St. Martin's Press.

Van Slooten, R. 1994. "The Case of the Montreal Protocol." In OECD, *Trade and the Environment: Processes and Production Methods* p. 87–91. Paris: OECD.

Chapter 12

The Importance of Trade for the Ratification of the 1992 Climate Change Convention

Per G. Fredriksson and Noel Gaston

1. Introduction

The *United Nations Framework Convention on Climate Change* (FCCC) was made available for signature at the *Earth Summit* held at Rio de Janeiro in June 1992. It entered into force in March 1994 after fifty countries had ratified the Convention.[1] The *Summit* was a response to the growing weight of scientific evidence that the Earth may be affected by climate change in the coming decades.[2]

As a framework treaty, the FCCC sets out principles as well as general commitments to adopt national programs for mitigating climate change and promote the conservation of greenhouse gas "sinks," such as forests. The FCCC differentiates between developing countries and former Eastern Bloc countries and OECD countries (the latter two groups are referred to as Annex One countries). By ratifying the Convention, the latter two groups committed themselves to "aim" to reduce emissions individually or jointly to their 1990 levels by the year 2000. Developing countries have no significant commitments under the FCCC, but are responsible for cooperation and promotion of the diffusion of technologies and practices that restrict emissions, that is, there is a "common but differentiated responsibility" of nations in confronting the global environmental problem. The OECD countries were obliged to make financial resources and abatement technologies available to developing countries in order to meet these obligations. According to Chayes and Chayes (1991), the majority of international environmental agreements are complied with by ratifying countries. Although no nation can be forced to strictly adhere to the conditions stipulated in any international environmental agreement, Carraro and Siniscalco (1992) and Barrett (1994) argue that due to their voluntary nature, such agreements are self-enforcing.[3]

The primary objective of this paper is to study the determination of the propensity of countries to participate in global environmental policy making by ratifying the FCCC. In particular, we are interested in *when* countries signed the FCCC, rather than whether they signed. In a departure from the existing related literature, we focus on the delay in the ratification of an environmental treaty, that is, the duration of time it takes for countries to formally take action.[4] We argue that countries that speedily ratify an environmental treaty have a more intense preference for the provisions it contains. Thus, in our context the date of eventual ratification proxies the relative intensity of preference for the provisions of the FCCC. A shorter delay in ratifying implies that a country sees the provisions in its immediate national self-interest. In Barrett's (1990) terminology, signatories (and ratifiers, in our view) act as "abatement leaders" and the others as "abatement followers." Ratification delay data of the type we use in this paper are informative about the characteristics of "leaders" and "followers" (that is, given that abatement takes place subsequent to ratification of the agreement). A characterization of these countries may facilitate an improvement in the design of future international environmental agreements (IEAs).

Working with ratification or delay times not only avoids the problem of choosing an arbitrary cutoff date to investigate determinants of treaty ratification, but also adds to our knowledge of the political process underlying treaty ratification. Those countries that delay their ratification of a treaty do so, either because they perceive the treaty provisions as too costly and severe or, lacking net benefits (or that it may be strategically worthwhile to "hold-out," in which case they risk non-implementation of the agreement).

Global environmental policy carried out by international treaties suffer from at least two drawbacks. First, since participation is voluntary for each sovereign state, both in the ratification and the compliance stages, an international environmental agreement is based on a consensus of all participants and must be self-enforcing. According to Sand (1991), agreed upon environmental standards tend to result in the lowest common denominator. Barrett (1994) and Murdoch and Sandler (1997) argue that the Montreal Protocol merely codified CFC reductions that the countries would have undertaken in the absence of any agreement. Second, ratification of an international environmental treaty by parliament results in a time lag, delaying the implementation of the provisions of the treaty. In addition, the stipulation that multilateral agreements be ratified by a certain number of countries further slows implementation.[5] While this condition is aimed at avoiding any free-riding by potential non-ratifiers, it delays the desired outcome to the time until the "slowest truck in the convoy" reaches its destination.[6]

Sand (1991) sees time lags and treaty ratification as one of the most serious drawbacks of the treaty approach to global environmental policymaking. Therefore, the question arises as to whether the traditional approach to multilateral agreements constitutes an effective way of undertaking international environmental policy. Since the target of the FCCC was to stabilize greenhouse gases within eight years, the exhibited ratification speed may have been important for the failure of many ratifiers to live up to the agreement.[7] Moreover, it is possible that countries behaved strategically looking ahead to Kyoto.[8] The negotiations on global warming issues are clearly an ongoing process. The Kyoto meeting held in December 1997 was decided upon less than three years subsequent to Rio. The timing of this process, with new rounds of negotiation occurring at such short time intervals, may have been an important reason for countries to have delayed their ratification and for the perceived subsequent failure of the FCCC.

Unfortunately, slow ratification by major emitters and competitors is likely to either dampen the enthusiasm of others to ratify the agreement, or alternatively, to reduce the interest in adhering to commitments made. The FCCC is a prime example of the voluntary provision of a public good. There is scope for free-riding both in the ratification and the implementation stages. A better understanding of the underlying behavior of countries in this process is important for the appropriate design of global policies. Hopefully, this paper represents a step forward in our understanding of why ratifying countries deviated from the FCCC agreement.

As well as its unique focus on delays in the ratification of an international environmental agreement, the paper contributes to the policy debate and the literature in several ways. We are particularly interested in the impact of the degree of openness to international trade on the ratification process. Trade-related issues arose during the Protocol negotiations when it became apparent that some countries considered that future mitigation measures could have strong trade impacts (see Assunção 1997). Based on the experience with the Convention on International Trade in Endangered Species of Wild Flora and Fauna (CITES) and the Montreal Protocol, some countries believed that trade restrictions might be used, both to limit emissions and to induce non-compliant parties to participate in the new Protocol. Profitable trading relationships between nations therefore have important implications for a country's willingness to take up the obligations under the FCCC.

Increased exposure to international markets may yield a "race to the bottom," or "political drag" in the enactment of environmental regulations (see Esty 1996; Esty and Geradin 1997; Stewart 1993). Consequently, countries may delay the ratification of international environmental agreements and the associated abatement efforts, for international "competitiveness" reasons.

In the next section, we describe the legislative delay time data. To our knowledge, this is one of the first papers that uses data on the FCCC. Section 3 describes our key hypotheses, and section 4 presents results from a proportional hazards regression model. Section 5 provides some concluding observations. A description of the empirical methodology and technical details are left for the Appendix.

2. The Data on Legislative Delay

The few empirical studies that have preceded ours on the determinants of signing environmental treaties have investigated the signatories and non-signatories at a particular point in time. Since the date of ratification is a continuous variable, this introduces an inevitable degree of arbitrariness in the choice of a cut-off date for an investigation. It also reduces the political environmental treaty ratification decision to a dichotomous choice. In contrast, we focus on delay times to ratification of the FCCC.

The FCCC was made available for ratification on June 4th, 1992. The date of ratification by the countries is recorded by the Convention. By definition, "left-censoring" is not a problem. That is, we know the date when the FCCC was made available for ratification by all countries. However, some spells are incomplete since some countries have not ratified the FCCC. That is, some of the data are "right-censored." This requires the use of special empirical techniques that have been developed to handle duration data. At the commencement date of the Kyoto meeting (December 1, 1997) twenty-one countries had still not ratified the convention.

The total sample size consists of 184 countries. The main part of the data are for countries that were members of the United Nations (UN) as of June 1992. For countries that came into existence after June 1992, we compute the delay time from the date of that country's admission into the UN.[9]

Figure 12.1 plots the (non-parametric) estimates of the survival distribution function for the delay time data. This survivor function specifies the probability that the delay time will exceed a certain number of days. The average delay time for the countries that ratified the FCCC is 810 days, while the median spell length is 728 days (indicating skewness in the delay time distribution). The quartiles of the delay time distribution are 375, 810, and 978 days. That is, more than a year had passed by the time a quarter of the countries had ratified and well over two years had elapsed before half the countries had done so.

Figure 12.1 Survival function estimates

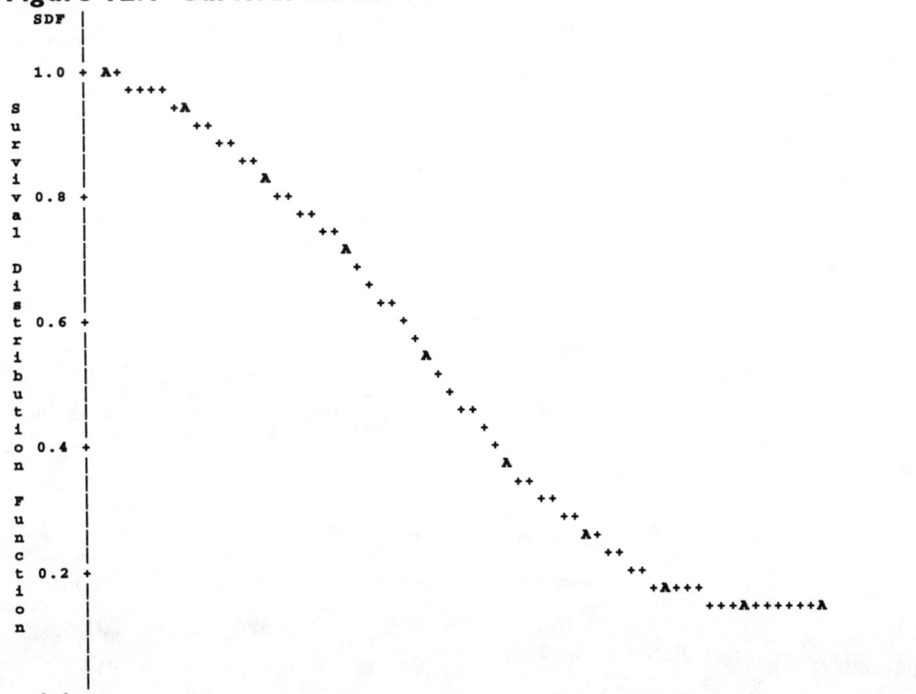

Figure 12.2 plots non-parametric estimates of the hazard function. The hazard rate is the rate at which countries will ratify the FCCC at any particular date (that is, conditional on them not having ratified up until that point in time). The single-peakedness indicates an initially increasing hazard or positive duration dependence and then a decreasing hazard or negative duration dependence. (The peak is at 98 countries, above the critical number of 50 countries required for ratification.) Negative duration dependence indicates that the longer a country has not ratified the FCCC, the less likely it is to do so. This latter fact points to the importance of early ratification.

Table 12.1 provides a breakdown by broad country "type," that is, OECD and former Eastern Bloc, and developing country. Despite the concessions granted, it is evident that developing countries tend to have longer delay times.[10] This suggests the importance of a variety of country characteristics as determinants of the ratification of international environmental agreement. We turn to this issue in the next section.

Figure 12.2 Hazard function estimates

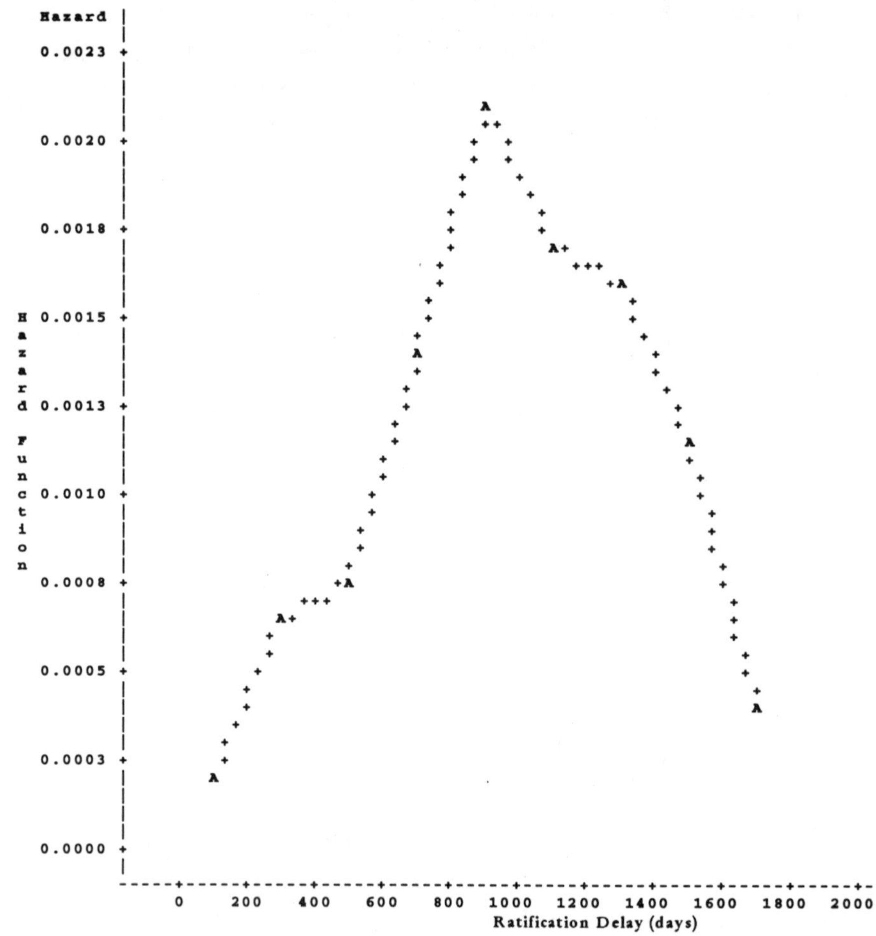

Table 12.1 Descriptive statistics for legislative delay times

Countries	*Complete*	*Mean*	*Std Dev*	*Median*	*Incomplete*
All	163	810	396	728	21
Developing country	130	849	402	914	19
OECD/Former Eastern Bloc	33	656	336	630	2

Source: Data on ratification dates are from the unfccc official web site (http://www.unfccc.de/).

3. The Determinants of Legislative Delay

The descriptive information is illuminating, but additional insights are gained from an analysis of probabilistic models that estimate the effects of various factors on ratification delay times. To deal with the censored nature of the data, we use the proportional hazards regression model (Cox 1972). Further details of the estimation and specification tests are left for the Appendix.

We link the delay time data with data on characteristics of the countries that are drawn from a number of different sources. All the data are publicly available. See table 12.2. Missing observations for some of the key explanatory variables reduce the sample size to 114 countries. The column containing correlations in table 12.2 provides some preliminary insights on some of the hypothesized relationships in this section.

The major focus of this paper is the association between trade relations and environmental policy making. Esty (1996) and Esty and Geradin (1997) discuss the issue of "political drag" in environmental policy making. Interpreted in our context, they have the following concern: Do countries delay the ratification of IEAs and the associated abatement efforts, for international "competitiveness" reasons?

Barrett (1997) studies the important relationship between trade and IEAs. He shows that if trade sanctions are a credible threat, full cooperation on global environmental policy can be sustained when a minimum participation requirement is used. He also argues that in the absence of trade sanctions, the environment is not protected at the Pareto efficient level.

Moreover, analogous to Fernandez' (1997) reasoning concerning regional trade areas, the commitment to environmental cooperation may work as a signaling device. That is, it signals that a country's industries are competitive, that the investment climate is attractive, and that future political relationships with other nations will remain healthy. All these factors stimulate investment and are therefore likely to make ratification of the FCCC more attractive.

Trade has been seen as a civilizing force for centuries (see Hirschman 1982; and Schiff and Winters 1997).[11] Chan (1984) argues that the level of conflict between any two nations diminishes if they are democratic. Polachek (1992, 1997) explains this result by the effect of democracy on trade. International trade between democracies is greater than between other countries. Trade also has a negative effect on the level of conflict and a positive effect on bilateral cooperation.

Hoel and Schneider (1997) argue that governments may ratify an IEA for fear of exclusion from future trade agreements. The costs of non-ratification, as well as of deviating after having ratified, are likely to be increasing in the total trade flows and openness of a country and in the number of trading partners. Hoel and Schneider (1997) argue that low income countries have little to lose by not joining an IEA because they have small non-environmental costs (such as a loss of reputation). Whereas exporters are likely to be concerned about both their reputation and abatement costs, import-competing sectors may care primarily about their costs, and thus trade may cause industries to take different lobbying stances on the FCCC.

In the area of international trade negotiations, and in the political game between superpowers, *reciprocity* is often invoked as the correct standard of behavior producing cooperation among states (Keohane 1986). Obligations are important and imply that agents behave in a generally acceptable fashion. The concept appears to apply to IEAs, such as the FCCC, as well as to trade agreements.

The sum of these arguments imply that nations which are relatively reliant on trade interact with other nations more frequently and exchange ideas more freely, and may therefore behave in a different way than autarkies. While the global benefits of ratification are commonly shared, the costs of non-ratification are likely to vary with each country's reliance on trade. The effect of openness, per se, is ambiguous. For example, it should also be noted that openness is also likely to affect compliance costs of an IEA as well as the trade-related costs associated with ratifying an IEA. However, conditional on compliance with IEAs, we hypothesize that EXPORTS are likely to be positively correlated with reputation costs and lead to shorter delay times and a higher hazard rate. However, greater total IMPORTS increase the inflow of foreign influences and ideas, as well as the amount of technology transfers and foreign competition.

We also include other controls and variables thought to be important determinants of the ratifica-

Table 12.2 Descriptive statistics for covariate analysis

Variable	*Label*	*N*	*Mean*	*Std Dev*	*Minm*	*Maxm*	$\rho^{\dagger}$	*Sources*
DELAY	Ratification delay, days after June 4, 1992	104	795.12	385.57	92.00	1959.00	.	a
ANNEX1	OECD/Former Eastern Bloc	114	0.23	0.42	0.00	1.00	-.28***	b
TROPICS	Tropics	114	0.61	0.49	0.00	1.00	.15	c
CAPRCORN	South of Tropic of Capricorn	114	0.05	0.22	0.00	1.00	.04	c
AREA	Total area, '000 sq km	114	877.71	1869.07	0.63	9976.14	-.42***	CIA
COASTLIN	Coastline, '000 km	114	5.68	23.78	0.00	243.79	-.30***	CIA
POPN	Population, 1994, mill.	114	43.64	142.87	0.21	1190.43	-.23**	CIA
LIFEEXP	Life expectancy, years	114	64.01	11.82	37.46	79.31	-.18*	CIA
EXPORTS	Exports 1992, bill. ($US)	114	26.00	65.56	0.04	449.00	-.35***	CIA
IMPORTS	Imports 1992, bill. ($US)	114	27.62	70.50	0.13	582.00	-.34***	CIA
NPCAPITA	National product pre capita, 1993 ($US)	114	6091.75	6500.01	500.00	24700.00	-.27***	CIA
SACHSIDX	Sachs-Warner trade openness index	104	0.37	0.48	0.00	1.00	-.12	SACHS
NOTFREE	Gastil civil rights index	114	4.26	2.04	1.00	7.00	.37***	SCULLY
SOCIALIST	Gastil economic system index	114	3.79	2.33	1.00	9.00	.15	SCULLY
GDPPER	GDP growth, 1983-93, %	114	2.48	3.00	-14.90	8.90	-.11	WRI table 7.1
CO2TOTAL	Total CO2 Emissions, 1992 (mill. tons)	114	143.84	532.68	0.02	4881.35	-.39***	WRI table 14.1
OILRES	Crude oil recoverable reserves (bill. tons)	65	2.00	5.44	0.00	35.62	.11	WRI table 12.3
SCOALRES	Soft coal recoverable reserves (bill. tons)	37	8.41	24.40	0.00	134.06	-.54***	WRI table 12.3
HCOALRES	Hard coal recoverable reserves (bill. tons)	46	8.43	22.41	0.00	106.50	-.40***	WRI table 12.3
OPEC	OPEC member country	114	0.09	0.28	0.00	1.00	.13	d

Notes: a. Data are from UNFCCC official web site (http://www.unfccc.de/). Sample consists of 114 countries of which 10 are non-ratifiers.
b. Dummy variable = 1, if country a member of OECD or former Eastern bloc.
c. Latitude calculated from geographic center of country.
d. OPEC country = 1.
CIA: Data from *The World Fact Book, 1996* (U. S. Central Intelligence Agency).
SCULLY: Data from Scully (1992), Appendix table 5.2, p.132–39.
SACHS: Data calculated from Sachs and Warner (1995). Open = 1.
WRI: Data from *World Resources: A Guide to the Global Environment, 1996-7*, World Resources Institute, various tables.
† Correlation with Log of Delay time. Statistically significant at 1 percent (***); 5 percent (**), 10 percent (*) level. N = 104.

tion of IEAs. First, the financial situation of the country is likely to play a role. Countries that are growing relatively quickly, for instance, may find it less costly on the margin to ratify an IEA than countries that grow more slowly. Slow income growth, which is associated with a growing unemployment problem, is often cited as the reason for resistance to entering into an IEA. Hence, higher percentage growth in income (GDPPER) is likely to be associated with shorter delay times and a higher hazard rate. Also, we use GDP per capita, NPCAPITA, as suggested by Congleton (1992). Murdoch and Sandler (1997) found a linear relationship between GNP and emission cutbacks which they interpreted as evidence in favor of the theory of the voluntary provision of public goods. To the extent that environmental quality is a normal good, NPCAPITA is likely to yield shorter delay times and a higher hazard rate (Bergstrom and others 1986).

Second, countries that emit more greenhouse gases and are more reliant on energy-intensive production may be more hesitant about ratification of the FCCC because their input costs are likely to rise relatively more. On the other hand, in a model with identical countries, Barrett (1994) finds that the greater is the ratio of the slope of each country's marginal abatement cost curve to the slope of the global marginal benefit function, the fewer are the number of countries that sign an IEA. If higher emissions imply a lower slope of the marginal abatement cost curve, then ratification of an IEA is more likely. Countries that emit more pollutants are also likely to be under greater international pressure to ratify an IEA, and the reputational effects of non-ratification are likely to be greater. A country's reputation may also affect international negotiations on other important issues, such as trade policy. We use CO2TOTAL as an indicator for greenhouse gas emissions.

Third, Congleton (1992) presents a theory which shows that autocratic countries select less stringent environmental regulations. He argues that dictators tend to have shorter time horizons and should be less likely, or take longer, to ratify an IEA, since the benefits of doing so are likely to accrue after they have left office, whereas the costs are incurred earlier.[12] The same argument implies a longer time before the FCCC is ratified. In addition, if more undemocratic governments do have a higher turnover, they are more likely to be out of office at the time of ratification. For reasons other than the purported shorter tenure of dictatorships, Olson (1993) argues that dictators wish to maximize tax revenues and thus oppose any policies that would reduce revenue, for example, those that result from increased abatement expenditures. Fredriksson (1997) argues that more democratic countries (in the sense that they put a greater emphasis on social welfare relative to lobbying activities) choose local environmental policies that are closer to being welfare-maximizing.[13] Consequently, democratic countries may therefore also be more likely to speedily ratify global environmental policies.

If a change in government or particular political group in favor has occurred from the time of the negotiations, the preferences of the legislative body have changed and thus a rapid ratification may be less likely. Iida (1996) argues that ratification failures are more likely when negotiators are uncertain about their constituency's preferences. We assert that a greater degree of representative democracy may be expected to yield better information about domestic legislative behavior. Furthermore, great internal divisions imply that legislatures are less likely to ratify international environmental agreements, although this can to some degree also be used by negotiators to extract concessions (see Milner and Rosendorff 1997).

It is also possible that the ratification of IEAs serves as a commitment to the idea of democracy. By participation in international agreements, countries can show that they fulfill the requirements for participation in various forms of cooperation (Fernandez 1997).[14]

Following previous authors (for example, Congleton 1992), we use Gastil's indices of civil liberties and political freedoms (NOTFREE) as well as an index of the type of economic system that a country has (SOCIALIST). Higher values of NOTFREE index *fewer* civil liberties; higher values of SOCIALIST index a greater degree of government control of property and less market-oriented or more socialistic economic systems (see Scully 1992).

Fourth, the population size (POPN) may influence the ratification date because a country with a small population may stand to gain more from an IEA than a large country. This is because in the negotiation process a small concession by a large country may imply a substantial gain for a small country (see Chen 1997). It may be easier for a small country to free-ride, however, since the effect on global pollution is lower. Alternatively, Congleton (1992) used POPN to proxy for a country's labor force. Hence, the extent to which this is correlated with worker concerns about unemployment is likely to delay ratification.

A country's resource base is positively related to personal income and negatively related to the marginal cost of environmental regulations (and therefore, positively correlated with the equilibrium stringency of environmental policies). We use land area (AREA) as a proxy for resource base (which is also correlated with fossil fuels). Available data for recoverable oil and coal reserves are poor, due to the large number of missing observations. However, we estimate some models with the reduced sample and also estimate models with an OPEC country dummy.

Next, the time horizon has implications for the costs and benefits derived from the reduction of emissions. Nordhaus (1991) argues that whereas the costs of environmental regulations are incurred immediately, the rewards of regulation are repaid only later. We use life expectancy at birth (LIFEEXP) as a proxy for the planning horizon.

Flooding is expected to increase as a result of global warming. We use total COASTLINE as a measure of the propensity for floods. Moreover, desertification and increased frequency of malaria are expected results of increased temperature. We use distance from the equator as measured by two dummies (TROPICS, CAPRICORN).

Finally, developing countries have no significant obligations under the FCCC. This is likely to reduce the costs of ratifying the agreement. We capture this effect by the ANNEX1, which takes a value of one for OECD and former Eastern Bloc countries. Preliminary evidence for this hypothesis is not supported by comparisons across the rows of table 12.1 and by the negative correlation in the penultimate column of table 12.2. This is, however, consistent with Hoel and Schneider (1997) who argue that the availability of side-payments, such as technology transfers, provided that a country does not commit itself to cooperation, may actually reduce the incentive to participate in IEAs.

4. The Results

Main findings: Table 12.3 contains the estimation results. Column (1) presents estimates of the main model specification. The findings reveal that the hazard rate, the conditional probability of ratifying the FCCC, is positively correlated with EXPORTS, GDPPER, CO2TOTAL, AREA, and ANNEX1 and negatively correlated with IMPORTS and NOTFREE.

The coefficient for EXPORTS indicates that large exporting countries were more likely to ratify the FCCC quickly. Exporters appear to take reputational effects into consideration, possibly because of fears of consumer boycotts or repercussions in other international forums, such as the World Trade Organisation. Moreover, they are likely to be more exposed and more receptive to ideas in the area of environmental policy and are therefore more open to cooperation as predicted by Polachek (1992, 1997). To the extent that faster ratification mirrors a greater preference for increased abatement efforts and stringent regulations, the finding provides no support for the "political drag" or "race to the bottom" effects induced by freer trade. On the other hand, the negative sign for IMPORTS is suggestive of a "political drag" or "race to the bottom." Large importing countries have been hesitant to ratify the FCCC, perhaps out of fear of loss of "competitiveness."[15] This indicates that lobbying by import-competing industries may have been successful in stalling the ratification process. Evidently, the inflow of novel ideas about environmental policies from abroad through imported goods and services has been minimal. The findings for trade are subjected to further scrutiny below.

The finding for CO2TOTAL indicates that countries generating greater *total* pollution had shorter ratification delay times. This suggests that large polluting countries were under great political pressure, either internally or externally, to ratify the FCCC. Reputational considerations or marginal abatement costs thus appear to be playing an important role.

The positive coefficient for GDPPER suggests that fast-growing countries perceive relatively greater benefits, or lower costs, from the ratification of the FCCC than slower-growing ones. The latter group of countries is more likely to be concerned with high unemployment and to have fewer funds available for environmental protection. We also studied the effect of per capita income. We estimated several models. All models excluded POPN, as population appears in the denominator of NPCAPITA. In many models, GDPPER was deleted. In addition, some of the other

Table 12.3 Estimates of proportional hazards model — Effects of trade measures

Variable	(1) Full	(2) No trade	(3) Scaled trade	(4) Openness	(5) Sachs-Warner
AREA(*10³)	0.152*	0.147	0.139	0.143	0.153
	(0.086)	(0.091)	(0.090)	(0.091)	(0.095)
POPN(*10²)	0.015	0.056	0.050	0.049	0.035
	(0.115)	(0.101)	(0.102)	(0.102)	(0.104)
EXPORTS	0.010**	.	1.319	.	.
	(0.005)		(1.038)		
IMPORTS	-0.012**	.	-1.616	.	.
	(0.006)		(1.150)		
OPENNESS	.	.	.	-0.165	-0.067
				(0.279)	(0.285)
NOTFREE	-0.275***	-0.243***	-0.275***	-0.240***	-0.222***
	(0.080)	(0.078)	(0.082)	(0.078)	(0.087)
SOCIALIST	0.041	0.050	0.061	0.054	0.043
	(0.055)	(0.055)	(0.055)	(0.055)	(0.057)
GDPPER	0.070*	0.069*	0.083*	0.073*	0.050
	(0.041)	(0.041)	(0.043)	(0.042)	(0.042)
CO2TOTAL(*10²)	0.106*	0.071**	0.069**	0.071**	0.067*
	(0.057)	(0.035)	(0.035)	(0.035)	(0.036)
ANNEX1	0.776*	0.597	0.618	0.605	0.518
	(0.402)	(0.391)	(0.388)	(0.388)	(0.392)
TROPICS	0.004	0.071	0.029	0.097	-0.060
	(0.357)	(0.356)	(0.359)	(0.358)	(0.369)
CAPRCORN	0.127	0.238	0.216	0.252	0.140
	(0.518)	(0.518)	(0.516)	(0.518)	(0.542)
COASTLIN	0.007	0.009	0.009	0.009	0.009
	(0.006)	(0.006)	(0.006)	(0.006)	(0.006)
LIFEEXP	-0.016	-0.013	-0.013	-0.010	-0.010
	(0.014)	(0.013)	(0.015)	(0.015)	(0.015)
N	114	114	114	114	104
-2 LOG L	749.783	755.266	753.227	754.886	683.115
Likelihood ratio	56.961	51.477	53.517	51.858	44.708
Score	111.695	106.381	106.916	106.381	96.695
Wald	62.301	54.664	55.687	54.810	48.397

Notes: i. Standard errors in parentheses. Statistically significant at 1%(***); 5%(**), 10%(*) level.
ii. Column (3): Exports and Imports are scaled by domestic consumption (GDP + Imports - Exports); Column (4): Openness index calculated as (Exports + Imports)/GDP; Column (5): Sachs and Warner (1995) Openness index.

size-related variables were rotated out of the some of the models. To the extent that total CO_2 emissions are positively correlated with a country's wealth, some models were also estimated without CO2TOTAL. In *all* cases, the income per capita variable *never* achieved significance (at the 10 percent level). Hence, our discussion in this section relates to the preferred model specification, which includes GDPPER, reported in column (1) of table 12.3.

The group identity variable (ANNEX1) had a significant and positive impact on the ratification speed. It lends some support to the theory by Hoel and Schneider (1997) that the availability of technology transfers to developing countries does not necessarily increase the incentive to cooperate. Since developing countries had no binding commitments under the FCCC, the ratification decision may best be viewed as having a low priority by their legislatures or other decision-making bodies.

Robustness of the findings: Unfortunately, there is some sensitivity in some of the parameter estimates. Alternative model specifications were also estimated because of a suspected multicollinearity problem between some of the variables (for example, the correlation of the size variables is quite high for our sample).[16] In some model specifications, many of the effects identified above, in connection with the results reported in column (1), generally have weak statistical significance. Across all the specifications that were estimated, the signs of significant coefficients were generally robust. In particular, NOTFREE—Gastil's civil liberties index—is always associated with a significantly lower hazard across *all* model specifications that were estimated, that is, greater civil liberties result in more rapid ratification. Using the point estimate in column (1), the marginal effect of a unit increase in NOTFREE on the hazard rate is -24 percent.[17]

Benedick (1991) argues that the experience with the CFC negotiations shows the importance of political leadership and resistance to lobby groups interested in impeding the legislative process. More democratic countries may also be less likely to use tardy ratification as a tool in the next negotiation round. The result underscores the importance of political and institutional factors for the ratification of IEAs.

Apart from NOTFREE, the only other variable that consistently retained both its coefficient sign and statistical significance across all the model specifications that were estimated was CO2TOTAL. However, this variable is likely to be correlated with economic size and wealth. Scaling this variable by a size variable such as POPN yields a statistically insignificant coefficient estimate. That is, CO_2 emissions *per capita* have an insignificant effect on ratification delay. Therefore, the most conservative conclusion that can be drawn is that larger, wealthier countries, which have greater pollution levels, were more likely to ratify the FCCC at any point in time.

Variables that capture endowments (such as AREA and POPN) or vulnerability to global warming (COASTLINE) generally appear to be less important, although AREA and COASTLINE are significant at the 10 percent significance level in column (4) with the expected signs. AREA is a proxy for resource abundance, that is the marginal cost of environmental regulations (which is falling in the available resources), and this has some influence on countries' behavior, which was also reported by Congleton (1992).[18] The risk of flooding (COASTLINE) does seem to have some effect, maybe because of pressure from local insurance companies. This is not a robust finding, however. Finally, the type of economic system (SOCIALIST), location (TROPICS, CAPRICORN), and planning horizon (LIFEEXP) have no significant effects.

A detailed examination of trade variables: One of our key interests is the effects of trade and trade-related variables on the ratification of the FCCC. The remaining columns of table 12.3 present the estimation results for different measures of trade and trade openness. Column (2) reports the results from a model specification without any trade-related variables, which once again highlights the importance of NOTFREE and CO2TOTAL. Also, note that omission of total trade flows, which are positively correlated with a country's size, does not increase the significance levels or change the coefficient signs of the size variables such as AREA and POPN. Column (3) scales imports and exports by domestic consumption (that is, GDP plus imports minus exports). These measures therefore capture some notion of the importance of imports and exports in the domestic economies of each country by scaling trade flows using market size. The findings now reveal that the hazard rate is unaffected by either import penetration or scaled exports. Thus, as above, the economic size of a country appears to be the overriding consideration.[19]

Columns (4) and (5) use two different measures of countries' outward orientation or trade openness. We use the ratio of total trade (imports plus exports) scaled by total output, as well as the measure of trade openness developed by Sachs and Warner (1995).[20] In both model specifications, the results indicate that only NOTFREE and CO2TOTAL are significant. The signs of the other covariates are also stable, albeit insignificant.

Overall, while there is some evidence that trade may well matter for the passage of the FCCC, specifically total exports and imports, we find no conclusive evidence for either the "race to the bottom" or the "race to the top" hypothesis. In addition, since the coefficients of the two trade measures are approximately equal in absolute value, multilateral trade liberalization is unlikely to have a significant impact on the speed of ratification. This is evidenced by the insignificant coefficients for openness and Sachs-Warner in columns (4) and (5) of table 12.3. The findings can possibly be explained by the offsetting behavior of import and export industry lobby groups in the legislative process. We note that the evidence on the importance of trade variables is far from conclusive and indicates the need for both further empirical investigation and, in our opinion, greater effort directed at theoretically modeling the precise avenues through which international trade and environmental policy interact with one another.

There are (at least) two possible interpretations of the estimated effects of trade related variables on the ratification of the FCCC. The conservative statistical conclusion is that the economic size of countries is of overriding importance and that trade, or trade openness, has had no effect on the speed of the ratification of the FCCC. A more controversial conclusion is that large exporting countries were quicker to ratify the agreement because of reputational concerns. On the other hand, large importing countries were guilty of dragging their heels with regards to ratification of the agreement. This may have been due to competitiveness pressures and lobbying by import-competing industries.

Our findings may have implications for the ratification of future IEAs as follows. If we take the conservative high road (that is, that trade is irrelevant), then trade sanctions against non-ratifiers will have no effect on the speed of ratification. In fact, linking trade sanctions and the ratification of IEAs is likely to be counterproductive. Such measures will likely result in social welfare losses and have no great impact on when ratification of IEAs is achieved.

Alternatively, if one takes the view that trade does matter, then the threat of trade sanctions may reinforce the reputational concerns for exporters. In other words, trade sanctions are a credible threat for exporters and may expedite the ratification process. On the other hand, the large importing countries are the laggards in the ratification process and sanctions imposed by those countries that are more likely to ratify (that is, the exporters with reputational concerns), would not be a credible threat. Even if sanctions are credible, then under the interpretation that international competitiveness concerns slow the ratification process, the use of measures that sanction exports to these countries would further mitigate these competitiveness concerns and not serve to accelerate the ratification process. This is an area where much work remains to be done.

5. Conclusion

This paper represents a unique study of the United Nations Framework Convention on Climate Change (FCCC). In particular, the study looked at the determinants of the delay in ratification of the FCCC. The legislative delays in ratifying the agreement were instrumental in preventing the timely entry of the FCCC into force. Consequently, this may have had important implications for the overall lack of success of the agreement. The deadline for reductions was 8 years after the Rio Earth Summit. The credibility of this agreement hinged on its *early* entry into force. By examining when countries ratified the FCCC, our approach enabled us to identify the intensity of each country's preference to ratify, or not to ratify, the FCCC. We consequently identified the characteristics of the "leaders" and the "followers" involved in the process of negotiations on the global warming issue.

Among the more interesting findings were that the conditional probability of signing the FCCC was positively related to total CO_2 emissions and the presence of civil liberties. The latter finding is highly significant and robust and is consistent with earlier research that found that democratic freedoms raised the probability of signing the Montreal Protocol. Assuming increased levels of democracy over time, existing forecasts of future emissions may overestimate future CO_2 levels. Future research on the ratification of global international environmental agreements should explicitly consider the political and democratic status of countries at any point in time. If countries are converging in their degree of democracy, ratification delay may also converge. Interestingly, converging income levels would not yield this effect. The finding for CO_2 emissions indicates that large, heavily polluting countries were under great political pressure, either internally or externally, to ratify the FCCC. This also indicates that the speed of ratification is indeed viewed as important.

Finally, we found mixed evidence that trade mattered for the ratification of the FCCC. Whereas total exports has a positive impact on the speed of ratification, the opposite is true of total imports. Not surprisingly then, more aggregate measures of trade openness indicate no effect of international trade flows on the probability of ratifying the FCCC, that is, we find no evidence of "political drag" in the ratification process due to international trade. Moreover, the effects of these trade variables disappear when they are scaled by variables capturing size or total wealth, such as GDP. The economic size of countries also seems to be an extremely important determinant of the decision about *when* to ratify an international environmental agreement.

Naturally, there are strategic issues involved since the CO_2 negotiations are an ongoing process. This game merits further analysis in our opinion. We consider that our findings may be important for projections of the future increase of greenhouse gases under various scenarios. If democracy spreads further among nations, future abatement efforts may prove to be more successful than are currently predicted. The diffusion of democratic ideas are thus an important consideration in the continuing attempts to reduce global greenhouse emissions.

Appendix

The essential ideas of a survival model are sketched briefly here. See Kiefer (1988) or Lancaster (1992) for more detailed treatments. The conditional hazard rate is modelled as

$$\lambda(t|X) = \lambda_0(t)\exp^{X\beta}. \quad \text{(A.1)}$$

$\lambda(t|X)$ is the rate at which countries will ratify the FCCC at any particular date, given that they have not ratified up until that point in time. Equation (A.1) specifies the hazard rate as the product of two components: a function of spell length (for example, delay time), $\lambda_0(t)$ or baseline hazard, and a function of the observable country characteristics, which are denoted by the vector X. The Cox nonparametric estimation method enables us to estimate β without having to make a distributional assumption about $\lambda_0(t)$. A central objective of this paper is to obtain unbiased estimates of the vector β.

For those readers used to thinking in terms of standard regression analysis, it is helpful to interpret the estimates of the elements of β as being negatively related to the respective element in the β vector estimated by an OLS regression of X on log delay time. For example, if a variable X_j has a coefficient $\hat{\beta}_j > 0$ in equation (A.1), this implies that the effect of X_j on the hazard rate is positive, for example, that the country characteristic X_j is associated with a *higher* hazard or greater conditional probability of exiting (for example, ratifying the FCCC). Alternatively, it implies that the variable X_j is associated with a *shorter* delay in the ratification of the FCCC. Note that such direct comparisons and interpretations of coefficients are only meaningful if the data are not heavily censored (see Kiefer 1988, p.665).

More formally, the *hazard rate* $\lambda(t)$ is the probability of exiting a state in the time interval $[t, t+h]$, conditional on having arrived at t in that state, and is defined as

$$\lambda(t)h = \lim_{h \to 0} \Pr(t \le T < t + h \mid T \ge t), \quad \text{(A.2)}$$

where the random variable T is the length of the duration in the state. Assuming T has a distribution function $F(t) = \Pr(T < t)$, with density $f(t)$, then

$$\lambda(t) = f(t)/(1 - F(t)) = f(t)/S(t), \quad \text{(A.3)}$$

where $S(t) = \Pr(T \ge t)$ is the survivor function, for example, the probability of "surviving" at least until t. The density of completed spells can be found from equation (A.3), for example, $f(t) = S(t)\lambda(t)$. In addition, note that

$$d \ln S(t)/dt = -f(t)/S(t) = -\lambda(t), \quad \text{(A.4)}$$

hence, from equations(A.3) and (A.4), the survivor function is

$$S(t) = \exp\left\{-\int_0^t \lambda(s)ds\right\}. \quad \text{(A.5)}$$

Thus, the density of completed spells can be computed from the *integrated hazard* rate function. For our purposes, note that "survival" means that the country has still not ratified the FCCC and that a "hazard" occurs when the country ratifies the FCCC. Also note that the time variable "t" is not calendar time but rather the delay time, which is measured in days.

To model the effect of covariates on delay times, the hazard rate can be written as a conditional function of country characteristics, which we denote by the vector X. The most widely-used specification of the conditional hazard rate is the *proportional hazards* model,

$$\lambda(t|X) = \lambda_0(t)\phi(X). \quad \text{(A.6)}$$

Equation(A.6) specifies the hazard rate as the product of two components: a function of spell length, $\lambda_0(t)$ or *baseline hazard*, and a function of the observables, $\phi(X)$. Letting $\phi(X) = \exp(X'\beta)$, and taking logs, equation (A.6) gives:

$$\ln \lambda(t|X) = \ln \lambda_0(t) + X'\beta. \quad \text{(A.7)}$$

Note that

$$\partial \ln \lambda(t|X)/\partial X_j = \beta_j, \quad \text{(A.8)}$$

so that $\hat{\beta}_j$ gives an estimate of the effect of explanatory variable X_j on the conditional probability of ratifying the FCCC.

One approach to estimating equation (A.7) is to assume a parametric form for $\lambda_0(t)$ and maximize the likelihood function constructed from the implied distribution of spell lengths. The Cox nonparametric estimation technique provides an alternative method for estimating β without risking the specification bias that may arise if an incorrect distribution is assumed for $\lambda_0(t)$ (Cox 1972). The basic idea of the Cox technique is that even in the absence of a functional form assumption for the baseline hazard, information about β is present in the ranking of the data by spell lengths. If countries with a high value of a certain characteristic X_j, for example, have shorter delay times than countries with a low value of characteristic X_j, the hazard rate is then positively correlated with X_j, and the Cox estimation technique assigns a positive value to β_j. The usual method of estimation of the Cox model is *partial likelihood,* and is dealt with in many econometrics texts (for example, Lancaster 1992).

Notes

The authors would like to thank Johannes Heister, Suhas Parandekar, Alan Winters, the participants of the Trade, Global Policy, and the Environment Conference, and in particular our discussant Scott Barrett for useful comments. Funding from the Swedish International Development Cooperation Agency (Sida) is gratefully acknowledged.

1. The *date of signature* is defined as the date when a state expresses its consent to be bound by a treaty (subject to its ratification). The *date of ratification* is the date when a state's legislature formally consents to be bound by a treaty. The agreement only enters into force for the countries that ratify the agreement.

2. Expected effects are an increase in malaria, a rise in sea levels that could displace millions of people, and significant changes in ecosystems such as deforestation and degradation of coral reefs. Economic costs have been estimated to lie between 1 and 1.5 percent of GDP for industrialized countries and up to 9 percent for developing countries (Cline 1992; Frankhauser 1995; Tol 1995). The earth's temperature could increase by 1.5 to 6.5 degrees Fahrenheit and sea levels rise by between 6 to 37 inches by the year 2100. Fossil fuel combustion is the most important reason for the increase in greenhouse gases such as carbon dioxide (CO_2), methane (CH_4), chloro-fluorocarbons (CFCs), nitrous oxide (N_2O), ozone (O_3), and water vapor. Only vapor concentrations are not directly affected by human activities.

3. Although they have not been used the Montreal Protocol has provisions for the use of trade sanctions.

4. Fredriksson and Gaston (1999a) investigate the implications of some alternative cutoff dates using logit estimation.

5. See Black and others (1993) for a discussion of the impact of the minimum participation requirement for a Climate Change agreement.

6. A United Nations Institute for Training and Research (UNITAR) study, cited by Sand (1991), found that patterns of "drag" in treaty acceptance postponed the date of effectiveness by between two to twelve years after formal agreements had been made (the average was about five years).

7. The *Law of the Sea* only entered into force after more than twelve years.

8. Schelling's (1960) conjecture states that an international negotiator may point to a hawkish domestic legislature to extract greater concessions from the foreign country. For example, Denmark obtained considerable concessions in the 1992 renegotiation of the Maastricht Treaty after an initial ratification failure (Iida 1996). It could thus be possible to gain from a slow ratification of the FCCC in order to obtain a better bargaining position in Kyoto. If a legislature is too "hawkish," the negotiator's threat to the foreign country becomes non-credible, and the Schelling conjecture does not hold (Milner and Rosendorff 1997).

9. Specifically, we make such calculations for the Czech Republic, Eritrea, Georgia, and Macedonia.

10. See the discussion in the next section on the effect of side-payments, for example, in the form of technology transfers (also see Hoel and Schneider 1997).

11. This paragraph draws on Schiff and Winters (1997).

12. Dictatorships face an inherent uncertainty regarding the time of succession (Olson 1993).

13. See Fredriksson and Gaston (1999b) and Fredriksson (1999) for other models of lobbying on environmental issues.

14. Fernandez (1997) argues that by entering into regional trade agreements countries can show a commitment to democracy, for example, the entry of Greece, Portugal, and Spain to the European Union, the signing by the countries of Central and Eastern Europe of the Europe Agreements (which are meant to lead to eventual accession), and possibly the creation of MERCOSUR.

15. It should be noted that much of the literature has found insignificant results or small effects for the effects of environmental regulations on international trade patterns (see Jaffe and others (1995) for a survey). However, Lucas and others (1992) and Low and Yeats (1992) find evidence of the relocation of polluting industries from OECD countries to developing countries.

16. For example, the simple correlation between AREA and POPN is 0.54.

17. For any independent variable *Xi*, the marginal effect is calculated as $[\exp(\beta_i) - 1]*100$.

18. We also estimated hazard models that included an OPEC dummy, as well as models that included measures of total oil and coal reserves. None of these variables proved to be significant at the 10 percent level. In models using coal and oil reserves measures, this could be due to missing observations, however (see table 12.2). In most cases, the sample size was so dramatically reduced, that the results were uninformative.

19. It is also the case that the coefficients on EXPORTS and IMPORTS each lose their statistical significance, when either of them are omitted. They are highly correlated with each other and highly correlated with the other size variables. The authors are grateful to Alan Winters for this observation.

20. The Sachs-Warner openness dummy is based on five criteria. A country is classified as *closed* if it fulfills any of them: average tariff level, quota coverage, black market premiums, the existence of export marketing boards, and the presence of a socialist regime. *Open* countries have a value of one.

References

Assunção, Lucas. 1997. "Trade-Related Issues and the Post-Kyoto Framework Convention on Climate Change." *Bridges* 1: 2 and 12. International Center for Trade and Sustainable Development.

Barrett, Scott. 1990. "The Problem of Global Environmental Protection." *Oxford Review of Economic Policy* 6: 68–79.

_____. 1994. "Self-enforcing International Environmental Agreements." *Oxford Economic Papers* 46: 878–94.

_____. 1997. "The Strategy of Trade Sanctions in International Environmental Agreements." *Resource and Energy Economics* 19: 345–61.

Benedick, Richard E. 1991. "Protecting the Ozone Layer: New Directions in Diplomacy." In J. H. Mathews, ed., *Preserving the Global Environment*. New York: W. W. Norton & Company.

Bergstrom, Theodore C., Lawrence E. Blume, and Hal R. Varian. 1986. "On the Private Provision of Public Goods." *Journal of Public Economics* 29: 25–49.

Black, Jane, Maurice D. Levi, and David De Meza. 1993. "Creating a Good Atmosphere: Minimum Participation for Tackling the 'Greenhouse Effect.'" *Economica* 60: 281–93.

Carraro, Carlo and Domenico Siniscalco. 1992. "The International Dimension of Environmental Policy." *European Economic Review* 36: 379–87.

Chan, Steve. 1984. "Mirror, Mirror on the Wall ... Are the Freer Countries More Pacific?" *Journal of Conflict Resolution* 28: 617–48.

Chayes, Abraham and Antonia H. Chayes. 1991. "Adjustment and Compliance Processes in International Regulatory Regimes." In J.H. Mathews, ed., *Preserving the Global Environment*. New York: W. W. Norton & Company.

Chen, Zhiqi. 1997. "Negotiating an Agreement on Global Warming: A Theoretical Analysis." *Journal of Environmental Economics and Management* 32: 170–88.

Cline, William R. 1992. *The Economics of Global Warming*. Washington, DC: Institute for International Economics.

Congleton, Roger D. 1992. "Political Institutions and Pollution Control." *Review of Economics and Statistics* 74: 412–21.

Cox, David R. 1972. "Regression Models and Life Tables." *Journal of the Royal Statistical Society* (*Series B*) 34: 187–220.

Esty, Daniel C. 1996. "Revitalizing Environmental Federalism." *Michigan Law Review* 95: 609–38.

Esty, Daniel C. and Damien Geradin. 1997. "Market Access, Competitiveness, and Harmonization: Environmental Protection in Regional Trade Agreements." *Harvard Environmental Law Review* 21: 265–336.

Fernandez, Raquel. 1997. "Returns to Regionalism. An Evaluation of Nontraditional Gains from Regional Trade Agreements." Policy Research Department working paper no.1816, The World Bank.

Frankhauser, Samuel. 1995. *Valuing Climate Change. The Economics of the Greenhouse*. London: Earthscan Publications Ltd.

Fredriksson, Per G. 1997. "The Political Economy of Pollution Taxes in a Small Open Economy." *Journal of Environmental Economics and Management* 33: 44–58.

_____. 1999. "The Siting of Hazardous Waste Facilities in Federal Systems: The Political Economy of NIMBY." (Forthcoming.) *Environmental and Resource Economics*.

Fredriksson, Per G., and Noel Gaston. 1999a. "Ratification of the 1992 Climate Change Convention: What Determines Legislative Delay?" (Forthcoming.) *Public Choice*.

_____. 1999b. "Environmental Governance in Federal Systems: The Effects of Capital Competition and Lobby Groups." (Forthcoming.) *Economic Inquiry*.

Grambsch, Patricia M., and Terry M. Therneau. 1994. "Proportional Hazards Tests and Diagnostics Based on Weighted Residuals." *Biometrika* 81: 515–26.

Hirschman, Albert O. 1982. "Rival Interpretations of Market Society: Civilizing, Destructive, or Feeble?" *Journal of Economic Literature* 20: 1463–84.

Hoel, Michael and Kerstin Schneider. 1997. "Incentives to Participate in an International Environmental Agreement." *Environmental and Resource Economics* 9: 153–70.

Iida, Keisuke. 1996. "Involuntary Defection in Two-level Games." *Public Choice* 89: 283–303.

Jaffe, Adam B., Steven R. Peterson, Paul R. Portney, and Robert Stavins. 1995. "Environmental Regulation and the Competitiveness of U.S. Manufacturing." *Journal of Economic Literature* 33: 132–63.

Keohane, Robert O. 1986. "Reciprocity in International Relations." *International Organization* 40: 1–27.

Kiefer, Nicholas M. 1988. "Economic Duration Data and Hazard Functions." *Journal of Economic Literature* 26: 646–79.

Lancaster, Tony. 1992. *The Econometric Analysis of Transition Data*. New York: Cambridge University Press.

Low, Patrick and Alexander Yeats. 1992. "Do 'Dirty' Industries Migrate?" In Patrick Low, ed., *International Trade and the Environment*. World Bank Discussion Paper no.159, Washington, DC: World Bank.

Lucas, Robert E. B., David Wheeler, and Hemamala Hettige. 1992. "Economic Development, Environmental Regulation and Pollution and the International Migration of Toxic Industrial Pollution: 1960–88." In Patrick Low, ed., *International Trade and the Environment*. World Bank Discussion Paper #159, Washington, DC: World Bank.

Milner, Helen V., and B. Peter Rosendorff. 1996. "Trade Negotiations, Information and Domestic Politics: The Role of Domestic Groups." *Economics and Politics* 8: 145–89.

_____. 1997. "Democratic Politics and International Trade Negotiations." *Journal of Conflict Resolution* 41: 117–46.

Murdoch, James C., and Todd Sandler. 1997. "The Voluntary Provision of a Pure Public Good: The Case of Reduced CFC Emissions and the Montreal Protocol." *Journal of Public Economics* 63: 331–49.

Nordhaus, William. 1991. "To Slow or Not to Slow: The Economics of the Greenhouse Effect." *Economic Journal* 101: 920–37.

Olson, Mancur. 1993. "Dictatorship, Democracy, and Development." *American Political Science Review* 87: 567–76.

Polachek, Solomon W. 1992. "Conflict and Trade: An Economics Approach to Political Interaction." In Walter Isard and Charles H. Anderton, eds., *Economics of Arms Reduction and the Peace Process*. Amsterdam: New Holland.

_____. 1997. "Why Democracies Cooperate More and Fight Less: The Relationship Between International Trade and Cooperation." *Review of International Economics* 5: 295–309.

Sachs, Jeffrey D., and Andrew Warner. 1995. "Economic Reform and the Process of Global Integration." *Brooking Papers on Economic Activity* 26: 1–118.

Sand, P. H. 1991. "International Cooperation: The Environmental Experience." In J. H. Mathews, ed., *Preserving the Global Environment*. New York: W. W. Norton & Company.

Schelling, Thomas. 1960. *The Strategy of Conflict*. Cambridge, MA: Harvard University Press.

Schiff, Maurice and L. Alan Winters. 1997. "Regional Integration as Diplomacy." Policy Research Working Paper no. 1801, The World Bank.

Scully, Gerald W. 1992. *Constitutional Environments and Economic Growth*. Princeton, NJ: Princeton University Press.

Stewart, Richard B. 1993. "Environmental Regulation and International Competitiveness." *Yale Law Journal* 102: 2039–106.

Tol, Richard S. J. 1995. "The Damage Cost of Climate Change: Towards More Comprehensive Calculations." *Environmental and Resource Economics* 5: 353–74.

Chapter 13

Achieving Carbon Emission Reductions through Joint Implementation

Will Martin

1. Introduction

Sustainable reduction in global greenhouse gas emissions requires internationally coordinated policy action. Reaching such a position is difficult because of the different interests of sovereign states, and the incentives for free riding on the actions of others. The solution must lie in a set of policies that reduce costs by being efficient in achieving greenhouse gas emissions, and equitable in the burden that it imposes on individual countries. While there is great uncertainty about the burden likely to be involved in the required reductions in emissions, it is clear from SO_2 emissions trading in the United States that efficient policies can greatly reduce the costs of any given reduction.[1]

Three broad policies have been proposed for achieving reductions in greenhouse gas emissions—quotas, taxes and joint implementation (JI) projects. Quota approaches have intuitive appeal in that they focus on achieving specific, tangible goals. However, except in extreme cases such as the ban on chlorofluorocarbons, national quotas are likely to be an inefficient approach to achieving any given reduction in global greenhouse gases. Fixed national quotas and emission reductions are likely to require reductions in some countries at much higher costs than in others. Approaches that move toward equalizing the marginal costs of reducing emissions across countries will lower the overall costs of achieving any given reduction in emissions and make it more likely that a sustainable agreement can be achieved.

One approach to the problem with national quotas would be to define national quotas and to allow them to be traded between countries. Countries with high costs of emission reductions would find it worthwhile to purchase quotas from countries where the costs of reducing emissions were lower. In the long run, the marginal costs of emission reduction would fall in the quota-purchasing countries and rise in the quota-selling countries. A problem with this approach is that it is likely to lead to very large international transfers of quota rents—perhaps more than could be sustained or enforced between sovereign countries.

McKibbin and Wilcoxen (1997) have proposed an interesting alternative policy involving an initial national quota supplemented by additional units of quota sold at an internationally agreed price. This would reduce the distributional problems associated with international transfers of quota rents,[2] and ensure that the marginal costs of emissions were equalized worldwide. At the margin, this policy would have essentially the same impacts as an internationally agreed tax on energy use.

Stiglitz (1997) reviews the approaches for reducing global carbon emissions, and emphasizes the need for developing countries to participate in reductions in greenhouse gas emissions. For one of the main greenhouse gases, carbon dioxide, he points out that developing countries already emit as much carbon from industrial processes as do developed countries. By the middle of the next century, carbon dioxide emissions from developing countries are likely to be twice those from the current OECD countries. This implies that the task of reducing emissions in developing countries will be enormous and increases the importance of sound policy design.

In the long run, some form of internationally agreed carbon tax or set price at which emission permits can be sold seems likely to be the most efficient solution to this problem. However, we are a long way from reaching the international consensus for such policies that would be required for their effective implementation. The recently agreed Kyoto Protocol provides for quotas on emissions in the industrial countries only, with the developing countries pointing out that the current stock of emissions is primarily the result of past and present emissions from today's industrial countries.

The Kyoto Protocol provides for some potential mitigation of the costs of a system of national quotas through provisions for a clean development mechanism (UNFCCC 1997). This could increase the efficiency with which reductions in greenhouse gas emissions are made by allowing countries to substitute lower-cost reductions overseas for higher-cost reductions at home.[3] Engineering evidence suggests that the costs of achieving given reductions in energy use are frequently lower in developing countries even without quotas in the industrial countries. These differentials are likely to become considerably larger if binding quotas are enforced in the industrial countries. As developed countries use up their lowest-cost abatement options, the marginal costs of achieving larger reductions will rise.

A difficulty faced by joint implementation approaches of the type envisaged by the Kyoto Protocol is the measurement of the reductions in greenhouse gas emissions. While quotas and taxes focus on the emissions of greenhouse gases, a project-based approach such as the clean development mechanism must focus on the somewhat more speculative concept of "reductions in emissions that are additional to any that would occur in the absence of the certified project activity" (UNFCCC 1997, p. 12).

A key step in estimating the impact of a joint implementation project on emissions is to take into account the direct impact of the project on the output of greenhouse gases per unit of output. The approach taken in this paper is that this input-output approach is necessary, but not sufficient for assessing the total impact of the project on emissions. The central point of this paper is that it is highly likely that the technical changes created by joint implementation will affect emissions indirectly by induced changes in the level and mix of energy and other inputs into production—and that these indirect effects may be large. The changes in technique brought about by joint implementation will also have impacts on consumer prices of some goods, and the consequent changes in the pattern of consumption may also need to be taken into account.

Once the impact of the technical change induced by a joint implementation project on the demand for carbon fuels has been identified, one further step is needed before the results can be compared with *ex post* reductions in emissions of the type achieved using emissions quotas. This step involves the price responsiveness of the supply of the different types of energy. If the price elasticities of supply for these energy sources are low, much of the impact of a reduction in demand may fall on the price of that fuel, rather than on the level of its use.

The next section of the paper deals with the nature of joint implementation projects, and the likely impacts of these projects on energy use patterns. The third section considers the elasticities and CO_2 intensities that are needed as a basis for evaluating the impacts of the joint implementation projects. The fourth section presents some simple numerical estimates designed both to provide an order of magnitude indication of the likely importance of the phenomenon under consideration for particular types of project. In the fifth section, the supply side of the energy market is considered. The final section presents some conclusions and suggestions on approaches for evaluation of joint implementation projects.

2. Joint Implementation and Technical Change

The joint implementation projects envisaged under the Kyoto Protocol have two stated goals: to assist developing countries in achieving sustainable development, and to assist the industrial countries by allowing them to use certified emission reductions against their reduction commitments. To achieve these objectives, the projects clearly must change the production processes used in the developing countries. One way in which they might do this is by substituting a less-polluting technology for the one currently in use, without necessarily improving the overall efficiency of production. Another way would be to introduce technology that is superior to that previously in operation in the country. Changes in technique of the first type would contribute to the carbon emission goal, but not necessarily to the development goal, while changes of the second type seem more likely to contribute to both goals.

A general framework for categorizing the various types of technical change that might be used in joint implementation is provided in Alston and Martin (1994). Using the producer profit function,[4] they categorize technical changes into three broad types: (a) those represented by direct incorporation of technical change variables in the profit function (Binswanger 1974; Kohli 1991); (b) those represented through a distinction between actual and effective quantities and prices (eg Dixon, Parmenter, Sutton and Vincent 1982); and (c) those represented through changes in the parameters of profit or production functions (eg Fulginiti and Perrin 1993).

For technical changes that affect variable inputs, these three different types of technical change may be represented as:

$$\text{(a)} \qquad \pi \;=\; g(p, v, \tau \mid \alpha)$$

$$\text{(b)} \qquad \pi \;=\; g(p(\tau), v \mid \alpha)$$

$$\text{(c)} \qquad \pi \;=\; g(p, v \mid \alpha(\tau))$$

where α is the producer profit from the activity under consideration; p is the vector of input and output prices facing producers in the country; v is a vector of fixed inputs (and perhaps outputs); a is the vector of parameters of the profit function; and τ a vector of parameters representing the technical changes under consideration.

The profit function approach to the specification of changes in techniques of production is particularly desirable when the objective of the analysis is to consider the welfare impacts of the technical change, and hence the contribution of the project to development. As shown by Martin and Alston (1997), the welfare consequences of particular types of technical change may be substantially greater than would be suggested by the producer surplus techniques that have typically been used to measure these benefits. For a cost-reducing technical change in a commodity supplied with an elasticity of 0.5, for example, the producer surplus methodology understates the welfare benefits by just over half.

The profit function approach outlined above is also a useful organizing framework for considering the impacts of different types of JI-induced technical changes on greenhouse gas emissions. For the evaluation of these projects, it seems likely that the most relevant form of technical change will be type (b), although some projects may perhaps usefully be categorized by type (c). Type (a) is typically used in relatively stylized representations of technical change, where the specific form of technical change is either not known, or cannot be specified with precision. Almost by definition, the nature of the change in technique is well known and understood when a JI project is undertaken.

Most practical applications of Type (b) technical change involve a distinction between physical and effective quantities of a particular good (that is, input or output). The relationship between the physical and the effective units of an input (or output) can be represented by $q_i^* = q_i.\tau_i$ where q_i^* is the effective quantity of the good; q_i is the actual quantity of the good; and τ_i is the level of input-augmenting technology.[5] A good example of such a technical change would be one that increased the efficiency with which a particular fuel could be converted into usable energy, for example, the use of improved combustion techniques that raised the energy efficiency of coal used in electricity generation from 25 to 35 percent. Using the definition above, this improvement raises the number of effective units in any given physical quantity of coal by 40 percent.

Clearly, increases in the number of effective units associated with a given physical quantity of fuel allow reductions in the quantity of fuel, and hence CO_2 emitted, in achieving any given outcome. The effects of this change in the input-output coefficients appears to be the main thing currently considered in evaluating the impacts of projects on greenhouse gas emissions (World Bank forthcoming).

Associated with the increase in the effective quantity of good i is a change in its effective price. The relationship between actual and effective prices is given by $p_i^* = p_i/\tau_i$ where p_i^* is the effective price of the good. Clearly, the impact of the improvement in efficiency considered above is to reduce the effective price of this type of energy. In most cases, however, it is not enough to consider the impact of the technical change on the input-output coefficients. Typically, the sponsor of a project has the ability to influence these coefficients, but not to fully control the operation of the project, or the industry of which it is a part, in the host country. Industrial managers can be expected to respond to the changes in the effective prices resulting from the technical change. Depending upon the relevant elasticities, this may substantially change the impact of the project on total carbon emissions.

From the above discussion, it is clear that changes in technology that change the effective prices of particular types of energy in a particular application have both output and substitution effects. The nature of these effects is very readily seen using a demand function for a particular energy input, such as the following linear demand curve resulting from differentiation with respect to effective prices of a normalized quadratic profit function specified in effective quantities and prices.

$$q_i^* = a_i + S_j b_{ij} p_j^* + S_k q_{ik} v_k \quad (1)$$

Since the physical quantity of the fuel consumed, rather than the effective quantity, typically determines the quantity of greenhouse gas emissions, we need to rewrite this equation in terms of actual prices and quantities, rather than effective prices and quantities.

$$q_i = 1/\tau_i (\alpha_i + \Sigma_j \beta_{ij} p_j^* + \Sigma_k \theta_{ik} v_k) = \quad (2)$$

$$1/\tau_i (\alpha_i + \Sigma_j \beta_{ij} p_j / \tau_j + \Sigma_k \theta_{ik} v_k)$$

a formulation which highlights the input-saving consequences of the technical change.

Since p_i^* is equal to p_i/τ_i the lowering of the effective price has an effect that depends upon the slope of the demand curve. The contribution of the two effects to demand for the physical product is shown in figure 13.1. The shift from Demand Curve D_0 to D_1 corresponds to the impact of the $1/\tau_1$ term at the front of the right hand side of equation (2). It causes the demand curve to rotate about the vertical axis. The impact of the effective price change is represented by the rotation of curve D_1 around the horizontal axis. The decline in the effective price of the input stimulates demand to an extent that depends on the slope of the demand curve and on the price level. This effect is represented by the rotation of the demand curve from D_1 to D_2. In the diagram, the input-saving effect of the technical change dominates and demand at price p is lower with the final demand curve D_2 than with the original demand curve. However, this would not have been the case at higher price levels, or with a more elastic demand curve.

While the impact of an input-augmenting technical change on the demand for any particular energy source is ambiguous in general, the elasticity of demand for the good gives a local approximation to the impact. If, for instance, the elasticity of demand for the good is less (greater) than one, the compensated[6] demand for the input will decline (increase) following an input-augmenting technical advance.

The ambiguous impact of the change in effective prices on own demand is not the end of the story because the change in the effective price of the good will also change the demand for other production inputs through substitution effects. In this case, at least, the direction of the impact is clear as long as the goods are substitutes—a reduction in the effective price of one fuel will reduce the demand for any substitute fuel. Even if the demand for a fuel rises following the technical change, this effect may offset the impact on aggregate carbon emissions. If the demand for an alternative fuel has fallen, then this substitution effect will augment the reduction in fuel use and carbon emissions. Whether the substitution effects will outweigh the own price impacts will depend a great deal on the carbon intensity of the fuels; if the fuel whose use is expanding is more carbon intensive than its substitutes, then overall emissions may rise as a consequence of the project.

While input-augmenting technical change seems likely to be the most relevant for most cases considered under joint implementation, type (c) technical change might be important in some applications. Changes in technology of this type are very difficult to implement in the flexible functional forms so widely used in modern applied studies because of the restrictions imposed by economic theory, including homogeneity of degree one in prices; symmetry of cross price effects; and the adding up restrictions. However, this approach has sometimes been used for broad technical changes such as the very large shift in demand towards more skilled labor in the industrial countries (Tyers and Yang 1997). For most applications likely to be encountered in joint implementation

Figure 13.1 Impacts of augmenting technical change on the demand for an input

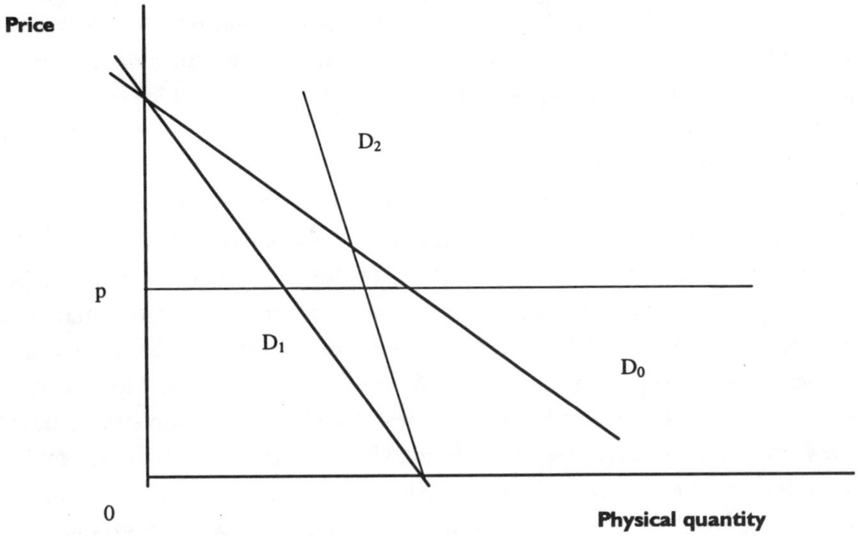

projects, the input-augmenting technical change approach appears likely to be the most useful.

3. Relevant Elasticities of Demand for Energy and Emissions Intensities

The practical importance of the changes in effective prices induced by the technical changes caused by joint implementation will depend a great deal on the magnitudes of the relevant elasticities of demand for energy inputs, and for energy-intensive final products. Where these elasticities are small, the induced impacts of changes in effective prices will almost always be small.

Three groups of elasticities need to be considered. The first is the elasticities of demand for particular energy sources. The second is the demand for energy as a whole. The third is the elasticity of demand for energy-intensive products.

As Atkinson and Manning (1995) observe, the literature on the elasticities of demand for energy is not in very satisfactory, with the range of estimates for different parameters being particularly wide, especially for the cross-price effects that are of importance in this analysis. Further, the full implications of recent developments in econometric techniques being only partially reflected in the stock of elasticity estimates. Despite this, some regularities do seem to emerge fairly strongly.

The own and cross price elasticities of demand for individual energy sources do generally seem to be larger than the elasticity of demand for energy as a whole. From the range of estimates presented by Atkinson and Manning (1995), it seems likely that the own-price elasticity of demand for energy as a whole is in the order of -0.2. The elasticities of demand for particular energy-intensive goods also seem likely to be relatively low. Further, the impact of a change in the effective price of a particular fuel has only an indirect impact on the price of the good in which it is embodied. Assuming the good is non-traded, and produced according to constant returns to scale, the maximum price impact will be given by the share of the fuel in the total cost of producing the good. Thus, except for goods such as aluminium or home-produced goods such as electric lighting, which are particularly energy intensive, it seems likely that the impacts of technical changes on consumption of final goods will be relatively minor. In a small country, such changes will be unobservable for traded goods because the price of the good will not be affected by changes in the domestic technology alone.

The elasticities of demand for individual fuels, such as gas, oil and coal generally appear to be much larger, with values above 1.0, and even above 2.0, in absolute value frequently appearing in the literature. Where the own price elasticities are large, the cross price elasticities typically are also large, making evaluation of the substitution effects considerably more important.

It seems likely that, with such large elasticities, both the own-price effects induced by input-augmenting technical change, and the substitution effects from this source, will be important. A simple numerical example is used to explore the potential sensitivity of the effects of projects that improve the efficiency with which particular types of energy are used.

To explore the effects of projects on overall energy use requires knowledge of the price elasticities of demand, and the CO_2 intensity of each fuel. The price elasticities need to be derived from comprehensive, system-based approaches because of the importance of the cross-price impacts that tend to be poorly estimated when traditional, single commodity estimation approaches are used. There are many levels at which an exploratory analysis might be undertaken. However, the area in which the best estimates of demand elasticities appear to be available is use in the industrial sector. Jones (1996) provides a comprehensive set of elasticity estimates for the G-7 countries utilizing a modern system-based econometric estimator, the linear-logit estimator applied to aggregate data. Pindyck (1979) provides a similar set of estimates obtained by applying the Translog estimator to national data for a group of OECD countries. Woodland (1993) provides estimates based on a panel of establishment-level data for New South Wales industrial firms over an eight-year period. Another set of estimates underlies the simulation modeling undertaken by McKibbin and Wilcoxen (1995a) using the G-Cubed model.

The elasticities estimated by Jones (1996) are based on inter-fuel substitution in the industrial sector. He allows for substitution between coal, oil, natural gas and electricity. Thus his results provide estimates of the direct usage of coal, oil and natural gas in the industrial sector, which should be comparable with the data on energy use and CO_2 emissions by sector provided by the International Energy Agency. He provides both short run and long run estimates. The long run elasticities are used here because of the long run focus of the global warming problem. The matrix of own and cross price elasticities of demand for direct use of coal, oil, and gas is provided in table 13.1.

The elasticities presented in table 13.1 are higher than many in the literature. However, they do not appear unreasonable as estimates of the long run values of elasticities allowing for inter-fuel substitution. Pindyck's comparable estimates of the own-price elasticity of demand for individual OECD countries were in the same range for coal, generally lower for oil, and generally higher for natural gas. Woodland's estimates based on data at the establishment level are generally somewhat lower for coal and substantially higher for natural gas. Jones' estimates are, however, considerably above the comparable estimates utilized by McKibbin and Wilcoxen, who apply an energy elasticity of substitution of 0.80 in the durable manufacturing sector and 1.0 in the non-durable sub-sector.

Table 13.1 Long run elasticities of demand in the industrial sector of the G-7

	Coal	*Oil*	*Gas*
Coal	-1.55	0.72	0.15
Oil	0.63	-2.23	0.78
Gas	0.13	0.79	-0.86

Unfortunately, there appears to be a dearth of recent system-based estimates of the elasticities of demand for fuels in developing countries. If the underlying parameters of the system are the same, it would be possible to utilize the estimates provided by Jones, together with information on the shares of each fuel in total energy use, to estimate elasticities for particular developing countries. However, it would be very desirable to have estimates actually obtained using data from developing countries. If joint implementation becomes an important feature of the implementation of global strategies for greenhouse gas mitigation, it will be particularly important to have such estimates.

The other information needed to investigate the impact of any given improvement in energy use efficiency is the importance of each fuel as a source both of energy and of emissions in the industrial sector. These data were obtained from the International Energy Agency (1997, 1991) and are presented in table 13.2. The first column shows estimated CO_2 emissions from direct use of each fuel in the industrial sector and the second the corresponding shares. The third column shows the delivered fuel emission factors, taking into account both the inherent carbon intensity of each fuel and the efficiency with which it used to provide usable energy. The final column shows the implied shares of each fuel in total usable energy availability from these fuels in the industrial sector.

This short survey of relevant elasticities and emission intensities points to some likely implications of different types of joint implementation that results in different types of improvements in fuel use efficiency. The much higher elasticities of demand for individual fuels, than for energy as a whole, implies that substitution between fuels is likely to be important for its effects on quantities of fuel used. The very different emissions intensities mean that changes in the mix of fuels used will have major impacts on fuel emissions. Projects that increase the efficiency of a fuel that is carbon intensive may induce greater use of that fuel relative to less emission-intensive fuels. Conversely, increases in the efficiency of a less carbon inten-

Table 13.2 International Energy Agency estimates of energy and emissions data for the industrial sector of ANNEX I parties

	CO_2 emissions Million Mt CO_2	*Emission shares %*	*Emission factors Mt C/Mtoe*	*Energy shares %*
Coal	945.5	40	1.14	32
Oil	677.3	29	0.89	29
Gas	734	31	0.73	39
Total	2356.8	100		100

sive fuel will shift energy usage towards that fuel, with potentially important second-round savings in carbon emissions. The importance of substitution between fuels means, however, that technical changes that increase efficiency for all fuels will create smaller induced substitution impacts.

4. Some Stylized Experiments

The experiments undertaken to highlight some of the important features of the problem were increases in energy use efficiency sufficient, with no other adjustments, to reduce total CO_2 emissions by ten percent. This target required improvements of 25 percent, 35 percent and 32 percent for coal, oil, and gas respectively. The results of this direct energy-saving effect on total emissions are shown in column 1 of table 13.3.

Because of the reduction in the effective price of each energy source resulting from the improvement in technology, there are impacts on the consumption both of the fuel itself and other fuels. The impact of the reduction in the effective price of each fuel on emissions directly from that fuel is shown in Column 2 of the table. The total effective price induced impact is shown in Column 3. These estimates differ from those in Column 2 by taking into account the substitution effects on usage of, and emissions from, other fuels.

The total impact of the change in efficiency is shown in Column 4 of the table. These estimates include both the direct impact on emissions, and that induced by the changes in effective price.

The improvement in coal use efficiency shown in the first row of the table would directly reduce total emissions by ten percent if there were no changes in the input or output mix. However, the own price effect of the reduction in the effective price of coal increases total emissions by over 15 percent as emission-intensive coal is substituted for oil and gas. This adverse effect is offset by the reductions in carbon emissions resulting from the induced reductions in oil and gas usage. The net impact of all the price-induced changes in the fuel mix on direct consumption of fossil fuels is an increase of ten percent. This increase of ten percent exactly offsets the direct reduction in consumption resulting from the increase in efficiency, leaving this increase in energy use efficiency completely ineffective in reducing CO_2 emissions.

The improvement in oil use efficiency has, by construction, the same impact on emissions as the efficiency improvement in coal. Because the elasticity of demand for oil is so high, this change in the effective price of oil has a larger impact on direct consumption of oil than was the case with coal. When only the own-price impact is taken into account, the effect on emissions is more strongly adverse than for coal, with a 22 percent increase in total emissions. However, the substitution effects are more strongly favorable both because of the elasticities, and because of the higher emission intensity of coal. With these substitution effects included, the total price-induced impact is an increase in emissions of 3.7 percent. Thus, in this case, the price-induced impact only partially offsets the direct energy-saving impact of the technical change.

The efficiency improvement in the use of natural gas presented in the third row of table 13.3 causes

Table 13.3 Impacts of improvements in fuel use efficiency on total CO_2 emissions (*percentages*)

	Direct impact	*Own effective price impacts*	*All effective price impacts*	*Total impact*
Coal efficiency	-10	15.5	10.0	0.0
Oil efficiency	-10	22.3	3.7	-6.3
Gas efficiency	-10	8.6	-0.5	-10.5
All fuels	-30	46.4	13.2	-16.8

an induced increase in natural gas usage. However, the increase in emissions resulting from this is more than offset by the induced reductions in the use of coal and oil, so that the total price-induced impact is -0.5 percent, reinforcing the direct reduction in the energy use. Had the own and cross-price elasticities been larger, as they were in Woodland's (1993) study, it is likely that the total price-induced impact would have been a substantially larger negative value, augmenting the direct impact to a much greater degree. The result from this experiment supports the general principle that, other things equal, an improvement in efficiency in what is already the most energy-efficient technology will have a more favorable impact on emissions than an improvement in a less efficient technology.

When simultaneous increases in efficiency in all fuels are considered, the direct reduction in emissions is 30 percent. The increase in emissions resulting from own-price induced increases in fuel usage is 46.4 percent, but this figure falls to only 13.2 percent once substitution effects are taken into account. Thus, the overall reduction in emissions resulting from this experiment is 16.8 percent. This experiment supports the general principle that substitution effects are less a concern for a broad-based improvement that increases efficiency for all fuels than for improvements concentrated only in emission-intensive fuels.

The numerical examples provided in this section are deliberately simplified and stylized. They represent only the impacts on direct use of fuels in industry, ignoring indirect consumption in the form of electricity (unless this is generated from nonpolluting or renewable sources). Further, they ignore the indirect impacts on energy consumption and emissions that arise from induced changes in demand for energy in total, and from induced effects on the prices of particular commodities. Their purpose is purely to highlight the potentially important, and frequently ignored, impacts of changes in effective prices on fuel consumption and on emission levels.

5. Supply Side Considerations

All of the analysis to this point has focused on the demand side of the market for energy. However, the impact of a reduction in the demand for fuel on its consumption will clearly also depend upon the price responsiveness of fuel supply. If the fuels are not in perfectly elastic supply, reductions in demand will not be translated directly into reductions in the quantity of fuel used. As demand declines, the price will fall, thus stimulating fuel use and partially offsetting the effects of the original decline in demand. This introduces another factor that may need to be taken into account when comparing joint implementation outcomes with those from outcome-based measures such as tradeable quotas.

On the supply side, the cross-price impacts are probably much smaller than on the demand side simply because of the diversity of the natural resource bases involved in the production of major fuels such as coal, oil and gas. While all produced goods are general equilibrium substitutes (or complements) in production simply through their demands for resources, it seems likely that these cross-price impacts are relatively small, and that attention can focus primarily on the own-price elasticities.

As long as the elasticity of fuel supply lies between zero and infinity, the impact of any technology-induced reduction in demand will fall partly on the price of the fuel, and partly on fuel usage. The reduction in price will to some degree offset the original reduction in demand, introducing an additional offset to the effectiveness of joint implementation that is quite different from the one discussed on the demand side. The magnitude of the reduction in price, for any given horizontal shift in the demand curve, will depend upon the sum of the elasticities of supply and demand. The exact impact of the shift on the demand for fuel depends, however, on the individual elasticities and on the nature of the shift in the demand curve. For example, for any given horizontal shift in the demand curve, the reduction in demand is greater, the higher is the absolute value of the supply elasticity. Similarly, the reduction in demand will be less, the larger is the absolute elasticity of demand.

In the short run, the elasticity of supply of the major fuels is probably fairly inelastic because of the quasi-fixed nature of investments in resource extraction. Over time, these elasticities tend to rise as it becomes possible to invest in new capital, and to invest in the discovery and proving of new reserves. Since the supply of capital and exploration services to these industries is highly elastic, it seems likely that the long run elasticities of supply for the major energy sources are quite elastic, substantially reducing the need to account for supply-side offsetting impacts of joint implementation projects.

The supply side effects considered in this section and the demand side impacts considered in the remainder of this paper can be integrated using computable general equilibrium models such as the GTAP model (Hertel 1997) or the G-Cubed model (McKibbin and Wilcoxen 1995b). These models include both the demand and supply side linkages. In any such analysis, it is particularly important to focus attention on the specification of the change in demand for energy, and on the effects of shifts in demand on energy supply.

6. Conclusions and Policy Implications

Much of the literature on evaluating the impacts of joint implementation projects appears to assume that an improvement in efficiency that reduces the amount of fuel required to achieve a particular objective by 10 percent will reduce the quantity of emissions by the same 10 percent. The main purpose of this paper is to point out that technological advances of the most common kind have two impacts—one through their direct energy-saving impact, and one through their impact on the effective price of the fuel in the use(s) under consideration. Unfortunately, this channel of effect appears to have been ignored in much of the recent literature on evaluation of jointly implemented projects or demand side management.

The direct impact of the reduction in the effective price of a fuel is an increase in the consumption of that fuel. In addition, there are substitution effects that will generally reduce the use of other fuels, and the emissions generated from that source. If the fuel whose efficiency is being improved is already the least emission-intensive, the combined impact of these price impacts is most likely to be favorable. If the fuel whose efficiency is being improved is initially the most emission-intensive, the combined impact of these price changes is less likely to be favorable, and may even result in an increase in emissions. In the numerical example considered in this paper, an increase in coal use efficiency was completely ineffective in reducing emissions because it resulted in emission-intensive coal being substituted for less polluting oil and gas.

The final impact of the demand shifts on fuel consumption and energy emissions will also depend on supply side responses in energy markets. As long as energy supply is less than perfectly elastic, reductions in energy demand resulting from joint implementation will reduce the market price of energy and stimulate energy use, partially offsetting the initial reduction in demand. These effects are likely to be substantially larger in the long run, reducing the magnitude of these offsets.

Many analysts have advocated ignoring the offsetting effects that are the focus of this paper on the grounds of lack of information. While the need to form some assessment of the magnitude of the relevant demand elasticities is a serious difficulty given the paucity of estimates of elasticities for developing countries, it need not be insuperable. Further, the general principles following from the analysis provide a (potentially rebuttable) case for favoring particular types of projects. Projects that improve the efficiency of the fuel that is already the least emission-intensive are likely to be more effective than projects focusing on more emission-intensive fuels. Projects that improve the efficiency of all fuels are unlikely to be offset by adverse substitution effects. By contrast, projects that improve the efficiency of an emission-intensive process may be completely ineffective in reducing carbon emissions.

Notes

Revised version of a paper presented to the World Bank Conference on Trade, Global Policy and the Environment, April 21–22, 1998. Thanks are due to Johannes Heister, Dorsati Madani, Shane Streifel and L. Alan Winters of the World Bank, Scott Vaughan of the WTO, and participants in the conference, for helpful comments.

1. The need to use the most efficient approach to emissions reduction will be particularly great if emissions are, as argued by Schmalensee, Stoker and Judson (1998), increasing at substantially higher rates than projected by the IPCC.

2. However, it would still not seem to deal with the international transfers between net energy exporters and importers that would follow from declining world prices of carbon-intensive energy products. Clearly, this distributional concern could potentially be dealt with by levying part of any agreed tax on the production side and part on the consumption side.

3. The Kyoto Convention uses the term joint implementation to refer to activities between the

industrial countries whose emissions are subject to agreed quotas (Article 6). Joint activities between industrial and developing countries are covered by the clean development mechanism (Article 12). The focus of this paper is on joint activities between industrial and developing countries and the term joint implementation is used to refer to these activities.

4. This profit function may be a simple, partial equilibrium profit function for a single industry able to purchase all of its inputs at fixed prices (see Binswanger (1974) for this general type of application), or an economy-wide profit function representing the technology for production of total GDP in the economy given predetermined endowments of aggregate factors such as labor and capital (see Kohli (1991) for this type of application).

5. For expositional ease, technical change has been specified so that an increase in t_i represents an improvement in technology.

6. That is, output-constant.

References

Alston, J., and Martin, W. 1994. "A Dual Approach to Evaluating Research Benefits in the Presence of Trade Distortions." *American Journal of Agricultural Economics* 76: 26–35.

Atkinson, J., and Manning, N. 1995. "A Survey of International Energy Elasticities." In T. Barker, P. Ekins, and N. Johnstone, eds., *Global Warming and Energy Demand.* Routledge, London.

Binswanger, H. 1974. "A Cost Function Approach to the Measurement of Elasticities of Factor Demand and Elasticities of Substitution." *American Journal of Agricultural Economics* 56: 377–86.

Dixon, P., B. Parmenter, J. Sutton, and D. Vincent. 1982. *ORANI: A Multisectoral Model of the Australian Economy.* North-Holland, Amsterdam.

Fulginiti, L., and R. Perrin. 1993. "Prices and Productivity in Agriculture." *Review of Economics and Statistics* 75: 471–82.

Hertel, T., ed. 1997. *Global Trade Analysis: Modeling and Applications.* Cambridge University Press, New York.

International Energy Agency. 1997. *CO_2 Emissions From Fuel Combustion: A New Basis for Comparing Emissions of a Major Greenhouse Gas.* OECD, Paris.

_____. 1991. *Energy Efficiency and the Environment.* OECD, Paris.

Jones, C.T. 1996. "A Pooled Dynamic Analysis of Interfuel Substitution in Industrial Energy Demand by the G-7 Countries." *Applied Economics* 28: 815–21.

Kohli, U. 1991. *Technology, Duality and Foreign Trade.* University of Michigan Press, Ann Arbor.

McKibbin, W., and P. Wilcoxen. 1995a. "Environmental Policy and International Trade." Brooking Discussion Paper in International Economics no. 117, The Brookings Institution, Washington DC.

_____. 1995b. "The Theoretical and Empirical Structure of the G-Cubed Model." Brookings Discussion Paper in International Economics no 118, The Brookings Institution, Washington DC.

_____. 1997. "A Better Way to Slow Global Climate Change" Brookings Policy Brief no. 17, The Brookings Institution, Washington DC. (available at www.brookings.edu).

Martin, W., and J. Alston. 1997. "Producer Surplus Without Apology? Evaluating investments in R&D." *Economic Record* 73(221): 146–58.

Pindyck, R. 1979. "Interfuel Substitution and the Industrial Demand for Energy: An International Comparison." *Review of Economics and Statistics* 61: 169–79.

Schmalensee, R., T. Stoker, and R. Judson. 1998. "World Carbon Dioxide Emissions: 1950–2050." *Review of Economics and Statistics* LXXX(1): 15–27.

Stiglitz, J. 1997. "Stepping Toward Balance: Addressing Global Climate Change." Paper presented to World Bank Conference on Environmentally and Socially Sustainable Development, Washington DC, October 6.

Tyers, R., and Y. Yang. 1997. "Trade with Asia and Skill Upgrading: Effects on Factor Markets in Older Industrial Countries." *Weltwirtschaftliches Archive* 133(3): 383–417.

UNFCCC. 1997. "Kyoto Protocol to the United Nations Framework Convention on Climate Change." United Nations Framework Convention on Climate Change, United Nations. (www.unfccc.de).

Woodland, A. 1993. "A Micro-econometric Analysis of Industrial Demand for Energy in NSW." *The Energy Journal* 14(2): 57–89.

World Bank. (Forthcoming). *Greenhouse Gas Assessment Handbook: A Practical Guidance Document for the Assessment of Project-Level Greenhouse Gas Emissions.* Environment Department, World Bank.

Chapter 14

Carbon Abatement

Lessons from second-best economics

Ian W. H. Parry

1. Introduction

According to the traditional approach in environmental economics, it is optimal to reduce emissions of a pollutant until the incremental environmental benefits (or damages avoided) equals the incremental economic cost. This optimum can be induced by either setting an emissions tax equal to marginal environmental damage, or issuing the appropriate quantity of emissions permits. The welfare gain from achieving this optimum is the difference between marginal environmental benefit and marginal abatement cost, integrated over the level of abatement. So far the attempts to develop a cost/benefit analysis of carbon dioxide (CO_2) abatement, in response to the possibility that atmospheric accumulations of this gas will cause future global climate change, have used this basic theory.[1] The conclusion from these studies is that the currently optimal tax on the carbon content of fossil fuels (the primary source of CO_2 emissions) is around $5 to $20 per ton (see below), although there is a good deal of uncertainty and controversy surrounding these estimates.

For our purposes, the key feature of these cost/benefit studies is that they assume a first-best world. That is, they focus on the CO_2 externality distortion in the fossil fuel market, but they do not take into account interactions between this market and other distorted markets in the economy. Even in a market-based economy like the United States, market imperfections are very pervasive, due to distortions created by taxes, regulations, imperfect competition, other externalities, and so on. Indeed there is a long tradition in the public finance literature warning that the outcomes from second-best analyses, which do capture the secondary welfare effects of policies in other distorted markets, can be very different from those implied by a first-best analysis (Lipsey and Lancaster 1956; Harberger 1974).

How important are these sources of pre-existing market distortions in the context of carbon abatement policies? Fortunately, many of these distortions are small in size and are in markets that are very distant from the fossil fuel market, and incorporating them into the analysis would have negligible empirical effect. For example, Oates and Strassmann (1984) found that allowing for imperfect competition in the U.S. economy had little empirical significance for implementing environmental policies in general, because the price distortions created by monopoly pricing are typically small. However, this is not the case for pre-existing distortions created by the tax system. Indeed some very recent studies have shown that allowing for taxes in factor markets can crucially affect not only the magnitude, but also the sign, of the welfare impact from environmental policies.[2]

Environmental policies interact with the tax system in two important respects (Goulder 1995a). First, to the extent that they cause the economy-wide level of employment or investment to fall, they compound the welfare cost of pre-existing taxes in these markets. Second, environmental policies can produce an efficiency gain to counteract this loss, if they raise revenues and these are used to cut the level of pre-existing distortionary taxes. Non-auctioned emissions quotas do not directly affect revenues, and do not produce this latter efficiency benefit. Indeed the net welfare loss from interactions with the tax system can be large enough to more than offset the traditional partial equilibrium gain from imposing an emissions quota, when environmental benefits are relatively modest. In contrast, because of the efficiency value of the revenues raised, an emissions tax is potentially welfare-improving, regardless of the level of environmental benefits.

The purpose of this paper is to pull together this recent literature on environmental policy in a second-best setting, and discuss the implications for carbon abatement policies. This is a very complex topic, so we proceed in stages. The next section summarizes the results from highly simplified analytical models, which have examined the interactions between environmental policies and a pre-existing tax distortion in the labor market. In these models, the overall welfare gain from introducing a balanced-budget environmental tax is generally lower in the presence of a labor tax, than when there is no labor tax. In addition, the second-best optimal emissions tax is somewhat below the first-best optimal tax, equal to marginal environmental damages. Probably the most important result, however, is that given existing "best estimates" for damages from carbon emissions, it is possible that only a revenue-raising instrument—a tax or auctioned carbon quota—can increase economic efficiency. Section 3 discusses the results from numerical models, which allow for more complex features of the tax system. In general, these results back up those from the analytical models. Section 4 briefly discusses some implications for carbon abatement policies in other countries. Section 5 concludes.

2. Results from Analytical Models

Several recent analytical papers have examined how a pre-existing tax in the labor market affects the welfare impact of an environmental tax (see Bovenberg and de Mooij 1994; Bovenberg and van der Ploeg 1994; Parry 1995).[3] The models have a similar structure. They assume households gain utility from consumption goods, leisure and environmental quality. Labor supplied by households is the only primary input (that is, there is no capital input), and labor supply plus leisure equals the aggregate household time endowment. Firms use labor to produce consumption goods and intermediate goods, under competition and constant returns to scale. Producing one of the goods (either a consumption or intermediate good) causes a proportional amount of waste emissions, which reduce environmental quality. The government levies a tax on labor income and also taxes emissions. These revenues finance an exogenous amount of non-distortionary spending.[4] The models focus on "revenue-neutral" or "balanced budget" environmental taxes; that is, extra revenues generated by increasing the environmental tax are recycled in labor tax cuts.

The labor tax drives a wedge between the gross wage paid by firms, and the net wage received by households. Since firms employ labor until the value marginal product equals the gross wage, and households supply labor until the value of foregone leisure time equals the net wage, the labor tax creates a welfare loss because the equilibrium quantity of employment is below the point where marginal social benefit equals marginal social cost.

Welfare impacts of a carbon tax

In this setting, the welfare effect of tax on emissions from a particular commodity, such as carbon emissions from fossil fuels, can be separated into three components.[5] First the *primary welfare gain*, that is the welfare gain in the regulated market from reducing the quantity of emissions, for which marginal social cost exceeds marginal social benefit. This is the focus of a first-best analysis. In the context of carbon abatement, it is the present discounted value of the benefits from avoided future climate change, less the current economic costs of abatement, due to the induced reduction in carbon-intensive fuels.

Second, the *revenue-recycling effect*. This is the efficiency gain from using the emissions tax revenues to reduce the rate of labor tax, relative to the case when these revenues are returned to households as lump sum transfers (and have no efficiency consequences). That is, the gain from reducing the wedge between the marginal social benefit and marginal social cost of labor, thereby increasing employment towards the socially efficient level.

Third the *tax-interaction effect*, which is the welfare loss from the reduction in aggregate labor supply indirectly caused by the emissions tax. If firms are charged a tax on their emissions, this increases their marginal cost of production, and will result in a higher final product price. Indeed, given the assumptions of competition and constant returns to scale, the full amount of the tax is passed on in a higher final product price, and there is no reduction in the net price received by producers. This causes a reduction in the real wage received by households (the nominal wage divided by an index of consumer goods prices). In general, the effect of this is to reduce aggregate labor supply, since the return to work effort relative to leisure falls. This produces a welfare loss in the labor market, because of the wedge between the marginal social benefit and marginal social cost of labor. In addition, the reduction in employment reduces labor tax revenues, and the tax-interaction effect also incorporates the resulting efficiency loss.[6]

The effect on aggregate employment from the tax-interaction effect will only be slight. In particular, it will be much less than the labor released from the (fossil fuel producing and consuming) industries that contract in response to the emissions tax, since most of this labor will be absorbed by other (substitute) industries rather than becoming "unemployed."[7] However, the welfare loss from the tax-interaction effect can still be important relative to the primary welfare effect, since the welfare loss per unit of labor is "large." This is because when we take into account federal and state income taxes, social security taxes, sales taxes, and benefit withdrawal as income rises, the marginal rate of tax on labor earnings faced by the average household is substantial: around 40 percent (Browning 1987).

The analytical models indicate (either explicitly or implicitly) that in general the tax-interaction effect dominates the revenue-recycling effect. That is, the net effect of the emissions tax is to reduce aggregate labor supply, hence producing a net welfare loss from interactions with the tax system. This means that raising additional revenue from an emissions tax involves a higher efficiency loss (ignoring environmental benefits) than raising the same amount of revenue by increasing the labor tax. There are two reasons for this.

First of all, assume that fossil fuels are used in fixed proportions to final output, that is, raising the price of fossil fuels does not induce firms to substitute labor and other inputs for fossil fuels in production. In this case, taxing fossil fuels is equivalent to taxing final output from industries that use fossil fuels. Call this output *X*, and all other consumption *Y*. Also, note that a tax on labor income received is equivalent to a uniform tax on consumption expenditure, in a static model (where there is no income from capital) and all labor income is spent. If the revenue-recycling effect were larger than the tax-interaction effect, then, holding total revenue constant, introducing a (small) tax on *X* and reducing the consumption (labor) tax would increase welfare. But we know from the theory of optimal commodity taxation (see, for example, Sandmo 1976) that this result could only hold if *X* were a sufficiently weaker substitute for leisure than *Y*. If *X* were an equal (or stronger) substitute for leisure, then this tax change would necessarily reduce welfare. This is because the base of the tax on *X* is smaller than the base of the consumption tax (*X*+*Y*). Therefore, raising a given amount of revenue requires a higher tax rate on *X*, than it would if the tax were levied on *X*+*Y*. In addition, it is easier for consumers to substitute away from *X* (into *Y* as well as leisure) in response to the tax, compared with the broader-based tax. Both of these factors raise the welfare cost of a tax on fossil fuels, relative to an equal revenue-yield labor tax.

The second reason is that the fossil fuel tax distorts the mix of inputs used in production, as well as the quantity of final goods and leisure. Relaxing the assumption of fixed proportions, the fossil fuel tax will lead to some replacement of fossil fuels by labor and other inputs in the production of *X*. This opens up another channel for substituting away from the taxed commodity, thereby increasing the welfare cost of the tax. A well-known result in public finance is that, for a given revenue-yield, taxing an input used in variable proportions, is more distortionary than taxing final output (Diamond and Mirrlees 1971; Wisecarver 1974). In contrast, since the labor tax is equivalent to a uniform consumption tax, it does not affect production efficiency (assuming labor is the only primary input).

In summary, only if final output from industries that use fossil fuels intensively were a sufficiently weaker substitute for leisure than other consumption goods, could the revenue-recycling effect outweigh the tax-interaction effect, in the analytical models described above. Fossil fuel-intensive consumption goods primarily consist of transportation and electricity-intensive goods. Very little is known about the relative degree of substitution between these goods and leisure, but there is no obvious reason to suggest that it would differ substantially from that for the average consumption good. Despite the net loss from interactions with the tax system, however, the analytical models show that the emissions tax is still potentially welfare-improving (unless the X sector is a very strong substitute for leisure relative to the Y sector). That is, the primary welfare gain still dominates the tax-interaction effect net of the revenue recycling effect.

The rise and fall of the double-dividend hypothesis

These studies, and the numerical work discussed below, have refuted the widely held view that there was a "double dividend" from environmental taxes. The essential idea behind the double dividend hypothesis was that environmental taxes could simultaneously correct environmental externality distortions, and provide other gains, when the revenues raised were used to cut other distortionary taxes. These gains were either defined in terms of increased economic efficiency, or other desirable goals such as reduced unemployment and increased investment. The double dividend argument took several different forms, and Goulder (1995a) has distinguished the following three:

(1) Weak form: this asserts that using emissions tax revenues to reduce other distortionary taxes will produce an efficiency gain, relative to the case when revenues are returned to taxpayers in a lump sum fashion.
(2) Intermediate form: the overall welfare impact of a balanced-budget emissions tax is greater in the presence of pre-existing tax distortions, than when there is no pre-existing tax.
(3) Strong form: not only is there a net welfare gain because of the pre-existing tax, but this gain more than offsets the primary costs of emissions reduction, within the regulated market.

The third form asserts that the gross cost of an emissions tax (that is, without subtracting environmental benefits) is negative. In this case, introducing a balanced-budget emissions tax could produce an efficiency gain, even if environmental benefits were very small, or even zero. This is a particularly appealing notion in the context of carbon abatement, where the benefits from emissions reduction are very difficult to quantify. It implies that we can do something to reduce the threat of possible future global climate change, and even if this threat turns out to be nonexistent, we will have incurred no costs, and possibly even positive economic benefits. The second form asserts that, in a static setting where the pre-existing tax is on labor income, the net effect of an emissions tax is to increase efficiency in the labor market by *increasing* employment. In this connection, Repetto and others (1992) suggested that using the revenues from a \$40 carbon tax in the United States to cut other distorting taxes could produce enormous efficiency gains of around \$20-30 billion each year, in addition to any efficiency gain from offsetting the carbon externality.[8] These claims caught the attention of policy makers in Western Europe, where unemployment seems to be "stuck" at rates often in excess of 12 percent. It was thought that, by imposing a carbon, or more broad-based energy tax, "two birds could be killed with one stone;" that is, emissions of carbon, and aggregate unemployment, could be reduced at the same time.

Unfortunately, as often the case in economics, there is no such free lunch. The double dividend hypothesis was based on an analysis which "tacked on" the revenue-recycling effect to partial equilibrium models of emissions abatement. As discussed above, a more complete analysis would take into account the tax-interaction effect, which generally negates the hypothesis in both its strong and intermediate form. Therefore, the large revenue potential from a carbon tax does *not* strengthen the case for introducing such a tax per se. However, the debate over the double dividend has at least made a very valuable contribution in drawing attention to the potentially large efficiency gains to be had, from using emissions tax revenues to cut distortionary taxes rather than for other purposes (this is discussed further below).[9]

Second-best optimal carbon tax

The analytical models indicate that (when output from the polluting sector is an average substitute for leisure) the marginal cost of emissions reduction in the presence of a labor tax, MC_t in figure 14.1, has a steeper slope than the primary, or partial equilibrium marginal cost MC_p. The first-best or Pigouvian tax t_p, equals marginal environmental benefit MB (assumed to be constant for simplicity), and induces an emis-

Figure 14.1 Pre-existing taxes and the marginal cost of abatement

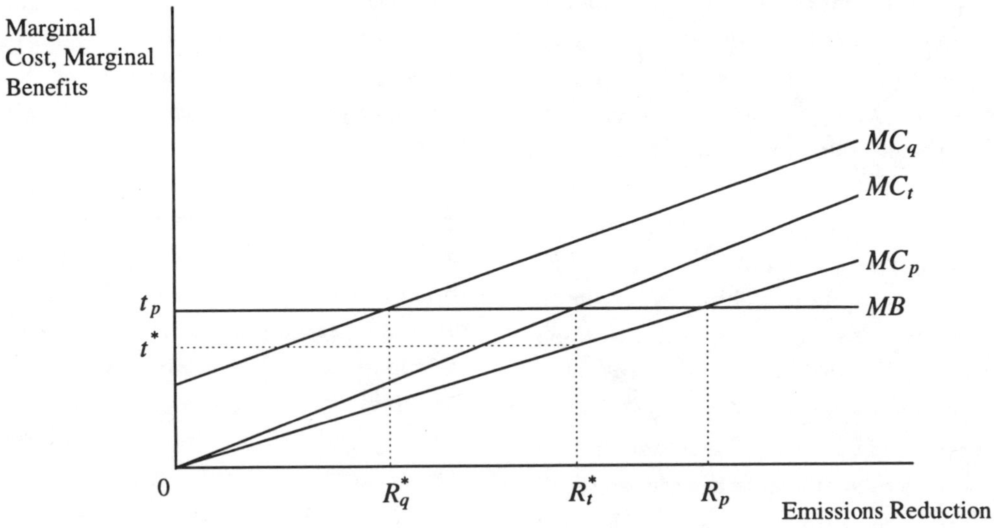

sions reduction of R_p. However, this tax is too high from an efficiency-maximizing perspective. The second-best optimal emissions reduction is R_t^* in Figure 14.1, where MC_t and MB intersect. To induce this requires a tax of t^*. Given existing estimates of the labor tax wedge and labor supply elasticities for the United States, the second-best optimal tax is about 90 percent of the Pigouvian tax in Bovenberg and Goulder's (1996a) analytical model, and 60-80 percent of the Pigouvian tax in Parry (1995).[10]

Earlier studies suggested that the discrepancy between the optimal environmental tax and the Pigouvian tax was positively related to marginal tax revenue (Lee and Misiolek 1986; Oates 1993). The latter declines with the level of abatement, and is negative beyond the revenue-maximizing tax, or peak of the Laffer curve. Therefore, these studies suggested that if marginal environmental benefits are low (high) relative to marginal abatement costs, then the optimal emissions tax is above (below) marginal environmental benefits. Indeed Nordhaus (1993a) estimated that the optimal tax on carbon in his model increased from $5 per ton to $59 per ton, when carbon tax revenues are used to cut other taxes. Again, these studies just focused on the revenue-raising effect. However, when allowance is also made for the tax-interaction effect, the optimal emissions tax can only exceed marginal environmental benefits under fairly restrictive conditions (Parry 1995).

Welfare impacts of a carbon quota

To date, much less attention has been paid to the welfare effects of emissions quotas (or permits) in the presence of distortionary taxes. The key difference between an emissions tax and a (non-auctioned) emissions quota in this respect, is that the former directly raises revenue while the latter does not. Two recent papers (Goulder and others 1997; and Parry 1997) have emphasized that this distinction can imply a significant empirical difference, and even a difference in sign, between the overall welfare effects of emissions taxes and quotas.

Using a similar model structure to that described above, Goulder and others (1997) and Parry (1997) indicate that a quota causes the same tax-interaction effect as an emissions tax. This is because the quota effectively creates a price or virtual tax on emissions (equal to the sale value of a quota), which increases marginal production costs, final product prices, and thereby reduces the real wage. For a given reduction in emissions, the tax-interaction effect is the same for both the emissions tax and quota.

Parry (1997) suggested that there is no revenue-recycling effect from the quota to offset the tax-interaction effect. However, Goulder and others (1997) point out that allocating quotas creates rents, by limiting entry into the regulated industry. These are reflected in higher firm profits which are subject to corporate income taxation, and personal income taxation when returned to households. Therefore, quotas do actually raise revenue, albeit indirectly. Still, since the effective tax rate on such rent income is around 40 percent,[11] the revenue-recycling effect from the quota is only around 40 percent of that in the emissions tax case.

This implies that, for a given level of emissions abatement, total abatement costs are higher under the quota than the tax. Indeed, in the context of SO_2 abatement, Goulder and others (1997) found this discrepancy is quite striking at modest levels of abatement. For example, if the emissions reduction is below 20 percent, then the cost of the quota is more than double the cost of the tax. However at higher levels of abatement, the discrepancy is much less substantial. The addition to the revenue-recycling effect from incremental increases in the emissions tax is declining, while the incremental addition to the tax-interaction effect is approximately constant. This is because the emissions tax base declines with abatement, and the revenue loss from incremental reductions in emissions increases as the emissions tax increases. At an emissions reduction of around 50 percent, increasing the emissions tax actually starts to reduce revenue. That is, the downward sloping part of the emissions tax Laffer curve is reached. In the limit, at 100 percent emissions reduction, the overall cost of the tax and quota are the same. This is because there is no revenue raised from the tax, and hence no revenue-recycling effect.

These results have important implications for welfare. Suppose the first-best level of emissions tax or quota is introduced. If marginal environmental benefits are modest relative to the primary marginal cost of abatement, then the overall welfare impact of the quota can be negative. That is, the net loss from interactions with the tax system can be large enough to more than offset the primary welfare gain. In this case, only the emissions tax can increase welfare. However when environmental damages are larger, implying the first-best emissions reduction would be in the order of 50 percent or more, Goulder and others (1997) find that the overall welfare impact of the quota is positive. Never-the-less, it can still be significantly lower than when there is no pre-existing labor tax. Returning to Figure 14.1, suppose that the first-best quantity of quotas is imposed, reducing emissions to R_p. This will reduce welfare if the area between MC_q and MB and R_q^* and R_p, exceeds that between MB and MC_q and 0 and R_q^*. Also, note that MC_q has a positive intercept. This means that if MB lies below this intercept, then no level of quota can increase welfare.

No empirical studies (that I am aware of) have been done comparing the efficiency effects of carbon quotas and carbon taxes in the presence of distorting taxes. However, in a simulation from Bovenberg and Goulder's (1997) numerical model, a carbon tax where the revenues are returned as lump sum transfers (rather than used to cut other taxes), reduces welfare unless the damages per ton of carbon exceed $50. Since lump sum transfers have no efficiency consequences, this policy is equivalent to a carbon quota, where none of the quota rents are received by the government. If instead, rent income is taxed at 40 percent, we can speculate that this threshold would be around $30 per ton.[12] Most of the "best estimates" (that is, using median parameter values from the economics and scientific literature) for carbon damages are actually *below* $30 per ton.[13] These estimates are relatively low, because most economic activity is not particularly sensitive to the modest changes in climate predicted over the next century, and because discounting over long periods of time substantially reduces the present value of economic impacts. However under more extreme scenarios for climate change, or when the utility of future generations is not discounted, then damages per ton can rise well above this threshold.[14]

In summary, although yet to be confirmed by rigorous empirical analysis, there would appear to be a compelling case on efficiency grounds for preferring carbon taxes to carbon quotas, if action is to be taken to reduce carbon emissions. Aside from more extreme scenarios for climate change, it seems possible that only the carbon tax can increase welfare using conventional cost/benefit criterion, and a quota is necessarily welfare-reducing. However, it is important to emphasize that this distinction arises entirely from the revenue-raising feature of the carbon tax. If carbon quotas were auctioned rather than given away free, they could potentially generate the same revenues as under the tax, and hence produce the same efficiency benefits from the revenue-recycling effect.

Some further issues

(1) Should carbon tax revenues be used for purposes other than cutting taxes?

Carbon tax revenues could be used for a variety of purposes, other than cutting distortionary taxes. For example, they could be earmarked for further carbon-reducing policies, such as subsidies for tree growing.[15] Alternatively, they could be used to neutralize the distributional consequences of the carbon tax. Since consumption goods that are produced intensively from fossil fuels, in particular electricity and gasoline, are necessities, their share of expenditure in total consumption expenditure is greater for lower income households. Therefore a carbon tax, which drives up the price of these goods, is regressive (Poterba 1991). This effect could be counteracted (albeit imperfectly) by, for example, using carbon tax revenues to finance an increase in the earned income tax credit, or higher means-tested benefits.[16] However, the opportunity cost of using revenues for these purposes rather than to cut other taxes is the revenue-recycling effect. Only if they generated benefits to society (in terms of increased efficiency, more desirable income distribution, etc.) in excess of the dollar cost plus the revenue-recycling effect, could they be justified on cost/benefit criterion.

(2) Should we tax economic "bads" (pollution) instead of "goods", such as employment?

At first glance, the answer to this question sounds obvious: is it not better to raise a given amount of revenue from taxes that discourage pollution, rather than taxes that discourage employment? However taxes on emissions are in fact implicit taxes on labor, since they reduce the real wage received by households. Therefore, both the emissions tax and the labor tax reduce employment. Indeed, as discussed above, to raise a given amount of revenue it is more efficient to use a labor tax than an emissions tax, since it has a broader base and does not distort production efficiency. Never-the-less environmental taxes are still part of an optimal tax system, albeit at a somewhat lower level than the first-best tax.

(3) Should we ever subsidize pollution?

The above discussion indicated that reducing emissions by a non-auctioned quota may sometimes reduce welfare. Does this mean that a subsidy for emissions, which increased production and employment, can be welfare-improving? In general, the answer to this is no. There are two effects of a subsidy, as well as the primary welfare effect, when the labor market is distorted by taxes. First, the welfare cost of financing the subsidy by distortionary taxation, which is the mirror image of the revenue-recycling effect for emissions taxes. Second the tax-interaction effect, which is now a welfare gain since the subsidy reduces the price of consumption goods, hence increasing the real wage and employment. In general there is a net loss from these two effects (Parry 1998), in addition to the primary welfare loss.

3. Results from Numerical Models

The analytical models described above can explain the key mechanisms by which environmental policies interact with the tax system, in a simple and intuitive fashion. However, their empirical usefulness is limited in a number of respects. First, although these models can be used to estimate the effects of incremental policy changes, they can only estimate the effects of "large" policy changes, if demand and the primary marginal cost of emissions reduction are taken to be linear. In general demand curves must be non-linear in order to satisfy various adding up properties associated with the household's budget constraint (Deaton and Muellbauer 1980), and the primary marginal cost of reducing carbon is thought to be convex (Nordhaus 1991b). Therefore, an analytical model can only generate second order welfare approximations, which may be unreliable for "large" reductions in emissions. Instead, solving the model by numerical simulation avoids this problem. Second, in the context of carbon abatement, numerical models are able to capture more complex features of the fossil fuel sector, and tax system, that are not tractable within an analytical model. This allows the sensitivity of the results from analytical models to be examined in a more general setting, with a variety of different channels for reducing carbon, and interactions with other tax distortions besides those in the labor market.

Important numerical contributions in this area include Bovenberg and Goulder (1996, 1997) which use a dynamic computable general equilibrium model of the U.S. economy. This model incorporates a particularly detailed treatment of how the tax system affects household consumption, saving and labor supply decisions; and firm's investment, output and input choices.[17]

The implications of taxes on capital

Bovenberg and Goulder (1997) address the important issue of whether incorporating capital accumulation, and the taxation of capital income, affects the results on environmental taxes discussed above. In this case, the tax-interaction effect is defined more broadly to include the welfare loss from any reduction in aggregate investment, as well as that from any reduction in aggregate labor supply, caused by an environmental tax. This more general setting, with two primary factor inputs, introduces the possibility of a *tax shifting* effect. Even though the tax wedge in the capital market in the United States is around the same magnitude as that in the labor market, the former is thought to be more distorting.[18] This is because a tax on capital discourages investment, while a tax on labor discourages work effort, and investment is estimated to be relatively more sensitive to tax increases than labor supply.[19] Therefore the efficiency cost of raising an extra dollar of revenue from taxes on capital is thought to be higher than that for taxes on labor;[20] that is, capital is "overtaxed" relative to labor. In this situation, a policy change which induced firms to substitute capital for labor at the economy-wide level, would produce an efficiency gain from the tax-shifting effect, and reduce the overall cost of the tax-interaction effect. This means that, even if output from the sector affected by an environmental tax is an average substitute for leisure, the net effect of the revenue-recycling and tax-interaction effects could be positive, and the environmental tax could produce a double dividend (in the intermediate form). A revenue-neutral environmental tax is more likely to produce such a double dividend by this mechanism when: (a) the environmental tax revenues are used to cut taxes on capital, rather than labor, thereby increasing the demand for capital relative to labor; and (b) the environmental tax is levied on a relatively labor intensive industry, so that a greater share of the tax-interaction effect is felt in the (less distorted) labor market, than in the capital market.

The numerical results in Bovenberg and Goulder (1997) confirm the significance of the tax-shifting effect. They examine two taxes which have been proposed to reduce carbon emissions and other pollutants: a gasoline tax and a Btu tax. The latter has a broader tax base, and therefore for a given revenue yield one might expect it to have a lower efficiency cost (ignoring environmental benefits) than the gasoline tax. However, the gasoline tax causes a significant tax-shifting effect, while the Btu tax does not, and this is large enough so that the overall efficiency cost is lower under the gasoline tax.

Never-the-less, Bovenberg and Goulder find that, even when the revenues from gasoline and Btu taxes are used to reduce taxes on capital, there is still no double dividend, under a wide variety of assumptions about key parameter values. This contrasts with Jorgenson and Wilcoxen (1995), who do find a significant double dividend from environmental taxes, if the revenues are specifically targeted to reduce the most distortionary taxes in the economy. Poterba (1993, p. 55) sums up the debate as follows:

> Simply demonstrating that raising the carbon tax and reducing other onerous taxes would lead to an efficiency gain does not imply that carbon taxes should be adopted. Rather, one must compare the carbon tax policy with the set of all feasible policies that could reduce the onerous taxes and achieve a balanced budget. On reflection, however, the revenue-recycling argument may make more sense. If there is a casual link between enacting a carbon tax and cutting particular other taxes, perhaps because

Table 14.1 Differences between Pigouvian and second-best taxes (*all rates in dollars per ton*)

Assumed Marginal Environmental Damages ($/ton)	*"Optimal" Pigouvian Tax*	*Optimal Tax Implied by Analytical Model (PIT Replacement)*	*Optimal Tax from Numerical Model:* *Realistic Benchmark, Lump-Sum Replacement*	*Realistic Benchmark, PIT Replacement*	*Optimized Benchmark, PIT Replacement*
25	25	22	0	7	17
50	50	45	0	27	41
75	75	67	13	48	64
100	100	89	31	68	85

Source: Bovenberg and Goulder (1996a).

of political constraints on raising existing taxes, then it *is* appropriate to consider how the funds are used in evaluating the net benefit from a carbon tax. Absent a strong basis for linking enactment of a carbon tax to other particular tax changes, a plausible assumption is that carbon taxes would be paired with a proportionate reduction in all existing revenue sources (in which case a double dividend seems unlikely).

The optimal carbon tax revisited

Table 14.1 presents Bovenberg and Goulder's (1996) estimates for the second-best optimal carbon tax in the United States, under damage scenarios varying from $25 to $100 per ton of carbon. The second column shows the optimum tax from a first-best analysis, which is just equal to the damages per ton. The third column shows the second-best optimal tax from Bovenberg's analytical model, discussed in Section 2, when carbon tax revenues finance reductions in taxes on labor income. This is equal to about 89 percent of the first-best tax, regardless of the level of damages per ton.

The fourth column shows the optimal carbon tax in the numerical model, when the revenues are returned as lump sum transfers to households. It is dramatically below the first-best tax, and is zero when damages are $50 per ton or below. This reflects the role of the tax-interaction effect in shifting up the overall marginal cost of emissions reduction, so that damages must be above a threshold level before abatement can increase welfare. In the fifth column, carbon tax revenues are used to increase efficiency by reducing the rate of personal income taxation (PIT). The optimal tax is higher in this case, about 55-65 percent of the first-best tax when damages are $50 or above, but is still significantly below that implied by the analytical model. Bovenberg and Goulder suggest that this discrepancy is due to the suboptimality of the existing tax system (which is captured in the numerical but not the analytical model). In addition, the gasoline tax is effectively a tax on carbon emissions from the transportation sector. Therefore, an optimal tax system is created in which the efficiency cost of raising an additional dollar of revenue is equalized across all taxes in the economy (and which yields the same total revenue as in the realistic tax case). This involves reducing the relative tax on capital, and eliminating taxes on intermediate inputs, industry outputs and consumer goods. In this case, the second-best optimal carbon tax (sixth column) is much closer to that in the analytical model. These results indicate therefore, that extending the analytical models of Section 2 to allow for more complex features of the tax system, leads to a further reduction in the second-best optimal carbon tax.

4. International Implications

This section briefly examines whether the revenue-recycling and tax-interaction effects are likely to be important in other countries, and whether a uniform carbon tax still minimizes abatement costs across countries.

The importance of pre-existing taxes in other countries

To date, empirical estimates of the revenue-recycling and tax-interaction effects have been made for the United States but not for other countries. In general, developed countries have a similar tax structure to that in the United States, with the huge bulk of revenues collected from taxes on labor and capital income, or broad-based consumption taxes (which cause similar distortions to a labor tax). Therefore, the key parameters which determine the revenue-recycling and tax-interaction effects in other developed countries, are essentially the same as in the United States. In the analytical models of Section 2, these parameters are the ratio of emissions to gross domestic product, the primary marginal cost of percentage emissions reductions, the tax wedge between the gross and net wage, and the labor supply elasticity.

Goulder and others (1997) illustrate that increasing the relative size of the polluting sector increases the absolute size of the revenue-recycling and tax-interaction effects, but has very little effect on their size relative to the primary welfare effect. This suggests that the proportionate increase in carbon abatement costs caused by pre-existing taxes, is not significantly affected by the ratio of carbon emissions to a country's gross domestic product. The primary marginal cost of emissions reduction is determined by the ease of substituting away from carbon using other fuels, energy-saving technologies, less energy-intensive consumption goods, and so on. These substitution possibilities may vary considerably across countries. However, estimates of the marginal cost of percentage reductions in carbon emissions for the United States do not differ markedly from those for other countries (see Nordhaus 1991b). Thus, if labor market parameters were the same, the proportionate increase in costs due to interactions with the tax system is likely to be similar in magnitude for the "average" developed country, as in the United States.

Labor tax rates are, however, significantly higher in many other countries than in the United States, since their governments play a greater role in the provision of goods and services. The fourth column in table 14.2 shows the effective tax wedge in the labor market for the G-7 countries, using estimates of labor income and consumption taxes in 1988 by Mendoza and others (1994).[21] Compared with the United States, this distortion is around 75 percent higher in France, 50 percent higher in Germany and Italy, 15 percent higher in Canada and the United Kingdom, and slightly lower in Japan.[22] There is a good deal of uncertainty over the labor supply elasticity, even in the United States which has been the focus of most studies (see the discussion in CBO 1996). This elasticity could be somewhat smaller in other countries than for the United States, given the lower labor force participation of women, and the more stringent regulations on the hiring and firing of workers in Western Europe. Therefore, despite higher effective labor taxes, the revenue-recycling and tax-interactions effects are not *necessarily* more important in other countries.

A further consideration is the extent of pre-existing tax or subsidy distortions within the energy sector. Given the gasoline tax, and the reduction in tax exemptions for exploration and mining of natural resources, on balance the United States taxes energy.[23] Gasoline taxes are considerably higher in Western Europe. However most developing countries subsidize energy. In particular, the price of electricity is typically well below long run marginal cost, and the production of fuels usually receives favorable tax treatment and/or explicit subsidies (Kosmo 1987). Shah and Larsen (1992) have estimated that total world energy subsidies exceeded $230 billion in 1990, which is equivalent to a negative carbon tax of $40 per ton! The removal of such subsidies would not only produce a primary welfare gain, but also, as discussed above, a likely gain from interactions with the tax system.

Another relevant feature of many developing countries is segmented labor markets. Part of the labor force may be employed in a formal sector where taxes are levied while the rest of the labor force might be in an informal sector that is not covered by the tax system. The effect of the tax system in this setting is to distort the allocation of production between the two sectors: the informal sector is effectively subsidized. Both sectors use energy inputs such as transportation and heating fuels. If these fuels are taxed to reduce carbon emissions and the revenues used to reduce taxes on the formal sector, up to a point this tax shift can reduce the overall efficiency costs of the tax system by reducing the effective subsidy to the informal sector. That is, segmented labor markets open up the possibility of a double dividend from environmental tax reform. It would be useful in future research to explore the potential empirical significance of this double dividend.[24]

Does a uniform carbon tax equalize marginal abatement costs across countries?

A familiar implication of the first-best environmental policy model is that, if all emissions sources face the same tax, they will reduce emissions until the prima-

Table 14.2 International comparison of tax rates

	Consumption tax rates	*Labor income tax rates*	*Effective tax wedge*
France	21.4	47.2	56.5
Germany	14.7	41.2	48.7
Italy	14.3	40.9	48.3
United Kingdom	16.9	26.8	37.4
Canada	13.1	28.0	36.3
United States	5.2	28.5	32.0
Japan	5.3	26.6	31.1

Source: Mendoza and others (1994), and author's calculations.

ry marginal cost is the same across all sources (and equal to the tax rate). This achieves a given aggregate emissions reduction at minimum cost. A uniform carbon tax across countries produces a parallel result, that is, the total cost of emissions reduction is minimized at the international level.

However, when there are pre-existing tax distortions, this result no longer holds. Returning again to figure 14.1, for a given tax on emissions the gap between MC_p and MC_t differs between countries, since they have different labor tax rates and labor supply elasticities. Therefore the second-best optimal tax is non-uniform across countries.[25] Unfortunately, achieving agreement among countries on a set of differentiated carbon taxes would be even more difficult than achieving agreement on a single tax rate for all.

5. Conclusion

Recent studies have indicated that environmental policies can be substantially more costly, when their effect on compounding pre-existing tax distortions in the economy is taken into account. This arises because these policies tend to reduce slightly the overall level of employment and investment in the economy. Due to pre-existing taxes the levels of employment and investment are already below levels that would maximize economic efficiency. Hence further reductions result in additional efficiency losses. However, if the policy raises revenues, and these are used to cut other distortionary taxes, then much of this additional economic cost can be offset. This suggests a strong efficiency case for preferring a revenue-raising instrument (an emissions tax or auctioned emissions quota) over a non-revenue-raising instrument (a non-auctioned emissions quota), should action be taken to slow atmospheric accumulations of carbon dioxide.

Of course there are a number of other factors to consider, besides pre-existing taxes distortions, in the choice of policy instruments to reduce carbon dioxide emissions. For example, affected industries may oppose a carbon tax that requires them to reduce emissions *and* pay taxes to the government more than a free carbon emissions permit program. Other important considerations include the potential impact of a given policy instrument on the private incentives to develop more energy-efficient technologies.

Nonetheless, minimizing the economic costs of any action to reduce carbon dioxide emissions is desirable not only for its own sake, but also to enhance the likelihood of a policy standing the test of time. Recent research warns that even modest emissions reductions might be especially costly if the policies used do not raise revenues for the government than are returned to the economy in other tax reductions.

Notes

I thank John Horrowitz and George Frisvold for comments on an earlier draft, and Brian Kropp for first-rate research assistance. The views expressed are entirely my own. This paper is forthcoming in Betsey A. Kuhn and George Frisvold (eds.), *Global Environmental Change and Agriculture: Assessing the Impacts*, Edward Elgar, and printed with permission from the publisher.

1. Emissions of methane, nitrous oxide and chlorofluorocarbons (CFCs) may also affect future global climate. However their potential contribution is small relative to that of CO_2. Moreover, methane and nitrous oxide are much more difficult to regulate than CO_2, and CFCs are being phased out, at least in developed countries, because of their effect on depleting the ozone layer.
2. See Bovenberg and Goulder (1996), Goulder and others (1997), and Parry (1997).
3. These models build on earlier contributions by Sandmo (1975) and Ng (1981).
4. That is, either a lump sum transfer to households, or a public good.
5. The following decomposition is discussed in Parry (1995) (who used a slightly different terminology), Oates (1995), and Goulder (1995a). The models by Bovenberg and collaborators do not separate out the tax-interaction and revenue-recycling effects defined below.
6. However, this reduction in revenue is generally small relative to the direct revenues raised by the emissions tax.
7. This is probably why the labor market consequences of environmental policies have been ignored in the past.
8. To put this figure in perspective, it is about 7 times the efficiency gain estimated by Harberger (1954) from eliminating all product market monopolies in the United States; and about 50 percent greater than the efficiency gains from eliminating a 10

percent inflation, estimated by Lucas (1981) (when these figures are converted into current dollars).

9. That is, the weak form of the double dividend is still correct.

10. One reason for this discrepancy is that Bovenberg and Goulder (1996) assume demand elasticities are constant, while Parry (1995) assumes constant price coefficients and variable elasticities.

11. See for example Lucas (1990).

12. The analytical models imply that the revenue-recycling effect equals the tax-interaction effect for the first unit reduction in emissions. Therefore, a 40 percent revenue-recycling effect would produce an offsetting gain of $20.

13. These include $7 per ton (Nordhaus 1991a), $12 (Peck and Teisberg 1993), $5 (Nordhaus 1994), and $20 (Frankhauser 1994).

14. In particular, the possibility of some discontinuity leading to dramatic climate change cannot be ruled out. For example, an induced change in North Atlantic Ocean currents could freeze Western Europe. In addition, Cline (1992) argues that the utility of future generations should not be discounted on ethical grounds. Cline (1991) also criticizes these damage estimates for neglecting some ecosystem impacts, and possibly adverse effects on the distribution of world income. However, Nordhaus (1993b) gives a convincing response to these criticisms.

15. A carbon tax does *not* reward activities which remove CO_2 from the atmosphere, such as tree growing.

16. The revenues could also be used to reduce the federal budget deficit. However this is equivalent to reducing future taxes, and therefore produces an efficiency gain analogous to the revenue-recycling effect.

17. The model also allows for imperfect capital mobility, which limits the ability of firms to shift the burden of new carbon taxes to other sectors; and the transition dynamics as firms substitute away from fossil fuels to synthetic fuels. See also Goulder (1994, 1995b), who find that the gross efficiency cost of a fossil fuel Btu tax and a $25 per ton carbon tax respectively, are positive. That is, they reject the strong form of the double dividend hypothesis.

18. Income from capital is subject to corporate income taxation, and personal income taxation at the federal and state level.

19. Actually, since part of labor earnings are saved, a tax on future consumption (that is, a capital tax) does discourage current work effort to some degree.

20. In Bovenberg and Goulder (1997), this efficiency cost is 0.43 per dollar of revenue for capital, and 0.31 for labor.

21. With no taxes, the real wage is the nominal wage (w) divided by the general price level (p). If wages are taxed at m percent, and there is a tax of t percent on the value of goods, the net wage is $(1\text{-}m)w/(1+t)p$. Therefore, the effective tax on real labor earnings is calculated by $1\text{-}[(1\text{-}m)/(1+t)]$.

22. These figures do not take account of benefit withdrawal as income rises, the other major determinant of marginal tax rates faced by the average household.

23. This does not necessarily mean that energy is taxed enough to internalize the full costs of (non-carbon) pollution externalities.

24. Of course the economic gain from reducing the distortionary costs of the tax system may be more than outweighed by possibly adverse distributional consequences from the tax shift.

25. The same problem would arise under an internationally tradable quota scheme, since the permit price in each country is equalized to MCp rather than MCq in Figure 14.1.

References

Bovenberg, A.L., and R.A. de Mooij. 1994. "Environmental Levies and Distortionary Taxation." *American Economic Review* 84: 1085–89.

Bovenberg, A.L., and F. van der Ploeg. 1994. "Environmental Policy, Public Finance and the Labor Market in a Second Best World." *Journal of Public Economics* 55: 349–90.

Bovenberg, A.L., and L.H. Goulder. 1996. "Optimal Environmental Taxation in the Presence of other Taxes: An Applied General Equilibrium Analysis." *American Economic Review* 86: 985–1000.

_____. 1997. "Costs of Environmentally-Motivated Taxes in the Presence of other Taxes: General Equilibrium Analyses." *National Tax Journal* 50: 59–88.

Browning, E.K. 1987. "On the Marginal Welfare Cost of Taxation." *American Economic Review* 77: 11–23.

CBO. 1996. "Labor Supply and Taxes." CBO Memorandum, Congressional Budget Office, Washington, DC.

Cline, W.R. 1992. *The Economics of Global Warming.* Institute for International Economics, Washington, DC.

Deaton, A., and J. Muellbauer. 1980. *Economics and Consumer Behavior.* Cambridge University Press, Cambridge, MA.

Diamond, P., and J. Mirrlees. 1971. "Optimal Taxation and Public Production I: Production Efficiency and II: Tax Rules." *American Economic Review* 61: 8–27 and 261–78.

Frankhauser, S. 1994. "The Social Costs of Greenhouse Gas Emissions: An Expected Value Approach." *The Energy Journal* 15: 157–84.

Goulder, L.H. 1995a. "Environmental Taxation and the 'Double Dividend:' A Reader's Guide." *International Tax and Public Finance* 2: 157–84.

Goulder, L.H. 1995b. "Effects of Carbon Taxes in an Economy with Prior Tax Distortions: An Intertemporal General Equilibrium Analysis." *Journal of Environmental Economics and Management* 29: 271–97.

Goulder, L.H. 1994. "Energy Taxes: Traditional Efficiency Effects and Environmental Implications." In J.M. Poterba, ed., *Tax Policy and the Economy 8.* MIT Press, Cambridge, MN.

Goulder, L.H., I.W.H. Parry, and D. Burtraw. 1997. "Revenue-Raising vs. other Approaches to Environmental Protection: The Critical Significance of Pre-Existing Tax Distortions." *RAND Journal of Economics* 28: 708–31.

Harberger, A.C. 1974. *Taxation and Welfare.* University of Chicago Press, Chicago.

_____. 1954. "Monopoly and Resource Allocation." *American Economic Review* 44: 77–87.

Jorgenson, D.W., and P.J. Wilcoxen. 1995. "Reducing US Carbon Emissions: An Econometric General Equilibrium Assessment." In D. Gaskins and J. Weyant, eds., *Reducing Global Carbon Dioxide Emissions: Costs and Policy Options.* Stanford University Press, Stanford, CA.

Kosmo, M. 1987. "Money to Burn: The High Cost of Energy Subsidies." Working Paper series, World Resources Institute, Washington, DC.

Lee, D.R., and W.S. Misiolek. 1986. "Substituting Pollution Taxation for General Taxation: Some Implications for Efficiency in Pollution Taxation." *Journal of Environmental Economics and Management* 13: 338–47.

Lipsey, R.G., and K. Lancaster. 1956. "The General Theory of the Second Best." *Review of Economic Studies* 24: 11–32.

Lucas, R.E. 1990. "Supply-Side Economics: An Analytical Review." *Oxford Economic Papers* 42: 292–316.

_____. 1981. Discussion of: Stanley Fischer, "Towards an Understanding of the Costs of Inflation: II." *Carnegie-Rochester Conference Series on Public Policy* 15: 43–52.

Mendoza, E.G., A. Razin, and L.L. Tesar. 1994. "Effective Tax Rates in Macroeconomics: Cross Country Estimates of Tax Rates on Factor Incomes and Consumption." *Journal of Monetary Economics* 34: 297–323.

Ng, Y.K. 1980. "Optimal Corrective Taxes or Subsidies when Revenue-Raising imposes an Excess Burden." *American Economic Review* 83: 313–17.

Nordhaus, W.D. 1994. *Managing the Global Commons.* MIT Press, Cambridge, MA.

_____. 1993a. "Optimal Greenhouse Gas Reductions and Tax Policy in the 'DICE' Model." *American Economic Review* 83: 313–17.

_____. 1993b. "Reflections on the Economics of Climate Change." *Journal of Economic Perspectives* 7: 11–26.

_____. 1991a. "To Slow or not to Slow: The Economics of the Greenhouse Effect." *The Economic Journal* 101: 920–37.

_____. 1991b. "The Costs of Slowing Climate Change: A Survey." *The Energy Journal* 12: 37–53.

Oates, W.E. 1995. "Green Taxes: Can we Protect the Environment and Improve the Tax System at the Same Time?" *Southern Economic Journal* 61: 914–22.

Oates, W.E., and D.L. Strassmann. 1984. "Effluent Fees and Market Structure." *Journal of Public Economics* 24: 29–46.

Parry, I.W.H. 1997. "Environmental Taxes and Quotas in the Presence of Distortionary Taxes in Factor Markets." *Resource and Energy Economics* 19: 203–220.

_____. 1998. "A Second-Best Analysis of Environmental Subsidies." *International Tax and Public Finance* 5: 153–70.

_____. 1995. "Pollution Taxes and Revenue Recycling." *Journal of Environmental Economics and Management* 29: S64–S77.

Peck, S.C., and T.J. Teisberg. 1993. "Global Warming Uncertainties and the Value of Information: An Analysis using CETA." *Resource and Energy Economics* 15: 71–98.

Poterba, J.M. 1993. "Global Warming: a Public Finance Perspective." *Journal of Economic Perspectives* 7: 47–63.

_____. 1991. "Tax Policy to Combat Global Warming: on Designing a Carbon Tax." In R. Dornbusch and J.M Poterba, eds., *Global Warming: Economic Policy Responses.* MIT Press Cambridge, MA.

Repetto, R., R.C. Dower, R. Jenkins, and J. Geoghegan. 1992. *Green Fees: How a Tax Shift can work for the Environment and the Economy.* World Resources Institute, Washington, D.C.

Sandmo, A. 1976. "Optimal Taxation—An Introduction to the Literature." *Journal of Public Economics* 6: 37–54.

_____. 1975. "Optimal Taxation in the Presence of Externalities." *Swedish Journal of Economics* 77: 86–98.

Shah, A., and B. Larsen. 1992. "Carbon Taxes, the Greenhouse Effect and Developing Countries." World Bank Policy Research Working Paper Series No. 957, World Bank, Washington, DC.

Wisecarver, D. 1974. "The Social Costs of Input Market Distortions." *American Economic Review* 64: 359–72.

Distributors of World Bank Group Publications

Prices and credit terms vary from country to country. Consult your local distributor before placing an order.

ARGENTINA
World Publications SA
Av. Cordoba 1877
1120 Ciudad de Buenos Aires
Tel: (54 11) 4815-8156
Fax: (54 11) 4815-8156
E-mail: wpbooks@infovia.com.ar

AUSTRALIA, FIJI, PAPUA NEW GUINEA, SOLOMON ISLANDS, VANUATU, AND SAMOA
D.A. Information Services
648 Whitehorse Road
Mitcham 3132, Victoria
Tel: (61) 3 9210 7777
Fax: (61) 3 9210 7788
E-mail: service@dadirect.com.au
URL: http://www.dadirect.com.au

AUSTRIA
Gerold and Co.
Weihburggasse 26
A-1011 Wien
Tel: (43 1) 512-47-31-0
Fax: (43 1) 512-47-31-29
URL: http://www.gerold.co/at.online

BANGLADESH
Micro Industries Development Assistance Society (MIDAS)
House 5, Road 16
Dhanmondi R/Area
Dhaka 1209
Tel: (880 2) 326427
Fax: (880 2) 811188

BELGIUM
Jean De Lannoy
Av. du Roi 202
1060 Brussels
Tel: (32 2) 538-5169
Fax: (32 2) 538-0841

BRAZIL
Publicacões Tecnicas Internacionais Ltda.
Rua Peixoto Gomide, 209
01409 Sao Paulo, SP.
Tel: (55 11) 259-6644
Fax: (55 11) 258-6990
E-mail: postmaster@pti.uol.br
URL: http://www.uol.br

CANADA
Renouf Publishing Co. Ltd.
5369 Canotek Road
Ottawa, Ontario K1J 9J3
Tel: (613) 745-2665
Fax: (613) 745-7660
E-mail: order.dept@renoufbooks.com
URL: http:// www.renoufbooks.com

CHINA
China Financial & Economic Publishing House
8, Da Fo Si Dong Jie
Beijing
Tel: (86 10) 6401-7365
Fax: (86 10) 6401-7365

China Book Import Centre
P.O. Box 2825
Beijing

Chinese Corporation for Promotion of Humanities
52, You Fang Hu Tong,
Xuan Nei Da Jie
Beijing
Tel: (86 10) 660 72 494
Fax: (86 10) 660 72 494

COLOMBIA
Infoenlace Ltda.
Carrera 6 No. 51-21
Apartado Aereo 34270
Santafé de Bogotá, D.C.
Tel: (57 1) 285-2798
Fax: (57 1) 285-2798

COTE D'IVOIRE
Center d'Edition et de Diffusion Africaines (CEDA)
04 B.P. 541
Abidjan 04
Tel: (225) 24 6510; 24 6511
Fax: (225) 25 0567

CYPRUS
Center for Applied Research
Cyprus College
6, Diogenes Street, Engomi
P.O. Box 2006
Nicosia
Tel: (357 2) 59-0730
Fax: (357 2) 66-2051

CZECH REPUBLIC
USIS, NIS Prodejna
Havelkova 22
130 00 Prague 3
Tel: (420 2) 2423 1486
Fax: (420 2) 2423 1114
URL: http://www.nis.cz/

DENMARK
SamfundsLitteratur
Rosenoerns Allé 11
DK-1970 Frederiksberg C
Tel: (45 35) 351942
Fax: (45 35) 357822
URL: http://www.sl.cbs.dk

ECUADOR
Libri Mundi
Libreria Internacional
P.O. Box 17-01-3029
Juan Leon Mera 851
Quito
Tel: (593 2) 521-606; (593 2) 544-185
Fax: (593 2) 504-209
E-mail: librimu1@librimundi.com.ec
E-mail: librimu2@librimundi.com.ec

CODEU
Ruiz de Castilla 763, Edif. Expocolor
Primer piso, Of. #2
Quito
Tel/Fax: (593 2) 507-383; 253-091
E-mail: codeu@impsat.net.ec

EGYPT, ARAB REPUBLIC OF
Al Ahram Distribution Agency
Al Galaa Street
Cairo
Tel: (20 2) 578-6083
Fax: (20 2) 578-6833

The Middle East Observer
41, Sherif Street
Cairo
Tel: (20 2) 393-9732
Fax: (20 2) 393-9732

FINLAND
Akateeminen Kirjakauppa
P.O. Box 128
FIN-00101 Helsinki
Tel: (358 0) 121 4418
Fax: (358 0) 121-4435
E-mail: akatilaus@stockmann.fi
URL: http://www.akateeminen.com

FRANCE
Editions Eska; DBJ
48, rue Gay Lussac
75005 Paris
Tel: (33-1) 55-42-73-08
Fax: (33-1) 43-29-91-67

GERMANY
UNO-Verlag
Poppelsdorfer Allee 55
53115 Bonn
Tel: (49 228) 949020
Fax: (49 228) 217492
URL: http://www.uno-verlag.de
E-mail: unoverlag@aol.com

GHANA
Epp Books Services
P.O. Box 44
TUC
Accra
Tel: 223 21 778843
Fax: 223 21 779099

GREECE
Papasotiriou S.A.
35, Stournara Str.
106 82 Athens
Tel: (30 1) 364-1826
Fax: (30 1) 364-8254

HAITI
Culture Diffusion
5, Rue Capois
C.P. 257
Port-au-Prince
Tel: (509) 23 9260
Fax: (509) 23 4858

HONG KONG, CHINA; MACAO
Asia 2000 Ltd.
Sales & Circulation Department
302 Seabird House
22-28 Wyndham Street, Central
Hong Kong, China
Tel: (852) 2530-1409
Fax: (852) 2526-1107
E-mail: sales@asia2000.com.hk
URL: http://www.asia2000.com.hk

HUNGARY
Euro Info Service
Margitszgeti Europa Haz
H-1138 Budapest
Tel: (36 1) 350 80 24, 350 80 25
Fax: (36 1) 350 90 32
E-mail: euroinfo@mail.matav.hu

INDIA
Allied Publishers Ltd.
751 Mount Road
Madras - 600 002
Tel: (91 44) 852-3938
Fax: (91 44) 852-0649

INDONESIA
Pt. Indira Limited
Jalan Borobudur 20
P.O. Box 181
Jakarta 10320
Tel: (62 21) 390-4290
Fax: (62 21) 390-4289

IRAN
Ketab Sara Co. Publishers
Khaled Eslamboli Ave., 6th Street
Delafrooz Alley No. 8
P.O. Box 15745-733
Tehran 15117
Tel: (98 21) 8717819; 8716104
Fax: (98 21) 8712479
E-mail: ketab-sara@neda.net.ir

Kowkab Publishers
P.O. Box 19575-511
Tehran
Tel: (98 21) 258-3723
Fax: (98 21) 258-3723

IRELAND
Government Supplies Agency
Oifig an tSoláthair
4-5 Harcourt Road
Dublin 2
Tel: (353 1) 661-3111
Fax: (353 1) 475-2670

ISRAEL
Yozmot Literature Ltd.
P.O. Box 56055
3 Yohanan Hasandlar Street
Tel Aviv 61560
Tel: (972 3) 5285-397
Fax: (972 3) 5285-397

R.O.Y. International
PO Box 13056
Tel Aviv 61130
Tel: (972 3) 649 9469
Fax: (972 3) 648 6039
E-mail: royil@netvision.net.il
URL: http://www.royint.co.il

Palestinian Authority/Middle East Index Information Services
P.O.B. 19502 Jerusalem
Tel: (972 2) 6271219
Fax: (972 2) 6271634

ITALY, LIBERIA
Licosa Commissionaria Sansoni SPA
Via Duca Di Calabria, 1/1
Casella Postale 552
50125 Firenze
Tel: (39 55) 645-415
Fax: (39 55) 641-257
E-mail: licosa@ftbcc.it
URL: http://www.ftbcc.it/licosa

JAMAICA
Ian Randle Publishers Ltd.
206 Old Hope Road, Kingston 6
Tel: 876-927-2085
Fax: 876-977-0243
E-mail: irpl@colis.com

JAPAN
Eastern Book Service
3-13 Hongo 3-chome, Bunkyo-ku
Tokyo 113
Tel: (81 3) 3818-0861
Fax: (81 3) 3818-0864
E-mail: orders@svt-ebs.co.jp
URL: http://www.bekkoame.or.jp/~svt-ebs

KENYA
Africa Book Service (E.A.) Ltd.
Quaran House, Mfangano Street
P.O. Box 45245
Nairobi
Tel: (254 2) 223 641
Fax: (254 2) 330 272

Legacy Books
Loita House
Mezzanine 1
P.O. Box 68077
Nairobi
Tel: (254) 2-330853, 221426
Fax: (254) 2-330854, 561654
E-mail: Legacy@form-net.com

KOREA, REPUBLIC OF
Dayang Books Trading Co.
International Division
783-20, Pangba Bon-Dong,
Socho-ku
Seoul
Tel: (82 2) 536-9555
Fax: (82 2) 536-0025
E-mail: seamap@chollian.net

Eulyoo Publishing Co., Ltd.
46-1, Susong-Dong
Jongro-Gu
Seoul
Tel: (82 2) 734-3515
Fax: (82 2) 732-9154

LEBANON
Librairie du Liban
P.O. Box 11-9232
Beirut
Tel: (961 9) 217 944
Fax: (961 9) 217 434
E-mail: hsayegh@librairie-du-liban.com.lb
URL: http://www.librairie-du-liban.com.lb

MALAYSIA
University of Malaya Cooperative Bookshop, Limited
P.O. Box 1127
Jalan Pantai Baru
59700 Kuala Lumpur
Tel: (60 3) 756-5000
Fax: (60 3) 755-4424
E-mail: umkoop@tm.net.my

MEXICO
INFOTEC
Av. San Fernando No. 37
Col. Toriello Guerra
14050 Mexico, D.F.
Tel: (52 5) 624-2800
Fax: (52 5) 624-2822
E-mail: infotec@rtn.net.mx
URL: http://rtn.net.mx

Mundi-Prensa Mexico S.A. de C.V.
c/Rio Panuco, 141-Colonia Cuauhtemoc
06500 Mexico, D.F.
Tel: (52 5) 533-5658
Fax: (52 5) 514-6799

NEPAL
Everest Media International Services (P.) Ltd.
GPO Box 5443
Kathmandu
Tel: (977 1) 416 026
Fax: (977 1) 224 431

NETHERLANDS
De Lindeboom/Internationale Publicaties b.v.-
P.O. Box 202, 7480 AE Haaksbergen
Tel: (31 53) 574-0004
Fax: (31 53) 572-9296
E-mail: lindeboo@worldonline.nl
URL: http://www.worldonline.nl/~lindeboo

NEW ZEALAND
EBSCO NZ Ltd.
Private Mail Bag 99914
New Market
Auckland
Tel: (64 9) 524-8119
Fax: (64 9) 524-8067

Oasis Official
P.O. Box 3627
Wellington
Tel: (64 4) 499 1551
Fax: (64 4) 499 1972
E-mail: oasis@actrix.gen.nz
URL: http://www.oasisbooks.co.nz/

NIGERIA
University Press Limited
Three Crowns Building Jericho
Private Mail Bag 5095
Ibadan
Tel: (234 22) 41-1356
Fax: (234 22) 41-2056

PAKISTAN
Mirza Book Agency
65, Shahrah-e-Quaid-e-Azam
Lahore 54000
Tel: (92 42) 735 3601
Fax: (92 42) 576 3714

Oxford University Press
5 Bangalore Town
Sharae Faisal
PO Box 13033
Karachi-75350
Tel: (92 21) 446307
Fax: (92 21) 4547640
E-mail: ouppak@TheOffice.net

Pak Book Corporation
Aziz Chambers 21, Queen's Road
Lahore
Tel: (92 42) 636 3222; 636 0885
Fax: (92 42) 636 2328
E-mail: pbc@brain.net.pk

PERU
Editorial Desarrollo SA
Apartado 3824, Ica 242 OF. 106
Lima 1
Tel: (51 14) 285380
Fax: (51 14) 286628

PHILIPPINES
International Booksource Center Inc.
1127-A Antipolo St, Barangay, Venezuela
Makati City
Tel: (63 2) 896 6501; 6505; 6507
Fax: (63 2) 896 1741

POLAND
International Publishing Service
Ul. Piekna 31/37
00-677 Warzawa
Tel: (48 2) 628-6089
Fax: (48 2) 621-7255
E-mail: books%ips@ikp.atm.com.pl
URL: http://www.ipscg.waw.pl/ips/export

PORTUGAL
Livraria Portugal
Apartado 2681, Rua Do Carm o 70-74
1200 Lisbon
Tel: (1) 347-4982
Fax: (1) 347-0264

ROMANIA
Compani De Librarii Bucuresti S.A.
Str. Lipscani no. 26, sector 3
Bucharest
Tel: (40 1) 313 9645
Fax: (40 1) 312 4000

RUSSIAN FEDERATION
Isdatelstvo <Ves Mir>
9a, Kolpachniy Pereulok
Moscow 101831
Tel: (7 095) 917 87 49
Fax: (7 095) 917 92 59
ozimarin@glasnet.ru

SINGAPORE; TAIWAN, CHINA MYANMAR; BRUNEI
Hemisphere Publication Services
41 Kallang Pudding Road #04-03
Golden Wheel Building
Singapore 349316
Tel: (65) 741-5166
Fax: (65) 742-9356
E-mail: ashgate@asianconnect.com

SLOVENIA
Gospodarski vestnik Publishing Group
Dunajska cesta 5
1000 Ljubljana
Tel: (386 61) 133 83 47; 132 12 30
Fax: (386 61) 133 80 30
E-mail: repansekj@gvestnik.si

SOUTH AFRICA, BOTSWANA
For single titles:
Oxford University Press Southern Africa
Vasco Boulevard, Goodwood
P.O. Box 12119, N1 City 7463
Cape Town
Tel: (27 21) 595 4400
Fax: (27 21) 595 4430
E-mail: oxford@oup.co.za

For subscription orders:
International Subscription Service
P.O. Box 41095
Craighall
Johannesburg 2024
Tel: (27 11) 880-1448
Fax: (27 11) 880-6248
E-mail: iss@is.co.za

SPAIN
Mundi-Prensa Libros, S.A.
Castello 37
28001 Madrid
Tel: (34 91) 4 363700
Fax: (34 91) 5 753998
E-mail: libreria@mundiprensa.es
URL: http://www.mundiprensa.com/

Mundi-Prensa Barcelona
Consell de Cent, 391
08009 Barcelona
Tel: (34 3) 488-3492
Fax: (34 3) 487-7659
E-mail: barcelona@mundiprensa.es

SRI LANKA, THE MALDIVES
Lake House Bookshop
100, Sir Chittampalam Gardiner Mawatha
Colombo 2
Tel: (94 1) 32105
Fax: (94 1) 432104
E-mail: LHL@sri.lanka.net

SWEDEN
Wennergren-Williams AB
P. O. Box 1305
S-171 25 Solna
Tel: (46 8) 705-97-50
Fax: (46 8) 27-00-71
E-mail: mail@wwi.se

SWITZERLAND
Librairie Payot Service Institutionnel
C(tm)tes-de-Montbenon 30
1002 Lausanne
Tel: (41 21) 341-3229
Fax: (41 21) 341-3235

ADECO Van Diermen EditionsTechniques
Ch. de Lacuez 41
CH1807 Blonay
Tel: (41 21) 943 2673
Fax: (41 21) 943 3605

THAILAND
Central Books Distribution
306 Silom Road
Bangkok 10500
Tel: (66 2) 2336930-9
Fax: (66 2) 237-8321

TRINIDAD & TOBAGO AND THE CARRIBBEAN
Systematics Studies Ltd.
St. Augustine Shopping Center
Eastern Main Road, St. Augustine
Trinidad & Tobago, West Indies
Tel: (868) 645-8466
Fax: (868) 645-8467
E-mail: tobe@trinidad.net

UGANDA
Gustro Ltd.
PO Box 9997, Madhvani Building
Plot 16/4 Jinja Rd.
Kampala
Tel: (256 41) 251 467
Fax: (256 41) 251 468
E-mail: gus@swiftuganda.com

UNITED KINGDOM
Microinfo Ltd.
P.O. Box 3, Omega Park, Alton,
Hampshire GU34 2PG
England
Tel: (44 1420) 86848
Fax: (44 1420) 89889
E-mail: wbank@microinfo.co.uk
URL: http://www.microinfo.co.uk

The Stationery Office
51 Nine Elms Lane
London SW8 5DR
Tel: (44 171) 873-8400
Fax: (44 171) 873-8242
URL: http://www.the-stationery-office.co.uk/

VENEZUELA
Tecni-Ciencia Libros, S.A.
Centro Cuidad Comercial Tamanco
Nivel C2, Caracas
Tel: (58 2) 959 5547; 5035; 0016
Fax: (58 2) 959 5636

ZAMBIA
University Bookshop, University of Zambia
Great East Road Campus
P.O. Box 32379
Lusaka
Tel: (260 1) 252 576
Fax: (260 1) 253 952

ZIMBABWE
Academic and Baobab Books (Pvt.) Ltd.
4 Conald Road, Graniteside
P.O. Box 567
Harare
Tel: 263 4 755035
Fax: 263 4 781913